S.S.F. PUBLIC LIBRARY
West Orange JAN 17
840 West Orange Avenue
South San Francisco, CA 94080

D0404113

1 Map

Dublin

"All you've got to do is decide to go
and the hardest part is over.

So go!"

TONY WHEELER, COFOUNDER – LONELY PLANET

THIS EDITION WRITTEN AND RESEARCHED BY

Fionn Davenport

Contents

Plan Your Trip 4

Explore Dublin 48

Understand Dublin 189

Survival Guide 215

Dublin Maps 237

(left) **St Patrick's Day**
Join the festivities.

(above) **Auld Dubliner**
p107 Enjoy the 'old
world' charm of a Dublin
pub.

(right) **Christ Church**
Cathedral p100
Witness this iconic
cathedral.

Welcome to Dublin

A small capital with a huge reputation, Dublin's mix of heritage and hedonism will not disappoint. All you have to do is show up.

Layers of History

Dublin has been in the news since the 9th century, and while traces of its Viking past have been largely washed away, the city is a living museum of its history since then, with medieval castles and cathedrals on display alongside the architectural splendours of its 18th-century heyday, when Dublin was the most handsome Georgian city of the British Empire and a fine reflection of the aspirations of its most privileged burghers. How power was wrested from their hands is another story, and you'll learn that one in its museums and on its walking tours.

Personality Goes a Long Way

Even Dubliners will admit that theirs isn't the most beautiful city in the world, telling you that pretty things are as easy to like as they are to forget...before showing you the showstopper Georgian bits to prove that Dublin has a fine line in sophisticated elegance. Their beloved capital, about which they can be brutally unsentimental, has personality, which is much more important and lasts far longer. Garrulous, amiable and witty, Dubliners at their ease are the greatest hosts of all, a charismatic bunch whose soul and sociability are so compelling and infectious that you mightn't ever want to leave.

A Few Scoops

To experience Dubliners at their most comfortable and convivial, you'll have to spend some time in a pub. Dublin's relationship with alcohol is complex and conflicted, but at its very best, a night out in the pub remains the city's favourite social lubricant and one of the most memorable experiences of a visit to Ireland. Everyone has their favourite pub: for some it's a never-changing traditional haunt; for others, it's wherever the beautiful people are currently at. Either way, you'll have over 1000 to choose from.

All the World Is Dublin

Dublin may be a small capital, but its cosmopolitan bone fides have been firmly established. Beyond its impressive collection of museums and galleries, and its choice of food from all four corners of the globe – in both restaurant and market form – this is a city that conspicuously embraces diversity and has been transformed by two decades of multiculturalism. It used to be said that 'real' Dubs had to be born within the canals like their parents and grandparents before them: these days, you're as likely to meet a Dub whose parents were born in Warsaw, Lagos or Beijing.

RICHARD I'ANSON / GETTY IMAGES ©

Why I Love Dublin

By Fionn Davenport, Writer

More than anything I love Dublin's intimacy. It's really just a big capital village, where going for a walk is as much an opportunity for socialising as actually making an arrangement to meet someone. As a travel writer, I've always played host to visitors from out of town, which means I get the chance to experience the city with an outsider's perspective, exploring those corners I often take for granted and discovering new bits to be enthusiastic about.

For more about our writers, see p260.

Top: O'Connell Bridge, River Liffey

Dublin's
Top 10

A Dublin Pub (p33)

1 'A good puzzle would be to cross Dublin without passing a pub', mused Leopold Bloom in James Joyce's *Ulysses*. A conundrum, given there's at least one on every street, but the answer is simple: go into each one you find. A hundred years later, the alpha and omega of all social life in Dublin remains the bar. There are over 1000, from traditional boozers like Kehoe's to the trendiest watering holes. It's where you'll meet Dubliners at their convivial, easy-going best and get a sense of what makes this city tick. BELOW LEFT: TEMPLE BAR PUB (P106)

🍷 *Drinking & Nightlife*

Trinity College (p54)

2 Since its foundation in 1592, Trinity College has become one of the world's most famous universities; it's the alma mater of Swift, Wilde and Beckett, and the home of the world's most famous illuminated Gospel, the *Book of Kells*. Its 16 hectares are an oasis of aesthetic elegance, its cobbled quadrangles lined with handsome neoclassical buildings that lend an air of magisterial calm to the campus, evident as soon as you walk through Front Arch.

◉ *Grafton Street & Around*

YOHAN LB/500PX / GETTY IMAGES ©

BRUCE YUANYUE BI / GETTY IMAGES ©

Dublin City Gallery – The Hugh Lane (p133)

3 Hanging on the walls of a magnificent Georgian pile is arguably the city's finest collection of modern and contemporary art, which runs the gamut from Impressionist masterpieces (Degas, Monet, Manet et al) to Irish artists such as Dorothy Cross and Sean Scully. The gallery's extra-special treat is Dublin-born Francis Bacon's actual London studio, brought over piece by piece and painstakingly reassembled in all its glorious mess.

👁 *North of the Liffey*

National Museum of Ireland (p84, p90, p134)

4 The artefacts of a nation are to be found in this eminent institution, which opened in 1890 with a fine collection of coins, medals and 'significant Irish antiquities'. The collection has grown significantly since then, and now numbers in excess of four million objects split across three separate museum buildings, including prehistoric archaeological finds and Celtic and medieval treasures, an extensive folklore collection, and the stuffed beasts and skeletons of the natural history section.

👁 *Merrion Square & Around; North of the Liffey*

Kilmainham Gaol *(p118)*

5 Ireland's struggle for independence was a bloody and tempestuous journey, and this forbidding prison played a role in it for nearly 150 years. Unoccupied since 1924, it is now a museum with an enthralling exhibit on the history of Irish nationalism. The guided tour of its grim cells and corridors is highly memorable and it finishes in the yard where the leaders of the failed 1916 Easter Rising were executed.

⊙ *Kilmainham & the Liberties*

Dining Scene *(p29)*

6 Unthinkable less than two decades ago, but Dublin's foodie scene is now one of the city's major highlights. There are restaurants to suit every taste and budget, but the most interesting ones are the places – like 101 Talbot – that are experimenting with the basic ingredients of Irish cuisine and transforming them into 'Modern Irish', a catholic style that absorbs influences from virtually every other cuisine in the world. BELOW: IRISH SEA-FOOD CHOWDER

✖ *Eating*

Guinness Storehouse *(p112)*

7 One of the world's most famous beer brands is Guinness, as inextricably linked with Dublin as James Joyce and… no, we can't think of anything else. An old fermentation plant in the St James's Gate Brewery has been converted into a seven-storey museum devoted to the beer, the company's history, how the beer is made and how it became the brand it is today. The top floor is an atrium bar, where you put the theory to the test and drink a pint.

◉ *Kilmainham & the Liberties*

6

HAQLIANG / GETTY IMAGES ©

7

Martello Tower, Sandycove

They halted while Haines surveyed the tower and said at last:
— Rather bleak in wintertime, I should say.
Martello you call it?
— Billy Pitt had them built, Buck Mulligan said,
when the French were on the sea. But ours is
the omphalos.

8

St Stephen's Green *(p63)*

8 Dublin is blessed with green spaces, but none is so popular or so beloved by its citizens than St Stephen's Green, the main entrance to which is through an arch at the southern end of Grafton St. When the sun burns through the cloud cover virtually every blade of grass is occupied, by students, lovers, and workers on a break. Many a business meeting is conducted along its pathways, which run by flower gardens, playgrounds and old Victorian bandstands.

⊙ *Grafton Street & Around*

Chester Beatty Library
(p62)

9 Alfred Chester Beatty was a mining magnate with exceedingly good taste, and the fruit of his aesthetic sensibility is gathered in this remarkable museum. Books, manuscripts and scrolls were his particular love, and his collection includes one of the world's finest gathering of Qu'rans (example pictured), the finest collection of Chinese jade books in existence, and some of the earliest biblical parchments ever found. The remainder of the collection is fleshed out with tablets, paintings, furniture and other beautiful objets d'art.

⊙ *Grafton Street & Around*

National Gallery *(p88)*

10 The state's art collection is an impressive one, a history of art spread across six centuries and 54 separate galleries, which have just been given a major spruce-up. The marquee names include Goya, Caravaggio and Van Gogh, but no less impressive are the paintings by luminaries like Orpen, Reynolds and Van Dongen. Don't miss the Jack B Yeats room; as you find your way there, you'll pass the odd Rembrandt, Velázquez and Vermeer.

⊙ *Merrion Square & Around*

What's New

Teeling Distillery, Dublin

The first new distillery in Dublin for 125 years opened in 2015, but it'll be a few years yet before what it makes is actually whiskey; in the meantime, the visitor centre explains how it's made. (p120)

Epic Ireland

Epic Ireland is an engaging, interactive museum telling the story of Irish emigration and the diaspora, which should appeal to the 70-odd million global citizens with Irish ancestry. (p152)

Northside Dining

For too long treated as a culinary wasteland, the north side is now a gourmet hotspot thanks to some old favourites like 101 Talbot and Chapter One, and a host of new cafes and restaurants including Cotto (p141), Oxmantown (p141) and M&L (p141), the latter the best Chinese restaurant in town.

City Assembly Hall

The first purpose-built art gallery in Dublin is the glorious City Assembly Hall, which has reopened after years of closure thanks to the curative efforts of the Irish Georgian Society, which is based on the ground floor. (p63)

National Gallery

A three-year, €20m refurbishment and the National Gallery is gleaming again, with state-of-the-art security and heating systems and new galleries never before open to the public. (p88)

Fab Food Trails

Get to grips with the raw ingredients of Dublin's foodie revolution with this excellent new walking tour, which brings you to meet local producers and graze at local markets. (p80)

Women's History of Ireland

For far too long the role of women in Irish history was either ignored or written out completely; this weekly tour at the Little Museum of Dublin looks to redress the balance and highlight how central women actually were. (p80)

The Dean

The newest addition to the hotelscape borrows heavily from hotels like the Ace in New York and the Hoxton in London – it's not just a place to sleep, but to work and play, in hyper-stylish environs designed to snare creatives and their ilk. (p180)

For more recommendations and reviews, see **lonelyplanet. com/Dublin**

Need to Know

For more information, see Survival Guide (p215)

Currency
Euro (€)

Language
English

Visas
Not required for citizens of Australia, New Zealand, USA and Canada. Citizens of European nations that belong to the European Economic Area (EEA) don't need one either.

Money
ATMs are widespread. Credit cards (with PIN) are accepted at most restaurants, hotels and shops.

Mobile Phones
All European and Australasian phones work in Dublin; some North American (non-GSM) phones don't. Check with provider. Prepaid SIM cards cost from €10.

Time
Western European Time (UTC/GMT November to March; plus one hour April to October)

Tourist Information
Dublin Visitor Centre (p225) has general visitor information on Dublin and Ireland, along with booking information and services..

Daily Costs

Budget:
Less than €100
➡ Dorm bed: €14–20

➡ Cheap meal in cafe or pub: €10–20

➡ Bus ticket: up to €2.80

➡ Sightseeing in museums with free admission: free

➡ Pint: €4.50–5

Midrange: €100–200
➡ Budget hotel double: €70–110

➡ Midrange hotel or townhouse double: €110–200

➡ Lunch and/or dinner in decent restaurant: €30

➡ Guided tours and admission to paid attractions: €20

Top End:
More than €200
➡ Double in top-end hotel: from €200

➡ Dinner in top-end restaurant: €50–100

Advance Planning

One month before Book accommodation, especially in summer. Book tickets for bigger live gigs, especially touring musicians and comedians.

Two weeks before Secure accommodation in low season. Book weekend performances for main theatres, and Friday or Saturday night reservations at top-end restaurants.

Three days before Book weekend tables at the trendiest or most popular restaurants.

Useful Websites

Dublin Tourism (www.visit dublin.com) Official website of Dublin Tourism.

Dublintown (www.dublintown. ie) Comprehensive list of events and goings on.

Failte Ireland (www.discover ireland.ie) Official tourist board website.

Lovin Dublin (www.lovindublin. com) Honest, sometimes scathing, reviews of bars, restaurants and other Dublin-related activities.

Totally Dublin (www.totallydub lin.ie) Latest news and reviews.

Lonely Planet (www.lonely planet.com/dublin) Destination information, hotel bookings, traveller forum and more.

WHEN TO GO

Weather is at its best from June to August, and September can be warm and sunny. November to February are cold, but dry; May sees rain and sun.

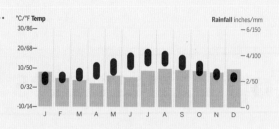

°C/°F Temp
30/86—
20/68—
10/50—
0/32—
-10/14—

Rainfall inches/mm
— 6/150
— 4/100
— 2/50
— 0

J F M A M J J A S O N D

Arriving in Dublin

Dublin Airport Buses to the city centre run every 10 to 15 minutes between 6am and midnight; taxis (€25) take around 45 minutes.

Dun Laoghaire ferry terminal DART (one-way €3.25) to Pearse Station (for south Dublin) or Connolly Station (for north Dublin); bus 46A to St Stephen's Green, or bus 7, 7A or 8 to Burgh Quay.

Dublin Port terminal Busáras buses (adult/child €3/1.50) are timed to coincide with arrivals and departures.

Busáras All Bus Eireann services arrive at Busáras; private operators have arrival points in different parts of the city.

Heuston and Connolly Stations Main-line trains from all over Ireland arrive at Heuston Station (for all destinations south and west of Dublin, including Wexford, Waterford, Cork, Limerick and Galway) or Connolly Station (all destinations northwest and north of Dublin, including Sligo and all trains from Northern Ireland).

For much more on **arrival** see p216

Getting Around

➡ **Bus** Useful for getting to the west side of the city and the suburbs.

➡ **Bicycle** The city's rent-and-ride Dublinbikes scheme is the ideal way to cover ground quickly.

➡ **DART** Suburban rail network that runs along the eastern edge of the city along Dublin Bay.

➡ **Luas** A two-line light-rail transport system that links the city centre with southern suburbs.

➡ **Taxi** Easily recognised by light-green-and-blue 'Taxi' sign on door; can be hailed or picked up at ranks in the city centre.

➡ **Walking** Dublin's city centre is compact, flat and eminently walkable – it's less than 2km from one end of the city centre to the other.

For much more on **getting around** see p217

Sleeping

As with most cities, the closer to the city centre you want to stay, the more you'll pay – and room sizes get smaller accordingly. Budget travellers will gravitate to the handful of good hostels in the city. There are good midrange options north of the Liffey, but the biggest spread of accommodation is south of the river, from mid-range Georgian townhouses to the city's top hotels. Excellent options also sprinkle the suburbs immediately south of the city centre. Expect prices to soar during summer and festivals.

Useful Websites

➡ **Dublin City Centre Hotels** (www.dublin.city-centre-hotels.com) Hotel bookings with a range of budget options.

➡ **Lonely Planet** (www.lonelyplanet.com/ireland/dublin/hotels) Writer-recommended reviews and online booking.

➡ **Daft.ie** (www.daft.ie) If you're looking to rent in Dublin, this is the site to search.

➡ **Dublin Tourism** (www.visitdublin.com) Good selection of rated accommodation.

For much more on **sleeping** see p177

Top Itineraries

Day One

Grafton Street & Around (p52)

 Start with a stroll through the grounds of **Trinity College**, visiting the **Book of Kells** and the **Long Room** before ambling up **Grafton St** to **St Stephen's Green**. For more beautiful books and artefacts, drop into the **Chester Beatty Library**. On your way, you can do a spot of retailing in **Powerscourt Townhouse Shopping Centre** or the many boutiques west of Grafton St.

> **Lunch** The two-course lunch special at Coppinger Row (p70) is a steal.

Merrion Square & Around (p82)

Pick your heavyweight institution, or visit all three: the **National Museum of Ireland – Archaeology** (if only for the Ardagh Chalice and Tara Brooch), the **National Gallery** (be sure to check out the Jack B Yeats room) and the **Museum of Natural History**, which the kids will surely enjoy.

> **Dinner** Fade Street Social (p69) serves up gourmet tapas.

Temple Bar (p98)

 Dublin's one-time party zone still likes to have a good time, and is definitely at its most animated in the evenings, where you have the choice of a **traditional music session**, some decent clubbing at **Mother** (Saturdays only) or just straight up drinking at any of the district's many **pubs**.

Day Two

Kilmainham & the Liberties (p110)

 Begin with a little penance at either (or both) of Dublin's medieval cathedrals, **St Patrick's** and **Christ Church**, before pursuing pleasure at Dublin's most popular tourist attraction, the **Guinness Storehouse**; make sure to sample the almost perfect Guinness you get at the end of the visit.

> **Lunch** Fumbally (p121) has great soups, sandwiches and coffee.

Kilmainham & the Liberties (p110)

Go further west to Kilmainham, visiting first the fine collection at the **Irish Museum of Modern Art** (don't forget to visit the gardens too) before going out the back entrance and stepping into **Kilmainham Gaol**, the tour of which offers one of the most illuminating and interesting insights into Ireland's struggle for independence. If the weather is good, a stroll in the **War Memorial Gardens** is also recommended.

> **Dinner** Organic grub at L Mulligan Grocer (p142), in Stoneybatter.

North of the Liffey (p128)

 Walshe's of Stoneybatter is a superb traditional bar, full of interesting locals and hipster blow-ins looking for a 'real' Dublin experience. Alternatively, you could take in a play at either the **Gate** or Ireland's national theatre, the **Abbey**. Use the Luas to get you from Stoneybatter (get on at the Museum stop) and alight at Abbey St.

SICI/ GETTY IMAGES ©

National Botanic Gardens (p136)

Day Three

North of the Liffey (p128)

 After walking the length of **O'Connell St**, and pausing to inspect the bullet holes in the **General Post Office**, explore the collection of the **Dublin City Museum – The Hugh Lane**, including Francis Bacon's reconstructed studio. The **Old Jameson Distillery**, to the west in Smithfield, is the place to learn about (and taste) Irish whiskey.

> **Lunch** Get great sandwiches, wraps and baps at Third Space (p141).

North of the Liffey (p128)

The collection of the **National Museum of Ireland – Decorative Arts & History** is excellent, but you'll be distracted by the stunning 18th-century barracks that is its home. The nearby **Arbour Hill Cemetery** is where the executed leaders of the 1916 Easter Rising are buried, while further west again is the broad expanse of **Phoenix Park**, the largest city park in Europe.

> **Dinner** Chapter One (p142) is ideal for a special occasion. Book ahead.

Grafton Street & Around (p52)

 The biggest choice of nightlife is in the streets around Grafton St. There are traditional **pubs**, trendy new **bars** and **music venues**. You can drink, talk and dance the night away, or go see a show at the **Gaiety Theatre**. Whatever you choose, everything is easily reached in what is a pretty compact district.

Day Four

North of the Liffey (p128)

 You'll get a particularly interesting insight into the vagaries of Irish history with a visit to **Glasnevin Cemetery**, the final resting place of so many Irish notables – but be sure to take the brilliant tour. The **National Botanic Gardens** are just around the corner, and well worth an amble. Sporting fans will enjoy the tour of **Croke Park**, Ireland's biggest stadium and the HQ of the Gaelic Athletic Association.

> **Lunch** Wuff (p142) in Stoneybatter has a great range of lunch options.

Howth (p168)

Hop on a DART and head northwards to the suburb of Howth, a nice fishing village at the foot of a bulbous headland overlooking Dublin Bay. There are great walks around the headland itself, but if you prefer something a little more sedate, there's a fine selection of **pubs** in the village and some excellent seafood **restaurants** along the pier. There's also a terrific **farmers' market** at weekends.

> **Dinner** The Winding Stair (p143) serves beautiful Irish cuisine.

Merrion Square & Around (p82)

 A visit to **O'Donoghue's** on Merrion Row is guaranteed to be memorable. It's a beautiful traditional bar that is always full of revellers, and there's a good chance there'll be a trad music session on.

If You Like...

Traditional Pubs

Kehoe's Beautiful traditional pub with elegant Victorian bar beloved of locals and visitors alike. (p72)

John Mulligan's This place has featured in films and is synonymous with the quiet, ticking-clock-style of Dublin pub. (p155)

Fallon's Great neighbourhood bar at the edge of the Liberties frequented by locals and hipsters in the know. (p122)

John Kavanagh's It's worth the trek to the north Dublin suburb of Glasnevin for this traditional classic. (p143)

Stag's Head The most picturesque of Dublin's traditional bars hasn't changed a jot since it was remodelled in 1895. (p73)

James Toner's Flagstone floors and an old-style bar make this a favourite boozer for the local business crowd, who come here to unwind. (p95)

Old Royal Oak Traditional pub in the western suburb of Kilmainham beloved of aficionados of the classic pub experience. (p122)

Walshe's Wonderful local pub frequented by old men in flat caps and young arty types in... flat caps. (p143)

Irish History

Kilmainham Gaol Ireland's troubled and bloody struggle for independence is revealed in a visit to this historic jail, where rebels were incarcerated and the leaders of the 1916 Easter Rising executed. (p118)

TONY WHEELER / GETTY IMAGES ©

Powerscourt Townhouse Shopping Centre (p76)

Glasnevin Cemetery Almost everyone who was anyone in the last two centuries of Irish history is interred at this cemetery, and their stories are brought to life (ahem) by the excellent tours. (p136)

1916 Rebellion Walking Tour A detailed and informative walking tour of all the sites and stories associated with the Easter Rising make this one of the best ways to get to grips with this particular episode in history. (p220)

Epic Ireland This new interactive museum explores the story of emigration and the diaspora. (p152)

Jeanie Johnston An exact replica of a 19th-century Famine ship that gives a first-hand impression of what it was like to sail across the Atlantic. (p152)

Admiring Art

Irish Museum of Modern Art Art from the 20th and 21st centuries hangs on its walls, but you'll soon be distracted by the elegant surroundings and beautiful gardens. (p119)

Dublin City Gallery – The Hugh Lane Impressionist masterpieces and Francis Bacon's actual studio, reconstructed piece by exacting piece, are the highlights of this wonderful gallery. (p133)

National Gallery Home of the Irish State's art collection, including a Caravaggio and a whole room dedicated to Jack B Yeats. (p88)

Royal Hibernian Academy (RHA) Gallagher Gallery Privately run gallery where installations, sound pieces and

other treats complement the contemporary paintings. (p91)

City Assembly Hall Dublin's original art gallery has started staging exhibitions again in a beautiful room. (p63)

Museum Meanders

National Museum of Ireland – Archaeology The country's most important cultural institution is the repository of its most valuable and sacred historical treasures. (p84)

Chester Beatty Library Best small museum in Ireland, with breathtaking collection of sacred books and objets d'art from the Middle East and Asia. (p62)

Little Museum of Dublin This museum tells the story of Dublin in the 20th century through items, photographs and objects donated by Dubliners themselves. (p63)

Museum of Natural History The Dead Zoo's collection of two million stuffed beasts has hardly changed since Scottish explorer Dr David Livingstone cut the ribbon in 1857. (p90)

National Print Museum Sounds dull, but is anything but – and if you've any interest in the printed word then it's a memorable visit. (p152)

Live Gigs

Workman's Club A great spot for left-of-centre stuff, from electronica to alt rock and beardy folk music. (p107)

Whelan's The spiritual home of the singer-songwriter, you can get up close and personal

For more top Dublin spots, see the following:
➡ Eating (p29)
➡ Drinking & Nightlife (p33)
➡ Entertainment (p38)
➡ Shopping (p42)
➡ Sports & Activities (p44)

at this terrifically intimate venue. (p75)

Vicar Street A mid-sized venue that generally hosts soul, folk and foreign music. (p124)

3 Arena The place to see your favourite touring international superstar, along with 23,000 others. (p156)

Wigwam First-class DJs do their thing in the basement bar. (p143)

Markets & Shopping

Powerscourt Townhouse Shopping Centre The city's most elegant shopping centre, replete with stores selling everything from hand-crafted leather bags to hats by Irish designers. (p76)

George's St Arcade Beneath the arches of this Victorian arcade you'll find everything from second-hand LPs to patchouli oil. (p76)

Temple Bar Food Market The best gourmet food market in town is the place to sample all kinds of goodies. (p107)

Ulysses Rare Books Rare books, maps and first editions are found in this beautiful bookshop, which specialises in Irish titles. (p76)

Barry Doyle Design Jewellers Fancy a bespoke bit of Celtic jewellery? This lovely shop in the George's St Arcade is the place to go. (p76)

Literary Locations

Marsh's Library Founded in 1701, Ireland's oldest library is home to more than 25,000 books and manuscripts dating back to the 1400s. (p120)

The Old Library, Trinity College The world's most famous illuminated Gospels (the *Book of Kells*) and the Long Room, a magnificent cathedral of books, scrolls and ancient manuscripts. (p55)

Dublin Writers Museum Dublin's literary heritage explored through writers' personal possessions, scribblings and memorabilia. (p134)

Bloomsday Edwardian gear is de rigueur on June 16 if you want to celebrate Dublin's unique tribute to James Joyce. (p22)

Green Spaces

St Stephen's Green The city's favourite sun trap, with every blade of its manicured lawns occupied by lounge lizards and lunchers. (p63)

Merrion Square Perfectly raked paths meander by beautifully maintained lawns and flower beds. (p89)

Phoenix Park Dublin's biggest park, home to deer, the zoo, the president and the US ambassador. (p130)

Iveagh Gardens Delightful, slightly dishevelled gardens hidden behind St Stephen's Green. (p66)

War Memorial Gardens The best-kept open secret in town are these magnificent gardens by the Liffey. (p120)

Georgian Buildings

Leinster House Richard Cassels built this home for the Duke of Leinster; it's now the home of the Irish parliament. (p90)

Charlemont House Lord Charlemont's city dwelling, now home to the Dublin City Gallery – The Hugh Lane, was one of the city's finest Georgian homes. (p133)

Powerscourt Townhouse Shopping Centre Once home to the third Viscount Powerscourt, Robert Mack's beautiful building is now a popular shopping centre. (p76)

Four Courts The home of the highest courts in the land is the joint effort of Thomas Cooley and James Gandon. (p137)

Custom House James Gandon announced his arrival in Dublin with this architectural stunner. (p152)

Bank of Ireland Now a bank, this was designed by Edward Lovett Pearce for the Irish parliament. (p64)

WAYNE WALTON / GETTY IMAGES ©

Bloomsday reading at the James Joyce Cultural Centre (p135)

Month by Month

January

It's cold and often wet, and the city is slowly getting over the Christmas break.

✨ New Year's Celebrations

Experience the birth of another year with a cheer among thousands of revellers at Dublin's iconic Christ Church Cathedral.

February

Bad weather makes February the perfect month for indoor activities. Some museums launch new exhibits.

☆ Audi Dublin International Film Festival

Most of Dublin's cinemas participate in the city's film festival, a two-week showcase for new films by Irish and international directors, which features local flicks, arty international films and advance releases of mainstream movies.

March

This month is all about one festival. Uncertain weather: often warmer but really cold spells are also common.

✨ St Patrick's Festival

The mother of all Irish festivals (www.stpatricksfestival. ie), where hundreds of thousands gather to 'honour' St Patrick on city streets and in venues throughout the centre over four days around 17 March.

April

The weather is getting better, the flowers are beginning to bloom and the festival season begins anew.

☆ Irish Grand National

Dublin loves horse racing, and the race that's loved the most is the Grand National, the showcase of the national hunt season that takes place at Fairyhouse in County Meath, 25km northwest of the city centre, on Easter.

May

The May bank holiday (on the first Monday) sees the first of the busy summer weekends as Dubliners take to the roads to enjoy the budding good weather.

☆ International Literature Festival Dublin

Four-day literature festival takes place in mid-May, attracting Irish and international writers to its readings, performances and talks.

✨ Bloom in the Park

Ireland's largest gardening expo sees over 90,000 visitors coming to Phoenix Park over one weekend midmonth to eat food, listen to music and, yes, test their green thumbs.

June

The bank holiday at the beginning of the month sees the city spoilt for choice as to what to do. There's a bunch of festivals to choose from in the good weather.

 Bloomsday

Edwardian dress and breakfast of 'the inner organs of beast and fowl' are but two of the elements of the Dublin festival celebrating 16 June, the day on which James Joyce's *Ulysses* takes place; the real highlight is retracing Leopold Bloom's steps.

Taste of Dublin

The city's best restaurateurs share their secrets and their dishes with each other and the public at the wonderful Taste of Dublin (http://dublin.tastefestivals.com) in the Iveagh Gardens, which takes place over a long weekend in June and features talks, demonstrations, lessons, and some extraordinary grub.

☆ Forbidden Fruit

An alternative-music festival (www.forbiddenfruit.ie) in the grounds of the Irish Museum of Modern Art over the first weekend in June.

July

There's something on every weekend, including the biggest music festival of the year.

☆ Dublin Horse Show

The international horsey set trot down to the Royal Dublin Society (RDS) for the social highlight of the year (www.dublinhorseshow.com). Particularly popular is the Aga Khan Cup, an international-class competition packed with often heart-stopping excitement in which eight nations participate.

☆ Longitude

A mini-Glastonbury in Dublin's Marlay Park, Longitude (www.longitude.ie) packs them in over three days in mid-July for a feast of EDM, nu-folk, rock and pop.

☆ Street Performance World Championships

The world's best street performers test their skills (www.spwc.ie) over two July weekends in Merrion Square – from jugglers to sword-swallowers.

August

Schools are closed, the sun is shining (or not!) and Dublin is in holiday mood. It's the busiest time of the year for visitors.

🏃 Liffey Swim

Five hundred lunatics swim 2.5km from Rory O'More Bridge to the Custom House in late August (www.leinsteropensea.ie) – one can't but admire their steel will.

September

Summer may be over, but September weather can be surprisingly good, so you can often enjoy the dwindling crowds amid an Indian summer.

☆ All-Ireland Finals

The climax of the year for fans of Gaelic games as the season's most successful county teams battle it out for the All-Ireland championships in hurling and football, on the second and fourth Sundays in September, respectively.

☆ Culture Night

For one night in September (www.culturenight.ie), free entry to museums, churches, galleries and historic homes throughout the city. These places host performances, workshops and talks.

☆ Dublin Fringe Festival

This excellent theatre showcase (www.fringefest.com) precedes the main theatre festival with 700 performers and 100 events – ranging from cutting edge to crap – and takes place over three weeks. It's held in the Famous Spiegeltent.

🍷 Irish Craft Beer Festival

The RDS hosts the country's largest celebration of craft beer, with plenty of music, cuisine and, of course, 200-plus craft beers.

October

The weather starts to turn cold, so it's time to move the fun indoors again. The calendar is still packed with activities and distractions, especially over the last weekend of the month.

☆ Dublin Theatre Festival

This two-week festival (www.dublintheatrefestival.com) at the beginning of the month is Europe's oldest theatre festival and showcases the best of Irish and international productions at various locations around town.

🏃 Dublin City Marathon

If you fancy a 42km running tour through the streets of

(Top) St Patrick's Festival revellers
(Bottom) Pub serving Guinness

CONLETH MC KERNAN / GETTY IMAGES ©

LONELY PLANET / GETTY IMAGES ©

Dublin on the last Monday of October, you'll have to register at least three months in advance. The winner crosses the finishing line on O'Connell St at around 10.30am.

☆ Hard Working Class Heroes

The only showcase in town for unsigned Irish acts, this three-day music festival features 100 bands and musicians playing at venues on and around Camden St on the south side of the city.

🎆 Samhain (Hallowe'en)

Tens of thousands take to the streets on 31 October for a night-time parade, fireworks, theatre, drinking and music in this traditional pagan festival celebrating the dead, end of the harvest and Celtic new year.

December

Christmas in Dublin is a big deal, with everyone looking forward to at least a week's holiday.

🏃 Christmas Dip

At 11am on Christmas Day, a group of very brave swimmers jump into the icy waters at the 40 Foot, just below the Martello Tower in the southern suburb of Sandycove, for a 20m swim to the rocks and back.

☆ Leopardstown Races

Blow your dough and your post-Christmas crankiness at this historic and hugely popular racing festival at one of Europe's loveliest courses. Races run from 26 to 30 December.

With Kids

Kid-friendly? You bet. Dublin loves the little 'uns, and will enthusiastically ooh and aah at the cuteness of your progeny. But alas such admiration hasn't fully translated into child services like widespread and accessible baby-changing facilities.

VICTOR WALSH PHOTOGRAPHY / GETTY IMAGES ©

Tiger, Dublin Zoo (p130)

Hands-On Museums

If your kids are between three and 14, spend an afternoon at Ark Children's Cultural Centre (p103), which runs activities aimed at stimulating participants' interests in science, the environment and the arts – but be sure to book well in advance.

Only five-minutes' walk from the Stillorgan stop on the Luas is **Imaginosity** (www.imaginosity.ie; The Plaza, Beacon South Quarter, Sandyford; adult/child €8/7; ☺9.30am-5.30pm Tue-Fri, 10am-6pm Sat & Sun, 1.30-5.30pm Mon), the country's only designated interactive museum for kids. Over the course of two hours they can learn, have fun and get distracted by the museum's exhibits and activities.

Viking Adventures

There are loads of ways to discover Dublin's Viking past, but Dublinia (p103), the city's Viking and medieval museum, has interactive exhibits that are specifically designed to appeal to younger visitors.

Kids of all ages will love a Viking Splash Tour (p81), where you board an amphibious vehicle, put on a plastic Viking hat and roar at passersby as you do a tour of the city before landing in the water at the Grand Canal basin.

Dublin Zoo

A recommended mobile option is a hop-on hop-off open-top bus tour (p220), which helps you get your bearings and lets the kids enjoy a bit of Dublin from the top deck. You can use the bus to get to Dublin Zoo (p130), where you can hop aboard the zoo train and visit the animals. There are roughly 400 animals from 100 different species across eight different habitats, which range from an Asian jungle to a family farm, where kids get to meet the inhabitants up close.

AITORMMFOTO / GETTY IMAGES ©

Viking Splash Tour (p81)

NEED TO KNOW

Public Transport Children under five years of age travel free on all public transport.

Pubs Unaccompanied minors are not allowed in pubs; accompanied children can remain until 9pm (10pm May to September).

Babysitting Agencies such as **Belgrave Agency** (☎01-280 9341; www.nanny.ie; 55 Mulgrave St, Dun Laoghaire; per hr €12 plus €25 agency booking fee & VAT at 23%.) provide professional nannies. The average charge is €15 per hour, plus taxi fare.

Resources Parents with young children should check out www.eumom. com; an excellent site about family-friendly accommodation is www.baby-goes2.com.

Only in Ireland

Across the river from Dublinia is the National Leprechaun Museum (p140), which despite its high-sounding name is really just a romper room for kids with a little bit of Irish folklore thrown in for good measure. The optical illusion tunnel (which makes you appear smaller to those at the other end), the room full of over-sized furniture, the wishing wells and, invariably, the pot of gold, are especially appealing for little ones.

Doll & Teddy-Bear Hospital

On the 2nd floor of the Powerscourt Town-house Shopping Centre is the Dolls Store (p76), which sells all kinds of dolls and doll houses, but should your little one's doll or teddy get 'ill', this is also the home of Ireland's only doll and teddy-bear hospital.

Wide Open Spaces

While it's always good to have a specific activity in mind, don't forget Dublin's parks – from St Stephen's Green (p63) to Merrion Square (p89) to Phoenix Park (p130), the city has plenty of green spaces for the kids to run wild in.

Like a Local

Dublin is, depending on your perspective, a small city or a very large village, which makes it at once easy to navigate but difficult to understand. Spend enough time here and you'll realise exactly what we mean.

Pints of Guinness, O'Donoghue's pub (p95)

'Slagging'

Dubliners are, for the most part, an informal and easy-going lot who don't stand on excessive ceremony and generally prefer not to make too much of a fuss. Which doesn't mean that they don't abide by certain rules, or that there isn't a preferred way of doing things in the city. But the transgressions of the unknowing are both forgiven and often enjoyed – the accidental faux pas is a great source of entertainment in a city that has made 'slagging', or teasing, a veritable art form. Indeed, slagging is a far more reliable indicator of the strength of friendship than virtually any kind of compliment: a fast, self-deprecating wit and an ability to take a joke in good spirits will win you plenty of friends. Mind you, even slagging has its hidden codes, and is only acceptable among friends: it wouldn't do at all to follow an introduction by making fun of their shoes!

Accents

Even in a small city like Dublin there is a lot of variation, ranging from suburban dialects that sound faintly American to working-class 'Dublinese' that is nearly incomprehensible to outsiders.

DORT Accent

Aka the D4 accent (after the posh south-side postal district). Borrows heavily from Home Counties British English and American English and is distinctive for its distorted vowels ('Dort' instead of 'DART'), liberal use of 'like' (pronounced 'loike') and use of upspeak, where every sentence ends with an upwards inflection, like a question.

'Inner City' Accent

Synonymous with working-class Dubliners, the most impenetrable of Dublin dialects, marked by cramped vowels and words that run into each other, coupled with the liberal insertion of extra consonants ('world' pronounced as 'wordled'). It is stigmatised as the uneducated accent of the city's poorer quarters, but of all the city's accents it is the closest to the earliest days of modern English.

ANDREW MONTGOMERY / LONELY PLANET / GETTY IMAGES ©

Suburban Accent

The easiest accent to understand, this is also the accent of the overwhelming majority of the city's middle-class population. It is self-consciously clear and enunciated, and has its origins in the efforts of post-independence educators to foster a well-spoken accent that was deliberately 'unBritish' instead filtering its clear diction and pronunciation through an Irish voice.

Dubliners & Sport

Dubliners can tell a lot about each other based on their preferred sport and favourite teams.

Gaelic Football

Generally the preserve of the middle-class suburbs of the north side and southwest Dublin, where most of the city's clubs are located. True fans will support not just 'the Dubs' but their local club too; the county championship is a highly competitive affair. The game is also popular in the working-class areas of the north inner city, where supporting Dublin is an expression of local pride.

Football

The most popular game in Dublin has support throughout the city, primarily in working-class and middle-class neighbourhoods, where it is known as 'football' or, simply, 'ball' (as in 'Did you watch the ball last night?'). Although the Dublin-based teams in the League of Ireland have trenchant support, your average football fan in Dublin is also a die-hard supporter of a team in the English Premier League, usually one of Manchester United, Liverpool or Arsenal, but also Aston Villa (particularly among fans born in the late 1970s and early 1980s, who came of age when Dublin legend Paul McGrath played for them) and, latterly, Manchester City and Chelsea (mostly young fans born since the millennium). Generally speaking, Dubliners who refer to the game as 'soccer' are doing so derisively.

Rugby

The traditional game of the city's elite – love and knowledge of rugby was a telltale indicator of privilege and elevated social status. The most exclusive schools in the city favour rugby over other sports, and to be a

NEED TO KNOW

Dinner Time At home, Dubliners dine early, between 6pm and 7pm; when they go out, they eat later, usually after 7pm.

Rounds If someone buys you a drink, you always need to return the favour – or at least offer to.

Drinking Water Don't bother with bottled water in restaurants; Dublin's tap water is perfectly safe, free and generally excellent.

PLAN YOUR TRIP LIKE A LOCAL

Blackrock boy (an exclusive boys school in the southern suburb of the same name) is code for privileged youngster whose greatest ambition is to line out for Ireland while taking a law or medical degree. The advent of professionalism, Ireland's repeated successes at international level and the Celtic Tiger changed all that, however, transforming rugby from an elitist pursuit to a more general expression of national pride (flavoured by the social aspirations that accompanied the disposable wealth of the Celtic Tiger years). The girls' equivalent is hockey, which is played at the most exclusive schools. But, like most sport played by girls in Dublin, it's generally out of the limelight.

The Rounds System

The rounds system – the simple custom where someone buys you a drink and you buy one back – is the bedrock of Irish pub culture. It's summed up in the Irish saying: 'It's impossible for two men to go to a pub for one drink.' Nothing will hasten your fall from social grace here like the failure to uphold this pub law. The Irish are extremely generous and one thing they can't abide is tight-fistedness.

Another golden rule about the system is that the next round starts when the first person has finished (or preferably just about to finish) their drink. It doesn't matter if you're only halfway through your pint, if it's your round, get them in.

Your greatest challenge will probably be trying to keep up with your fellow drinkers, who may keep buying you drinks in every round even when you've still got a clatter of unfinished pints in front of you and you're sliding face first down the bar.

For Free

Dublin has a reputation for being expensive and there's no doubt you can haemorrhage cash without too much effort. But the good news is you can see and experience much of what's great about Dublin without having to spend a cent.

Museums

The nation's cultural and historical legacy is yours to enjoy at no cost.

National Museum of Ireland All three Dublin branches of the National Museum – Archaeology (p84), Decorative Arts & History (p134) and Natural History (p90) – are free of charge, and you're welcome to wander in and explore its myriad treasures and fascinating exhibits at your leisure.

National Gallery (p88) The State's proud collection of art, from the Middle Ages up to the modern age, is well-represented on the walls of the National Gallery.

Chester Beatty Library (p62) The city's foremost small museum is a treasure trove of ancient books, illuminated manuscripts, precious scrolls and other gorgeous objets d'art.

Science Gallery (p64) Tap into your inner nerd and discover how interesting it all is...for absolutely nothing.

Green Spaces

Dublin is blessed with green spaces, all but one of which is open to the public.

St Stephen's Green (p63) The city's most popular park is always packed with folks looking to take advantage of the good weather.

Merrion Square (p89) The most elegant of Dublin's free parks has beautiful lawns, delicate flower beds and a statue of Oscar Wilde (among others).

Iveagh Gardens (p66) A little wilder and not as well known as the city's other parks is this bit of countryside smack in the middle of the city.

Phoenix Park (p130) The largest non-wildlife enclosed park in Europe is huge – big enough to house the president, the American ambassador, the zoo, a herd of fallow deer and more green space than you could ever need.

No-Cost Tours

Áras an Uachtaráin (p131) Guided tours of the presidential residence are free.

Glasnevin Cemetery Tours (p136) Excellent free guided tours of the country's most famous resting place.

iWalks (www.visitdublin.com/iwalks) Download your own walking tour from the tourist-office website and explore the city with an expert's voice leading the way.

LVNST- / GETTY IMAGES ©

Traditional Dublin coddle

Eating

There has never been a better time to eat out in Dublin. Not only is the range of choices better than ever, but the quality of the cuisine has reached levels never before enjoyed in a city that is a relative latecomer (in European terms, anyway) to the pleasures of the palate.

Local Specialities

It's a wonder the Irish retain their good humour amid the perpetual potato-baiting they endure. But, despite the stereotyping, potatoes are still paramount here and you'll see lots of them on Dublin menus. The mashed potato dishes colcannon and champ (with cabbage and spring onion respectively) are two of the tastiest recipes you'll find.

Most meals are usually meat based, with beef, lamb and pork common options. The most Dublin of dishes is coddle, a working-class concoction of bacon rashers, sausages,

onions, potato and plenty of black pepper. More easily available is the national edible icon, Irish stew, the slow-simmered one-pot wonder of lamb, potatoes, onions, parsley and thyme (note, no carrots).

The most famous Irish bread, and one of the signature tastes of Ireland, is soda bread. Irish flour is soft and doesn't take well to yeast as a raising agent, so Irish bakers of the 19th century leavened their bread with bicarbonate of soda. Combined with buttermilk, it makes a superbly light-textured and tasty bread, and is often on the breakfast menus at B&Bs. Scones, tarts and biscuits are specialities too.

NEED TO KNOW

Opening Hours

➡ **Cafes** 8am to 5pm Monday to Saturday

➡ **Restaurants** noon to 10pm (or midnight); food service generally ends around 9pm. Top-end restaurants often close between 3pm and 6pm; restaurants serving brunch open around 10am.

Price Ranges

The following price ranges refer to a main course:

€ less than €15

€€ €15–€28

€€€ more than €28

Booking Tables

You'll need to reserve a table for most city-centre restaurants Thursday to Saturday, and all week for the trendy spots. Most restaurants operate multiple sittings, which means 'Yes, you can have a table at seven, but we'll need it back by nine'. A recent trend is to adopt a no-reservations policy in favour of a get-on-the-list, get-in-line policy where you leave your number and wait for your table over a drink in a nearby pub.

Tipping

It's industry standard these days to tip between 10% and 12% of the bill, unless the waiter has dumped the dinner in your lap and given you the finger, while the gratuity for exceptional service is only limited by your generosity and/or level of inebriation. If you're really unhappy, don't be afraid to leave absolutely nothing, though it will very rarely come to that.

Veggie Bites

Vegetarians are having it increasingly easier in Dublin as the capital has veered away from the belief that food isn't food until your incisors have had to rip flesh from bone, and towards an understanding that healthy eating leads to, well, longer lives.

There's a selection of general restaurants that cater to vegetarians beyond the token dish of mixed greens and pulses – places like M&L (p141), Yamamori (p70) and Chameleon (p105). The Wednesday night dinner at the Fumbally (p121) always includes a tasty vegetarian option, while Assassination Custard (p67) strikes an even balance between meat and non-meat dishes.

Solidly vegetarian places include Blazing Salads (p68), with organic breads, Californian-style salads and pizza; Cornucopia (p68), Dublin's best-known vegetarian restaurant, serving wholesome salads, sandwiches and a selection of hot main courses; and Govinda's (p69), an authentic beans-and-pulses place run by the Hare Krishna.

Organic & Farmers' Markets

For more info on local markets, check out www.irishfarmersmarkets.ie, www.irishvillagemarkets.com or local county council sites such as www.dlrcoco.ie/markets.

Dublin Food Co-op (p125) Everything in this market hall is organic and/or eco-friendly. Saturday is when it's all on display – Dubliners from all over drop in for their responsible weekly shop.

Coppinger Row Market It's small but packs a proper organic punch, with freshly baked breads, delicious hummus and other goodies.

Harcourt Street Food Market (Map p242; www.irishfarmersmarkets.ie; Park Pl, Station Bldgs, Upper Hatch St; ⊗noon-2pm Thu; ▣all city centre) Organic veggies, cheeses, olives and meats made into dishes from all over the world.

People's Park Market (☑087 957 3647; People's Park, Dun Laoghaire; ⊗11am-4pm Sun) Organic meat and veg, local seafood, Irish fruit and farm cheeses.

Restaurant Patrick Guilbaud (p94)

When to Eat

Breakfast Usually eaten before 9am, although hotels and B&Bs will serve until 11am Monday to Friday, and to noon at weekends. Many cafes serve an all-day breakfast.

Lunch Usually a sandwich or a light meal between 12.30pm and 2pm. On weekends Dubliners have a big meal (called dinner) between 2pm and 4pm.

Tea No, not the drink, but the evening meal – also confusingly called dinner. A Dubliner's main daily meal, usually eaten around 6.30pm.

Eating by Neighbourhood

➡ **Grafton Street & Around** The best choice of restaurants and cafes in all price brackets. (p67)

➡ **Merrion Square & Around** Sandwich bars and Michelin-starred gourmet experiences, but little in between. (p92)

➡ **Temple Bar** A fine selection of food-as-fuel eateries and ethnic cuisine, including the best Japanese restaurant in town. (p104)

➡ **Kilmainham & the Liberties** Limited to a couple of great spots and Dublin's most famous chipper. (p121)

➡ **North of the Liffey** The most transformed of the city's neighbourhoods, with a fine selection of cafes, midrange restaurants and ethnic cuisine. (p141)

➡ **Docklands & the Grand Canal** A handful of vaguely trendy restaurants. (p153)

Lonely Planet's Top Choices

Chapter One (p142) Sublime cuisine, fabulous service and a wonderfully relaxed atmosphere.

101 Talbot (p141) Buzzy spot serving Mediterranean cuisine allegedly favoured by members of a certain Dublin supergroup.

Fade Street Social (p69) Gourmet tapas and traditional mains by Dublin superchef Dylan McGrath.

Fumbally (p121) Beautiful warehouse cafe beloved of Dublin's hipster crowd.

Banyi Japanese Dining (p105) Authentic Japanese cuisine – including the city's best sushi.

Best to Linger

Simon's Place (p68) Grab a sandwich and stare out at the world through the windows.

Third Space (p141) Perpetual refills, great music…is that the time?

L Mulligan Grocer (p142) When you're done eating, stay for the beer.

Best Asian

Yamamori (p70) Tasty Japanese classics north and south of the Liffey.

Musashi Noodles & Sushi Bar (p142) Lovely atmosphere, tasty food.

Banyi Japanese Dining (p105) Hands down the best sushi in town.

Saba (p71) Thai and Vietnamese classics in a handsome darkwood room.

Best Italian

Bottega Toffoli (p67) Tiny, tucked-away cafe serving mouth-watering food from the chef's family recipe book.

Paulie's Pizza (p153) Excellent, authentic pizza.

Honest to Goodness (p67) Superb city-centre pizza out of a stone oven.

La Dolce Vita (p105) Excellent antipasti dishes to be washed down with lashings of good wine.

Best Quick Bites

Honest to Goodness (p67) Tasty sandwiches and hot stuff to go.

Assassination Custard (p67) Great sandwiches on the fly.

Soup Dragon (p141) Get in line for the city's best liquid lunches.

Lemon (p68) Crêpes both savoury and sweet like you'd get in France.

Oxmantown (p141) Breakfast and sandwiches to go.

Best Irish Cuisine

Chapter One (p142) Nobody knew Irish cuisine could taste this good!

101 Talbot (p141) A stalwart with an always excellent menu.

Workshop Gastropub (p153) The standard bearer for pub grub in Dublin.

'The Dead' Dinner Experience (p122) Time-travel back to the late 19th century!

Winding Stair (p143) Classic Irish dishes given an elegant twist.

Union8 (p121) Beautifully presented modern Irish cuisine.

Best by Budget

€

Fumbally (p121) Great warehouse space with filling sandwiches and good coffee.

Honest to Goodness (p67) Compact eatery that is always full.

M&L (p141) The most authentic Chinese restaurant in town.

Gerry's (p68) Traditional greasy spoon with a proper greasy breakfast.

Crackbird (p104) All kinds of deep-fried chicken with tasty sides.

Cotto (p141) Lovely flavours of the Mediterranean.

€€

Fade Street Social (p69) Gourmet tapas in a gorgeous room.

Richmond (p69) Classic dishes done to perfection.

Banyi Japanese Dining (p105) The best Japanese food in town.

€€€

Chapter One (p142) The food is sublime, the atmosphere is wonderfully relaxed.

L'Ecrivain (p94) Excellent cuisine à la française.

Restaurant Patrick Guilbaud (p94) Perhaps the best restaurant in Ireland, where everything is just right.

Thornton's (p71) Modern cuisine by one of the best chefs in the country.

Sign outside O'Donoghue's (p95)

🍷 Drinking & Nightlife

If there's one constant about life in Dublin, it's that Dubliners will always take a drink. Come hell or high water, the city's pubs will never be short of customers, and we suspect that exploring a variety of Dublin's legendary pubs and bars ranks pretty high on the list of reasons you're here.

NEED TO KNOW

Opening Hours

Last orders are at 11.30pm Monday to Thursday, 12.30am Friday and Saturday and 11pm Sunday, with 30 minutes' drinking-up time each night. However, many central pubs have secured late licences to serve until 1.30am or even 2.30am (usually pubs that double up as dance clubs).

Made to Measure

➡ When drinking stout, beer or ale, the usual measure is a 'pint' (568mL).

➡ Half a pint is called a 'glass'.

➡ If you come to Ireland via Britain and drink spirits (or 'shorts' as they're called here), watch out: the English measure is a measly 25mL, while in Dublin you get a whopping 35mL, nearly 50% more.

Tipping

The American-style gratuity is not customary in bars. If there's table service, it's polite to give your server the coins in your change (up to €1).

Pubs

The pub – or indeed anywhere people gather to have a drink and a chat – remains the heart of the city's social existence and the broadest window through which you can experience the essence of the city's culture, in all its myriad forms. There are pubs for every taste and sensibility, although the traditional haunts populated by flat-capped pensioners bursting with insightful anecdotes are about as rare as hen's teeth and most Dubliners opt for their favourite among a wide selection of trendy bars, designer boozers and hipster locales. But despair not, for it is not the spit or sawdust that makes a great Dublin pub but the patrons themselves, who provide a reassuring guarantee that Dublin's reputation as the pub capital of the world remains in perfectly safe (if occasionally unsteady!) hands.

Grogan's Castle Lounge (p72)

Bars & Clubs

Dubliners like to throw down some dance-floor moves, but for the most part they do it in bars equipped with a late licence, a decent sound system and a space on the floor. It's all changed from even a decade ago, when clubbing was all the rage: these days fewer people pay to simply go dancing, preferring instead the option of dancing in a bar they've been in most of the evening. DJs are an increasingly rare breed, but the ones that thrive usually play it pretty safe; the handful of more creative DJs (including occasional international guests) play in an increasingly restricted number of venues.

The busiest nights are Thursday to Saturday, and most clubs are free if you arrive before 11pm. After that, you'll pay between €5 and €10.

Cafes

Dublin's coffee junkies are everywhere, looking for that perfect barista fix that will kill the hunger until the next one. You can top-up at any of the chains – including that one from Seattle (with multiple branches throughout the city centre) – but we reckon your caffeine craving will get the best fix at places such as Clement & Pekoe (p73), Brother Hubbard (p141), Wall and Keogh (Map p242; www.wallandkeogh.ie; 45 S Richmond St; 8.30am-8.30pm Mon-Fri, 11am-7pm Sat & Sun; all city centre) and Kaph (p73).

Above: Exterior of Oliver St John Gogarty pub (p106), Temple Bar

Right: After-work crowds on Grafton Street (p72)

STEPHEN SAKS / GETTY IMAGES ©

Drinking & Nightlife

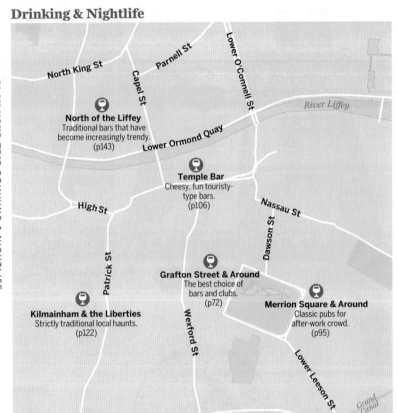

North of the Liffey
Traditional bars that have
become increasingly trendy.
(p143)

Temple Bar
Cheesy, fun touristy-
type bars.
(p106)

Grafton Street & Around
The best choice of
bars and clubs.
(p72)

Merrion Square & Around
Classic pubs for
after-work crowd.
(p95)

Kilmainham & the Liberties
Strictly traditional local haunts.
(p122)

Where to Drink

With over 1000 pubs spread across the city, you'll have your choice of where to wet your beak. The plethora of pubs in Temple Bar are a favourite place to start – here you'll find a selection of contemporary bars (some with gaudy themes) and 'traditional' boozers (strangely devoid of locals but full of Spanish tourists). We urge you to explore further afield: the pubs around Grafton St are a great mix of old-style pubs and stylish modern spots. Camden St, southwest of St Stephen's Green, is very popular, as is Dawson St and Merrion Row – the latter has a couple of long-established favourites.

North of the Liffey has a selection of fine old pubs and genuine locals (read: visitors will be given the once-over), but there are a handful of popular bars, including the city's best gay bar, on Capel St.

Lonely Planet's Top Choices

Anseo (p72) Unpretentious, un-affected and incredibly popular.

Grogan's Castle Lounge (p72) Favourite haunt of Dublin's writers and painters.

James Toner's (p95) Closest thing you'll get to a country pub in the heart of the city.

Kehoe's (p72) Atmospheric pub in the city centre.

Long Hall (p72) One of the city's most beautiful and best-loved pubs.

No Name Bar (p72) Great bar in a restored Victorian townhouse.

John Mulligan's (p155) Established in 1782, this old boozer is still going strong.

Best Pint of Guinness

Kehoe's (p72) Stalwart popular with locals and tourists.

John Mulligan's (p155) Perfect setting for a perfect pint.

Grogan's Castle Lounge (p72) Great because the locals demand it!

Fallon's (p122) Centuries of experience.

Best Choice of Beer

L Mulligan Grocer (p142) A wide range of cask ales.

Porterhouse (p106) Serves its own delicious brews.

Wigwam (p143) Big selection of craft beers.

P.Mac's (p72) Thirty different IPAs as well as established brews.

Best Musical Pubs

O'Donoghue's (p95) The unofficial HQ of folk music.

Devitt's (p75) Trad music most nights.

Cobblestone (p143) Best sessions in town.

Auld Dubliner (p107) Traditional sessions for tourists.

Best New Bars

P.Mac's (p72) Old-style new hipster hangout.

Opium Rooms (p74) Dublin's version of Hakkasan.

Bow Lane (p72) Elegant bar.

Chelsea Drug Store (p73) Art deco hang-out.

Best Club Nights

Jazz Jam Open, free jazz jam session at **Grand Social** (p144) on Monday.

C U Next Tuesday Student night of R & B, hip hop and pop at **Opium Rooms** (p74) on Tuesday.

DJs Indie, house and disco in different rooms on Friday at the **Workman's Club** (p107).

Mother Disco, electro and pop on Saturday at **Mother** (p106)… not for the faint-hearted.

Reflektor Indie rock at **Whelan's** (p75) on Thursday.

Best DJ Bars

Whelan's (p75) Classic and contemporary rock.

Dice Bar (p143) Dive bar with an eclectic range, from rock to lounge and dance.

Bernard Shaw (p74) Great DJs playing a mix of tunes.

Workman's Club (p107) Regular line-up of excellent DJs.

Wigwam (p143) Basement bar with rockin' DJs.

Best Traditional Pubs

John Mulligan's (p155) The gold standard of traditional.

Long Hall (p72) Stylishly old-fashioned.

Hartigan's (p95) The bare essentials.

Stag's Head (p73) Popular with journalists and students.

Old Royal Oak (p122) A proper neighbourhood pub.

Best for a Solitary Pint

Kehoe's (p72) Best in the early afternoon.

John Mulligan's (p155) Just a ticking clock for noise.

Grogan's Castle Lounge (p72) Artistic contemplation.

PLAN YOUR TRIP DRINKING & NIGHTLIFE

Props on stage at Gate Theatre (p144)

 # Entertainment

Believe it or not, there is life beyond the pub or, more accurately, around it. There are comedy clubs and classical concerts, recitals and readings, marionettes and music – lots and lots of music. The other great Dublin treat is the theatre, where you can enjoy a light-hearted musical alongside the more serious stuff by Beckett, Yeats and O'Casey – not to mention a host of new talents.

Theatre

Despite Dublin's rich theatrical heritage, times are tough for the city's thespians. Once upon a time, everybody went to the theatre to see the latest offering by Synge, Yeats or O'Casey. Nowadays, a night at the theatre is the preserve of the passionate few, which has resulted in the city's bigger theatres taking a conservative approach to their programming and many fringe companies having to make do with non-theatrical spaces to showcase their skills – and that's if they manage to stay afloat at all: 24 companies went to the wall between 2009 and 2013 due to the recession.

Nevertheless, a Dublin performance of, say, O'Casey's *Plough and the Stars* or Synge's *The Playboy of the Western World* remains a special experience. The Abbey and the Gate are the city's most important theatres, but you'll also find shows in pubs, offices and other spaces appropriated for the purpose.

Theatre bookings can usually be made by quoting a credit-card number over the phone, then you can collect your tickets just before the performance. Expect to pay anything between €12 and €25 for most shows, with some costing as much as €30. Most plays begin between 8pm and 8.30pm. Check www.irishtheatreonline.com to see what's playing.

Comedy

The Irish have a reputation for hilarity – mostly off-the-cuff, iconoclastic humour – and the funniest of them generally find their way out of Ireland and onto bigger stages. Notable among these are Dara O'Briain, Dylan Moran and Chris O'Dowd, who's a bona fide star thanks to films such as *Bridesmaids* (2011) and *This Is 40* (2012).

One of the biggest breakout stars of 2015 was Sharon Horgan, the Irish-born, London-based creator and star of TV sitcom *Catastrophe,* which was hugely successful in the UK and, latterly, the US; in 2016 she was busy writing a new series for HBO starring Sarah Jessica Parker. Another big talent is David O'Doherty, who's been a regular festival winner since the early noughties but in 2015-16 toured the world with his hit show *We Are All in the Gutter, But Some of Us Are Looking at David O'Doherty*.

Film

Of the five cinemas in the city centre, two (Irish Film Institute and Lighthouse) offer a more offbeat list of foreign releases and art-house films. Save yourself the hassle of queuing and book your tickets online, especially for Sunday-evening screenings of popular first-run films. After drinking sessions on Friday and Saturday nights, most Dubliners have neither the energy nor the cash for more of the same, so it's a trip to the cinema at the end of the weekend. Admission prices are generally around €6 for afternoon shows, rising to €10 after 5pm. If you have a student card, you pay only €6 for all shows.

Live Music
POPULAR

Dubliners love their live music and are as enthusiastic about supporting local acts as they are about cheering touring international stars – even if the latter command the bigger crowds and ticket prices. You can sometimes buy tickets at the venue itself, but you're probably better off going through an agent. Prices for gigs range dramatically, from as

NEED TO KNOW

Bookings

Theatre, comedy and classical concerts are usually booked directly through the venue. Tickets for touring international bands and big-name local talent are either sold at the venue or through a booking agency like Ticketmaster (p40), which sells tickets to every genre of big- and medium-sized show – but be aware that it charges between 9% and 12.5% service charge *per ticket*.

Pre-Theatre Deals

Look out for good-value pre-theatre menus in some restaurants, which will serve dinner before opening curtain and coffee and drinks after the final act.

Opening Hours

➡ Doors for most gigs open at 7pm.

➡ By law, gigs in bigger venues and arenas finish by 11pm.

Newspaper Listings

The Herald (www.herald.ie; €1.30) Thursday edition has a good listings page.

Hot Press (www.hotpress.com) Fortnightly music mag; Ireland's answer to *NME* or *Rolling Stone*.

Irish Times (www.irishtimes.com; €2) Friday listings pullout called 'The Ticket'.

Irish Independent (www.independent.ie; €1.90) 'Night/Day' listings pullout on Friday.

Online Listings

Entertainment.ie (www.entertainment.ie) For all events.

MCD (www.mcd.ie) Biggest promoter in Ireland.

Nialler9 (www.nialler9.com) Excellent indie blog with listings.

Sweebe (www.sweebe.com) Over 200 venues listed.

Totally Dublin (http://totallydublin.ie) Comprehensive listings and reviews.

What's On In (www.whatsonin.ie) From markets to gigs and club nights.

low as €5 for a tiny local act to anywhere up to €90 for the really big international stars.

THEATRE FESTIVALS

For two weeks in October most of the city's theatres participate in the **Dublin Theatre Festival** (www.dublintheatrefestival.com; ☉Oct), originally founded in 1957 and today a glittering parade of quality productions and elaborate shows.

Initially a festival for those shows too 'out-there' or insignificant to be considered for the main festival, **Dublin Fringe Festival** (www.fringefest.com; ☉Sep) is now a three-week extravaganza with more than 100 events and over 700 performances. The established critics may keep their ink for the bigger do, but we strongly recommend the Fringe for its daring and diversity.

The listings sections of both paper and on-line resources will have all the gigs.

TRADITIONAL & FOLK

The best place to hear traditional music is in the pub, where the 'session' – improvised or scheduled – is still best attended by foreign visitors who appreciate the form far more than most Dubs and will relish any opportunity to drink and toe-tap to some extraordinary virtuoso performances.

Also worth checking out is the **Temple Bar Trad Festival** (www.templebartrad.com; ☉Jan), which takes place in the pubs of Temple Bar over the last weekend in January. For online info on sessions, check out www.dublinsessions.ie.

CLASSICAL

Classical music is constantly fighting an uphill battle in Dublin, with inadequate funding, poor management and questionable repertoires all contributing to its limited appeal. Resources are appalling, and there's neither the talent nor the funding to match their European counterparts. But before lambasting Ireland's commitment to classical forms, it's well worth bearing in mind that this country has never had a tradition of classical music or lyric opera – the musical talents round these parts naturally focused their attentions on Ireland's home-grown repertoire of traditional music. And still they managed to produce one of the great lyric tenors of the 20th century in Count John McCormack (1884–1945).

But it's not all doom and gloom. Classical music may be small fry, but it survives thanks to the efforts of a number of (sub-sidised) orchestras and the Opera Theatre Company, which works to keep opera alive. Bookings for all classical gigs can be made either at the venues or through **Ticketmaster** (Map p244; ☑0818 719 300; www.ticketmaster.ie; Stephen's Green Shopping Centre).

Entertainment by Neighbourhood

➡ **Grafton Street & Around** The entertainment heartland of Dublin has something for everyone. (p75)

➡ **Merrion Square & Around** Quiet at night-time except for the pubs, some of which have live music. (p95)

➡ **Temple Bar** From clubbing to live traditional music, you'll find a version of it in Temple Bar. (p107)

➡ **Kilmainham & the Liberties** The Irish Museum of Modern Art hosts the occasional concert. (p124)

➡ **North of the Liffey** Live gigs, traditional music and the city's two most historic theatres dominate the entertainment skyline. (p144)

➡ **Docklands & the Grand Canal** Make your way eastward along the Liffey to Dublin's biggest theatre. (p155)

Lonely Planet's Top Choices

Cobblestone (p143) Best traditional music sessions in town.

Dublin Fringe Festival (p40) Exciting new theatre.

Gate Theatre (p144) Masterfully presented classics.

Bord Gáis Energy Theatre (p155) Top-class club venue.

Whelan's (p75) For the intimate gig.

Workman's Club (p107) To see the best new bands.

Best Comedy

Ha'Penny Bridge Inn (p107) Local humour hits and misses.

International Bar (p73) Rising crop of Irish talent.

Laughter Lounge (p145) Established names and visiting stars.

Best High Culture

Abbey Theatre (p144) Top names in Irish theatre.

Bloomsday (p22) Making sense of *Ulysses*.

Culture Night (p22) Art, architecture and heritage.

Best Festivals

Dublin Fringe Festival (p40) Best of contemporary theatre.

St Patrick's Festival (p21) A city goes wild.

Temple Bar Trad Festival (p40) One of the best knees up of the year.

Taste of Dublin (p22) A weekend of gourmet goodness.

Forbidden Fruit (p22) Excellent alternative music fest.

Best Theatres

Gate Theatre (p144) Wonderful old classic.

Project Arts Centre (p107) For interesting fringe plays.

Bord Gáis Energy Theatre (p155) The best indoor venue in town.

Best Live-Music Venues

Cobblestone (p143) For traditional music.

3 Arena (p156) Big-name acts only.

Whelan's (p75) Singer-songwriter HQ.

Workman's Club (p107) Who's cool, right now.

PLAN YOUR TRIP ENTERTAINMENT

CHRISTIAN KOBER / ROBERTHARDING / GETTY IMAGES ©

Performers in the St Patrick's Day parade, part of St Patrick's Festival (p21)

Shopping

If it's made in Ireland – or pretty much anywhere else – you can find it in Dublin. Grafton St is home to a range of largely British-owned high-street chain stores; you'll find the best local boutiques in the surrounding streets. On the north side, pedestrianised Henry St has international chain stores, as well as Dublin's best department store, Arnott's.

Traditional Irish Products

Traditional Irish products such as crystal and knitwear remain popular choices, and you can increasingly find innovative modern takes on the classics. But steer clear of the mass-produced junk whose joke value isn't worth the hassle of carting it home on the plane: trust us, there's no such thing as a genuine *shillelagh* (Irish fighting stick) for sale anywhere in town.

Markets

In recent years Dublin has gone gaga for markets. Which is kind of ironic, considering the city's traditional markets, like Moore St, were ignored by those same folks who now can't get enough of the homemade hummus on sale at the new gourmet spots. It's all so... continental.

Shopping by Neighbourhood

➤ **Grafton Street & Around** Grafton St has traditionally been the shopping street, but the preponderance of British-owned chain stores means you'll find the same kind of stuff you can get almost anywhere. To really get the most of the area's retail allure, get off Grafton St and head into the grid of streets surrounding it, especially to the west, where you'll find some of Dublin's most interesting outlets. (p75)

➤ **Temple Bar** Dublin's most touristy neighbourhood has a pretty diverse mix of shops, from tourist-only tat retailers to the weird and (sometimes) wonderful; it's a place where you can get everything from a Celtic-design wall-hanging to a handcrafted bong. A couple of Dublin's best markets take place in this area on Saturday. (p107)

➤ **North of the Liffey** North-side shopping is all about the high-street chain store and the easy-access shopping centre, which is mighty convenient for Dubliners looking for everyday wear at decent prices. (p145)

Lonely Planet's Top Choices

Avoca Handweavers (p76) Irish knits and handicrafts.

Barry Doyle Design Jewellers (p76) Beautiful bespoke creations.

Ulysses Rare Books (p76) For that rare first edition.

Claddagh Records (p108) Traditional and folk music.

Article (p75) Homewares and gift ideas.

Sheridan's Cheesemongers (p76) A proper cheese shop.

Best Markets

Book Fair (p109) Rummage through second-hand books.

Cow's Lane Designer Mart (p109) A real market for hipsters bringing together over 60 of the best clothing, accessory and craft stalls.

Temple Bar Food Market (p107) The city's best open-air food market.

Moore Street Market (p147) Open-air, steadfastly 'Old Dublin' market, with fruit, fish and flowers.

Best Fashion

Louis Copeland (p78) Fabulous suits made to measure, as well as ready-to-wear suits by international designers.

Costume (p78) Exclusive contracts with some of Europe's most innovative designers.

Nowhere (p76) The very latest fashions for young men.

Maven (p78) The latest international fashions for women.

Best Guaranteed Irish

Avoca Handweavers (p76) Our favourite department store in the city has myriad homemade gift ideas.

Irish Design Shop (p75) Wonderful handicrafts carefully sourced.

Barry Doyle Design Jewellers (p76) Exquisite handcrafted jewellery with unique contemporary designs.

Ulysses Rare Books (p76) For that priceless first edition or a beautiful, leather-bound copy of Joyce's *Dubliners*.

Louis Copeland (p78) Dublin's very own top tailor with made-to-measure suits.

Best Homewares

Martin Fennelly Antiques (p125) Fine furniture and furnishings from the Georgian, Victorian and Edwardian eras.

Industry (p78) Scandi-style homewares with an Irish touch.

Article (p75) Beautiful tableware and decorative home accessories made by Irish designers.

Avoca Handweavers (p76) Stylish but homey brand of modern Irish life.

Best Jewellery

Appleby (p78) High-quality silver and gold jewellery.

Loulerie (p76) Beautiful selection of delicate jewellery.

Barry Doyle Design Jewellers (p76) Handmade jewellery exceptional in its beauty and simplicity.

Rhinestones (p78) Fine antique and quirky costume jewellery from the 1920s to 1970s.

Hurley sticks, used in the Gaelic game of Hurling

Sports & Activities

To many Dubliners, sport is a religion. For an ever-increasing number, it's all about faith through good works such as jogging, amateur football, cycling and yoga; for everyone else, observance is enough, especially from the living-room chair or the pub stool.

Activities

Public sporting facilities are limited – there are only a handful of public tennis courts, for instance – so most visitors have to make do with their hotel gym or a run in the park.

GOLF

A round of golf is a highlight of many an Irish visit. Dublin's suburban courses are almost all private clubs, but many of them allow visitors on a pay-to-play basis. Tough times means reduced green fees, especially if you book online beforehand. You'll generally need your own transport if you wish to head to any of the major courses.

The best courses within reach of the city are **Killeen Castle** (www.killeencastle. com; Dunsany, Co Meath; green fee €50-90) in Dunsany, County Meath; **Carton House** (www.cartonhousegolf.com; Carton House; green fees weekday/weekends €50/65), just outside Maynooth in County Kildare; **Portmarnock** (☑01-846 2968; www.portmarnockgolfclub.ie; Golf Links Rd, Portmarnock; green fee weekday/weekend €175/200), by the sea in north county Dublin; and **Druid's Glen** (☑01-287 0800; www. druidsglenresort.com; Newtownmountkennedy, Co

OONAT / GETTY IMAGES ©

Wicklow; weekdays/weekends €55/65), 45km
south of the city in County Wicklow.

Spectator Sport
GAELIC FOOTBALL & HURLING
Gaelic games are at the core of Irishness;
they are enmeshed in the fabric of Irish
life and hold a unique place in the heart
of its culture. Of the two main games,
football is by far the most popular – and
Dublin (www.dublingaa.ie) is the second-
most successful county with 25 All-Ireland
Senior Championship titles, after its great
rival Kerry (who have 37). Hurling has
traditionally never been as popular, but
in recent years the Dublin team has done
very well.

The big event in both sports is the All-
Ireland championship, a knockout contest
that begins in April and ends on the first
(for hurling) and third (for football) Sunday in September with the All-Ireland
Final, played at a jam-packed **Croke Park**
(01-836 3222; www.crokepark.ie; Clonliffe Rd;
 3, 11, 11A, 16, 16A, 123 from O'Connell St), which
is also where the Dubs play all of their
championship matches. The All-Ireland's
poorer cousin is the National Football
League (there's also a National Hurling
League), which runs from February to
mid-April. Dublin plays its league matches
at **Parnell Park** (Clantarkey Rd, Donnycarney;
adult/child €10/7; 20A, 20B, 27, 27A, 42, 42B,
43, 103 from Lower Abbey St or Beresford Pl),
which is smaller and infinitely less impressive than Croke Park but a great place to
see these games up close. Tickets for league
games can be easily bought at the ground;
tickets for All-Ireland matches get tougher
to find the further on the competition is,
but those that are available can be bought
online (https://gaa.tickets.ie) or at most
Centra and SuperValu convenience stores
throughout the city centre.

FOOTBALL
Although Dubliners are football (soccer)
mad, the five Dublin teams that play in
the **League of Ireland** (www.leagueofireland.
com) are semi-pro, as the best players are
all drawn to the glamour of the English
Premier League. The season runs from
April to November; tickets are available at
all grounds.

The national side plays its home games at
the **Aviva Stadium** (p156; a relatively high
pricing structure and the general mediocrity
of the team means that home matches don't

NEED TO KNOW
Sporting Seasons
➡ **Football** April to October
➡ **Gaelic Sports** April to September
➡ **Rugby Internationals** February to
April

Planning Ahead
➡ **Two months** Tickets for rugby in-
ternationals or the latter stages of the
Gaelic championship
➡ **One month** Leinster rugby matches
in the Heineken Cup
➡ **One week** Local football matches and
Gaelic league games

Online Resources
Gaelic Athletic Association (www.gaa.ie)
Football Association of Ireland (www.
fai.ie)
Irish Rugby Football Union (www.irfu.ie)
Horse Racing Ireland (www.goracing.ie)
Golf Union of Ireland (www.gui.ie)
Ladies Gaelic Football Association
(www.ladiesgaelic.ie)

usually sell out. You can buy tickets (€30 to
€60) from the **Football Association of
Ireland** (FAI; 01-676 6864; www.fai.ie).

HORSE & GREYHOUND RACING
Horse racing is a big deal in Dublin, especially when you consider that Irish trainers
are among the best in the world and Irish
jockeys dominate the field in British racing.
There are several racecourses within driving
distance of the city centre that host good-
quality meetings throughout the year. These
include the **Curragh** (045-441 205; www.cur
ragh.ie; admission €15-40; mid-Apr–Oct), which
hosts five classic flat races between May
and September; **Fairyhouse** (01-825 6167;
www.fairyhouse.ie; Fairyhouse Road, Ratoath, Co
Meath; €14-22; special from Busáras), home of
the Grand National on Easter Monday; and
Leopardstown (01-289 3607; www.leopards
town.com; special from Eden Quay), where the
big event is February's Hennessy Gold Cup.
The flat racing season runs from March to
November, while the National Hunt season –
when horses jump over things – is October to
April. There are also events in summer.

BEST DUBLIN SPORTING MOMENTS

➡ A cheeky intercept try by Brian O'Driscoll results in Leinster beating perennial rivals Munster in front of 80,000 fans during the 2009 Heineken Cup.

➡ Dublin beating Kerry 0-12 to 0-9 in the 2015 All-Ireland Final for their third title in five years, their 25th overall.

➡ Ireland beating England 1-0 in 1988 during the European Championship finals in Stuttgart, the first – and only – time the Irish soccer team has ever beaten England competitively.

➡ The Irish rugby team beating England by a record-margin 43-13 on 24 February 2007 at Croke Park: history and victory wrapped up in one delicious moment.

➡ Boxer Katie Taylor winning Olympic gold at the 2012 games in London.

Traditionally the poor-man's punt, greyhound racing ('the dogs') has been smartened up in recent years and partly turned into a corporate outing. It offers a cheaper alternative to horse racing. Dublin's two dog tracks are **Harold's Cross Park** (✆01-497 1081; www.igb.ie; 151 Harold's Cross Rd; adult/child €12/8; ⊘6.30-10.30pm Tue & Fri; ☐16, 16A from city centre) and **Shelbourne Park** (p156).

Swimming & Water Sports

Dublin might have miles of beachy coastline, but swimming and water sports aren't as big a deal as they might be in, say, a destination where the climate is more conducive to being wet and outdoors. There are boating aficionados (and designated clubs) in the seaside suburbs of Dun Laoghaire, Howth and Malahide, but when it comes to regular old swimming, there's relatively little choice, although one of these is an international-standard **aquatic centre** (www.nationalaquaticcentre.ie; Snugborough Rd; adult/child & student €14/13; ⊘6am-10pm Mon-Fri, 9am-8pm Sat & Sun; ☐38A from Hawkins St). The relatively new sport of wakeboarding (p156) is also available in the Docklands.

Sports & Activities by Neighbourhood

➡ **Kilmainham & the Liberties** Jogging and walking in the War Memorial Gardens. (p125)

➡ **North of the Liffey** Running, football, cycling in Phoenix Park, also cricket and polo. (p147)

➡ **Docklands & the Grand Canal** Wakeboarding in the Grand Canal Dock, jogging along the canal. (p156)

Above: Gaelic football

Right: Golf tournament, Killeen Castle (p44)

PATRICK BOLGER / STRINGER / GETTY IMAGES ©

CARLOS SANCHEZ PEREYRA / GETTY IMAGES ©

Explore Dublin

DUBLIN'S
TOP SIGHTS

Neighbourhoods at a Glance

❶ Grafton Street & Around p52

Dublin's bustling heart is the area on and around Grafton St. Most of the action takes place within its easily walkable confines, where you'll find the biggest range of pubs and restaurants, and where most Dubliners come to blow off some retail steam. Many of the city's most important sights and museums are here, as is Dublin's best-loved city park, St Stephen's Green.

❷ Merrion Square & Around p82

Genteel, sophisticated and elegant, the exquisite Georgian architecture spread around

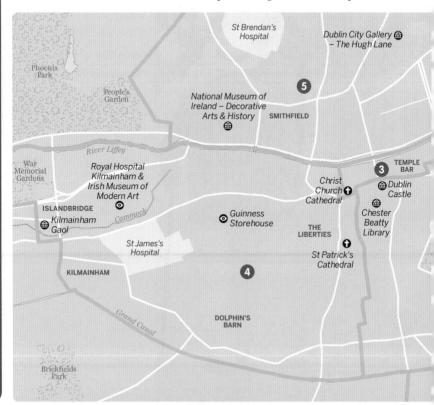

handsome Merrion Sq is a near-perfect mix of imposing public buildings, museums, and private offices and residences. It is round these parts that much of moneyed Dublin works and plays, amid the neoclassical beauties thrown up during Dublin's 18th-century prime. These include the home of the Irish parliament at Leinster House and, immediately surrounding it, the National Gallery, the main branch of the National Museum of Ireland and the Museum of Natural History.

❸ Temple Bar p98

Dublin's best-known district is the cobbled playpen of Temple Bar, where mayhem and merriment is standard fare, especially on summer weekends when the pubs are full and the party spills out onto the streets. During daylight hours there are shops and galleries to discover, which at least lend some truth to the area's title as the city's 'cultural quarter'.

❹ Kilmainham & the Liberties p110

Dublin's oldest and most traditional neighbourhoods would scarcely draw a crowd were it not for the presence of the Guinness Storehouse, home to Dublin's most visited museum. Keeping watch over the ancient Liberties is St Patrick's Cathedral, the most important of Dublin's three (!) cathedrals, while to the west of the city centre are the country's premier modern-art museum and a Victorian prison that played a central role in Irish history.

❺ North of the Liffey p128

Grittier than its more genteel southside counterpart, the neighbourhoods immediately north of the River Liffey offer a fascinating mix of 18th-century grandeur, traditional city life and the multicultural melting pot that is contemporary Dublin. Beyond its widest, most elegant boulevard you'll find art museums and whiskey museums, bustling markets and some of the best ethnic eateries in town. Oh, and Europe's largest enclosed park – home to the president, the US ambassador and the zoo.

❻ Docklands & the Grand Canal p150

Dublin's Docklands were once a symbol of the ambitious development of the Celtic Tiger, especially the area around Grand Canal Dock, on the south side of the Liffey east of the city centre. A couple of architectural beauties – most notably a theatre designed by Daniel Libeskind – stand out among the modern apartment and office blocks.

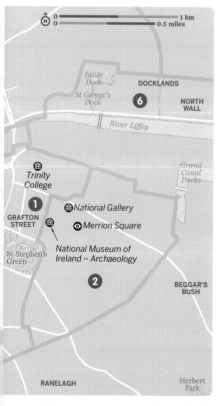

Grafton Street & Around

Neighbourhood Top Five

1 **Chester Beatty Library** (p62) Basking quietly in the aesthetic glow of the magnificent collection at one of the finest museums in Ireland.

2 **Old Library** (p55) Staring in wonderment at the colourful pages of the *Book of Kells,* the world's most

famous illuminated gospel, before visiting the majestic Long Room.

3 **St Stephen's Green** (p63) Enjoying a sunny, summer afternoon on the grass, where Dubliners come to rest, romance and remind themselves of what makes life worth living.

4 **Little Museum of Dublin** (p63) Exploring the marvellous collection of donated historical objects.

5 **A night out** (p72) Eating dinner in one of the area's fabulous restaurants followed by a pint or more in a pub, such as Kehoe's.

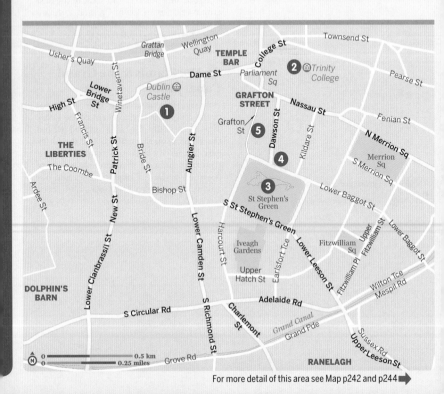

For more detail of this area see Map p242 and p244

Explore Grafton Street & Around

Grafton St and its surrounding precinct are something of a flexible feast of activities and sights, but it'll take you two days to even begin to do them justice – and much longer if you really want to get to the heart of what this part of the city is all about. The main attraction is Trinity College, whose pleasures and treasures can be explored in no more than a couple of hours; right on its doorstep is Grafton St itself, always worth an amble for a little retail experience or just to take in the sound of one of its many buskers. Just south of Grafton St is the centrepiece of Georgian Dublin, St Stephen's Green, beautifully landscaped and dotted with statuary that provides a veritable who's who of Irish history. But to get the most out of the neighbourhood, you'll need to get off Grafton St and into the warren of narrow lanes and streets to the west of it – here you'll find a great mix of shops and boutiques, some of our favourite eateries, and a handful of the best bars in the city. Further west again is Dublin Castle and the Chester Beatty Library, both of which can be explored in half a day. Thankfully, Dublin's compact size means you don't have to stay here to have it all at your doorstep, but if you do, be aware that most of the lodgings are among the priciest in town.

Local Life

➡ **Hang-outs** Grogan's Castle Lounge (p72) is the artiest of the city's bohemian pubs; the Stag's Head (p73) is a Victorian classic; sit at the window in hip Clement & Pekoe (p73) and watch the fashion parade outside.

➡ **Retail** Costume (p78) is the place for high-end women's fashions and Nowhere (p76) the men's equivalent; wander the boutiques of the Powerscourt Townhouse (p76) for quirky one-offs and local fashions.

➡ **Sustenance** Fade Street Social (p69) is great for a splashy night out; otherwise Honest to Goodness (p67) has divine pizzas and Super Miss Sue (p69) the best fish.

➡ **Markets** Every Thursday you can load up on goodies at the small Coppinger Row Market (p30).

Getting There & Away

➡ **Bus** All cross-city buses make their way to – or through, at least – this part of the city.

➡ **Tram** The Luas Green Line has its terminus at the south end of Grafton St, on the west side of St Stephen's Green.

➡ **On Foot** Grafton St is in the heart of the city and no more than 500m from all other neighbourhoods (including the western edge of the Docklands).

Lonely Planet's Top Tip

The most interesting shops in town are in the warren of streets between Grafton St and South Great George's St; here you'll also find some of the best lunch deals.

Best Places to Eat

➡ Assassination Custard (p67)

➡ Honest to Goodness (p67)

➡ Fade Street Social (p69)

➡ Richmond (p69)

For reviews, see p67 ➡

Best Places to Sleep

➡ Westbury Hotel (p182)

➡ Fitzwilliam Hotel (p182)

➡ Radisson Blu Royal Hotel (p182)

For reviews, see p180 ➡

Best Places to Shop

➡ Article (p75)

➡ Costume (p78)

➡ Nowhere (p76)

➡ Irish Design Shop (p75)

For reviews, see p75 ➡

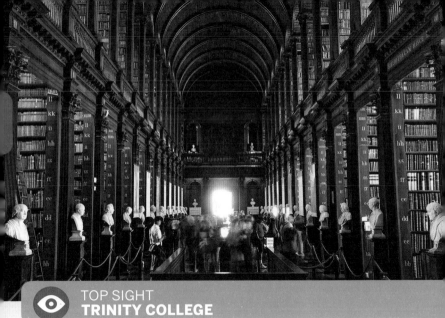

ANDREW MONTGOMERY / GETTY IMAGES ©

TOP SIGHT
TRINITY COLLEGE

This calm and cordial retreat from the bustle of contemporary Dublin is Ireland's most prestigious university, a collection of elegant Georgian and Victorian buildings, cobbled squares and manicured lawns that is among the most delightful places to wander.

History

The college was established by Elizabeth I in 1592 on land confiscated from an Augustinian priory in an effort to stop the brain drain of young Protestant Dubliners, who were skipping across to continental Europe for an education and becoming 'infected with popery'. Trinity went on to become one of Europe's most outstanding universities, producing a host of notable graduates – how about Jonathan Swift, Oscar Wilde and Samuel Beckett at the same alumni dinner?

Front Row & Parliament Square

The elegant **Regent House entrance** on College Green is guarded by statues of the writer Oliver Goldsmith (1730–74) and the orator Edmund Burke (1729–97). The railings outside are a popular meeting spot.

Through the entrance, past the Students Union, are Front Sq and Parliament Sq, the latter dominated by the 30m-high **Campanile** (Map p244; Trinity College; ☐all city centre), designed by Edward Lanyon and erected from 1852 to 1853 on what was believed to be the centre of the monastery that preceded the college. According to superstition, students who pass beneath it when the bells toll will fail their exams. To the north of the Campanile is a **statue of George Salmon**, the college provost from 1886 to 1904, who fought bitterly to keep women out of the college. He carried out his threat to permit them

DON'T MISS

➡ Long Room
➡ *Book of Kells*
➡ Science Gallery
➡ Walking Tour

PRACTICALITIES

➡ Map p244, G2
➡ ☎01-896 1000
➡ www.tcd.ie
➡ College Green
➡ admission free
➡ ⊘8am-10pm
➡ ☐all city centre

in 'over his dead body' by dropping dead when the worst happened. To the south of the Campanile is a **statue of historian WEH Lecky** (1838–1903).

Chapel & Dining Hall

North of Parliament Sq is the 1799 **Chapel** (Map p244; ☑01-896 1260; Trinity College; ⊙8.30am-5pm, admission by special permission only; ⬚all city centre), designed by William Chambers and featuring fine plasterwork by Michael Stapleton, Ionic columns and painted-glass windows. It has been open to all denominations since 1972 and is only accessible by organised tour. Next is the **Dining Hall** (Map p244; Parliament Sq, Trinity College; ⊙closed to public; ⬚all city centre), originally built by Richard Cassels in the mid-18th century. The great architect must have had an off day because the vault collapsed twice and the entire structure was dismantled 15 years later. The replacement was completed in 1761, but extensively restored after a fire in 1984.

Library Square

On the far east of Library Sq, the red-brick **Rubrics Building** (Map p244; Trinity College; ⊙closed to the public; ⬚all Trinity College) dates from around 1690, making it the oldest building in the college. Extensively altered in an 1894 restoration, it underwent serious structural modification in the 1970s.

If you are following the less-studious-looking throng, you'll find yourself drawn south of Library Sq to the **Old Library** (Map p244; Library Sq; ⊙9.30am-5pm Mon-Sat year-round, noon-4.30pm Sun Oct-Apr, 9.30am-4.30pm Sun May-Sep; ⬚all city centre), home to Trinity's prize possession and biggest crowd-puller, the astonishingly beautiful *Book of Kells*.

Upstairs is the highlight of Thomas Burgh's building, the magnificent 65m Long Room (p57) with its barrel-vaulted ceiling. It's lined with shelves containing 200,000 of the library's oldest manuscripts, busts of scholars, a 14th-century harp and an original copy of the Proclamation of the Irish Republic.

Fellows' Square

West of the brutalist, brilliant **Berkeley Library** (Map p244; Fellows' Sq; ⊙closed to public), designed by Paul Koralek in 1967 and now closed to the public, the Arts & Social Science Building is home to the **Douglas Hyde Gallery**, one of the country's leading contemporary galleries. It hosts regularly rotating shows presenting the works of top-class Irish and international artists across a range of media.

GRAFTON STREET & AROUND TRINITY COLLEGE

A CATHOLIC BAN

Trinity was exclusively Protestant until 1793, but even when the university relented and began to admit Catholics, the Church forbade it; until 1970, any Catholic who enrolled here could consider themselves excommunicated.

A great way to see the grounds is on a walking tour (p80), which depart from the College Green entrance.

Book a fast-track ticket online to get cheaper and speedier access to the Book of Kells and the Long Room.

SWORDS & GUNS

For nearly two centuries students weren't allowed through the grounds without a sword – and duels with pistols were not uncommon in the 17th and 18th centuries.

Trinity College, Dublin

STEP INTO THE PAST

Ireland's most prestigious university, founded on the order of Queen Elizabeth I in 1592, is an architectural masterpiece, a cordial retreat from the bustle of modern life in the middle of the city. Step through its main entrance and you step back in time, the cobbled stones transporting you to another era, when the elite discussed philosophy and argued passionately in favour of empire.

Standing in Front Square, the 30m-high **Campanile ❶** is directly in front of you with the **Dining Hall ❷** to your left. On the far side of the square is the Old Library building, the centrepiece of which is the magnificent **Long Room ❸**, which was the inspiration for the computer-generated imagery of the Jedi Archive in *Star Wars Episode II: Attack of the Clones*. Here you'll find the university's greatest treasure, the **Book of Kells ❹**. You'll probably have to queue to see this masterpiece, and then only for a brief visit, but it's very much worth it.

Just beyond the Old Library is the very modern **Berkeley Library ❺**, which nevertheless fits perfectly into the campus' overall aesthetic: directly in front of it is the distinctive **Sphere Within a Sphere ❻**, the most elegant of the university's sculptures.

DON'T MISS

» Douglas Hyde Gallery, the campus' designated modern-art museum.

» cricket match on pitch, the most elegant of pastimes.

» pint in the Pavilion Bar, preferably while watching the cricket.

» visit to the Science Gallery, where science is made completely relevant.

RAQUEL PEDROSA PEREZ / GETTY IMAGES ©

Campanile
Trinity College's most iconic bit of masonry was designed in the mid-19th century by Sir Charles Lanyon; the attached sculptures were created by Thomas Kirk.

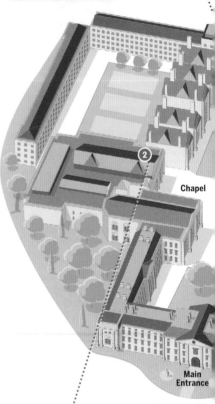

Chapel

Main Entrance

Dining Hall
Richard Cassels' original building was designed to mirror the Examination Hall directly opposite on Front Square: the hall collapsed twice and was rebuilt from scratch in 1761.

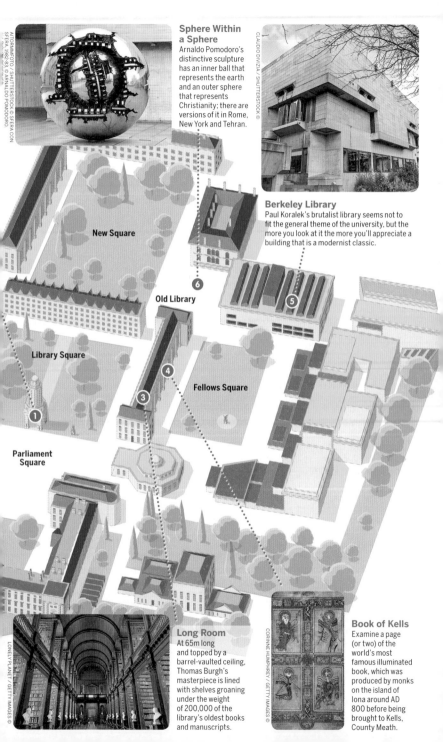

Sphere Within a Sphere
Arnaldo Pomodoro's distinctive sculpture has an inner ball that represents the earth and an outer sphere that represents Christianity; there are versions of it in Rome, New York and Tehran.

Berkeley Library
Paul Koralek's brutalist library seems not to fit the general theme of the university, but the more you look at it the more you'll appreciate a building that is a modernist classic.

New Square

Old Library

Library Square

Fellows Square

Parliament Square

Long Room
At 65m long and topped by a barrel-vaulted ceiling, Thomas Burgh's masterpiece is lined with shelves groaning under the weight of 200,000 of the library's oldest books and manuscripts.

Book of Kells
Examine a page (or two) of the world's most famous illuminated book, which was produced by monks on the island of Iona around AD 800 before being brought to Kells, County Meath.

AITORMMFOTO / SHUTTERSTOCK © SFERA, 1982-83, © ARNALDO POMODORO.CON

CLAUDIO DIVIZIA / SHUTTERSTOCK ©

LONELY PLANET / GETTY IMAGES ©

CORINNE HUMPHREY / GETTY IMAGES ©

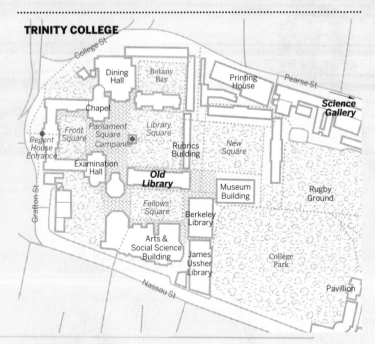

Examination Hall

On the way back towards the main entrance, past the Reading Room, is the late-18th-century Palladian **Examination Hall** (Map p244; Trinity College; ☉9am-6pm during exams only; ☐all city centre), which closely resembles the chapel opposite because it too was the work of William Chambers. It contains an oak chandelier rescued from the Irish parliament (now the Bank of Ireland).

College Park

Towards the eastern end of the complex, **College Park** is a lovely place to lounge around on a sunny day and occasionally you'll catch a game of cricket, a bizarre sight in Ireland. Keep in mind that **Lincoln Place Gate** is located in the southeast corner of the grounds, providing a handy shortcut to Merrion Sq.

Science Gallery

Although part of the campus, you'll have to walk along Pearse St to get into Trinity's newest attraction, the Science Gallery (p64). Since opening in 2008, it has proven immensely popular with everyone for its refreshingly lively and informative exploration of the relationship between science, art and the world we live in. Exhibits have touched on a range of fascinating topics including the science of desire and an exploration of the relationship between music and the human body. The ground-floor cafe (p64), bathed in floor-to-ceiling light, is a pretty good spot to take a load off.

GERMAN-IMAGES / GETTY IMAGES ©

TOP SIGHT
DUBLIN CASTLE

If you're looking for a medieval castle straight out of central casting you'll be disappointed; the stronghold of British power here for 700 years is principally an 18th-century creation that is more hotch-potch palace than turreted castle.

History

Only the Record Tower survives from the original Anglo-Norman fortress, which was built in the early 13th century and served as the centre of English colonial administration until 1922.

When Henry VIII's firm-handed representative in Ireland, Lord Deputy Henry Sidney, took charge in 1565, he declared the castle to be 'ruinous, foul, filthy and great decayed' – and he wasn't far wrong. Until then most of the King's deputies in Ireland had been Anglo-Irish lords who preferred living in their own castles than taking up residence at Dublin Castle, and so it fell into disrepair. Sidney oversaw a 13-year building program that saw the construction of a 'a verie faire house for the Lord Deputie or Chief Governor to reside in' as well as a new chapel and the Clock Tower.

Sidney's new castle became the permanent residence of the monarch's chief representative – known at different times as the Justiciar, Chief Lieutenant, Lord Lieutenant or Viceroy – until the construction of the vice-regal lodge in the Phoenix Park in 1781 (now Áras an Uachtaráin, the residence of the President).

The new castle reflected the changing status of English power in Ireland – Henry's conquest of the whole island ('beyond the Pale') and his demolition of the old Anglo-Irish hegemony resulted in the castle no longer being a colonial outpost but the seat of English

DON'T MISS
- ⇒ Chapel Royal
- ⇒ State Apartments
- ⇒ Upper Yard

PRACTICALITIES
- ⇒ Map p242, A2
- ⇒ ☎ 01-677 7129
- ⇒ www.dublincastle.ie
- ⇒ Dame St
- ⇒ adult/child €8.50/6.50
- ⇒ ⏱ 9.45am-4.45pm Mon-Sat, noon-4.45pm Sun
- ⇒ ▣ all city centre

CASTLE CALENDAR

During British rule the Castle's social calendar was busiest for the six weeks leading up to St Patrick's Day, with a series of lavish dinners, levées and balls for the city's aristocratic residents – even during the Famine years.

The only way you'll get to see the castle's most interesting bits is by guided tour. The castle is occasionally used for government functions, so parts may be closed to the public.

CASTLE CATHOLICS

Until independence, Catholic Dubliners who were deemed to be too friendly with or sympathetic to the British crown were derisively termed 'Castle Catholics'.

power and the administrative centre for all of Ireland – a new role that brought with it a huge civil service.

The Irish Parliament met in the Great Hall, which burnt down (along with most of the rest of the castle) in the great fire of 1684 – the Parliament eventually moved in 1731 to what is now the Bank of Ireland building in College Green.

Below ground, the castle dungeons were home to the state's most notorious prisoners, including – most famously – 'Silken' Thomas Fitzgerald, whose defeated challenge to Henry VIII in 1534 kicked off Henry's invasion of Ireland in the first place. Needless to say, the native Irish came to view the castle as the most menacing symbol of their oppressed state.

When it was officially handed over to Michael Collins on behalf of the Irish Free State in 1922, the British viceroy is reported to have rebuked Collins for being seven minutes late. Collins replied, 'We've been waiting 700 years, you can wait seven minutes.' The castle is now used by the Irish government for meetings and functions, and can only be visited on a guided tour.

Chapel Royal

As you walk in to the grounds from the main Dame St entrance, there's a good example of extravagant 19th-century Irish architecture: on your left is the Victorian Chapel Royal (occasionally part of the Dublin Castle tours), decorated with more than 90 heads of various Irish personages and saints carved out of Tullamore limestone. The interior is wildly exuberant, with fan vaulting alongside quadripartite vaulting, wooden galleries, stained glass and lots of lively looking sculpted angels.

Upper Yard

The Upper Yard enclosure roughly corresponds with the dimensions of the original medieval castle. On your right is a **Figure of Justice** with her back turned to the city, reckoned by Dubliners to be an appropriate symbol for British justice. Next to it is the **Bedford Tower**, built in 1761 on the site of the original Norman gate. The Irish Crown Jewels were stolen from the tower in 1907 and never recovered.

Guided Tours

The 45-minute **guided tours** (departing every 20 to 30 minutes, depending on numbers) are pretty dry, seemingly pitched at tourists more likely to ooh and aah over period furniture than historical anecdotes, but they're included in the entry fee. You get to visit the **State Apartments**, many of which are decorated

DUBLIN CASTLE

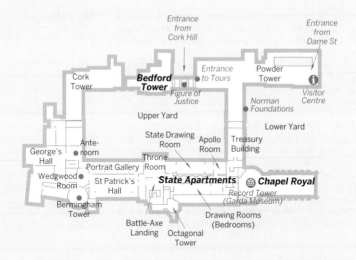

in dubious taste. There are beautiful chandeliers (ooh!), plush Irish carpets (aah!), splendid rococo ceilings, a Van Dyck portrait and the throne of King George V. You also get to see **St Patrick's Hall**, where Irish presidents are inaugurated and foreign dignitaries toasted, and the room in which the wounded James Connolly was tied to a chair while convalescing after the 1916 Easter Rising – brought back to health to be executed by firing squad.

The highlight is a visit to the **subterranean excavations** of the old castle, discovered by accident in 1986. They include foundations built by the Vikings (whose long-lasting mortar was made of ox blood, eggshells and horse hair), the hand-polished exterior of the castle walls that prevented attackers from climbing them, the steps leading down to the moat and the trickle of the historic River Poddle, which once filled the moat on its way to join the Liffey.

The Rest of the Castle

Beside the Victorian Chapel Royal is the Norman **Record Tower**, the last intact medieval tower in Dublin. On your right is the **Georgian Treasury Building**, the oldest office block in Dublin, and behind you, yikes, is the uglier-than-sin **Revenue Commissioners Building** of 1960.

The world-famous Chester Beatty Library, housed in the Clock Tower at the back of Dublin Castle, is not just Ireland's best small museum, but one of the best you'll find anywhere in Europe.

This extraordinary collection, so lovingly and expertly gathered by New York mining magnate Alfred Chester Beatty, is breathtakingly beautiful and virtually guaranteed to impress.

Alfred Chester Beatty

An avid traveller and collector, Alfred Chester Beatty (1875–1968) was fascinated by different cultures and amassed more than 20,000 manuscripts, rare books, miniature paintings, clay tablets, costumes and any other objets d'art that caught his fancy and could tell him something about the world. Fortunately for Dublin, he also happened to take quite a shine to the city and made it his adopted home. In return, the Irish made him their first honorary citizen in 1957.

Art of the Book

The collection is spread over two levels. On the ground floor you'll find the Art of the Book, a compact but stunning collection of artworks from the Western, Islamic and East Asian worlds. Highlights include the finest collection of Chinese jade books in the world and illuminated European texts featuring exquisite calligraphy that stand up in comparison with the *Book of Kells*. Audiovisual displays explain the process of bookbinding, paper-making and printing.

Sacred Traditions

The 2nd floor is home to Sacred Traditions, a wonderful exploration of the world's major religions through decorative and religious art, enlightening text and a cool cultural-pastiche video at the entrance. The collection of Qu'rans dating from the 9th to the 19th centuries (the library has more than 270 of them) is considered by experts to be the best example of illuminated Islamic texts in the world. There are also outstanding examples of ancient papyri, including renowned Egyptian love poems from the 12th century, and some of the earliest illuminated gospels in the world, dating from around AD 200. The collection is rounded off with some exquisite scrolls and artwork from China, Japan, Tibet and Southeast Asia, including the two-volume Japanese *Chogonka Scroll,* painted in the 17th century by Kano Sansetu.

The Building

As if all of this wasn't enough for one visit, the library also hosts temporary exhibits that are usually too good to be missed. Not only are the contents of the museum outstanding, but the layout, design and location are also unparalleled, from the marvellous Silk Road Café (p68) and gift shop, to the Zen rooftop terrace and the beautiful landscaped garden out the front. These features alone would make this an absolute Dublin must-do.

DON'T MISS

➡ Nara e-hon scrolls, The East Asian Collection, Sacred Traditions

➡ Ibn al-Bawwab Qu'ran, The Qu'ran Collection, Sacred Traditions

➡ New Testament papyri, The Western Collection, Sacred Traditions

PRACTICALITIES

➡ Map p242, A2

➡ 📞01-407 0750

➡ www.cbl.ie

➡ Dublin Castle

➡ admission free

➡ ⏱10am-5pm Mon-Fri, 11am-5pm Sat, 1-5pm Sun year-round, closed Mon Nov-Feb, free tours 1pm Wed, 3pm & 4pm Sun

➡ 🚌all city centre

 **SIGHTS**

TRINITY COLLEGE HISTORIC BUILDING
See p54.

DUBLIN CASTLE HISTORIC BUILDING
See p59.

CHESTER BEATTY LIBRARY MUSEUM
See p62.

★**ST STEPHEN'S GREEN** PARK
Map p242 (☺dawn-dusk; ▣all city centre, ▣St
Stephen's Green) As you watch the assorted
groups of friends, lovers and individuals
splaying themselves across the nine elegantly landscaped hectares of Dublin's
most popular green lung, St Stephen's
Green, consider that those same hectares
once formed a common for public whip-
pings, burnings and hangings. These
days, the harshest treatment you'll get is
the warden chucking you off the grass for
playing football or Frisbee.

The buildings around the square date
mainly from the mid-18th century, when
the green was landscaped and became the
centrepiece of Georgian Dublin. The northern side was known as the Beaux Walk
and it's still one of Dublin's most esteemed
stretches, home to Dublin's original society
hotel, the Shelbourne (p183). Nearby is the
tiny Huguenot Cemetery (p92), established
in 1693 by French Protestant refugees.

Railings and locked gates were erected
in 1814, when an annual fee of one guinea
was charged to use the green. This private
use continued until 1877 when Sir Arthur
Edward Guinness pushed an act through
parliament opening the green to the public once again. He also financed the central
park's gardens and ponds, which date from
1880.

The main entrance to the green today
is beneath **Fusiliers' Arch** (Map p244; St Stephen's Green; ▣all city centre), at the top of
Grafton St. Modelled to look like a smaller
version of the Arch of Titus in Rome, the
arch commemorates the 212 soldiers of
the Royal Dublin Fusiliers who were killed
fighting for the British in the Boer War
(1899–1902).

Spread across the green's lawns and
walkways are some notable artworks; the
most imposing of these is a **monument to
Wolfe Tone** (Map p242; St Stephen's Green;
▣all city centre), the leader of the abortive
1798 rebellion. Occupying the northeastern

corner of the green, the vertical slabs serving as a backdrop to the statue have been
dubbed 'Tonehenge'. At this entrance is a
memorial (Map p242; St Stephen's Green; ▣all
city centre) to all those who died in the Potato Famine (1845–51).

On the eastern side of the green is a
children's playground and to the south
there's a fine old **bandstand**, erected to
celebrate Queen Victoria's jubilee in 1887.
Musical performances often take place
here in summer. Near the bandstand is a
bust of James Joyce.

CITY ASSEMBLY HALL HISTORIC BUILDING
Map p244 (58 South William St; ☺11am-6pm
Mon-Fri, 12.30-6pm Sun; ▣all city centre) `FREE`
This elegant Georgian townhouse was
built between 1766 and 1771 by the Society
of Artists as the first purpose-built public
exhibition room in the British Isles. During the 19th century it served as an unofficial city hall – Daniel O'Connell once
spoke here for four hours – but is now
the headquarters of the Irish Georgian
Society, who are restoring it to its original
purpose. It now hosts exhibitions.

LITTLE MUSEUM OF DUBLIN MUSEUM
Map p244 (☏01-661 1000; www.littlemuseum.
ie; 15 St Stephen's Green N; adult/student €8/6;
☺9.30am-5pm Mon-Fri, to 8pm Thu; ▣all city
centre, ▣St Stephen's Green) The idea is
ingeniously simple: a museum, spread
across two rooms of an elegant Georgian
building, devoted to the history of Dublin
in the 20th century, made up of memorabilia contributed by the general public. You
don't need to know anything about Irish
history or Dublin to appreciate it: visits
by guided tour and everyone is presented
with a handsome booklet on the history of
the city.

Since opening in 2011, the contributions have been impressive. Amid the nos-
talgic posters, time-worn bric-a-brac and
wonderful photographs of personages and
cityscapes of yesteryear are some extraordinary finds, including a lectern used by
JFK on his 1963 visit to Ireland and an
original copy of the fateful letter given to
the Irish envoys to the treaty negotiations
of 1921, whose contradictory instructions
were at the heart of the split that resulted in
the Civil War. Curator Sarah Costigan also
runs a weekly tour of the exhibits focusing
on women and their role in Irish history.

DOUGLAS HYDE
GALLERY OF MODERN ART   GALLERY

Map p244 (www.douglashydegallery.com; Trinity College; ⊙11am-6pm Mon-Wed & Fri, to 7pm Thu, to 4.45pm Sat; 🖳all city centre) **FREE** This is one of those marvellous galleries that seems to have escaped the public radar, partly because of its location tucked away on campus at Trinity. Its ambitious contemporary program stays firmly in the cutting-edge camp; exhibitions here are often 'enhanced' with film, live music or performance-driven sideshows.

SCIENCE GALLERY   MUSEUM

(Map p248; www.sciencegallery.ie; Naughton Gallery, Pearse St; ⊙exhibitions usually noon-8pm Tue-Fri, to 6pm Sat & Sun; 🖳all city centre) **FREE** Demonstrating that science is fun, engaging and relevant to our everyday lives in more ways than we could even imagine is the mission statement of this immensely popular gallery, which hosts an ever-changing mix of compelling exhibits. Recent shows included a study of trauma and an exploration of domestic life. The ground-floor **cafe** (Map p248; Pearse St; €4-8; ⊙8am-8pm Tue-Fri, noon-6pm Sat & Sun) is lovely.

BANK OF IRELAND   NOTABLE BUILDING

Map p244 (📞01-671 1488; College Green; ⊙10am-4pm Mon-Wed & Fri, to 5pm Thu; 🖳all city centre) A sweeping Palladian pile occupying one side of College Green, this magnificent building was the Irish Parliament House until 1801 and is the first purpose-built parliament building in the world. The original building – the central colonnaded section that distinguishes the present-day structure – was designed by Sir Edward Lovett Pearce in 1729 and completed by James Gandon in 1733.

When the parliament voted itself out of existence through the 1801 Act of Union, the building was sold under the condition that the interior would be altered to prevent it ever again being used as a debating chamber. It was a spiteful strike at Irish parliamentary aspirations, but while the central House of Commons was remodelled and offers little hint of its former role, the smaller **House of Lords** (admission free) survived and is much more interesting. It has Irish oak woodwork, a mahogany longcase parliament clock and a late-18th-century Dublin crystal chandelier. Its design was copied for the construction of the original House of Representatives in Washington, DC, now the National Statuary Hall. The House of Lords is open to visitors during banking hours but Dublin historian Sean Ó Laocha does pre-arranged tours of the chamber on Tuesdays between 10.30am and 12.30pm.

CITY HALL   MUSEUM

Map p242 (www.dublincity.ie/dublincityhall; Dame St; adult/student/child €4/2/1.50; ⊙10am-5.15pm Mon-Sat; 🖳all city centre) This beautiful Georgian structure was originally built by Thomas Cooley as the Royal Exchange between 1769 and 1779, and botched in the mid-19th century when it became the offices of the local government (hence its name). Thankfully, a more recent renovation (2000) has restored it to its gleaming Georgian best. The basement has an exhibit on the city's history.

The rotunda and its ambulatory form a breathtaking interior, bathed in natural light from enormous windows to the east. A vast marble statue of former mayor and Catholic emancipator Daniel O'Connell stands here as a reminder of the building's links with Irish nationalism (the funerals of both Charles Stewart Parnell and Michael Collins were held here). Dublin City Council still meets here on the first Monday of the month, gathering to discuss the city's business in the Council Chamber, which was the original building's coffee room.

There was a sordid precursor to City Hall on this spot in the shape of the Lucas Coffee House and the adjoining Eagle Tavern, in which the notorious Hellfire Club was founded by Richard Parsons, Earl of Rosse, in 1735. Although the city abounded with gentlemen's clubs, this particular one gained a reputation for messing about in the arenas of sex and Satan, two topics that were guaranteed to fire the lurid imaginings of city's gossipmongers.

Located in the striking vaulted basement, **The Story of the Capital** is a multimedia exhibition that traces the history of the city from its earliest beginnings to its hoped-for future – with ne'er a mention of sex and Satan. More's the pity, as the info is quite overwhelming and the exhibits are a little text-heavy. Still, it's a pretty slick museum with informative audiovisual displays.

ROYAL IRISH ACADEMY   LIBRARY

Map p244 (📞01-676 2570; www.ria.ie; 19 Dawson St; ⊙10am-5.30pm Mon-Thu, to 5pm Fri; 🖳all city centre, 🚆St Stephen's Green) **FREE** Ireland's

THE PAGE OF KELLS

The history of the *Book of Kells* is almost as fascinating as its illuminations. It is thought to have been created around AD 800 by the monks at St Colmcille's Monastery on Iona, a remote island off the coast of Scotland; repeated looting by marauding Vikings forced the monks to flee to Kells, County Meath, along with their masterpiece. It was stolen in 1007, then rediscovered three months later buried underground.

The *Book of Kells* was brought to Trinity College for safekeeping in 1654, and is now housed in the **Old Library** (p55), with half a million visitors queueing up to see it annually. The 680-page (340-folio) book was rebound in four calfskin volumes in 1953.

And here the problems begin. Of the 680 pages, only two are on display – one showing an illumination, the other showing text – hence the 'page of Kells' moniker. No getting around that one, though: you can hardly expect the right to thumb through a priceless treasure at random. No, the real problem is its immense popularity, which makes viewing it a rather unsatisfactory pleasure. Punters are herded through the specially constructed viewing room at near lightning pace, making for a quick-look-and-move-along kind of experience.

To really appreciate the book, you can get your own reproduction copy for a mere €22,000. Failing that, the Old Library bookshop stocks a plethora of souvenirs and other memorabilia, including Otto Simm's excellent *Exploring the Book of Kells* (€11.99), a thorough guide with attractive colour plates, and a popular DVD showing all 680 pages for €31.95.

GRAFTON STREET & AROUND SIGHTS

pre-eminent society of letters has an 18th-century library that is home to several important documents, including a collection of ancient manuscripts such as the *Book of Dun Cow;* the *Cathach of St Columba;* and the entire collection of 19th-century poet Thomas Moore (1779–1852).

NEWMAN UNIVERSITY CHURCH   CHURCH

Map p242 (☑01-475 9674; www.universitychurch.ie; 87a St Stephen's Green S; ⊗8am-6pm; ☑10, 11, 13, 14 or 15A, ☑St Stephen's Green) **FREE** Cardinal Newman didn't care too much for the Gothic style of his day, so the 1856 church attached to his Catholic University of Ireland at Newman House is a neo-Byzantine charmer. Its richly decorated interior was mocked at first but has since become the preferred surroundings for Dublin's most fashionable weddings.

NEWMAN HOUSE   NOTABLE BUILDING

Map p242 (☑01-477 9810; www.ucd.ie; 85-86 St Stephen's Green S; adult €7; ⊗tours 2pm Tue, also by arrangement; ☑10, 11, 13, 14 or 15A, ☑St Stephen's Green) Among the finest examples of Georgian architecture in Dublin are these two townhouses, founded by Cardinal Newman as the Catholic University of Ireland in 1865, along with an adjoining Victorian hall. The college was founded as an alternative to the Protestant hegemony of Trinity College, which was then the only option available to those seeking third-level education in Ireland. The alma mater of James Joyce, Pádraig Pearse and Eamon de Valera can be visited by **guided tour**.

Newman House is still part of the college, which later decamped to the suburb of Belfield and changed its name to University College Dublin.

The house comprises two exquisitely restored town houses; No 85, the granite-faced original, was designed by Richard Cassels in 1738 for parliamentarian Hugh Montgomery, who sold it to Richard Chapel Whaley, MP, in 1765. Whaley wanted a grander home, so he commissioned another house next door at No 86.

Aside from Cassels' wonderful design, the highlight of the building is the plasterwork, perhaps the finest in the city. For No 85, the artists were the Italian stuccodores Paolo and Filippo LaFranchini, whose work is best appreciated in the wonderfully detailed Apollo Room on the ground floor. The plasterwork in No 86 was done by Robert West, but it is not quite up to the high standard of next door. When the newly founded, Jesuit-run Catholic University of Ireland took possession of the house in 1865, alterations were made to some of the more graphic plasterwork, supplying the nude figures with 'modesty vests'.

COLLEGE GREEN STATUARY

The imposing grey sculptures adorning College Green are monuments to two of Ireland's most notable patriots. In front of the bank is Henry Grattan (1746–1820), a distinguished parliamentary orator, while nearby is a modern memorial to the patriot Thomas Davis (1814–45). Where College St meets Pearse St, another traffic island is topped by a 1986 sculpted copy of the *Steyne* (the Viking word for 'stone'), which was erected on the riverbank in the 9th century to stop ships from grounding and removed in 1720.

During Whaley's residency, the house developed a certain notoriety, largely due to the activities of his son, Buck, a notorious gambler and hell-raiser who once walked all the way to Jerusalem for a bet and somehow connived to have himself elected to parliament at the tender age of 17. During the university's tenure, however, the residents were a far more temperate lot. The Jesuit priest and wonderful poet Gerard Manley Hopkins lived here during his time as professor of classics, from 1884 until his death in 1889. Hopkins's bedroom is preserved as it would have been during his residence, as is the classroom where the young James Joyce studied while obtaining his Bachelor of Arts degree between 1899 and 1902.

MOLLY MALONE STATUE   STATUE

Map p244 Dublin's most famous statue is that of fictional fishmonger (and lady of dubious morals) Molly Malone, she of the song alive, alive-o. Pending the ongoing expansion of the Luas tram system, she's been moved from the bottom of Grafton St to Suffolk St, but that doesn't halt the never-ending procession of visitors looking for a selfie with her.

IVEAGH GARDENS   GARDENS

Map p242 (☉dawn-dusk; 🚊all city centre, 🚊St Stephen's Green) FREE These beautiful gardens may not have the sculpted elegance of the other city parks, but they never get too crowded and the warden won't bark at you if you walk on the grass. They were designed by Ninian Niven in 1863 as the private grounds of **Iveagh House**, and include a rustic grotto, a cascade, a fountain, a maze and a rosarium. Enter the gardens from Clonmel St, off Harcourt St.

ROYAL COLLEGE OF SURGEONS   UNIVERSITY

Map p242 (www.rcsi.ie; 123 St Stephen's Green W; ☉closed to the public; 🚊all city centre) The early-19th-century Royal College of Surgeons has one of the finest facades on St Stephen's Green. During the 1916 Easter Rising, the building was occupied by rebel forces led by the colourful Countess Markievicz (1868–1927), an Irish Nationalist married to a supposed Polish count. The columns are scarred from the bullet holes. Today it continues to produce doctors, and is especially popular with students from overseas.

ST WERBURGH'S CHURCH   CHURCH

Map p242 (📞01-478 3710; Werburgh St; ☉services 11am 1st & 3rd Sun of month, call for access at other times; 🚌50, 50A or 56A from Aston Quay, 54 or 54A from Burgh Quay) West of Dublin Castle, St Werburgh's Church stands upon ancient foundations (probably from the 12th century), but was rebuilt several times during the 17th and 18th centuries. The church's tall spire was dismantled after Robert Emmet's rising in 1803, for fear that future rebels might use it as a vantage point for snipers.

Interred in the vault is Lord Edward Fitzgerald, who turned against Britain, joined the United Irishmen and was a leader of the 1798 Rising. In what was a frequent theme of Irish uprisings, compatriots gave him away and his death resulted from the wounds he received when captured. Coincidentally, Major Henry Sirr, the man who captured him, is buried out in the graveyard. On the porch you will notice two fire pumps that date from the time when Dublin's fire department was composed of church volunteers. The interior is rather more cheerful than the exterior, although the church is rarely used. Phone, or see the caretaker at 8 Castle St, to see inside. Donations welcome.

MANSION HOUSE   NOTABLE BUILDING

Map p244 (Dawson St; ☉closed to the public; 🚊all city centre, 🚊St Stephen's Green) Built in 1710 by Joshua Dawson – after whom the street is named – this has been the official residence of Dublin's mayor since 1715, and was the site of the 1919 Declaration of Independence and the meeting of the first parliament. The building's original brick Queen Anne style has all but disappeared behind a stucco facade added in the Victorian era.

IRISH-JEWISH MUSEUM
MUSEUM

Map p242 (☎01-453 1797; www.jewishmu seum.ie; 3 Walworth Rd; ☺11am-3pm Sun-Thu May-Sep, 10.30am-2.30pm Sun Oct-Apr) `FREE` Housed in an old synagogue, this museum recounts the history and cultural heritage of Ireland's small but prolific Jewish community. It was opened in 1985 by the Belfast-born, then-Israeli president, Chaim Herzog. The various memorabilia includes photographs, paintings, certificates, books and other artefacts.

WHITEFRIARS STREET CARMELITE CHURCH
CHURCH

Map p244 (☎01-475 8821; 56 Aungier St; ☺8am-6.30pm Mon & Wed-Fri, 8am-9.30pm Tue, 8am-7pm Sat, 8am-7.30pm Sun; ☐16, 19, 19A, 83 or 122 from Trinity College) If you find yourself mulling over the timing of a certain proposal – or know someone who needs some prompting – walk through the automated glass doors of this church and head for the remains of none other than St Valentine, donated by Pope Gregory XVI in 1836.

The Carmelites returned to this site in 1827, when they re-established their former church, which had been seized by Henry VIII in the 16th century. In the northeastern corner is a 16th-century Flemish oak statue of the Virgin and Child, believed to be the only wooden statue in Ireland to have escaped the Reformation unscathed.

✖ EATING

HONEST TO GOODNESS
PIZZA $

Map p244 (www.honesttogoodness.ie; 12 Dame Ct; mains €6-15; ☺8am-5pm Mon, to 10pm Tue & Wed, to 11pm Thu & Fri, 9am-11pm Sat, 10am-4pm Sun; ☐all city centre) By day, the downstairs cafe serves wholesome sandwiches, tasty soups and a near-legendary sloppy joe. By night, the upstairs restaurant serves what might be the best pizza in town – authentic enough to earn a Neapolitan's approval. Terrific staff, wonderful atmosphere.

PEPPERPOT
CAFE $

Map p244 (www.thepepperpot.ie; Powerscourt Townhouse Shopping Centre; mains €5-9; ☺10am-6pm Mon-Wed & Fri, to 8pm Thu, 9am-6pm Sat, noon-6pm Sun; ☐all city centre) Everything is baked and made daily at the lovely cafe on the 1st-floor balcony of the Powerscourt Townhouse. The salads with homemade brown bread are delicious but the real treat is the soup of the day (€4.50) – the ideal liquid lunch.

ASSASSINATION CUSTARD
CAFE $

Map p242 (19 Kevin St; mains €3.50-5; ☺8am-3.30pm Mon-Fri; ☐all city centre) A cafe so small you'd almost miss it, but then you'd miss one of the tastiest treats in town – how about roasted cauliflower with toasted dukkah, or broccoli with spicy Italian 'nduja pork sausage and Toonsbridge ricotta? And if you're feeling really adventurous, try the tripe sandwich. The name comes from a phrase coined by Samuel Beckett.

AZTECA
MEXICAN $

Map p242 (19 Lord Edward St; burritos €8.50; ☺10am-10pm Mon-Fri, noon-10pm Sat, noon-6pm Sun; ☐all city centre) This spot near Dublin Castle has been around for a few years but rarely features on anyone's 'must-eat' list. Their loss, because the burritos here are contenders for best in Dublin.

LISTONS
SANDWICHES $

Map p242 (www.listonsfoodstore.ie; 25 Lower Camden St; lunch €5-12; ☺9am-6.30pm Mon-Fri, 10am-6pm Sat; ☐all city centre) They've been making gourmet sandwiches for so long here that it's hard to imagine them getting any better. Besides the delicacies you put between slices of bread, this excellent spot also does roasted-vegetable quiches, rosemary potato cakes and sublime salads. On fine days, take your gourmet picnic to the nearby Iveagh Gardens.

BOTTEGA TOFFOLI
ITALIAN $

Map p242 (34 Castle St; sandwiches & salads €9-14; ☺8am-4pm Tue & Wed, 8am-9pm Thu & Fri, 11am-8pm Sat, 1-8pm Sun; ☐all city centre) Tucked away on a side street that runs alongside Dublin Castle is this superb Italian cafe, the loving creation of its Irish-Italian owners. Terrific sandwiches (beautifully cut prosciutto, baby tomatoes and rocket salad drizzled with imported olive oil on homemade *piadina,* a type of rustic bread), and the pizzas are as good as any you'd get out of a Neapolitan oven.

GERRY'S
CAFE $

Map p242 (6 Montague St; Irish fry €6.50; ⊙8am-7pm Mon-Fri, to 2.30pm Sat; 🖳all city centre) A no-nonsense, old-school 'caff' (the British Isles' equivalent of the greasy-spoon) is rarer than hen's teeth in the city centre these days, which makes Gerry's something of a treasure. You won't find a more authentic spot to enjoy a traditional Irish fry-up – and if you want healthy, it always does porridge, but what's the point?

BLAZING SALADS
VEGETARIAN $

Map p244 (42 Drury St; salads €5-10; ⊙10am-6pm Mon-Wed, Fri & Sat, to 8pm Thu; 🍴; 🖳all city centre) Organic breads (including many special diet varieties), Californian-style salads from a serve-yourself salad bar, smoothies and pizza slices can all be taken away from this delicious deli.

NEON
ASIAN $

Map p242 (🖉01-405 2222; www.neon17.ie; 17 Lower Camden St; mains €10-12; ⊙noon-11pm; 🖳all city centre) A brilliant spot that specialises in authentic Thai and Vietnamese street food, served in takeaway boxes, which you can eat at home or in the canteen-style dining room. Hardened palates can jump right into the super-spicy *pad ki mow* noodles; more delicate taste buds can live with a delicious massaman curry. It also delivers (from 5pm).

BUNSEN
BURGERS $

Map p242 (www.bunsen.ie; 36 Wexford St; burgers €7-9; ⊙noon-9.30pm Mon-Wed, noon-10.30pm Thu-Sat, 1-9.30pm Sun; 🖳all city centre) Homemade, succulent artisan burgers so big and tasty, they're almost sinful. Its latest **branch** (🖉01-652 1022; 3 S Anne St) is nearby on S Anne St.

SIMON'S PLACE
CAFE $

Map p244 (George's St Arcade, S Great George's St; sandwiches €5; ⊙8.30am-5pm Mon-Sat; 🍴; 🖳all city centre) Simon's soup-and-sandwich joint is a city stalwart, impervious to the fluctuating fortunes of the world around it mostly because its doorstep sandwiches and wholesome vegetarian soups are delicious and affordable. As trustworthy cafes go, this is the real deal.

LEMON
CREPERIE $

Map p244 (66 S William St; pancakes from €5.95; ⊙7.30am-7.30pm Mon-Fri, to 9pm Thu, 8.30am-7.30pm Sat, 9.40am-6.30pm Sun; 🖳all city centre) Dublin's best pancake joint has branches on both sides of Grafton St, one on South William and the other on Dawson St (p68). Each serves up a wide range of sweet and savoury crêpes – those paper-thin ones stuffed with a variety of goodies and smothered in toppings – along with super coffee in a buzzy atmosphere.

SILK ROAD CAFÉ
MIDDLE EASTERN $

Map p242 (Chester Beatty Library, Dublin Castle; mains €11; ⊙10am-4.45pm Mon-Fri, from 11am Sat & Sun May-Sep, closed Mon Nov-Apr; 🚌50, 51B, 77, 78A or 123) This vaguely Middle Eastern–North African–Mediterranean gem on the ground floor of the Chester Beatty Library (p62) is no ordinary museum cafe. Complementing house specialities including Greek moussaka and spinach lasagne are daily specials such as *djaj mehshi* (chicken stuffed with spices, rice, dried fruit, almonds and pine nuts). All dishes are halal and kosher.

The cafe also serves an Afternoon Tea with a Twist (€23), which features no cucumber sandwiches or scones but treats from 15 different countries such as sushi, chicken schwarma parcels and Persian love cakes.

FALLON & BYRNE
DELI $

Map p244 (www.fallonandbyrne.com; Exchequer St; mains €5-10; ⊙8am-9pm Mon-Wed, 8am-10pm Thu & Fri, 9am-9pm Sat, 11am-7pm Sun; 🖳all city centre) Dublin's answer to the American Dean and DeLuca chain is this upmarket food hall and wine cellar, which is where discerning Dubliners come to buy their favourite cheeses and imported delicacies, as well as to get a superb lunch-to-go from the deli counter.

Upstairs is an elegant **brasserie** (Map p244; 🖉01-472 1000; www.fallonandbyrne. com; Exchequer St; mains €12-16; ⊙noon-3pm & 5.30-9pm Sun-Tue, to 10pm Wed & Thu, to 11pm Fri & Sat; 🖳all city centre) that serves Irish-influenced Mediterranean cuisine.

CORNUCOPIA
VEGETARIAN $

Map p244 (www.cornucopia.ie; 19 Wicklow St; salads €5.50-10.95; ⊙8.30am-9pm Mon & Tue, 8.30am-10.15pm Wed-Sat, noon-9pm Sun; 🍴) Dublin's best-known vegetarian restaurant is this terrific eatery that serves wholesome salads, sandwiches and a selection of hot main courses from a daily changing menu. It's so popular it's recently expanded onto the 2nd floor.

LITTLE ASS BURRITO BAR   MEXICAN $

Map p244 (32 Dawson St; mains €7-8; ⊙11.30am-8pm Mon & Sun, to 9pm Tue & Wed, to 10pm Thu, to 2am Fri & Sat; ᴪall city centre, ᴪSt Stephen's Green) Tacos, quesadillas and burritos to go (this place is far too small to linger). They're tasty and pretty authentic, not that it would bother those queuing for late-night munchies.

GOVINDA'S   VEGETARIAN $

Map p244 (www.govindas.ie; 4 Aungier St; mains €7-10; ⊙noon-9pm Mon-Sat;) An authentic beans-and-pulses place run by the Hare Krishna, with three branches in the city centre. Its cheap, wholesome mix of salads and Indian-influenced hot daily specials is filling and tasty.

GREEN NINETEEN   IRISH $

Map p242 (☏01-478 9626; www.green19.ie; 19 Lower Camden St; mains €10-19; ⊙8.30am-11pm; ☏; ᴪall city centre) A firm favourite on Camden St's corridor of cool is this sleek restaurant that specialises in locally sourced, organic grub – without the fancy price tag. Braised lamb chump, corned beef, pot roast chicken and the ubiquitous burger are but the meaty part of the menu, which also includes salads and veggie options.

★FADE STREET SOCIAL   MODERN IRISH $$

Map p244 (☏01-604 0066; www.fadestreetsocial.com; 4-6 Fade St; mains €19-32, tapas €5-12; ⊙12.30-10.30pm Mon-Fri, 5-10.30pm Sat & Sun; ☏; ᴪall city centre) Two eateries in one, courtesy of renowned chef Dylan McGrath: at the front, the buzzy tapas bar, which serves up gourmet bites from a beautiful open kitchen. At the back, the more muted restaurant specialises in Irish cuts of meat – from veal to rabbit – served with home grown, organic vegetables. There's a bar upstairs too. Reservations suggested.

SUPER MISS SUE   SEAFOOD $$

Map p244 (www.supermisssue.com; 2-3 Drury St; mains €19-32; ⊙cafe noon-10pm Mon-Wed, to 11pm Thu-Sat, to 4pm Sun; Luna 5-11pm Wed-Sat) Super Miss Sue is not one restaurant, but three: on the ground floor is a bright cafe-style dining room that serves mostly

seafood, including lots of types of oysters and a shellfish platter to die for. Downstairs is Luna, where the focus is Italian and the menu favours meat dishes. There's also Cerva, a takeaway fish-and-chip shop.

SOPHIE'S @ THE DEAN   ITALIAN $$

Map p244 (www.sophies.ie; 33 Harcourt St; mains €15-28; ⊙7am-midnight; ᴪ10, 11, 13, 14 or 15A, ᴪSt Stephen's Green) There's perhaps no better setting in all of Dublin – a top-floor glasshouse restaurant with superb views of the city – to enjoy this quirky take on Italian cuisine, where delicious pizzas come with non-traditional toppings (pulled pork with BBQ sauce?) and the 8oz fillet steak is done to perfection. A good spot for breakfast too.

BOW LANE   INTERNATIONAL $$

Map p244 (www.bowlane.ie; 18 Aungier St; mains €19-29; ⊙3pm-late Sun-Thu, from 10.30am Fri & Sat; ᴪall city centre) It's a cocktail bar, but with a standout menu. On offer are dinner mains as diverse as rabbit pie and tandoori chicken, while the excellent brunch menu does it with a twist. Sure, you can order eggs Benedict, but you can also go for Korean BBQ beef with shrimp and *kim chi* fried rice and a poached egg.

RICHMOND   MODERN IRISH $$

Map p242 (☏01-478 8783; www.richmondrestaurant.ie; 43 S Richmond St; mains €16-22; ⊙5.30-9.30pm Wed-Sun, plus 11am-3pm Sat & Sun; ᴪ14, 15, 65 or 83) At first glance the menu offers nothing particularly novel, just a nice selection of favourites from a burger to a roasted breast of duck. But it's the way it's prepared and presented that makes this place one of the best recent openings in Dublin, and proof that expertise in the kitchen trumps everything else. Brunch is a particular favourite.

DADA   MOROCCAN $$

Map p244 (www.dadarestaurant.ie; 45 S William St; mains €18-24; ⊙5-11pm Mon-Thu, 1.30pm-12.30am Fri & Sat, 2.30-11pm Sun; ᴪall city centre) This bustling Moroccan restaurant has an atmospheric, low-lit dining room spread about lots of alcoves so as to give the feel of a medina and a substantial menu of North African favourites. The emphasis is on lamb (three separate tagines and a seven-hour roasted lamb shoulder) but there's also fish, chicken and decent vegetarian options.

PICHET FRENCH **$$**

Map p244 (☑01-677 1060; www.pichetrestaurant.ie; 14-15 Trinity St; mains €17-26; ⊗noon-3pm & 5-10pm Mon-Sat, 11am-4pm & 5-9pm Sun; ▣all city centre) Head chef Stephen Gibson (formerly of L'Ecrivain) delivers his version of modern French cuisine to this elongated dining room replete with blue leather chairs and lots of windows to stare out of. The result is pretty good indeed, the food excellent – we expected nothing less – and the service impeccable. Sit in the back for atmosphere.

GREEN HEN FRENCH **$$**

Map p244 (☑01-670 7238; www.greenhen.ie; 33 Exchequer St; mains €18-27; ⊗noon-3pm daily, plus 5-11pm Sun-Thu, 5pm-1am Fri & Sat; ▣all city centre) New York's SoHo meets Parisian brasserie at this stylish eatery, where elegance and economy live side-by-side. If you don't fancy gorging on oysters or tucking into a divine Irish Hereford rib-eye, you can opt for the *plat du jour* or avail yourself of the early-bird menus; watch out for its killer cocktails. Reservations recommended for dinner.

COPPINGER ROW MEDITERRANEAN **$$**

Map p244 (www.coppingerrow.com; Coppinger Row; mains €17-26; ⊗noon-5.30pm & 6-11pm Mon-Sat, 12.30-4pm & 6-9pm Sun; ▣all city centre) Virtually all of the Mediterranean basin is represented on the ever-changing, imaginative menu here. Choices include the likes of pan-fried sea bass with roast baby fennel, tomato and olives; or rump of lamb with spiced aubergine and dried apricots. A nice touch are the filtered still and sparkling waters (€1): 50% of the cost goes to cancer research.

YAMAMORI JAPANESE **$$**

Map p244 (☑01-475 5001; www.yamamorinoodles.ie; 71 S Great George's St; mains €16-26, lunch bentos €9.95; ⊗12.30-11pm; ☑; ▣all city centre) Hip and inexpensive, Yamamori rarely disappoints with its bubbly service and vivacious cooking that swoops from sushi and sashimi to whopping great plates of noodles, with plenty in between. The lunch bento is one of the best deals in town. There's another branch (p142) north of the river.

DUNNE & CRESCENZI ITALIAN **$$**

Map p244 (www.dunneandcrescenzi.com; 14-16 S Frederick St; mains €10-14, 3-course evening menu €35; ⊗8am-11pm Mon-Sat, 9.30am-11pm Sun; ▣all city centre) This exceptional Italian eatery delights its regulars with a basic menu of rustic pleasures, such as panini, a single pasta dish and a superb plate of mixed antipasto drizzled in olive oil. It's always full, and the tables are just that little bit too close to one another, but the coffee is perfect and the desserts are sinfully good.

GOOD WORLD CHINESE **$$**

Map p244 (18 S Great George's St; dim sum €4-6, mains €12-20; ⊗12.30pm-2.30am; ▣all city centre) To truly appreciate the quality of the south side's best Chinese restaurant, ignore the green Western-style menu and stick to the black-covered one, which is packed with dishes and delicacies that have made it a favourite with Dublin's Chinese community for two decades. It's a great option for a late-night, post-pub bite if you're looking to avoid fast food.

PITT BROS BBQ BARBECUE **$$**

Map p244 (www.pittbrosbbq.com; Unit 1, Wicklow House, S Great George's St; mains €13.95; ⊗noon-midnight Mon-Fri, 12.30pm-late Sat & Sun; ▣all city centre) Delicious, Southern-style barbecue – you have a choice of pulled pork, brisket, ribs, sausage or half a chicken – served amid loud music and a hipster-fuelled atmosphere that says Brooklyn, New York rather than Birmingham, Alabama. For dessert, there's a DIY ice-cream dispenser. Locals grumble that it's a straight rip-off of Bison Bar, but the happy clientele doesn't care.

DRURY BUILDINGS ITALIAN **$$**

Map p244 (☑01-960 2095; www.drurybuildings.com; 52-55 Drury St; mains €17.50-29.50; ⊗5-10.30pm daily, plus noon-3pm Sat & Sun; ▣all city centre) An elegant, 1st-floor restaurant in a converted rag-trade warehouse... sounds like New York's SoHo, and that's exactly what it's trying to emulate. The food – Italian dishes made with local produce and infused with an international twist – is excellent. The ground-floor cocktail bar (p73) has an Italian lunch menu of sandwiches, salads and other titbits.

777 MEXICAN **$$**

Map p244 (www.777.ie; 7 Castle House, S Great George's St; mains €20-32, tapas €9-12; ⊗5.30-10pm Mon-Wed, 5.30-11pm Thu, 5pm-midnight Fri & Sat, 2-10pm Sun; ▣all city centre) You won't eat better, more authentic Mexican cuisine – the *tostadas* (crispy corn tortillas with various toppings) and *taquitos* (filled, soft corn tortillas) are great nibbles, and the perfect accompaniment for a tequila fest (it serves 22 different types). The all-dishes-for-€7.77 on Sunday is one of the best deals in town.

OPIUM ROOMS
ASIAN $$

Map p242 (☎01-475 8555; www.thevillagevenue.com; 26 Wexford St; mains €16-19; ⊙noon-10pm Mon-Wed, noon-2.30am Thu & Fri, from 1pm Sat, 12.30-9pm Sun) Modelled on Hakkasan in London, Opium Rooms is a late-night restaurant and bar that serves tasty pan-Asian cuisine with a soundtrack, and when you're done dining you can retire to the cocktail bar or the late-night club (p74).

PIG'S EAR
MODERN IRISH $$

Map p244 (☎01-670 3865; www.thepigsear.com; 4 Nassau St; mains €12-25; ⊙noon-2.45pm & 5.30-10pm Mon-Sat; ▣all city centre) Looking over the playing fields of Trinity College – which counts as a view in Dublin – this fashionably formal restaurant is spread over two floors and is renowned for its exquisite and innovative Irish cuisine, including dishes such as crispy pork croquettes and slow-cooked beef cheeks. Trust us, it tastes better than it sounds.

L'GUEULETON
FRENCH $$

Map p244 (www.lgueuleton.com; 1 Fade St; mains €22-26; ⊙12.30-4pm & 5.30-10pm Mon-Sat, noon-4pm & 5.30-9pm Sun; ▣all city centre) Despite the tongue-twister name (it means 'gluttonous feast' in French), L'Gueuleton is a firm favourite with locals for its robust (meaty, filling) take on French rustic cuisine – it does a mean onion soup and the steak frites is a big crowd pleaser. It has a no-reservations, leave-your-name-at-the-door policy; just go for a drink and wait for the call.

SÖDER + KO
ASIAN, FUSION $$

Map p244 (www.soderandko.ie; 64 S Great George's St; plates €6-10, mains €12-22; ▣all city centre, ▣St Stephen's Green) This fusion of Scandinavian style and Asian food was the spot for Dublin's pretty young things to drink and dine in 2016. The menu, by ex-Cliff Townhouse chef Kwanghi Chan, has a range of sharing platters and tapas-style dishes as well as mains featuring tofu, fish and venison. Generous portions of excellent cuisine.

AVOCA
CAFE $$

Map p244 (www.avoca.ie; 11-13 Suffolk St; mains €11-14; ⊙9.30am-6pm Mon-Wed & Sat, to 7pm Thu & Fri, 11am-6pm Sun; ▣all city centre) The upstairs cafe of the city's best designer crafts shop has long been a favourite spot of the Ladies Who Lunch. Designer bags can get very heavy, and there's nothing better to restore flagging energy than the simple, rustic delights on offer here: organic shepherd's pie, roast lamb with couscous, or sumptuous salads from the Avoca kitchen.

There's also a takeaway salad bar and hot-food counter in the basement.

SABA
ASIAN, FUSION $$

Map p244 (☎01-679 2000; www.sabadublin.com; 26-28 Clarendon St; lunch mains €13-19, dinner mains €24.95; ⊙noon-11pm; ▣all city centre) The name means 'happy meeting place' and this Thai-Vietnamese fusion restaurant is just that. The buzzy atmosphere is all designer cool, the Southeast Asian fare a tad shy of being truly authentic (but still very tasty), and it's a good night out. There's a newer branch on Baggot St.

SHANAHAN'S ON THE GREEN
STEAK $$$

Map p242 (☎01-407 0939; www.shanahans.ie; 119 St Stephen's Green W; mains €35-49; ⊙from 6pm Sat-Thu, from noon Fri; ▣all city centre) You could order seafood or a plate of vegetables, but you'd be missing the point of this supremely elegant steakhouse: the finest cuts of juicy and tender Irish Angus beef you'll find anywhere. The ambience is upscale Americana – the bar downstairs is called the Oval Office and pride of place goes to a rocking chair owned by JFK.

THORNTON'S
FRENCH $$$

Map p244 (☎01-478 7000; www.thorntonsrestaurant.com; 128 St Stephen's Green W; 2-/3-course lunch €35/45, dinner tasting menus €75-85; ⊙12.30-2pm & 7-10pm Tue-Sat; ▣all city centre) Chef Kevin Thornton's culinary genius is to take new French cuisine and give it a theatrical, Irish revamp: the result is a wonderful mix of succulent seafood dishes and meatier fare such as noisette of milk-fed Wicklow lamb. A nice touch is when Kevin himself comes out to greet his guests and explain his creations. Reservations are essential.

CLIFF TOWNHOUSE
IRISH $$$

Map p242 (☎01-638 3939; www.theclifftownhouse.com; 22 St Stephen's Green N; mains

€17-36; ⊘noon-2.30pm & 6-11pm Mon-Sat, noon-4pm & 6-10pm Sun; 🖵all city centre) Sean Smith's menu is a confident expression of the very best of Irish cuisine – Warrenpoint fish pie, organic fillet of pork and a loin of venison share the menu with a masterful fish and chips. The dining room is supremely elegant – lots of white linen, beautiful art on the wall and deep-blue leather booths.

TROCADERO INTERNATIONAL $$$
Map p244 (📞01-677 5545; www.trocadero.ie; 3 St Andrew's St; mains €19-31.50; ⊘4.30pm-midnight Mon-Fri, from 4pm Sat; 🖵all city centre) As old school as a Dublin restaurant gets, this art-deco classic has been the social hub of the city's theatrical world for 50 years, a favourite of thespians and other luminaries. It's more of a nostalgia trip now, but the food remains uniformly good – a bunch of classics solidly made – as does the terrific atmosphere.

DESELBYS MEDITERRANEAN $$$
Map p242 (9 Lower Camden St; ⊘10am–3.30pm Mon & Tue, 10am–3.30pm & 6–10pm Wed-Fri, 11am-3.30pm & 6–11pm Sat, 11am–3.30pm Sun; 🖵all city centre) The lunchtime menu is all about tasty sandwiches (the crab is divine), flatbreads and salads; the evening menu offers mussels, oysters, terrines and a variety of Mediterranean-style meat dishes. The room, decorated like a 1920s cafe in Madrid or Rome, is one of the nicest in Dublin.

🍷 DRINKING & NIGHTLIFE

★NO NAME BAR BAR
Map p244 (3 Fade St; ⊘12.30-11.30pm Sun-Wed, to 1am Thu, to 2.30am Fri & Sat; 🖵all city centre) A low-key entrance just next to the trendy French restaurant L'Gueuleton leads upstairs to one of the nicest bar spaces in town, consisting of three huge rooms in a restored Victorian townhouse plus a sizeable heated patio area for smokers. There's no sign or a name – folks just refer to it as the No Name Bar.

★KEHOE'S PUB
Map p244 (9 S Anne St; ⊘10.30am-11.30pm Mon-Thu, to 12.30am Fri & Sat, noon-11pm Sun; 🖵all city centre) This is one of the most atmospheric pubs in the city centre and a favourite with all kinds of Dubliners. It has a beautiful Vic-

torian bar, a wonderful snug, and plenty of other little nooks and crannies. Upstairs, drinks are served in what was once the publican's living room – and looks it!

★LONG HALL PUB
Map p244 (51 S Great George's St; ⊘10.30am-11.30pm Mon-Thu, to 12.30am Fri & Sat, noon-11pm Sun; 🖵all city centre) Luxuriating in full Victorian splendour, this is one of the city's most beautiful and best-loved pubs. Check out the ornate carvings in the woodwork behind the bar and the elegant chandeliers. The bartenders are experts at their craft, an increasingly rare attribute in Dublin these days.

★GROGAN'S CASTLE LOUNGE PUB
Map p244 (www.groganspub.ie; 15 S William St; ⊘10.30am-11.30pm Mon-Thu, to 12.30am Fri & Sat, 12.30-11pm Sun) This place, known simply as Grogan's (after the original owner), is a city-centre institution. It has long been a favourite haunt of Dublin's writers and painters, as well as others from the alternative bohemian set, who enjoy a fine Guinness while they wait for that inevitable moment when they're discovered.

★ANSEO BAR
Map p242 (18 Lower Camden St; ⊘10.30am-11.30pm Mon-Thu, to 12.30am Fri & Sat, 11am-11pm Sun; 🖵all city centre) Unpretentious, unaffected and incredibly popular, this cosy alternative bar – which is pronounced 'an-*shuh*', the Irish for 'here' – is a favourite with those who live by the credo that to try too hard is far worse than not trying at all. The pub's soundtrack is an eclectic mix; you're as likely to hear Peggy Lee as Lee Perry.

P.MAC'S BAR
Map p244 (30 Lower Stephen St; ⊘noon-midnight Mon-Thu, to 1am Fri & Sat, to 11.30pm Sun; 🖵all city centre) One of the 'in' bars of 2015 and 2016 is this hipster heaven, full of mismatched vintage furniture, American-style pint glasses and an alternative soundtrack veering towards the '90s. It also has 30-odd taps serving a huge variety of craft beers.

BOW LANE COCKTAIL BAR
Map p244 (17 Aungier St; mains €16-29; ⊘3pm-late Sun-Thu, from 10.30am Fri & Sat; 🖵all city centre) This new late-night cocktail lounge has an 'industrial art-deco' design but the dark, moody atmosphere of a '50s Vegas bar, where the pretty young things order

fancy drinks and nibbles off the excellent menu (p69). The weekend brunch is one of the best in town.

CLEMENT & PEKOE
CAFE

Map p244 (www.clementandpekoe.com; 50 S William St; ◷8am-7pm Mon-Fri, 10am-6pm Sat, noon-6pm Sun; 🚇all city centre) Our favourite cafe in town is this hipster version of an Edwardian tea room. Walnut floors, art-deco chandeliers and wall-to-wall displays of handsome tea jars are the perfect setting in which to enjoy the huge range of loose leaf teas and carefully made coffees, along with a selection of cakes.

STAG'S HEAD
PUB

Map p244 (www.louisfitzgerald.com/stagshead; 1 Dame Ct; ◷10.30am-1am Mon-Sat, to midnight Sun; 🚇all city centre) The Stag's Head was built in 1770, remodelled in 1895 and thankfully not changed a bit since then. It's a superb pub: so picturesque that it often appears in films, and also featured in a postage-stamp series on Irish bars. A bloody great pub, no doubt.

MCDAID'S
PUB

Map p244 (☎01-679 4395; 3 Harry St; ◷10.30am-11.30pm Mon-Thu, 10.30am-12.30am Fri & Sat, 12.30-11pm Sun; 🚇all city centre) One of Dublin's best-known literary pubs, this classic boozer was Brendan Behan's local (until he was barred) and it still oozes character. The pints are perfect, and best appreciated during the day when it's less busy. Thankfully, there's no music – just conversation and raucous laughter.

HOGAN'S
BAR

Map p244 (35 S Great George's St; ◷1pm-11.30am Mon-Wed, to 1am Thu, to 2.30am Fri & Sat, 4-11pm Sun; 🚇all city centre, 🚇St Stephen's Green) Midweek this big contemporary bar is a relaxing hang-out for young professionals, and restaurant and bar workers on a night off. But come the weekend the sweat bin downstairs pulls them in for some serious music courtesy of the usually excellent DJs.

CHELSEA DRUG STORE
BAR

Map p244 (25 S Great George's St; ◷4pm-midnight Mon-Fri, noon-1.30am Sat, 4-11pm Sun; 🚇all city centre) It doesn't matter that its name seems plucked out of a hipster focus group and the decor carefully curated to reflect current trends (art-deco elements, old-looking-like-new), this is actually a beautiful

bar that in 2016 was full of young creatives ordering cocktails with names like The Truth Behind Augustus and Penicillin.

KAPH
CAFE

Map p244 (31 Drury St; ◷9am-6pm Mon-Sat, noon-6pm Sun; 🚇all city centre) One of the new breed of cafes in town where the barista's creations are considered caffeinated art. Order a flat white and use it to dunk one of the (homemade) madeleines.

DRURY BUILDINGS
COCKTAIL BAR
COCKTAIL BAR

Map p244 (www.drurybuildings.com; 52-55 Drury St; mains €10; ◷noon-11.30pm Sun-Thu, to 12.30am Fri-Sat) The Drury Buildings' (p70) ground-floor cocktail bar is popular for pre-dinner drinks. It also has an Italian lunch menu of sandwiches, salads and other titbits.

LOST SOCIETY
CLUB

Map p244 (Bassment; ☎01-677 0014; www.lostsociety.ie; Powerscourt Townhouse Shopping Centre, S William St; admission €6-10; ◷10pm-3am; 🚇all city centre) Part of the magnificent 18th-century Powerscourt complex, Lost Society (Twitter: @lostsocdublin) offers two distinct nightlife experiences for the price of one ticket. Upstairs, spread across three levels and a host of rooms, the music is eclectic and the crowd beautifully self-aware. Downstairs is the Bassment, where the music is thumping and the dancing is hot and sweaty.

PYGMALION
BAR

Map p244 (☎01-674 6712; www.bodytonicmusic.com; Powerscourt Townhouse Shopping Centre, 59 S William St; ◷noon-12.30am Mon-Wed, to 1am Thu & Sun, to 3am Fri & Sat; 🚇all city centre) Currently one of the busiest bars in town, the 'Pyg' caters to a largely student crowd with its €10 pitchers, pounding music and labyrinthine nooks and crannies (perfect for a naughty hideaway). The owner thought it best to line the walls with carpet – perhaps they're worried that the action on the dance floor might get a little too crazy?

INTERNATIONAL BAR
PUB

Map p244 (23 Wicklow St; ◷10.30am-11.30pm Mon-Thu, to 12.30am Fri & Sat, noon-11pm Sun; 🚇7 & 44 from city centre) This smallish pub with a huge personality is a top spot for an afternoon pint. It has a long bar,

GRAFTON STREET & AROUND DRINKING & NIGHTLIFE

stained-glass windows, red-velour seating and a convivial atmosphere. Some of Ireland's most celebrated comedians stuttered through their first set in the **Comedy Cellar**, which is, of course, upstairs.

OPIUM ROOMS
BAR

Map p242 (www.opiumrooms.ie; 26 Wexford St; admission €5-11; ☺11pm-2.30am Thu-Sat) Clubbers familiar with the Hakkasan experience – whether in London or in Las Vegas – will recognise that the Opium Rooms is trying to do the same thing, albeit on a less grand scale: the DJs it gets aren't as famous, but the dance floor is just as full and the sound is excellent. Downstairs there's a lovely restaurant and bar.

BERNARD SHAW
BAR

Map p242 (www.bodytonicmusic.com; 11-12 S Richmond St; ☺8am-11.30pm Mon-Thu, to 1am Fri, 10am-1am Sat, 2-11.30pm Sun; ☐7 & 44 from city centre) This deliberately ramshackle boozer is probably the coolest bar in town for its marvellous mix of music (courtesy of its owners, the Bodytonic production crew) and diverse menu of events such as afternoon car-boot sales, storytelling nights and fun competitions like having a 'tag-off' between a bunch of graffiti artists.

DAVY BYRNE'S
BAR

Map p244 (☑01-677 5217; www.davybyrnes. com; 21 Duke St; ☺11am-11.30pm Mon-Thu, to 12.30am Fri, 9am-12.30am Sat, 11am-11pm Sun; ☐all city centre) James Joyce would barely recognise the bar that Leopold Bloom popped into for a Gorgonzola sandwich and a glass of burgundy in *Ulysses*. It doesn't stop Davy Byrne's from making the most of its Joycean connections, even though today's version is strictly for out-of-towners and the rugby crowd.

BRUXELLES
PUB

Map p244 (7-8 Harry St; ☺9.30am-1.30am Sun-Thu, to 2.30am Fri & Sat; ☐all city centre) Bruxelles is a raucous music bar split across different areas. It's comparatively trendy on the ground floor, while downstairs is a great, loud and dingy rock bar with live music each weekend. Just outside, a bronze Phil Lynott (p75) is there to remind us of Bruxelles' impeccable rock credentials.

GEORGE
GAY

Map p244 (www.thegeorge.ie; 89 S Great George's St; ☺2-11.30pm Mon, 2pm-2.30am Tue-Fri, 12.30pm-2.30am Sat, 12.30pm-1.30am Sun; ☐all city centre) The purple mother of Dublin's gay bars is a long-standing institution, having lived through the years when it was the only place in town where the gay crowd could, well, be gay. Shirley's legendary Sunday night bingo is as popular as ever, while Wednesday's Space N Veda is a terrific night of cabaret and drag.

COPPER FACE JACKS
CLUB

Map p242 (www.copperfacejacks.ie; 29-30 Harcourt St, Jackson Court Hotel; admission free-€10; ☺10.30pm-3am; ☐10, 11, 13, 14 or 15A, ☐St Stephen's Green) In rural Ireland you don't go clubbing; you go to 'the disco' for a drink, a dance and – hopefully – 'the shift', a particularly Irish way of describing making out. Copper (Twitter: @CopperFaceJacks) is a slice of country clubbing in the middle of the capital, and it's all the more popular for it.

37 DAWSON STREET
BAR

Map p244 (☑01-902 2908; www.37dawsonstreet. ie; 37 Dawson St; ☺10.30am-11.30pm Mon-Thu, to 12.30am Fri & Sat, noon-11pm Sun; ☐all city centre) Antiques, eye-catching art and elegant bric-a-brac adorn this bar that quickly established itself as a favourite with the trendy crowd. At the back is a Whiskey Bar, a '50s-style bar that Don Draper & co would feel comfortable sipping a fine scotch at; upstairs is an elegant restaurant that serves a terrific brunch.

NEARY'S
PUB

Map p244 (☑01-677 8596; 1 Chatham St; ☺10.30am-11.30pm Mon-Thu, to 12.30am Fri & Sat, 12.30-11pm Sun; ☐all city centre) One of a string of off–Grafton St, classic Victorian boozers once patronised by Dublin's legless literati, Neary's is a perfect stop-off day or night. It combines great service, a bohemian atmosphere and attractively worn furnishings, and is popular with actors from the nearby Gaiety Theatre.

CAFÉ EN SEINE
BAR

Map p244 (☑01-677 4369; 40 Dawson St; ☺noon-midnight Mon & Tue, noon-3am Wed-Sat, noon-11pm Sun; ☐all city centre) The wildly extravagant art-nouveau style of this huge bar has been a massive hit since it first opened in 1995, and while it may not be the 'in' place it once was, it is still very popular with suburbanites, the after-work crowd and out-of-towners. Maybe it's the glass panelling, or the real 12m-high trees; but

PICKING ON POOR PHILO

Thin Lizzy's Phil Lynott may have been one of the most loved of all Irish rock stars, but the **statue** (Map p244; Harry St; all city centre) dedicated to him has seen its fair share of trouble since its erection in 2005. In 2013 vandals knocked it off its plinth, resulting in its removal for extensive repairs, but no sooner did it reappear than a motorist ran into it, breaking a piece of the bass guitar. Thankfully, the driver stepped forward and took full responsibility and the repairs only took a few weeks.

most likely it's the beautiful people propping up the wood-and-marble bar.

DAWSON LOUNGE   PUB

Map p244 (25 Dawson St; ⊙10.30am-11.30pm Mon-Thu, to 12.30am Fri & Sat, noon-11pm Sun; all city centre, St Stephen's Green) To see *the* smallest bar in Dublin, go through a small doorway, down a narrow flight of steps and into two tiny rooms that always seem to be filled with a couple of bedraggled drunks who look like they're hiding.

 ENTERTAINMENT

WHELAN'S   LIVE MUSIC

Map p242 (☎01-478 0766; www.whelanslive. com; 25 Wexford St; 16, 122 from city centre) Perhaps the city's most beloved live-music venue is this midsized room attached to a traditional bar. This is the singer-songwriter's spiritual home: when they're done pouring out the contents of their hearts on stage, you can find them filling up in the bar along with their fans.

DEVITT'S   LIVE MUSIC

Map p242 (☎01-475 3414; 78 Lower Camden St; ⊙from 9pm Thu-Sat; all city centre) Devitt's – aka the Cusack Stand – is one of the favourite places for the city's talented musicians to display their wares, with sessions as good as any you'll hear in the city centre. Highly recommended.

NATIONAL CONCERT HALL   LIVE MUSIC

Map p242 (☎01-417 0000; www.nch.ie; Earlsfort Tce; all city centre) Ireland's premier orchestral hall hosts a variety of concerts year-round, including a series of lunchtime concerts from 1.05pm to 2pm on Tuesdays from June to August.

GAIETY THEATRE   THEATRE

Map p244 (☎01-677 1717; www.gaietytheatre. com; S King St; all city centre) The 'Grand Old Lady of South King St' is more than 150 years old and has for much of that time thrived on a diet of fun-for-all-the-family fare: West End hits, musicals, Christmas pantos and classic Irish plays keep the more serious-minded away, leaving more room for those simply looking to be entertained.

JJ SMYTH'S   LIVE MUSIC

Map p244 (☎01-475 2565; www.jjsmyths.com; 12 Aungier St; €8-12; ⊙8-11.30pm; all city centre) There's live music in the upstairs room of this old bar every night, from country rock to jazz, performed by some extraordinary players. Check the website for listings.

BANKER'S   COMEDY

Map p244 (☎01-679 3697; 16 Trinity St; €8; ⊙9-11pm Fri & Sat; all city centre) The basement room of this decent bar hosts two nights of comedy: the Craic Club on Fridays and the usually excellent Stand Up at the Banker's on Saturday nights. There's decent talent on stage – some of whom have made it onto TV.

SHOPPING

IRISH DESIGN SHOP   CRAFTS

Map p244 (41 Drury St; ⊙10am-6pm Mon-Wed, Fri & Sat, to 7pm Thu, 1-5pm Sun; all city centre) Beautiful, imaginatively crafted items – from jewellery to kitchenware – carefully curated by owners Clare Grennan and Laura Caffrey. If you're looking for a stylish, Irish-made memento or gift, you'll surely find it here.

ARTICLE   HOMEWARES

Map p244 (1st fl, Powerscourt Townhouse Shopping Centre, S William St; ⊙10.30am-6pm Mon-Wed, Fri & Sat, to 7pm Thu, 1-5pm Sun) Beautiful tableware and decorative home accessories all made by Irish designers. Ideal for unique, tasteful gifts.

★**AVOCA HANDWEAVERS** HANDICRAFTS
Map p244 (📞01-677 4215; www.avoca.ie; 11-13 Suffolk St; ⏰9.30am-6pm Mon-Wed & Sat, to 7pm Thu & Fri, 11am-6pm Sun; 🚇all city centre) Combining clothing, homewares, a basement food hall and an excellent top-floor cafe (p71), Avoca promotes a stylish but homey brand of modern Irish life – and is one of the best places to find an original present. Many of the garments are woven, knitted and naturally dyed at its Wicklow factory. There's a terrific kids' section.

★**ULYSSES RARE BOOKS** BOOKS
Map p244 (📞01-671 8676; www.rarebooks.ie; 10 Duke St; ⏰9.30am-5.45pm Mon-Sat; 🚇all city centre) Our favourite bookshop in the city stocks a rich and remarkable collection of Irish-interest books, with a particular emphasis on 20th-century literature and a large selection of first editions, including rare ones by the big guns: Joyce, Yeats, Beckett and Wilde.

★**BARRY DOYLE**
DESIGN JEWELLERS JEWELLERY
Map p244 (📞01-671 2838; 30 George's St Arcade; ⏰10am-6pm Mon-Wed, Fri & Sat, to 7pm Thu; 🚇all city centre) Goldsmith Barry Doyle's upstairs shop is one of the best of its kind in Dublin. The handmade jewellery – using white gold, silver, and some truly gorgeous precious and semiprecious stones – is exceptional in its beauty and simplicity. Most of the pieces have Afro-Celtic influences.

★**SHERIDAN'S CHEESEMONGERS** FOOD
Map p244 (📞01-679 3143; www.sheridans cheesemongers.com; 11 S Anne St; ⏰10am-6pm Mon-Fri, 9.30am-6pm Sat; 🚇all city centre) If heaven were a cheese shop, this would be it. Wooden shelves are laden with rounds of farmhouse cheeses, sourced from around the country by Kevin and Seamus Sheridan, who have almost single-handedly revived cheese-making in Ireland.

KILKENNY SHOP HANDICRAFTS
Map p244 (📞01-677 7066; www.kilkennyshop. com; 6 Nassau St; ⏰8.30am-7pm Mon-Wed & Fri, to 8pm Thu, to 6pm Sat, 10am-6pm Sun; 🚇all city centre) A large, long-running repository for contemporary, innovative Irish crafts, including multicoloured, modern Irish knits, designer clothing, Orla Kiely bags and lovely silver jewellery. The glassware and pottery is beautiful and sourced from

workshops around the country. A great source for presents.

LOULERIE JEWELLERY
Map p244 (14B Chatham St; ⏰10am-6pm Mon-Wed, Fri & Sat, to 7pm Thu; 🚇all city centre) Owner Louise Stokes learnt her craft in New York, and has since returned with an unerring eye for finding that individual piece of jewellery – rings, necklaces, earrings etc – to suit every mood and occasion.

MOMUSE JEWELLERY
Map p244 (Powerscourt Townhouse Shopping Centre; ⏰10.30am-6pm Mon-Wed, Fri & Sat, to 7pm Thu, 1-5pm Sun; 🚇all city centre) Exquisite jewellery by designer Margaret O'Rourke, with many of the pieces finished in this lovely boutique on the ground floor of Powerscourt Townhouse.

NOWHERE FASHION
Map p244 (www.anowhereman.com; 64 Aungier St; ⏰noon-6pm Tue, Wed, Fri & Sat, to 7pm Thu; 🚇all city centre) Men's clothing and accessories by hip designers such as CMMN_SWDN, Christopher Raeburn and A Kind of Guise. It operates an extensive online shop too.

DOLLS STORE TOYS
Map p244 (www.dollstore.ie; Powerscourt Townhouse Shopping Centre; ⏰10am-6pm Mon-Sat; 🚇all city centre) Dolls, doll's houses and toys stock the shelves of this lovely shop on the 2nd floor of the Powerscourt Centre, but our favourite bit is the wonderful dolls hospital and teddy bear clinic, where children whose dolls or teddies have had the misfortune to fall 'ill' can be treated with a little TLC (and maybe even a stitch).

POWERSCOURT TOWNHOUSE
SHOPPING CENTRE SHOPPING CENTRE
Map p244 (📞01-679 4144; 59 S William St; ⏰10am-6pm Mon-Wed & Fri, to 8pm Thu, 9am-6pm Sat, noon-6pm Sun; 🚇all city centre) This absolutely gorgeous and stylish centre is in a carefully refurbished Georgian townhouse, built between 1741 and 1744. These days it's best known for its cafes and restaurants but it also does a top-end, selective trade in high fashion, art, exquisite handicrafts and other chichi sundries.

GEORGE'S STREET ARCADE MARKET
Map p244 (www.georgesstreetarcade.ie; btwn S Great George's St & Drury St; ⏰9am-6.30pm Mon-Wed, Fri & Sat, 9am-8pm Thu, noon-6pm

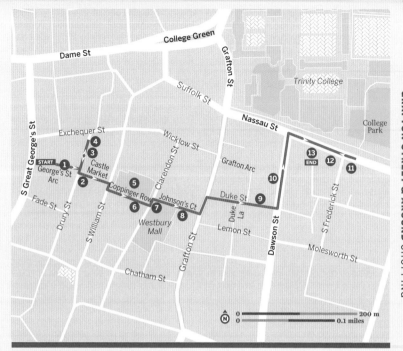

🚶 Neighbourhood Walk
A Retail Stroll

START GEORGE'S ST ARCADE
END KNOBS & KNOCKERS
LENGTH 1.1KM; TWO HOURS

Start your adventure in the ❶ **George's Street Arcade** (p76), with its range of interesting stalls selling all kinds of alternative wares. In the midst of all this bohemia, take a look at the beautiful pieces in Barry Doyle Design Jewellers and browse the shelves of Stokes Books.

Exit at the Drury St side and cross onto Castle Market, stopping to browse the high-end women's fashions in ❷ **Costume** (p78) or, if you prefer, go north on Drury St to the gorgeous homewares and handicrafts in ❸ **Industry** (p78) or, next door, the excellent ❹ **Irish Design Shop** (p75).

From Castle Market, cross S William St and enter the ❺ **Powerscourt Townhouse Shopping Centre** (p76), the city's most elegant retail space – you'll find cafes and a host of wonderful shops, including Article, for homewares and gifts, and, on the top floor, the Design Centre, a top-end boutique.

Exit the centre on S William St and walk south, taking the first left onto Coppinger Row. The ❻ **eponymous restaurant** (p70) is a great spot for a little lunch.

Continue east and cross Clarendon St. At the corner is ❼ **Magills** (p78), an old-fashioned grocer selling cheeses and cold cuts. On Johnson's Ct, the southern side is lined with jewellery stores, including ❽ **Appleby** (p78); you'll find something worth coveting in the elegant windows.

Take a left on Grafton St and turn right onto Duke St: on your left is ❾ **Ulysses Rare Books** (p76), the city's best seller of rare books. The biggest bookshop in town is ❿ **Hodges Figgis** (p79), around the corner on Dawson St. From here walk down to Nassau St and take a right to ⓫ **Kilkenny Shop** (p76), which has locally produced handicrafts, knits, glassware and silverware.

If you still need to pick up some Irish gifts, retrace your tracks along Nassau St, stopping at ⓬ **House of Names** (p79) (for coasters with your family's coat of arms) and ⓭ **Knobs & Knockers** (p78) for that replica Georgian door handle!

Sun; all city centre) Dublin's best nonfood market is sheltered within an elegant Victorian Gothic arcade. Apart from shops and stalls selling new and old clothes, secondhand books, hats, posters, jewellery and records, there's a fortune teller, some gourmet nibbles, and a fish and chipper that does a roaring trade.

DESIGN CENTRE CLOTHING
Map p244 (01-679 5718; www.designcentre.ie; Powerscourt Townhouse Shopping Centre, S William St; 10am-6pm Mon-Wed & Fri, 10am-8pm Thu, 9.30am-6pm Sat; all city centre) Mostly dedicated to Irish designer womenswear, featuring well-made classic suits, evening wear and knitwear. Irish labels include Jill De Burca, Philip Treacy, Caroline Kilkenny and Erickson Beamon – a favourite with Michelle Obama.

COSTUME CLOTHING
Map p244 (01-679 5200; www.costumedublin. ie; 10 Castle Market; 10am-6pm Mon-Wed, Fri & Sat, to 7pm Thu; all city centre) Costume is considered a genuine pacesetter by Dublin's fashionistas; it has exclusive contracts with innovative designers such as Isabel Marant, Cedric Charlier and Yves Salomon.

MAVEN FASHION
Map p244 (29 Wicklow St; 11am-6pm Tue, Wed & Sat, 11am-7pm Thu-Fri; all city centre) This upstairs boutique is pitched at stylishly on-trend women, which really means it stocks labels still cool enough to be worn by fashionistas who are well ahead of the curve. Sounds a mite obnoxious, but this shop is anything but and the labels – including Irish designers Sian Jacobs and JBK knitwear – are very elegant.

LOUIS COPELAND CLOTHING
Map p244 (01-872 1600; www.louiscopeland. com; 18-19 Wicklow St; 9am-5.30pm Mon-Wed, Fri & Sat, to 7.30pm Thu; all city centre) Dublin's answer to the famed tailors of London's Savile Row, this shop makes fabulous suits to measure, and stocks plenty of ready-to-wear suits by international designers.

APPLEBY JEWELLERY
Map p244 (01-679 9572; 5-6 Johnson's Ct; 9.30am-5.30pm Mon-Wed & Fri, to 7pm Thu, to 6pm Sat; all city centre) The best known of the jewellery shops that line narrow Johnson's Ct, Appleby is renowned for the high quality of its gold and silver jewellery, which tends towards more conventional designs. This is the place for serious stuff – diamond rings, sapphire-encrusted cufflinks and Raymond Weil watches.

MAGILLS FOOD
Map p244 (01-671 3830; 14 Clarendon St; 9.30am-5.45pm Mon-Sat; all city centre) With its characterful old facade and tiny dark interior Magills' old-world charm reminds you how Clarendon St must have once looked. At this family-run place, you get the distinct feeling that every Irish and French cheese, olive oil, packet of Italian pasta and salami was hand-picked.

WEIR & SON'S JEWELLERY
Map p244 (01-677 9678; www.weirandsons. ie; 96-99 Grafton St; 9am-5.30pm Mon-Wed, Fri & Sat, 9am-8pm Thu; all city centre) The largest jeweller in Ireland, this huge store on Grafton St first opened in 1869 and still has its original wooden cabinets and a workshop on the premises. There's new and antique Irish jewellery (including Celtic designs) and a huge selection of watches, Irish crystal, porcelain, leather and travel goods.

KNOBS & KNOCKERS HANDICRAFTS
Map p244 (01-671 0288; 19 Nassau St; 10am-6pm Mon-Wed, Fri & Sat, 10am-8pm Thu, 11am-6pm Sun; all city centre) Replica Georgian door-knockers are a great souvenir of your Dublin visit, but there are plenty of other souvenir door adornments to look at here.

INDUSTRY HOMEWARES
Map p244 (www.industrydesign.ie; 41 Drury St; 10am-6pm Mon-Sat, noon-6pm Sun; all city centre) 'Curated vintage' is the tag line at this super-cool independently owned design shop, where you can pick up everything from kids' booties to a birch veneer desk.

RHINESTONES JEWELLERY
Map p244 (01-679 0759; 18 St Andrew's St; 9am-6.30pm Mon-Wed, Fri & Sat, 9am-8pm Thu, noon-6pm Sun; all city centre) Exceptionally fine antique and quirky costume jewellery from the 1920s to 1970s, with pieces priced from €25 to €2000. Victorian jet, 1950s enamel, art-deco turquoise, 1930s mother-of-pearl, cut-glass and rhinestone necklaces, bracelets, brooches and rings are displayed in old-fashioned cabinets.

DANKER ANTIQUES HANDICRAFTS

Map p244 (☑01-677 4009; www.dankerantiques.com; 4-5 Royal Hibernian Way; ⊗9.30am-5pm Mon-Sat; ⊠all city centre) Chock-full of exquisite treasures, this shop specialises in Irish and English antique silver, jewellery and objets d'art. You can find period suites of antique cutlery, candlesticks and candelabra as well as unusual items like potato rings – dish rings to insulate tables from hot bowls.

BROWN THOMAS DEPARTMENT STORE

Map p244 (☑01-605 6666; www.brownthomas.com; 92 Grafton St; ⊗9.30am-8pm Mon, Wed & Fri, 10am-8pm Tue, 9.30am-9pm Thu, 9am-8pm Sat, 11am-7pm Sun; ⊠all city centre) Soak up the Jo Malone–laden rarefied atmosphere of Dublin's most exclusive shop, where presentation is virtually artistic. Here you'll find fantastic cosmetics, shoes to die for, exotic homewares and a host of Irish and international fashion labels such as Balenciaga, Lainey Keogh and Philip Treacy. The 3rd-floor Bottom Drawer outlet stocks the finest Irish linen you'll find anywhere.

DUBRAY BOOKS BOOKS

Map p244 (☑01-677 5568; 36 Grafton St; ⊗9am-7pm Mon-Wed & Sat, 9am-9pm Thu & Fri, 11am-6pm Sun; ⊠all city centre) Three roomy floors devoted to bestsellers, recent releases, coffee-table books and a huge travel section make this one of the better bookshops in town. It can't compete with its larger, British-owned rivals on price, but it holds its own with a helpful staff and a lovely atmosphere that encourages you to linger.

WALTON'S MUSIC

Map p244 (☑01-475 0661; 69-70 S Great George's St; ⊗9am-6pm Mon-Wed, Fri & Sat, to 7pm Thu; ⊠all city centre) This is the place to go if you're looking for your very own *bodhrán* (goat-skin drum) or any other musical instrument associated with Irish traditional music. It also has an excellent selection of sheet music and recorded music.

DESIGNYARD HANDICRAFTS

Map p244 (☑01-474 1011; www.designyard.ie; 25 S Frederick St; ⊗10am-5.30pm Tue, Wed & Fri, to 8pm Thu, to 6pm Sat; ⊠all city centre) A high-end, craft-as-art shop where everything you see – glass, batik, sculpture, painting – is one-off and handmade in Ireland. It also showcases contemporary jewellery stock from young international designers. Perfect

for that bespoke engagement ring or a very special present.

HOUSE OF NAMES HANDICRAFTS

Map p244 (☑01-679 7287; www.houseofnames.ie; 26 Nassau St; ⊗10am-6pm Mon-Wed, Fri & Sat, 10am-8pm Thu, 11am-6pm Sun; ⊠all city centre) Impress your friends by serving them drinks on coasters emblazoned with your family's coat of arms, matching the sweatshirt you're wearing and, of course, the glasses or mugs the drinks are served in. All this and more can be yours from the House of Names, so long as you have a surname with Irish roots.

HODGES FIGGIS BOOKS

Map p244 (☑01-677 4754; 56-58 Dawson St; ⊗9am-7pm Mon-Wed & Fri, to 8pm Thu, to 6pm Sat, noon-6pm Sun; ⊠all city centre) The mother of all Dublin bookshops has books on every conceivable subject for every kind of reader spread across three huge floors, including a substantial Irish section on the ground floor.

WESTBURY MALL SHOPPING ARCADE

Map p244 (Clarendon St; ⊗10am-6pm Mon-Sat, noon-5pm Sun; ⊠all city centre) Wedged between the five-star Westbury Hotel and the expensive jewellery stores of Johnson's Ct, this small mall has a handful of pricey, specialist shops selling everything from Persian rugs to buttons and lace or tasteful children's wooden toys.

ST STEPHEN'S GREEN SHOPPING CENTRE SHOPPING CENTRE

Map p244 (☑01-478 0888; St Stephen's Green W; ⊗9am-7pm Mon-Wed, Fri & Sat, 9am-9pm Thu, 11am-6pm Sun; ⊠all city centre) A 1980s version of a 19th-century shopping arcade, the dramatic, balconied interior and central courtyard are a bit too grand for the nondescript chain stores within. There's Boots, Benetton and a large Dunnes Store with supermarket, as well as last-season designer warehouse TK Maxx.

JENNY VANDER CLOTHING

Map p244 (☑01-677 0406; 50 Drury St; ⊗10am-6pm Mon-Sat, noon-6pm Sun; ⊠all city centre) This secondhand shop oozes elegance and sophistication. Discerning fashionistas and film stylists snap up the exquisite beaded handbags, fur-trimmed coats, richly patterned dresses, and costume jewellery priced as if it were the real thing.

ACTIVITIES

★ HISTORICAL
WALKING TOUR
WALKING TOUR

Map p244 (☏01-878 0227; www.historicaltours.ie; Trinity College Gate; adult/child €12/free; ☺11am & 3pm May-Sep, 11am Apr & Oct, 11am Fri-Sun Nov-Mar; ⊟all city centre) Trinity College history graduates lead this 'seminar on the street' that explores the Potato Famine, Easter Rising, Civil War and Partition. Sights include Trinity, City Hall, Dublin Castle and Four Courts. In summer, themed tours on architecture, women in Irish history and the birth of the Irish state are held. Tours depart from the College Green entrance.

FAB FOOD TRAILS
WALKING TOUR

(www.fabfoodtrails.ie; €55; ☺10am Sat) Two-and-a-half-hour tasting walks throughout the city centre taking in the very best of culinary Dublin. You'll visit bakeries, cheesemongers, markets and delis, learning about the food culture of each neighbourhood you explore. You meet in the city centre.

WOMEN'S HISTORY
OF IRELAND TOUR
TOUR

Map p244 (www.littlemuseum.ie; 15 St Stephen's Green, Little Museum of Dublin; adult/concession €8/6; ☺4pm Thu; ⊟all city centre, ⊞St Stephen's Green) A weekly tour of the museum exhibits with a focus on women and their key role in Irish history.

1916 REBELLION
WALKING TOUR
WALKING TOUR

Map p244 (☏086 858 3847; www.1916rising.com; 23 Wicklow St; €13; ☺11.30am Mon-Sat, 1pm Sun Mar-Oct; ⊟7 & 44 from city centre) Superb two-hour tour starting in the International Bar (p73), Wicklow St. Lots of information, humour and irreverence to boot. The guides – all Trinity graduates – are uniformly excellent and will not say no to the offer of a pint back in the International at tour's end.

DUBLIN LITERARY
PUB CRAWL
WALKING TOUR

Map p244 (☏01-670 5602; www.dublinpubcrawl.com; 9 Duke St; adult/student €12/10; ☺7.30pm daily Apr-Oct, 7.30pm Thu-Sun Nov-Mar; ⊟all city centre) A tour of pubs associated with famous Dublin writers is a sure-fire recipe for success, and this 2½-hour tour-performance by two actors – which includes them acting out the funny bits – is a riotous laugh. There's plenty of drink taken, which makes it all the more popular. It leaves from the Duke on Duke St; get there by 7pm to reserve a spot for the evening tour.

PAT LIDDY WALKING TOURS
WALKING TOUR

Map p244 (☏01-831 1109; www.walkingtours.ie; Visit Dublin Centre, 25 Suffolk St; €10-14; ⊟all city centre) Dublin's best-known tour guide is local historian Pat Liddy, who leads a variety of guided walks including Dublin Highlights & Hidden Corners and The Best of Dublin – The Complete Heritage Walking Tour. He is also available for private guided walks. Check the website for timings. He also has a bunch of **podcast walks** (www.visitdublin.com/iwalks) available for download.

TRINITY COLLEGE
WALKING TOUR
WALKING TOUR

Map p244 (Authenticity Tours; www.tcd.ie/Library/bookofkells/trinity-tours; Trinity College; tours €6, incl Book of Kells €13; ☺10.15am-3.40pm Mon-Sat, to 3.15pm Sun May-Sep, fewer midweek tours Oct & Feb-Apr) A great way to see Trinity's grounds is on a student-led walking tour, which departs from the College Green entrance every 20 to 40 minutes.

CARRIAGE TOURS
TOUR

Map p244 (St Stephen's Green N; 1-4 adults €20-50; ☺Apr-Oct; ⊟all city centre, ⊞St Stephen's Green) Horse-drawn carriage tours of Dublin. Pick-up is at the northwestern corner of St Stephen's Green.

SEE DUBLIN BY BIKE
BICYCLE TOUR

Map p244 (☏01-280 1899; www.seedublinbybike.ie; Fade St; €25-30; ⊟all city centre) Three-hour themed tours that start outside Cafe Rothar on Fade St and take in the city's highlights and not-so-obvious sights. The Taste of Dublin is the main tour, but you can also take a U2's Dublin tour and a literary Dublin tour. Bikes, helmets and a hi-vis vests included.

DUBLIN BUS TOURS
BUS TOUR

Map p244 (☏01-872 0000; www.dublinsightseeing.ie; adult €22-28) A selection of bus tours including a hop-on, hop-off city tour (€22), a ghostbus tour (€28) and two half-day tours: the four-hour South Coast & Gardens Tour (€27; including Powerscourt) and the North Coast & Castle Tour (€25; including Malahide Castle).

SANDEMAN'S

NEW DUBLIN TOUR   WALKING TOUR

Map p242 (☑01-878 8547; www.newdublintours. com; City Hall, Castle St; free-€22; ☺11am & 2pm; ☑all city centre) A high-energy and thoroughly enjoyable three-hour walking tour of the city's greatest hits for free: tip only if you enjoyed the tour (guides make sure you do). They also do a Howth Day tour (€22), a famine tour (€12) and a pub crawl (€12). You can also get a pick up at the Visit Dublin Centre (p225) at 10.30am.

VIKING SPLASH TOURS   BUS TOUR, BOAT TOUR

Map p244 (☑01-707 6000; www.vikingsplash. ie; St Stephen's Green N; adult/child €22/12; ☺every 30-90min 10am-3pm; ☑all city centre, ☐St Stephen's Green) Go on, what's the big deal? You stick a plastic Viking's helmet on your head and yell 'yay' at the urging of your guide, but the upshot is you'll get a 1¼-hour semiamphibious tour that ends up in the Grand Canal Dock. 'Strictly for tourists' seems so...superfluous.

Merrion Square & Around

Neighborhood Top Five

1 **Merrion Square** (p89) Exploring this oasis of calm steeped in Irish history and flanked by a handful of heavyweight museums.

2 **National Gallery** (p88) Perusing the collection at Ireland's pre-eminent gallery, packed with art from eight centuries of European tradition.

3 **Museum of Natural History** (p90) Visiting this antiquated museum, which has changed little since it was opened in the middle of the 19th century.

4 **National Museum of Ireland – Archaeology** (p84) Uncovering the fascinating treasures of the most important repository

of Irish culture, from finely worked gold to prehistoric bodies.

5 **O'Donoghue's** (p95) Enjoying a night of music and beer in the very epitome of an Irish traditional pub.

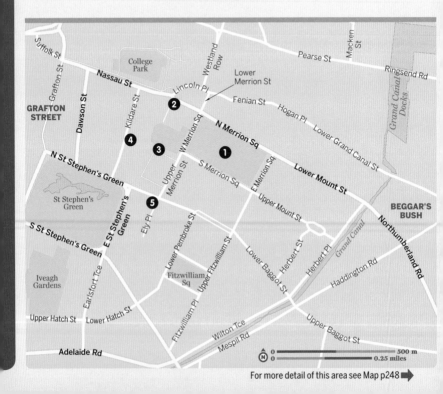

For more detail of this area see Map p248 ➡

Explore Merrion Square & Around

Ireland's national collections of art, history and natural history are to be found in the imposing neoclassical buildings that line the elegant Georgian streets and parks of the city's best-maintained 18th-century neighbourhood. Depending on your level of interest you'll need to devote as much as half a day to each, or just an hour or two if you're only interested in an overview. You'll also want to spend some time looking at the private residences that line Merrion and Fitzwilliam Sqs – the many plaques on these Georgian buildings remind us that it was behind these brightly coloured doors that the likes of Oscar Wilde and William Butler Yeats hung their hats. These streets also house the offices of some of the country's most important businesses, so when there's even a hint of sunshine, workers pour out into the various parks, or follow the lead of poet Patrick Kavanagh and lounge along the banks of the Grand Canal. When they clock off, these same workers head to the wonderfully atmospheric and historical pubs of Baggot St and Merrion Row for a couple of scoops of chips and some unwinding banter. There are also some smart restaurants, including several of Dublin's best.

Local Life

➡ **High Art** The Jack B Yeats collection in the National Gallery (p88) soothes a Dubliner's troubled soul, while the Royal Hibernian Academy (p91) is an excellent showcase of contemporary art. For something a little more affordable, the weekend art market (p95) along the railings of Merrion Sq displays surprisingly good-quality work.

➡ **Beer Power** Follow the power-brokers, politicians and business crowd as they unwind in some of the city's best traditional boozers: James Toner's (p95) and Doheny & Nesbitt's (p95) are established favourites, but O'Donoghue's (p95) of Merrion Row is in a league of its own.

➡ **Fine Dining** The critics regularly praise Restaurant Patrick Guilbaud (p94) as the best in the country; whatever debate there is exists as a result of restaurants like L'Ecrivain (p94), but there's also a bunch of less exalted spots worth checking out, like Etto (p92).

Getting There & Away

➡ **Bus** Most cross-city buses will get you here (or near enough).

➡ **Train** The most convenient DART stop is Pearse St, with the station entrance on Westland Row.

➡ **On Foot** Merrion Sq is less than 500m from St Stephen's Green (and Grafton St).

Lonely Planet's Top Tip

The Vaughan Collection of watercolours by JMW Turner at the **National Gallery** (p88) is only displayed during the month of January, when the light is just right to appreciate the delicacy and beauty of these masterpieces.

⊙ Best Examples of Irish Art

➡ Yeats Room, National Gallery (p88)

➡ Treasury, National Museum of Ireland – Archaeology (p84)

➡ Royal Hibernian Academy (RHA) Gallagher Gallery (p91)

For reviews, see p84 ➡

⊙ Best Places to Eat

➡ Restaurant Patrick Guilbaud (p94)

➡ L'Ecrivain (p94)

➡ Xico (p92)

➡ Etto (p92)

For reviews, see p92 ➡

⊙ Best Drinking & Nightlife

➡ O'Donoghue's (p95)

➡ James Toner's (p95)

➡ Doheny & Nesbitt's (p95)

For reviews, see p95 ➡

MERRION SQUARE & AROUND

JOHN FREEMAN / GETTY IMAGES ©

TOP SIGHT
NATIONAL MUSEUM OF IRELAND – ARCHAEOLOGY

This is the mother of all Irish museums and the country's most important cultural institution. One of four branches, this is the most important, home to Europe's finest collection of Bronze and Iron Age gold artefacts, the most complete collection of medieval Celtic metalwork in the world, and fascinating prehistoric and Viking artefacts.

Treasury

The Treasury is perhaps the most famous part of the collection, and its centrepieces are Ireland's two most famous crafted artefacts, the **Ardagh Chalice** and the **Tara Brooch**. The 12th-century Ardagh Chalice is made of gold, silver, bronze, brass, copper and lead; it measures 17.8cm high and 24.2cm in diameter and, put simply, is the finest example of Celtic art ever found. The equally renowned Tara Brooch was crafted around AD 700, primarily in white bronze, but with traces of gold, silver, glass, copper, enamel and wire beading, and was used as a clasp for a cloak. It was discovered on a beach in Bettystown, County Meath, in 1850, but later came into the hands of an art dealer who named it after the hill of Tara, the historic seat of the ancient high kings. It doesn't have quite the same ring to it, but it was the Bettystown Brooch that sparked a revival of interest in Celtic jewellery that hasn't let up to this day. There are many other pieces that testify to Ireland's history as the land of saints and scholars.

Ór – Ireland's Gold

Elsewhere in the Treasury is the Ór – Ireland's Gold exhibition, featuring stunning jewellery and decorative objects created by Celtic artisans in the Bronze and Iron Ages. Among them are the **Broighter Hoard**, which includes a 1st-century-BC large gold collar,

DON'T MISS

➡ Tara Brooch
➡ Ardagh Chalice
➡ Loughnasade War Trumpet
➡ Kingship & Sacrifice exhibition

PRACTICALITIES

➡ Map p248, A3
➡ www.museum.ie
➡ Kildare St
➡ admission free
➡ ⏰10am-5pm Tue-Sat, 2-5pm Sun
➡ 🚌all city centre

unsurpassed anywhere in Europe, and an extraordinarily delicate gold boat. There's also the wonderful **Loughnasade bronze war trumpet**, which dates from the 1st century BC. It is 1.86m long and made of sheets of bronze, riveted together, with an intricately designed disc at the mouth. It produces a sound similar to the Australian didgeridoo, though you'll have to take our word for it. Running alongside the wall is a **15m log boat**, which was dropped into the water to soften, abandoned and then pulled out 4000 years later, almost perfectly preserved in the peat bog.

Kingship & Sacrifice

One of the museum's biggest showstoppers is the collection of Iron Age 'bog bodies' in the Kingship and Sacrifice exhibit – four figures in varying states of preservation dug out of the midland bogs. The bodies' various eerily preserved details – a distinctive tangle of hair, sinewy legs and fingers with fingernails intact – are memorable, but it's the accompanying detail that will make you pause: scholars now believe that all of these bodies were victims of the most horrendous ritualistic torture and sacrifice – the cost of being notable figures in the Celtic world.

Other Exhibits

If you can cope with any more history, upstairs are **Medieval Ireland 1150–1550**, **Viking Age Ireland** – which features exhibits from the excavations at Wood Quay, the area between Christ Church Cathedral and the river – and our own favourite, the aptly named **Clothes from Bogs in Ireland**, a collection of 16th- and 17th-century woollen garments recovered from the bog. Enthralling stuff!

WHAT'S IN A NAME?

Virtually all of the treasures held here are named after the location in which they were found. It's interesting to note that most of them were discovered not by archaeologists' trowels but by bemused farmers out ploughing their fields, cutting peat or, in the case of the Ardagh Chalice, digging for spuds.

If you don't mind groups, the themed guided tours will help you wade through the myriad exhibits. If you want to avoid crowds, the best time to visit is weekday afternoons, when school groups have gone, and never during Irish school holidays.

MERRION SQUARE & AROUND NATIONAL MUSEUM OF IRELAND – ARCHAEOLOGY

National Museum of Ireland

NATIONAL TREASURES

Ireland's most important cultural institution is the National Museum, and its most important branch is the original one, housed in this fine neoclassical (or Victorian Palladian) building designed by Sir Thomas Newenham Deane and finished in 1890. Squeezed in between the rear entrance of Leinster House – the Irish parliament – and a nondescript building from the 1960s, it's easy to pass by the museum. But within its fairly cramped confines you'll find the most extensive collection of Bronze and Iron Age gold artefacts in Europe and the extraordinary collection of the Treasury. This includes the stunning **Ardagh Chalice 1** and the delicately crafted **Tara Brooch 2**. Amid all the lustre, look out for the **Broighter Gold Collar 3** and the impressively crafted **Loughnashade War Trumpet 4**, both extraordinary examples of Celtic art. Finally, pay a visit to the exquisite **Cross of Cong 5**, which was created after the other pieces but is just as beautiful.

As you visit these treasures – all created after the arrival of Christianity in the 5th century – bear in mind that they were produced with the most rudimentary of instruments.

VIKING DUBLIN

Archaeological excavations in Dublin between 1961 and 1981 unearthed evidence of a Viking town and cemeteries along the banks of the River Liffey. The graves contained weapons such as swords and spears, together with jewellery and personal items. Craftsmen's tools, weights and scales, silver ingots and coins show that the Vikings, as well as marauding and raiding, were also engaged in commercial activities. The Viking artefacts are now part of the National Museum's collection.

LUNCH BREAK

Enjoy homemade pasta along with a nice glass of Italian red at the very authentic Dunne & Crescenzi (14–16 South Frederick St), or a pancake on the go from Lemon (Dawson St).

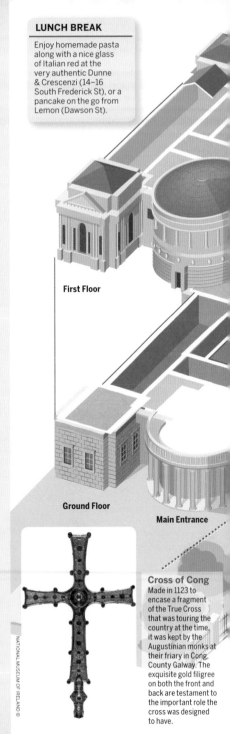

First Floor

Ground Floor

Main Entrance

NATIONAL MUSEUM OF IRELAND ©

Cross of Cong
Made in 1123 to encase a fragment of the True Cross that was touring the country at the time, it was kept by the Augustinian monks at their friary in Cong, County Galway. The exquisite gold filigree on both the front and back are testament to the important role the cross was designed to have.

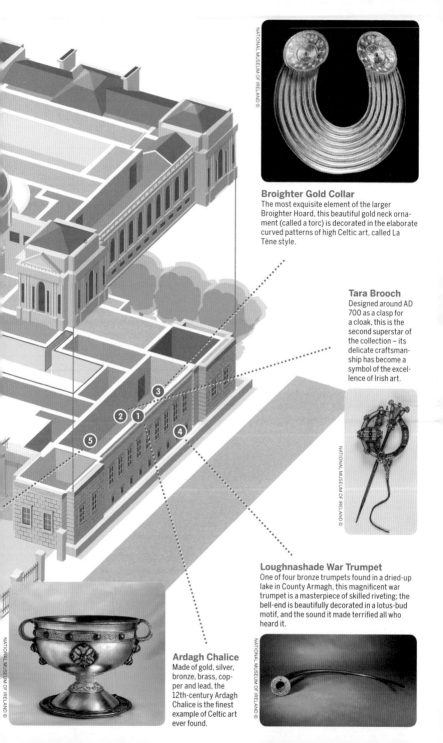

Broighter Gold Collar
The most exquisite element of the larger Broighter Hoard, this beautiful gold neck ornament (called a torc) is decorated in the elaborate curved patterns of high Celtic art, called La Tène style.

Tara Brooch
Designed around AD 700 as a clasp for a cloak, this is the second superstar of the collection – its delicate craftsmanship has become a symbol of the excellence of Irish art.

Loughnashade War Trumpet
One of four bronze trumpets found in a dried-up lake in County Armagh, this magnificent war trumpet is a masterpiece of skilled riveting; the bell-end is beautifully decorated in a lotus-bud motif, and the sound it made terrified all who heard it.

Ardagh Chalice
Made of gold, silver, bronze, brass, copper and lead, the 12th-century Ardagh Chalice is the finest example of Celtic art ever found.

NATIONAL MUSEUM OF IRELAND ©

A stunning Caravaggio and a room full of Ireland's pre-eminent artist, Jack B Yeats, are just a couple of highlights from this fine collection.

Its original collection of 125 paintings has grown, mainly through bequests, to over 13,000 artworks, including oils, watercolours, sketches, prints and sculptures.

The Building

The building itself was designed by Francis Fowke (1823–65), whose architectural credits also include London's Victoria & Albert Museum. The entire building comprises 54 galleries; works are divided by history, school, geography and theme. There are four wings: the original **Dargan Wing**, the **Milltown Wing** (1899–1903), the **Beit Wing** (1964–68) and the **Millennium Wing** (2002). A major refurbishment was completed in 2016.

The Collection

The collection spans works from the 14th to the 20th centuries and includes all the major continental schools.

There is an emphasis on Irish art, and among the works to look out for are William Orpen's *Sunlight,* Roderic O'Conor's *Reclining Nude* and *Young Breton Girl,* and Paul Henry's *The Potato Diggers.* But the highlight, and one you should definitely take time to explore, is the **Yeats Room**, devoted to and containing more than 30 paintings by Jack B Yeats, a uniquely Irish impressionist and arguably the country's greatest artist. Some of his finest moments are *The Liffey Swim, Men of Destiny* and *Above the Fair.*

Caravaggio's Taking of the Christ

The absolute star exhibit from a pupil of the European schools is Caravaggio's sublime *The Taking of Christ,* in which the troubled Italian genius attempts to light the scene figuratively and metaphorically (the artist himself is portrayed holding the lantern on the far right). Fra Angelico, Titian and Tintoretto are all in this neighbourhood. Facing Caravaggio, way down the opposite end of the gallery, is *A Genovese Boy Standing on a Terrace* by Van Dyck. Old Dutch and Flemish masters line up in between, but all defer to Vermeer's *A Lady Writing a Letter,* which is lucky to be here at all, having been stolen by Dublin gangster Martin Cahill in 1992, as featured in the film *The General.*

French Collection

The French section contains Jules Breton's famous 19th-century *The Gleaners,* along with works by Monet, Degas, Pissarro and Delacroix, while Spain chips in with an unusually scruffy *Still Life with Mandolin* by Picasso, as well as paintings by El Greco and Goya, and an early Velázquez. There is a small British collection with works by Reynolds, Hogarth and Gainsborough (*The Cottage Girl* is especially beautiful).

Joseph Turner

One of the most popular exhibitions occurs only in January, when the gallery hosts its annual display of the **Vaughan Collection**, featuring watercolours by Joseph Turner. The 35 works in the collection are best viewed at this time due to the particular quality of the winter light.

DON'T MISS

➡ The Yeats Room
➡ *The Taking of Christ* (Caravaggio)
➡ *A Lady Writing a Letter* (Vermeer)
➡ Vaughan Collection

PRACTICALITIES

➡ Map p248, B2
➡ www.nationalgallery.ie
➡ West Merrion Sq
➡ admission free
➡ ⊙9.30am-5.30pm Mon-Wed, Fri & Sat, to 8.30pm Thu, noon-5.30pm Sun
➡ 🚌7, 44 from city centre

TOP SIGHT
MERRION SQUARE

Elegant Merrion Sq was laid out in 1762 and is to this day the most prestigious of Dublin's squares. Its well-kept lawns and beautifully tended flower beds are flanked on three sides by gorgeous Georgian houses with colourful doors and peacock fanlights; and on the remaining side by the National Gallery, Leinster House and the Natural History Museum.

DON'T MISS
....
➡ Oscar Wilde Statue
➡ Happening Open Air Cinema
➡ Georgian houses

PRACTICALITIES
....
➡ Map p248, C3
➡ ☉dawn-dusk
➡ ☐7 & 44 from city centre

Oscar Wilde Statue

Just inside the southeastern corner of the square is a flamboyant **statue of Oscar Wilde** (Map p248; Merrion Sq; ☉dawn-dusk; ☐7 & 44 from city centre), who grew up across the street at **No 1**. This was the first residence built on the square (1762) and during the Wilde tenancy was renowned for the literary salon hosted by his mother, Lady 'Speranza' Wilde. Alas, you can't visit the restored house (used exclusively by students of the American College Dublin) so you'll have to make do with the statue of Wilde, wearing his customary smoking jacket and reclining on a rock. Wilde may well be sneering at Dublin and his old home, although the expression may have more to do with the artist's attempt to depict the deeply divided nature of the man: from one side he looks to be smiling and happy; from the other, gloomy and preoccupied. Atop one of the plinths, daubed with witty one-liners and Wildean throwaways, is a small green statue of Oscar's pregnant wife.

Troubled Times

Despite the air of affluent calm, life around here hasn't always been a well-pruned bed of roses. During the Famine, the lawns of the square teemed with destitute rural refugees who lived off the soup kitchen organised here. The British Embassy was at 39 East Merrion Sq until 1972, when it was burnt out in protest against the killing of 13 civilians on Bloody Sunday in Derry.

Damage to fine Dublin buildings hasn't always been the prerogative of vandals, terrorists or protesters. East Merrion Sq once continued into Lower Fitzwilliam St in the longest unbroken series of Georgian houses in Europe. Despite this, in 1961 the Electricity Supply Board (ESB) knocked down 26 of them to build an office block – just another in a long list of crimes against architectural aesthetics that plagued the city in the latter half of the 20th century. The Royal Institute of the Architects of Ireland is rather more respectful of its Georgian address and hosts regular exhibitions.

⊙ SIGHTS

NATIONAL MUSEUM OF IRELAND –
ARCHAEOLOGY   MUSEUM
See p84.

NATIONAL GALLERY   MUSEUM
See p88.

MERRION SQUARE   PARK
See p89.

★MUSEUM OF
NATURAL HISTORY   MUSEUM
Map p248 (National Museum of Ireland – Natural History; www.museum.ie; Upper Merrion St; ⊙10am-5pm Tue-Sat, 2-5pm Sun; ☐7, 44 from city centre) **FREE** Dusty, weird and utterly compelling, this window into Victorian times has barely changed since Scottish explorer Dr David Livingstone opened it in 1857 – before disappearing into the African jungle for a meeting with Henry Stanley. It is a fine example of Victorian charm and scientific wonderment, and its enormous collection is a testament to the skill of taxidermy.

The **Irish Room** on the ground floor is filled with mammals, sea creatures, birds and some butterflies all found in Ireland at some point, including the skeletons of three 10,000-year-old Irish elk that greet you as you enter. The **World Animals Collection**, spread across three levels, has as its centrepiece the skeleton of a 20m-long fin whale found beached in County Sligo. Evolutionists will love the line-up of orang-utan, chimpanzee, gorilla and human skeletons on the 1st floor.

A more recent addition is the **Discovery Zone**, where visitors can do some first-hand exploring of their own, handling taxidermy specimens and opening drawers. Other notables include the Tasmanian tiger (an extinct Australian marsupial, mislabelled as a Tasmanian wolf), a giant panda from China, and several African and Asian rhinoceros. The wonderful **Blaschka Collection** comprises finely detailed glass models of marine creatures whose zoological accuracy is incomparable.

NUMBER 29 LOWER
FITZWILLIAM STREET   HISTORIC BUILDING
Map p248 (www.esb.ie/numbertwentynine; 29 Lower Fitzwilliam St; adult/student/child €6/3/free; ⊙10am-5pm Tue-Sat mid-Feb–mid-Dec; ☐7 & 44 from city centre) In an effort to atone (partly) for its sins against Dublin's Georgian heritage –

it broke up Europe's most perfect Georgian row to build its headquarters – the Electricity Supply Board (ESB) carefully restored this home to give an impression of genteel family life at the beginning of the 18th century.

From rat-traps in the kitchen basement to handmade wallpaper and Georgian cabinets, the attention to detail is impressive, but the regular tours (the 11am tour is reserved for pre-booked groups, leaving only the 3pm tour on a first-come, first-served basis) are disappointingly dry.

LEINSTER HOUSE   NOTABLE BUILDING
Map p248 (Oireachtas Éireann; ☑01-618 3271; www.oireachtas.ie; Kildare St; ⊙observation galleries 2.30-8.30pm Tue, 10.30am-8.30pm Wed, 10.30am-5.30pm Thu Nov-May; ☐all city centre) All the big decisions are made at the Oireachtas (parliament). This Palladian mansion was built as a city residence for James Fitzgerald, the Duke of Leinster and Earl of Kildare, by Richard Cassels between 1745 and 1748. Prearranged guided tours (p95) are available when parliament is in session (but not sitting); entry tickets to the observation galleries are available.

The Kildare St facade looks like a townhouse (which inspired Irish architect James Hoban's design for the US White House), whereas the Merrion Sq frontage resembles a country mansion. The obelisk in front of the building is dedicated to Arthur Griffith, Michael Collins and Kevin O'Higgins, the architects of independent Ireland.

The first government of the Irish Free State moved in from 1922, and both the Dáil (lower house) and Seanad (senate, or upper house) still meet here to discuss the affairs of the nation and gossip at the exclusive members bar. The 60-member Seanad meets for fairly low-key sessions in the north-wing saloon, while there are usually more sparks and tantrums when the 166-member Dáil bangs heads in a less-interesting room, formerly a lecture theatre, which was added to the original building in 1897. Parliament sits for 90 days a year.

GOVERNMENT BUILDINGS   NOTABLE BUILDING
Map p248 (www.taoiseach.gov.ie; Upper Merrion St; ⊙tours hourly 10.30am-1.30pm Sat; ☐7 & 44 from city centre) **FREE** This gleaming Edwardian pile was the last building (almost) completed by the British before they were evicted; it opened as the Royal College of Science in 1911. When the college vacated in 1989, the then-Taoiseach Charles Haughey

TRACING YOUR ANCESTORS

Go on, you're dying to see if you've got a bit of Irish in you, and maybe tracking down your roots is the main reason for your visit. It will have made things much easier if you did some preliminary research in your home country – particularly finding out the precise date and point of entry of your ancestors – but you might still be able to plot your family tree even if you're acting on impulse.

The **Genealogy Advisory Service** at the **National Library** (p91) will advise you on how to trace your ancestry, which is a good way to begin your research if you have no other experience. For information on commercial agencies that will do the research for you, contact the **Association of Professional Genealogists in Ireland** (APGI; www. apgi.ie; c/o the Genealogy Advisory Service, Kildare St). The **Births, Deaths & Marriages Register** (☑01-671 1863; www.birthsdeathsmarriages.ie; Joyce House, East Lombard St; ⊙9.30am-12.30pm & 2.15-4.30pm Mon-Fri; ⬛56A from city centre) and the files of the National Library and the **National Archives** (☑01-407 2300; www.nationalarchives.ie; Bishop St, Dublin 8; ⊙10am-5pm Mon-Fri) are all potential sources of genealogical information.

There are also lots of books on the subject, with *Irish Roots Guide*, by Tony McCarthy, serving as a useful introduction. Other publications include *Tracing Your Irish Roots* by Christine Kinealy and *Tracing Your Irish Ancestors: A Comprehensive Guide* by John Grenham. All these, and other items of genealogical concern, can be obtained from the Genealogy Bookshop at **Heraldic Artists** (p95).

and his government moved in and spent a fortune refurbishing the complex.

Free 40-minute **tours** visit the Taoiseach's office, the Cabinet Room, the ceremonial staircase with a stunning stained-glass window – designed by Evie Hone (1894–1955) for the 1939 New York Trade Fair – and many fine examples of modern Irish arts and crafts.

ROYAL HIBERNIAN ACADEMY
(RHA) GALLAGHER GALLERY   GALLERY
Map p248 (☑01-661 2558; www.rhagallery.ie; 15 Ely Pl; ⊙11am-5pm Mon-Sat, till 8pm Wed, noon-5pm Sun; ⬛10, 11, 13B or 51X from city centre) **FREE** This large, well-lit gallery at the end of a serene Georgian street has a grand name to fit its exalted reputation as one of the most prestigious exhibition spaces for modern and contemporary art in Ireland – although it's worked hard to shrug off a reputation for being a little dowdy and conservative in its tastes.

The big event is the Annual Exhibition, held in May, which shows the work of those artists deemed worthy enough by the selection committee that is made up of members of the academy (easily identified amid the huge throng that attends the opening by their scholars' gowns). The show is a mix of technically proficient artists, Sunday painters and the odd outstanding talent.

NATIONAL LIBRARY   HISTORIC BUILDING
Map p248 (www.nli.ie; Kildare St; ⊙9.30am-7.45pm Mon-Wed, to 4.45pm Thu & Fri, 10am-12.45pm Sat; ⬛all city centre) **FREE** Suitably sedate and elegant, the National Library was built from 1884 to 1890 by Sir Thomas Newenham Deane, at the same time and to a similar design as the National Museum of Ireland – Archaeology. Its extensive collection has many valuable early manuscripts, first editions and maps.

Parts of the library are open to the public, including the domed reading room where Stephen Dedalus expounded his views on Shakespeare in James Joyce's *Ulysses*.

There's a **Genealogy Advisory Service** on the 2nd floor, where you can obtain free information on how best to trace your Irish roots.

For those prints that are worth a thousand words, you'll have to head down to Temple Bar to the National Photographic Archive (p103) extension of the library, for which you'll need to pick up a reader's ticket (look for the Readers Ticket Office in the main building).

ST STEPHEN'S
'PEPPER CANISTER' CHURCH   CHURCH
Map p248 (☑01-288 0663; www.peppercanister. ie; Upper Mount St; ⊙open for concerts only; ⬛4, 7, 8 or 120 from city centre) **FREE** Built in 1825 in Greek Revival style and commonly known as the 'pepper canister' on account of its appearance, St Stephen's is one of Dublin's most attractive and distinctive churches, and looks particularly fetching at twilight when its exterior lights have just come on.

It occasionally hosts classical concerts, but don't go out of your way to see the interior. It's only open during services, usually held at 11am Sunday and 11.30am Wednesday, with an extra one at 11am on Friday in July and August.

FITZWILLIAM SQUARE
PARK

Map p248 (⊘closed to public; 🚍10, 11, 13B or 46A from city centre) The smallest of Dublin's great Georgian squares was completed in 1825. It's the only one left where the central garden is still the private domain of the square's residents. William Dargan (1799–1867), the railway pioneer and founder of the National Gallery, lived at No 2, and the artist Jack B Yeats (1871–1957) lived at No 18.

Look out for the attractive 18th- and 19th-century metal coal-hole covers. The square is now a centre for the medical profession.

HUGUENOT CEMETERY
CEMETERY

Map p248 (St Stephen's Green; ⊘dawn-dusk; 🚍all city centre) This tiny cemetery was established in 1693 by French Protestant refugees.

✗ EATING

ETTO
ITALIAN $$

Map p248 (🖉01-678 8872; www.etto.ie; 18 Merrion Row; mains €18-23; ⊘noon-10pm Mon-Fri, 12.30-10pm Sat) A superb restaurant and wine bar that does contemporary versions of classic Italian cuisine. All the ingredients are fresh, the presentation is exquisite and the service is just right. Portions are small, but the food is so rich you won't leave hungry. The only downside is the relatively quick turnover; lingering over the excellent wine would be nice. Book ahead.

XICO
MEXICAN $$

Map p248 (www.xico.ie; 143 Lower Baggot St; mains €10-15; ⊘5pm-midnight) A relatively new arrival on the block is this underground Mexican restaurant, where the music is loud and the food – tacos, tostadas and main courses such as tuna ceviche and a fine chilli bowl – is washed down with margaritas. Yes, it's a restaurant, but you'd better be in the mood for a fiesta.

MARCEL'S
FRENCH $$

Map p248 (www.marcels.ie; 13 Merrion Row; mains €20-34; ⊘noon-1am; 🚍all city centre) An elegant brasserie with Hermès orange-coloured chairs, blue-and-white Churchill china and superb, French-inspired cuisine – just the

🏃 Neighbourhood Walk
A Georgian Block

START KILDARE ST
END NATIONAL GALLERY
LENGTH 1.7KM; ONE HOUR

Although Dublin is rightfully known as a Georgian city and many of its buildings were built between 1720 and 1814, the style cast such a tall shadow over Dublin design that for more than a century afterwards it was still being copied.

Begin your amble at the bottom (northern) end of Kildare St, opposite the walls of Trinity College Dublin. This street is named after James Fitzgerald, Duke of Leinster and the Earl of Kildare, who broke with 18th-century convention and opted to build his city mansion on the south side of the Liffey, away from the elegant neighbourhoods of the north side where most of his aristocratic peers lived. 'Where I go,' he confidently predicted, 'society will follow.'

He was right, and over the following century the street was lined with impressive buildings. On the left-hand side as you begin is the old Kildare Street Lords Club, a members' club famous for 'aristocracy, claret and whist' that was founded in 1782. In 1860 the original building was replaced by this Byzantine-style construction, designed by Thomas Newenham Deane, where it remained until 1976. It is now the home of the ❶**Alliance Française**.

On the same side a little further up is the ❷**National Library** (p91), another one of Deane's designs; immediately after the library, the imposing black gates and police presence protect ❸**Leinster House** (p90), the Palladian city pile that Fitzgerald commissioned Richard Cassels to build for him between 1745 and 1748. It is now the seat of both houses of the Irish parliament. From this side American visitors might think the building oddly familiar: the townhouse look is what inspired James Hoban, 1780 winner of the Duke of Leinster's medal for drawings of 'brackets, stairs and roofs', to submit a design that won the competition to build the White House in 1792.

The next building along the street is the ❹**National Museum of Ireland – Archaeology** (p84), another Deane

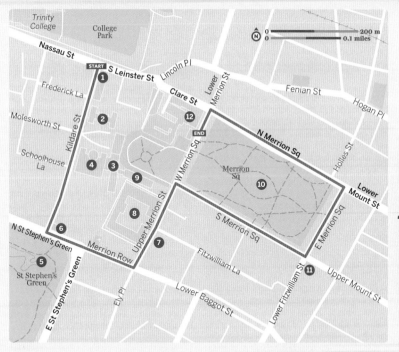

building, which opened in 1890 and has since been the repository of the state's most valuable cultural treasures. As you reach the top of the street, the greenery in front of you is that of **5 St Stephen's Green** (p63), the city's best-loved public square. Once a common used for punishments and hangings, the green was landscaped with Guinness money in the mid-18th century and quickly became the aristocracy's favourite spot to take a walk.

Turn left onto Merrion Row and walk along the green. You'll pass the **6 Shelbourne** (p183), Dublin's most historic hotel. During the Easter Rising of 1916 it treated the injured from both rebel and British sides, and the Irish Constitution of 1922 was framed in Room 112. The hotel even has a tenuous link to Hitler: his half-brother Alois worked as a waiter here. Take another left onto Merrion St. On your right, No 24 in the row of elegant Georgian houses is reputed to be the birthplace of Arthur Wellesley, the Duke of Wellington, who dealt with jibes about being born in Ireland by snippily responding that 'being born in a stable does not make one a horse'. That 'stable' is now part of the city's most elegant hotel, the **7 Merrion** (p183).

On your left-hand side you'll pass the **8 Government Buildings** (p90), where the current government runs its day-to-day affairs, and just past it, the rear entrance to Leinster House; from here it looks more like a country mansion. The smaller building wedged in between Government Buildings and Leinster House is the **9 Natural History Museum** (p90), opened in 1857.

On your right is **10 Merrion Square** (p89), the most elegant of Dublin's public spaces. The park itself is gorgeous, while the houses that surround it are magnificent: their doorways and fanlights are the most photographed of the city's Georgian heritage and a disproportionate number of Dublin's most famous residents lived on it at one point or another. If you want to see inside a typical Georgian home, **11 No 29 Lower Fitzwilliam Street** (p90), at the square's southeastern corner, has been carefully restored.

Walk around or through Merrion Sq, making your way back to West Merrion Sq and the **12 National Gallery** (p88), which opened in 1864 and was built by Francis Fowke after a design by Charles Lanyon. For the sake of symmetry, the facade is a copy of that of the Natural History Museum.

way they'd eat it in New York. It's owned by the same crowd as the Green Hen (p70), and the similarities are obvious and complementary. To one side is a bar – done in traditional Irish style. Bookings recommended.

ELY
MODERN IRISH $$

Map p248 (☑01-676 8986; www.elywinebar.ie; 22 Ely Pl; mains €15-28; ⊙noon-11.30pm Mon-Fri, 5pm-12.30am Sat; ⊟all city centre) ✐ Scrummy homemade burgers, bangers and mash, and wild smoked salmon salad are some of the dishes you can find in this basement restaurant. Meals are prepared with organic and free-range produce from the owner's family farm in County Clare, so you can rest assured of the quality. There are two more branches on either side of the Liffey.

DOBBINS
FRENCH $$

Map p248 (☑01-676 4679; www.dobbins.ie; 15 Stephen's Lane; mains €21-28; ⊙12.30-2.30pm & 6-10pm Wed-Fri, 6-10pm Sat, 12.30-4pm Sun; ⊟all city centre) Completely refurbished after 25 years as a stalwart of the city's top-end dining scene, Dobbins 2.0 is still a classy spot for an elegant dinner of established favourites – fish, chicken, duck and a good steak. Nothing too radical, just popular dishes done well. The service is excellent.

★RESTAURANT PATRICK GUILBAUD
FRENCH $$$

Map p248 (☑01-676 4192; www.restaurantpatrickguilbaud.ie; 21 Upper Merrion St; 2-/3-course set lunch €45/55, dinner menus €90-185; ⊙12.30-2.30pm & 7.30-10.30pm Tue-Sat; ☐7 & 44 from the city centre) Ireland's only Michelin two-star is understandably considered the best in the country by its devotees, who proclaim Guillaume Lebrun's French haute cuisine the most exalted expression of the culinary arts. If you like formal dining, this is as good as it gets: the lunch menu is an absolute steal, at least in this stratosphere.

The food is innovative without being fiddly, beautifully cooked and superbly presented.

The room itself is all contemporary elegance and the service expertly formal yet friendly – the staff are meticulously trained and are as skilled at answering queries and addressing requests as they are at making sure not one breadcrumb lingers too long on the immaculate tablecloths. Owner Patrick Guilbaud usually does the rounds of the tables in the evening to salute regular customers and charm first-timers into returning. Reservations are absolutely necessary.

L'ECRIVAIN
FRENCH $$$

Map p248 (☑01-661 1919; www.lecrivain.com; 109a Lower Baggot St; 3-course lunch menus €40, 8-course tasting menus €75, mains €40-47; ⊙12.30-2pm Thu & Fri, 6.30-10pm Mon-Sat; ☐38 & 39 from city centre) Head chef Derry Clarke is considered a gourmet god for the exquisite simplicity of his creations, which put the emphasis on flavour and the best local ingredients – all given the French once over and turned into something that approaches divine dining. The Michelin people like it too and awarded it one of their stars.

UNICORN
ITALIAN $$$

Map p248 (☑01-662 4757; www.theunicorn.restaurant; 12b Merrion Ct, Merrion Row; mains €26-32.50; ⊙12.30-2.30pm & 5-11pm Mon-Wed, 12.30-11pm Thu-Sat, 1-9pm Sun; ⊟all city centre) Saturday lunch at this Italian restaurant in a laneway off Merrion Row is a tradition for Dublin's media types, socialites, politicos and their cronies who guffaw and clink glasses in conspiratorial rapture. The extensive lunchtime antipasto bar is popular, but we still prefer the meaty à la carte menu. There are pasta and fish dishes to cater to all palates.

BANG CAFÉ
MODERN EUROPEAN $$$

Map p248 (☑01-400 4229; www.bangrestaurant. com; 11 Merrion Row; mains €22-33; ⊙5.30-10pm

LITERARY ADDRESSES

Merrion Sq has long been the favoured address of Dublin's affluent intelligentsia. Oscar Wilde spent much of his youth at 1 North Merrion Sq, now the campus of the American College Dublin. Grumpy WB Yeats (1865–1939) lived at 52 East Merrion Sq and later, from 1922 to 1928, at 82 South Merrion Sq. George (AE) Russell (1867–1935), the self-described 'poet, mystic, painter and cooperator', worked at No 84. The great Liberator Daniel O'Connell (1775–1847) was a resident of No 58 in his later years. Austrian Erwin Schrödinger (1887–1961), co-winner of the 1933 Nobel Prize for Physics, lived at No 65 from 1940 to 1956. Dublin seems to attract writers of horror stories and Joseph Sheridan Le Fanu (1814–73), who penned the vampire classic *Camilla*, was a resident of No 70.

Mon-Thu, to 11pm Fri & Sat, to 9.30pm Sun; all city centre) Fashionistas and foodies alike have been aficionados of this stylish spot for over a decade, which changed hands a few years ago but still continues to turn out top-notch contemporary Irish fare, including slow-cooked beef cheek and a delicious chargrilled, dry aged rib eye.

DRINKING & NIGHTLIFE

⭐ JAMES TONER'S   PUB
Map p248 (139 Lower Baggot St; ⊙10.30am-11.30pm Mon-Thu, to 12.30am Fri & Sat, noon-11pm Sun; 7, 44 from city centre) Toner's, with its stone floors and antique snugs, has changed little over the years and is the closest thing you'll get to a country pub in the heart of the city. The shelves and drawers are reminders that it once doubled as a grocery shop.

The writer Oliver St John Gogarty once brought WB Yeats here, after the upper-class poet – who lived just around the corner – decided he wanted to visit a pub. After a silent sherry in the noisy bar, Yeats turned to his friend and said, 'I have seen the pub, now please take me home.' We always suspected he was a little too precious for normal people, and he would probably be horrified by the good-natured business crowd making the racket these days too. His loss.

⭐ O'DONOGHUE'S   PUB
Map p248 (15 Merrion Row; ⊙10.30am-11.30pm Mon-Thu, to 12.30am Fri & Sat, noon-11pm Sun; all city centre) Once the most renowned traditional music bar in all Dublin, this is where the world-famous folk group the Dubliners refined their raspish brand of trad in the 1960s. On summer evenings a young, international crowd spills out into the courtyard beside the pub. It's also a famous rugby pub and the Dublin HQ for many Irish and visiting fans.

DOHENY & NESBITT'S   PUB
Map p248 (☑01-676 2945; www.dohenyandnesbitts.ie; 5 Lower Baggot St; ⊙10am-11.30pm Mon-Thu, 10am-2am Fri & Sat, noon-11pm Sun; all city centre) A standout, even in a city of wonderful pubs, Nesbitt's is equipped with antique snugs and is a favourite place for the high-powered gossip of politicians and journalists; Leinster House is only a short stroll away.

HARTIGAN'S   PUB
Map p248 (100 Lower Leeson St; ⊙10.30am-11.30pm Mon-Thu, to 12.30am Fri & Sat, noon-11pm

LOCAL KNOWLEDGE

STREET ART
At weekends, the wrought-iron fences of Merrion Sq convert to gallery walls for the traditional open-air **art market** (Map p248; Merrion Sq; ⊙10am-6pm Sat & Sun; all city centre). At any given time you'll find the work of 150 artists, mostly Sunday-painter types with a penchant for landscapes and still lifes, some of whom are very talented indeed.

Sun; all city centre) This is about as spartan a bar as you'll find in the city, and the daytime home of some serious drinkers, who appreciate the quiet, no-frills surroundings. In the evening it's popular with students from the medical faculty of University College Dublin (UCD).

☆ ENTERTAINMENT

HAPPENING OPEN AIR CINEMA   CINEMA
Map p248 (www.happenings.ie; Merrion Sq; €5; ⊙8pm Thu May-Sep; all city centre) Grab a blanket and take a seat on the grass of Merrion Sq for a summer screening al fresco.

SUGAR CLUB   LIVE MUSIC
Map p248 (☑01-678 7188; www.thesugarclub.com; 8 Lower Leeson St; €7-20; ⊙7pm-late; St Stephen's Green) There's live jazz, cabaret and soul music at weekends in this comfortable theatre-style venue on the corner of St Stephen's Green.

🛍 SHOPPING

HERALDIC ARTISTS   BOOKS
Map p248 (3 Nassau St; ⊙1-6pm Mon-Sat) Hand-painted heraldic plaques and scrolls, as well as an extensive research facility on genealogy, with plenty of books to aid both professional and amateur researchers.

🏃 ACTIVITIES

GUIDED TOUR OF OIREACHTAS   TOUR
Map p248 (www.oireachtas.ie; Kildare St; ⊙10.30am, 11.30am, 2.30pm & 3.30pm Mon-Fri; all city centre) **FREE** Pre-arranged guided tours of the Oireachtas (houses of parliament) are available when parliament is in session (but not sitting).

TIM GRAHAM / GETTY IMAGES ©

1. Georgian Architecture (p212)
The area around Merrion Square is renowned for its Georgian architecture.

2. Merrion Square (p82)
One of Dublin's best-maintained 18th century neighbourhoods.

3. Green Spaces (p89)
Merrion Square, pictured, is doubtless Dublin's most prestigious public squares.

4. Grafton Street (p52)
This pedestrian-friendly street, full of activities and sights, is a Dublin must-see.

DE AGOSTINI / GETTY IMAGES ©

Temple Bar

Neighborhood Top Five

1 **Temple Bar Food Market** (p107) Feast on organic and exotic nibbles from all over at Dublin's most exciting food market.

2 **Gallery of Photography** (p103) Explore the creative reach of photography at this small but excellent gallery, with a fine bookshop on the ground floor.

3 **Cow's Lane Designer Mart** (p109) Rummage for designer gear, radical fashions and oddball knickknacks by local producers at this weekend market.

4 **Ark Children's Cultural Centre** (p103) Awaken your child's inner performer and creator at this wonderful cultural centre.

5 **Gutter Bookshop** (p108) This locally owned bookshop is one of the best in town because it is the kind of place that encourages you to browse and linger.

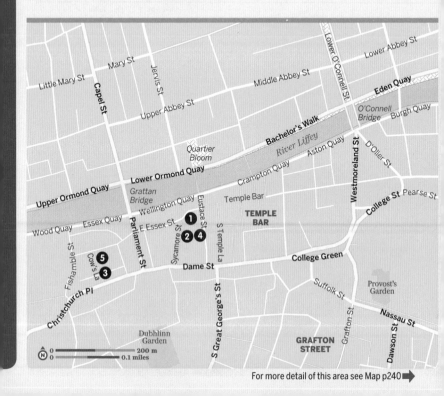

For more detail of this area see Map p240 ➡

Explore Temple Bar

You can visit all of Temple Bar's attractions in less than half a day, but that's not really the point: this cobbled neighbourhood, for so long the city's most infamous party zone, is really more about ambience than attractions. If you visit during the day, the district's bohemian bent is on display. You can browse for vintage clothes, get your nipples pierced, nibble on Mongolian barbecue, buy organic food, pick up the latest musical releases and buy books on every conceivable subject. You can check out the latest art installations or join in a pulsating drum circle. By night – or at the weekend – it's a different story altogether, as the area's bars are packed to the rafters with revellers looking to tap into their inner Bacchus: it's loud, raucous and usually a lot of fun. Temple Bar is also Dublin's official 'cultural quarter', so you shouldn't ignore its more high-minded offerings like the progressive Project Arts Centre, Temple Bar Gallery & Studios and the Irish Film Institute (IFI).

Local Life

→**Markets** The Temple Bar Food Market (p107) is all about gourmet goodies and organic foodstuffs; the Cow's Lane Designer Mart (p109) is a showcase of local art and clothing; while the Book Fair (p109) is the place to pick up second-hand novels and CDs.

→**Nightlife** A live-music gig at the Button Factory (p107) or the Workman's Club (p107) is always a great night out, and you can really get your grind on at Mother (p106) on a Saturday night.

→**Dining** Soaking up the excesses of the night before is a favourite weekend activity, and we recommend the marvellous mayhem at the Elephant & Castle (p105) or the sublime sushi at Banyi (p105), a favourite with the city's Japanese population.

Getting There & Away

→**Bus** As Temple Bar is right in the heart of the city, all cross-city buses will deposit you by the cobbled, largely pedestrianised streets, making access – and escape – that bit easier.

→**On Foot** Temple Bar is easily accessible on foot from Grafton St to the southeast, Kilmainham to the west and the north side of the river to the north.

Lonely Planet's Top Tip

Unless you're in for a no-holds-barred, knees-up weekend and don't care too much about sleeping, don't overnight in Temple Bar – hotel rooms are generally more cramped and noisier here than elsewhere. Temple Bar's central location and the city's size mean you can get in and out of here with relative ease.

TEMPLE BAR

✕ Best Places to Eat

→ Crackbird (p104)
→ Bunsen (p104)
→ Banyi Japanese Dining (p105)
→ Elephant & Castle (p105)

For reviews, see p104 ➡

☕ Best Places to Drink

→ Vintage Cocktail Club (p106)
→ Palace Bar (p106)
→ Front Lounge (p106)
→ Mother (p106)

For reviews, see p106 ➡

🔒 Best Places to Shop

→ Cow's Lane Designer Mart (p109)
→ Gutter Bookshop (p108)
→ Claddagh Records (p108)
→ Siopaella Design Exchange (p108)

For reviews, see p107 ➡

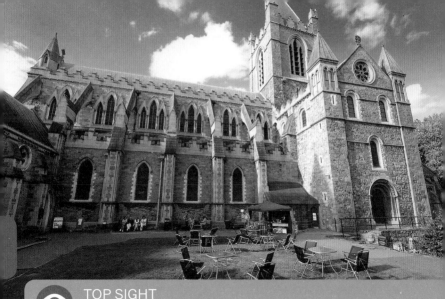

DRAGOS COSMIN PHOTOS / GETTY IMAGES ©

◉ TOP SIGHT
CHRIST CHURCH CATHEDRAL

Its hilltop location and eye-catching flying buttresses make this the most photogenic of Dublin's three cathedrals as well as one of the capital's most recognisable symbols.

Early Beginnings

A wooden church was first erected here by Dunán, the first bishop of Dublin, and Sitric, the Viking king, around 1030, at the southern edge of Dublin's Viking settlement. In 1163, however, the secular clergy was replaced by a group of Augustinian monks installed by the patron saint of Dublin, Archbishop Laurence O'Toole. Six years later, the Normans of Richard de Clare, Earl of Pembroke (better known as Strongbow), blew into town and got themselves into the church-building business, arranging with O'Toole (and his successor John Cumin) for the construction of a new stone cathedral that would symbolise Anglo-Norman glory. The new cathedral opened its doors late in the 12th century, by which time Strongbow, O'Toole and Cumin were long dead.

Above ground, the north wall, the transepts and the western part of the choir are almost all that remain from the original. It has been restored several times over the centuries and, despite its apparent uniformity, is a hotchpotch of different styles, ranging from Romanesque to English Gothic.

Hard Times

Until the disestablishment of the Church of Ireland in 1869, senior representatives of the Crown all swore their allegiance here. The church's fortunes, however, were not

DON'T MISS

→ Mummified Cat & Rat
→ The Treasury
→ Strongbow Monument

PRACTICALITIES

→ Church of the Holy Trinity
→ Map p240, A5
→ www.christchurch cathedral.ie
→ Christ Church Pl
→ adult/student/child €6/4.50/2
→ ⊘9am-5pm Mon-Sat, 12.30-2.30pm Sun year-round, longer hours Jun-Aug
→ 🚌50, 50A, 56A from Aston Quay, 54, 54A from Burgh Quay

guaranteed. By the turn of the 18th century its popularity waned along with the district as the upper echelons of Dublin society fled north, where they attended a new favourite, St Mary's Abbey. Through much of its history, Christ Church vied for supremacy with nearby St Patrick's Cathedral, but both fell on hard times in the 18th and 19th centuries. Christ Church was virtually derelict – the nave had been used as a market and the crypt had earlier housed taverns – by the time restoration took place. Whiskey distiller Henry Roe donated the equivalent of €30 million to save the church, which was substantially rebuilt from 1871 to 1878. Ironically, both of the great Church of Ireland cathedrals are essentially outsiders in a Catholic nation today, dependent on tourist donations for their very survival.

From its inception, Christ Church was the State Church of Ireland, and when Henry VIII dissolved the monasteries in the 16th century, the Augustinian priory that managed the church was replaced with a new Anglican clergy, which still runs the church today.

Chapterhouse & Northern Wall
From the southeastern entrance to the churchyard you walk past ruins of the **chapterhouse**, which dates from 1230. The **main entrance** to the cathedral is at the southwestern corner, and as you enter, you face the ancient **northern wall**. This survived the collapse of its southern counterpart but has also suffered from subsiding foundations (much of the church was built on a peat bog) and, from its eastern end, it leans visibly.

Strongbow Monument
The southern aisle has a **monument to the legendary Strongbow**. The armoured figure on the tomb is unlikely to be of Strongbow (it's more probably the Earl of Drogheda), but his internal organs may have been buried here. A popular legend relates an especially visceral version of the daddy-didn't-love-me tale: the half-figure beside the tomb is supposed to be Strongbow's son, who was cut in two by his loving father when his bravery in battle was suspect – an act that surely would have saved the kid a fortune in therapist's bills.

South Transept
The south transept contains the super baroque **tomb of the 19th earl of Kildare**, who died in 1734. His grandson, Lord Edward Fitzgerald, was a member of the United Irishmen and died in the abortive 1798 Rising. The entrance to the **Chapel**

DID YOU KNOW?

In March 2012, the heart of St Laurence O'Toole, which had been kept in the church for 890 years, was stolen by a gang linked to the international trade of rhino horns.

The combination ticket that includes Dublinia is excellent value if you're visiting with kids. The cathedral also has a weekly schedule of sung masses, which can be very beautiful; check the website for details.

TEMPLE BAR CHRIST CHURCH CATHEDRAL

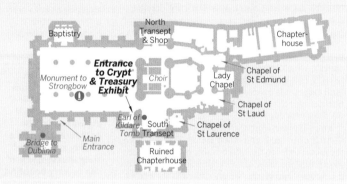

of St Laurence is off the south transept and contains two effigies, one of them reputed to be of either Strongbow's wife or sister.

Crypt

An entrance by the south transept descends to the unusually large arched **crypt**, which dates back to the original Viking church. Curiosities in the crypt include a glass display-case housing a mummified cat in the act of chasing a mummified rat (aka Tom & Jerry), frozen midpursuit inside an organ pipe in the 1860s. Also on display are the stocks from the old 'liberty' of Christ Church, used when church authorities meted out civil punishments to wrongdoers. The **Treasury** exhibit includes rare coins, the Stuart coat of arms and gold given to the church by William of Orange after the Battle of the Boyne. From the main entrance, a **bridge**, part of the 1871–78 restoration, leads to Dublinia.

 SIGHTS

CHRIST CHURCH CATHEDRAL CHURCH

See p100.

DUBLINIA & THE VIKING WORLD MUSEUM

Map p240 (☑01-679 4611; www.dublinia. ie; Christ Church Pl; adult/student/child €8.50/7.50/5.50; ⊗10am-5.30pm Mar-Sep, to 4.30pm Oct-Feb; ☐50, 50A, 56A from Aston Quay, 54, 54A from Burgh Quay) A must for the kids, the old Synod Hall, added to Christ Church Cathedral (p100) during its late-19th-century restoration, is home to the seemingly perennial Dublinia, a lively and kitschy attempt to bring medieval Dublin to life. Models, streetscapes and somewhat old-fashioned interactive displays do a fairly decent job of it, at least for kids. Your ticket gets you into Christ Church Cathedral free, via the link bridge.

The model of a medieval quayside and a cobbler's shop are both excellent, as is the scale model of the medieval city. Up one floor is **Viking World**, which has a large selection of objects recovered from Wood Quay, the world's largest Viking archaeological site. Interactive exhibits tell the story of Dublin's 9th- and 10th-century Scandinavian invaders, but the real treat is exploring life aboard the recreated longboat. Finally, you can climb neighbouring **St Michael's Tower** and peek through its grubby windows for views over the city to the Dublin hills. There is also a pleasant cafe and the inevitable souvenir shop.

GALLERY OF PHOTOGRAPHY GALLERY

Map p240 (www.galleryofphotography.ie; Meeting House Sq; ⊗11am-6pm Mon-Sat, 1-6pm Sun; ☐all city centre) **FREE** This small gallery devoted to the photograph is set in an airy three-level space overlooking Meeting House Sq. It features a constantly changing menu of local and international work, and while it's a little too small to be considered a really good gallery, the downstairs shop is well stocked with all manner of photographic tomes and manuals.

**NATIONAL
PHOTOGRAPHIC ARCHIVE** MUSEUM

Map p240 (www.nli.ie; Meeting House Sq; ⊗10am-1pm Tue-Thu & 2.30-4.30pm Wed; ☐all city centre) **FREE** The archive of photographs taken from the mid-19th century onward are part of the collection of the National Library, and so are open by appointment only

and only with a reader's ticket, which can be obtained from the main branch (p91) on Kildare St.

NATIONAL WAX MUSEUM PLUS MUSEUM

Map p240 (www.waxmuseumplus.ie; The Armoury, Foster Pl; adult/child/concession €14/9/12; ⊗10am-7pm; ☐all city centre) More a mini history museum in wax than Dublin's version of Madame Tussauds. The quality of the waxworks is inconsistent – some look like the result of a hastily conceived school project. Still, the Chamber of Horrors (Dracula has a starring role) is pretty good. The 'plus' in the name refers to the interactive use of video and music. Buy tickets online for a 10% discount.

HA'PENNY BRIDGE BRIDGE

Map p252 (☐all city centre) The Ha'penny Bridge – officially known as the Liffey Bridge – was built in 1816 and remains one of the world's oldest cast-iron bridges. It was built to replace the seven ferries that plied a busy route between the two banks of the river and it gets its name from the ha'penny toll that was charged until 1919 (for a time the toll was one and a half pence, and so it was called the Penny Ha'penny Bridge).

**HANDEL'S HOTEL (SITE OF
NEAL'S NEW MUSICK HALL)** HISTORIC SITE

Map p240 (☐all city centre) The clue is the name: on the site of this hotel was once Neal's New Musick Hall, where on 13 April 1742, the nearly broke GF Handel conducted the very first performance of his epic work *Messiah*. All that's left now is the original arch, restored to something like its elegant original. Every year the *Messiah* is performed in an open-air concert on Fishamble St – Dublin's oldest street – to commemorate the event.

Ironically, Jonathan Swift – author of *Gulliver's Travels* and dean of St Patrick's Cathedral – suggested the choirs of St Patrick's and Christ Church participate in the original performance, but then he revoked his invitation, vowing to punish vicars who took part for their 'disobedience, rebellion, perfidy and ingratitude'. The concert went ahead nonetheless.

**ARK CHILDREN'S
CULTURAL CENTRE** CULTURAL CENTRE

Map p240 (www.ark.ie; 11a Eustace St; ☐all city centre) Aimed at youngsters between the ages of three and 14, the Ark is enormously

TEMPLE BAR SIGHTS

A SAUCY PAST

Purists may cry foul that Temple Bar never lived up to its cultural quarter moniker, but in many ways it's just staying true to its heritage. Imagine yourself back in 1742, for instance, when Handel was conducting the first-ever performance of his *Messiah* in Fishamble St, while just down the road on Bagnio Slip – now Lower Fownes St – gentlemen were lining up for an altogether different kind of distraction. Bagnio, from the Italian for bath house, had by then become the term for a brothel, and Temple Bar had plenty of them. It seems that pleasures of the flesh and of the mind have never been that far apart!

popular – and perpetually booked out. The centre runs age-specific activities aimed at stimulating participants' interests in science, the environment and the arts. The centre also has an open-air stage for summer events.

SUNLIGHT CHAMBERS NOTABLE BUILDING

Map p240 (Parliament St; closed to the public; all city centre) On the southern banks of the Liffey, Sunlight Chambers, designed by Liverpool architect Edward Ould (designer of Port Sunlight), stands out among the Georgian and modern architecture for its romantic Italianate style and beautiful art nouveau frieze-work by German sculptor Conrad Dressler. Sunlight was a brand of soap made by Lever Brothers and the frieze shows the Lever Brothers' view of the world: men make clothes dirty, women wash them.

CONTEMPORARY MUSIC CENTRE ARTS CENTRE

Map p240 (01-490 1857; www.cmc.ie; 19 Fishamble St; 10am-5.30pm Mon-Fri; all city centre) FREE Anyone with an interest in Irish contemporary music must visit the CMC's national archive where you can hear (and play around with on an electronic organ) 10,000 samples from composers of this and the last century. There's also a good reference library where you can attend courses and meet composers.

TEMPLE BAR GALLERY & STUDIOS GALLERY

Map p240 (01-671 0073; www.templebargallery.com; 5 Temple Bar; 10am-6pm Tue, Wed, Fri & Sat, 10am-7pm Thu; all city centre) FREE This multistorey gallery showcases the works of dozens of up-and-coming Irish artists at any one time, and is a great spot to see cutting-edge Irish art across a range of media. The gallery runs occasional open days where you can explore the work of artists beavering away in the studios that are part of the complex.

EATING

CRACKBIRD FAST FOOD $

Map p240 (www.joburger.ie; 60 Dame St; mains €10-12.50; noon-10pm Mon-Wed, noon-11pm Thu-Sat, noon-9pm Sun; ; all city centre) A buzzy, trendy spot that only serves chicken that's been dipped in batter and breadcrumbs and then deep-fried...sounds a bit limited, right? But the chicken is excellent, and the sides – choose from the likes of potato salad, chipotle baked beans or carrot and cranberry salad – add taste and variety to what might otherwise just be fancy chicken in a bucket.

BUNSEN BURGERS $

Map p240 (www.bunsen.ie; 22 Essex St E; burgers €7-10; noon-9.30pm Mon-Wed, noon-10.30pm Thu-Sat, 1-9.30pm Sun; all city centre) The tagline says Straight Up Burgers, but Bunsen serves only the tastiest, most succulent lumps of prime beef cooked to perfection and served between two halves of a homemade bap. Want fries? You've a choice between skinny, chunky or sweet potato. Order the double at your peril. There are two other branches: on Wexford Street (p68) and South Anne St.

KLAW SEAFOOD $

Map p240 (www.klaw.ie; 5a Crown Alley; mains €8-14; noon-10pm Mon-Wed & Sun, noon-11pm Thu-Sat; all city centre) There's nothing sophisticated about this crabshack-style place except the food: Irish oysters served naked, dressed or torched; Lambay Island crab claws served with a yuzu aioli or half a lobster. Whatever you go for it's all delicious, even if the music is a little loud and not every 'c' word needs to start with a 'k'.

BISON BAR & BBQ BARBECUE $

Map p240 (086 056 3144; www.bisonbar.ie; 11 Wellington Quay; mains €13.95; noon-9pm; all city centre) Beer, whiskey sours and finger-lickingly good Texas-style barbecue – served on throwaway plates along with tasty sides such as slaw or mac 'n' cheese – is the fare at this boisterous restaurant. The cowboy theme is taken to the limit with the saddle chairs (yes, actual saddles); this is a place to eat, drink and be merry.

DWARF JAR
CAFE $

Map p240 (1 Wellington Quay; cakes €2-4; ☉8am-8.30pm; 🚇all city centre) A friendly coffee shop with a view, the Dwarf Jar serves excellent coffee, expertly made – not always the case in Temple Bar – in a lovely, glass-encased room. The cakes are all lovely too.

QUEEN OF TARTS
CAFE $

Map p240 (www.queenoftarts.ie; 4 Cork Hill; mains €5-10; ☉8am-7pm Mon-Fri, 9am-7pm Sat & Sun; 🚇all city centre) This cute little cake shop does a fine line in tarts, meringues, crumbles, cookies and brownies, not to mention a decent breakfast: the smoked bacon and leek-potato cakes with eggs and cherry tomatoes are excellent. There's another, bigger, branch around the corner at **Cow's Lane** (Map p240; www.queenoftarts.ie; 3-4 Cow's Lane; mains €5-10; ☉8am-7pm Mon-Fri, 9am-7pm Sat & Sun; 🚇all city centre).

SKINFLINT
PIZZA $

Map p240 (19 Crane Lane; pizzas €9-15; ☉noon-10.30pm Tue-Sat, noon-9pm Sun-Mon; 🚇all city centre) Tables made out of old doors and kitchen paper as tablecloths...this is industrial-style pizza brought to you by the people who run Crackbird around the corner. The pizzas – all with girls' names like Viv, Breda and Philomena – are all super-thin and rectangular, and they use Irish rather than Type 00 Italian flour. The result is OK.

⭐ BANYI JAPANESE DINING
JAPANESE $$

Map p240 (☎01-675 0669; www.banyijapanese dining.com; 3-4 Bedford Row; small/large sushi platter €14.90/26.90; €10.90, ☉noon-11pm; 🚇all city centre) This compact restaurant in the heart of Temple Bar has arguably the best Japanese cuisine in Dublin. The rolls are divine, and the sushi as good as any you'll eat at twice the price. If you don't fancy raw fish, the classic Japanese main courses are excellent, as are the lunchtime bento boxes. Dinner reservations are advised, particularly at weekends.

ELEPHANT & CASTLE
AMERICAN $$

Map p240 (☎01-679 3121; www.elephantand castle.ie; 18 Temple Bar; mains €12-26; ☉8am-11.30pm Mon-Fri, 10.30am-11.30pm Sat & Sun; 🚇all city centre) If it's massive New York–style sandwiches or sticky chicken wings you're after, this bustling upmarket diner is just the joint. Be prepared to queue, though, especially at weekends when the place heaves with the hassled parents of wandering toddlers and 20-somethings looking for a carb cure for the night before.

CLEAVER EAST
MODERN IRISH $$

Map p240 (☎01-531 3500; www.cleavereast. ie; Clarence, 6-8 Wellington Quay; tasting plates €9.95-12.50, main courses €19-26; ☉12.30-3pm Fri-Sun & 5.30-10.30pm Mon-Sun; 🚇all city centre) Michelin-starred chef Oliver Dunne has brought his cooking chops to bear in Cleaver East, where the decor (think New York brasserie but with cleavers everywhere) is macho but the food is anything but. Instead, it's a real treat comprising a series of delicate tasting plates (the six-course Surprise Tasting is excellent) and expertly prepared main courses.

LA DOLCE VITA
ITALIAN $$

Map p240 (☎01-707 9786; 5 Cow's Lane; mains €9-20; ☉9am-11.30pm; 🚇all city centre) This easygoing place serves proper Italian antipasti, dished up in sharing plates and named after Fellini movies. You can get mixed cheese platters (Il Viaggio di Mastorna), prosciutto samplers (Amarcord) or a mix of both (La Strada). The pasta dishes are authentic enough to earn Mamma's approval. Wash it all down with a selection of wines by the glass.

IL BACCARO
ITALIAN $$

Map p240 (☎01-671 4597; www.ilbaccarodublin. com; Meeting House Sq; mains €13-26; ☉5.30-10.30pm Sun-Fri, 1-10.30pm Sat; 🚇all city centre) Want a free Italian lesson? Drop in to eavesdrop at this fabulous trattoria that is like a rustic piece of the Old Boot. The food is exuberantly authentic, and includes bruschetta, homemade pasta, Italian sausage and the like. The Italian wines are *buonissimi*.

CHAMELEON
INDONESIAN $$

Map p240 (☎01-671 0362; www.chameleon restaurant.com; 1 Lower Fownes St; set menus €30-40, tapas €7.50-10.95; ☉5-11pm Mon-Sat, to 10pm Sun; ☏; 🚇all city centre) Friendly, cute and full of character, Chameleon is draped in exotic fabrics and serves up perky renditions of Indonesian classics such as satay, *gado gado* and *nasi goreng*. The *rijsttafel* set menus are a popular choice, as is the selection of smaller tapas-style dishes. The top floor has low seating on cushions, which is perfect for intimate group get-togethers.

🍷 DRINKING & NIGHTLIFE

PALACE BAR
PUB

Map p240 (21 Fleet St; ⊙10.30am-11.30pm Mon-Thu, to 12.30am Fri & Sat, noon-11pm Sun; ⊠all city centre) With its mirrors and wooden niches, the Palace (established in 1823) is one of Dublin's great Victorian pubs and a stubborn stalwart against the modernising influences of the last half century. Patrick Kavanagh and Flann O'Brien were once regulars and it was for a long time the unofficial head office of the *Irish Times.*

VINTAGE COCKTAIL CLUB
BAR

Map p240 (www.vintagecocktailclub.com; Crown Alley; ⊙5pm-1.30am Mon-Fri, from 12.30pm Sat & Sun; ⊠all city centre) Behind the inconspicuous, unlit doorway initialled with the letters 'VCC' is one of the coolest bars in Dublin, a '60s-style London members' club or Vegas Rat Pack hang-out. The emphasis is on expertly made (if expensive) cocktails served in a super-stylish setting: the 2nd-floor smoking lounge is easily the most elegant place in town in which to light up.

MOTHER
CLUB

Map p240 (twitter.com/motherdublin; Copper Alley, Exchange St; €10; ⊙11pm-3.30am Sat; ⊠all city centre) The best club night in the city is ostensibly a gay night, but does not discriminate: clubbers of every sexual orientation come for the sensational DJs who throw down a mixed bag of disco, modern synth-pop and other danceable styles.

FRONT LOUNGE
BAR

Map p240 (33 Parliament St; ⊙10.30am-11.30pm Mon-Thu, to 12.30am Fri & Sat, noon-11pm Sun; ⊠all city centre) The unofficially gay 'Flounge' is a sophisticated and friendly bar that stands out from other gay joints in that it is quieter, more demure and popular with a mixed crowd. Here, sexual orientation is

strictly secondary to having a drink and a laugh with friends, even though the 'Back Lounge', towards the back of the bar, is traditionally predominantly gay.

IVY
BAR

Map p240 (⏰01-670 7220; 1 Parliament St; ⊠all city centre) Blue velvet chairs, handsome leather booths and walls adorned in prints of Georgian Dublin set a sophisticated tone for this new bar, which has taken the place of the once beloved Thomas Read. It has a whole shelf devoted to Negronis and a cocktail menu straight out of the roaring twenties. A touch of class.

FITZSIMONS
BAR

Map p240 (⏰01-677 9315; www.fitzsimonshotel.com; 21-22 Wellington Quay; ⊙10.30am-3am Mon-Sat, noon-2am Sun; ⊠all city centre) The epitome of Temple Bar's commitment to a kind of loud and wonderfully unsophisticated nightlife is this sprawling hotel bar (four bars on five floors), which serves booze, sports and cheesy music to a crowd of pumped revellers. At weekends, it gets so busy the bouncers don't even try to keep the crowd from spilling out onto cobbled streets.

OLIVER ST JOHN GOGARTY
PUB

Map p240 (58-59 Fleet St; ⊙10.30am-11.30pm Mon-Thu, to 12.30am Fri & Sat, noon-11pm Sun; ⊠all city centre) You won't see too many Dubs ordering drinks in this bar, which is almost entirely given over to tourists who come for the carefully manufactured slice of authentic traditionalism...and the knee-slappin', toe-tappin' sessions that run throughout the day. The kitchen serves up dishes that most Irish cooks have consigned to the culinary dustbin.

PORTERHOUSE
BAR

Map p240 (16-18 Parliament St; ⊙11.30am-midnight Mon-Wed & Sun, to 1am Thu, to 2am Fri & Sat; ⊠all city centre) The second-biggest brewery in Dublin, the Porterhouse looks like a cross between a Wild West bar and a Hieronymus Bosch painting. It has lots of its own delicious brews, including its Plain Porter (some say it's the best stout in town) as well as unfamiliar imported beers.

TEMPLE BAR
BAR

Map p240 (⏰01-677 3807; 48 Temple Bar; ⊙10.30am-1.30am Mon-Wed, to 2.30am Thu-Sat, 11.30am-1am Sun; ⊠all city centre) The most photographed pub facade in Dublin, perhaps the world, the Temple Bar (aka Flannery's) is smack bang in the middle of the tourist precinct and is usually chock-a-block with visitors. It's good craic, though, and presses all the right buttons, with traditional musicians, a buzzy atmosphere and even a beer garden.

AULD DUBLINER   PUB

Map p240 (☑01-677 0527; www.aulddubliner.ie; 24-25 Temple Bar; ☺10.30am-11.30pm Mon-Tue, 10.30am-2.30am Wed-Sat, 12.30-11pm Sun; ☐all city centre) Predominantly patronised by tourists, 'the Auld Foreigner', as locals have dubbed it, has a carefully manicured 'old world' charm that has been preserved – or refined – after a couple of renovations. It's a reliable place for a singsong and a laugh, as long as you don't mind taking 15 minutes to get to and from the jax (toilets).

⭐ ENTERTAINMENT

WORKMAN'S CLUB   LIVE MUSIC

Map p240 (☑01-670 6692; www.theworkmansclub.com; 10 Wellington Quay; free-€20; ☺5pm-3am; ☐all city centre) A 300-capacity venue and bar in the former workingmen's club of Dublin, the emphasis is on keeping away from the mainstream, which means everything from singer-songwriters to electronic cabaret. When the live music at the Workman's Club (Twitter: @WorkmansClubs) is over, DJs take to the stage, playing rockabilly, hip hop, indie, house and more.

IRISH FILM INSTITUTE   CINEMA

Map p240 (IFI; ☑01-679 5744; www.ifi.ie; 6 Eustace St; ☺11am-11pm; ☐all city centre) The IFI has a couple of screens and shows classics and new art-house films. The complex also has a bar, a cafe and a bookshop.

PROJECT ARTS CENTRE   THEATRE

Map p240 (☑1850 260 027; www.projectartscentre.ie; 39 Essex St E; ☺open 45min before showtime; ☐all city centre) The city's most interesting venue for challenging new work – be it drama, dance, live art or film. Three separate spaces allow for maximum versatility. You never know what to expect, which makes it all that more fun: we've seen some awful rubbish here, but we've also seen some of the best shows in town.

BUTTON FACTORY   LIVE MUSIC

Map p240 (☑01-670 0533; www.buttonfactory.ie; Curved St; €10-20; ☺7.30-11.30pm Mon-Thu, 7.30pm-2.30am Fri-Sun; ☐all city centre) A multipurpose venue where one night you might be shaking your glow light to a thumping live set by a top DJ, and the next you'll be shifting from foot to foot as an esoteric Finnish band drag their violin bows over their electric guitar strings.

HA'PENNY BRIDGE INN   COMEDY, LIVE MUSIC

Map p240 (☑01-677 0616; 42 Wellington Quay; €6; ☺7.30-11.30pm; ☐all city centre) A traditional old bar that features local comics on the rise upstairs at the Unhinged Comedy Club on Sunday and Irish music downstairs on Sunday and Wednesdays.

OLYMPIA THEATRE   THEATRE

Map p240 (☑01-677 7744; www.olympia.ie; 72 Dame St; tickets €30-60; ☺shows from 7pm; ☐all city centre) This theatre specialises in light plays and, at Christmastime, pantomimes. It also hosts some terrific live gigs.

CHAPLINS COMEDY CLUB   COMEDY

Map p240 (www.chaplinscomedy.com; Chaplin's Bar, 2 Hawkins St; €10; ☺7-11pm Fri & Sat; ☐all city centre) A regularly changing line-up of up-and-coming and local talent look for laughs at this all-seater club; failing that, there's always pizza and craft beer to guarantee a decent night out.

NEW THEATRE   THEATRE

Map p240 (☑01-670 3361; www.thenewtheatre.com; 43 Essex St E; adult/concession €16/12.50; ☺shows 7.30pm Mon-Fri, 2.30pm & 7.30pm Sat; ☐all city centre) This small theatre's location above a left-wing bookshop should be a guide to the kind of thinking that informs most of the performances taking place on its small stage. It's all about having a social conscience, whether by promoting new work by emerging playwrights or putting on established works that highlight society's injustices.

SHOPPING

⭐ TEMPLE BAR FOOD MARKET   MARKET

Map p240 (www.templebar.ie; Meeting House Sq; ☺10am-4.30pm Sat; ☐all city centre) From sushi to salsa, this is the city's best open-air food market; pick, prod and poke your way through the organic foods of the world with a compact stroll through gourmet lane. There are tastes of everywhere, from cured Spanish chorizo and paellas to Irish farmhouse cheeses, via handmade chocolates, freshly made crêpes, homemade jams and freshly squeezed juices.

★**CLADDAGH RECORDS**   MUSIC

Map p240 (☎01-677 0262; 2 Cecilia St; ⊘10am-6pm Mon-Sat, noon-6pm Sun; ▣all city centre) An excellent collection of good-quality traditional and folk music is the mainstay at this centrally located record shop. The profoundly knowledgeable staff should be able to locate even the most elusive recording for you. There's also a decent selection of world music; there's another **branch** (Map p240; ☎01-888 3600; www.claddagh records.com; 5 Westmoreland St; ⊘10am-6pm Mon-Sat, noon-6pm Sun; ▣all city centre) on Westmoreland St.

TAMP & STITCH   FASHION

Map p240 (Unit 3, Scarlet Row, Essex St W; ⊘10am-5.30pm Mon-Fri, to 6pm Sat; ▣all city centre) The latest midrange fashions and a trendy little cafe doing nearly perfect coffee.

ALL CITY RECORDS   MUSIC

Map p240 (4 Crow St; ⊘11am-7pm Mon-Wed & Fri-Sat, to 8pm Thu, noon-6pm Sun; ▣all city centre) Vinyl in all genres, especially EDM, hip hop and alternative beats. It also sells spray paint for graffiti artists. Downstairs is the **Cut & Sew** (Map p240; 4-6 Crow St; ⊘10am-7pm Mon-Wed & Fri-Sat, to 8pm Thu; ▣all city centre) barber shop.

LIBRARY PROJECT   BOOKS

Map p240 (4 Temple Bar; ⊘11am-6pm Mon-Fri, noon-6pm Sat & Sun; ▣all city centre) A bookshop and library of contemporary images from all over the world.

RORY'S FISHING TACKLE   FISHING

Map p240 (17A Temple Bar; ⊘9.30am-6pm Mon-Sat, noon-5pm Sun; ▣all city centre) Temple Bar's most incongruous shop is this long-established tackle and fishing equipment emporium.

SCOUT   CLOTHING

Map p240 (www.scoutdublin.com; 5 Smock Alley Ct, Essex St W; ⊘10.30am-6pm Mon-Wed & Fri-Sat, to 7pm Thu, noon-5pm Sun; ▣all city centre) Owner Wendy carefully selects every

item of vintage clothing, and Irish and international labels including Armor Lux and Manley, plus accessories by Baggu and footwear by Grenson.

SIOPAELLA DESIGN EXCHANGE   VINTAGE

Map p240 (www.siopaella.com; 25 Temple Lane South; ⊘noon-6pm, also 10pm-midnight Tue-Wed & Fri-Sat; ▣all city centre) A second-hand shop like no other in Dublin: you're as likely to find a vintage Chanel bag priced at €3000 as you are a beautiful preloved shirt for €5. You can exchange clothes for cash, or clothes for other clothes. One of the best shopping experiences in town.

COW'S LANE DESIGNER MART   MARKET

Map p240 (St Michael's & St John's Banquet Hall, Essex St W; ⊘10am-5pm Oct-May; ▣all city centre) A real market for hipsters, bringing together the best clothing, accessory and craft stalls in town; from June to September it moves just around the corner to Cow's Lane.

URBAN OUTFITTERS   FASHION, MUSIC

Map p240 (☎01-670 6202; www.urbanoutfitters. com; 4 Cecilia St; ⊘10am-7pm Mon-Wed & Sat, 10am-8pm Thu & Fri, noon-6pm Sun; ▣all city centre) With a blaring techno soundtrack, the only Irish branch of this American chain sells ridiculously cool clothes to discerning young buyers. Besides clothing, the shop stocks all kinds of interesting gadgets, accessories and furniture. On the 2nd floor you'll find a hypertrendy record shop (hence the techno).

GUTTER BOOKSHOP   BOOKS

Map p240 (☎01-679 9206; www.gutterbookshop. com; Cow's Lane; ⊘10am-6.30pm Mon-Wed & Fri-Sat, 10am-7pm Thu, 11am-6pm Sun; ▣all city centre) Taking its name from Oscar Wilde's famous line from *Lady Windermere's Fan,* 'We are all in the gutter, but some of us are looking at the stars', this fabulous place is flying the flag for the downtrodden independent bookshop, stocking a mix of new novels, children's books, travel literature and other assorted titles.

CONNOLLY BOOKS   BOOKS

Map p240 (☎01-670 8707; www.communistparty ofireland.ie/cbooks; 43 Essex St E; ⊘9.30am-6pm Mon-Sat; ▣all city centre) Left-wing bookshop beloved of Marxists and radicals.

COW'S LANE DESIGNER MART   MARKET

Map p240 (Cow's Lane; ⊙10am-5pm Sat Jun-Sep; all city centre) A real market for hipsters, on the steps of Cow's Lane, this market brings together over 60 of the best clothing, accessory and craft stalls in town. It's open from June to September; the rest of the year it moves indoors to St Michael's and St John's Banquet Hall (p108), just around the corner.

Buy cutting-edge designer duds from the likes of Drunk Monk, punky T-shirts, retro handbags, costume jewellery by Kink Bijoux and even clubby babywear.

BOOK FAIR   MARKET

Map p240 (Temple Bar Sq; ⊙10am-5pm Sat; all city centre) Bad second-hand potboilers, sci-fi, picture books and other assorted titles invite you to rummage about on Saturday afternoons. If you look hard enough, you're bound to find something worthwhile.

FLIP   CLOTHING & ACCESSORIES

Map p240 (☑01-671 4299; 4 Upper Fownes St; ⊙10am-6pm Mon-Wed & Fri, 10am-7pm Thu & Sat, 1.30-6pm Sun; all city centre) This hip Irish label takes the best male fashion moods of the 1950s and serves them back to us, minus the mothball smell. US college shirts, logo T-shirts, Oriental and Hawaiian shirts, Fonz-style leather jackets and well-cut jeans mix it with the genuine secondhand gear upstairs.

 # ACTIVITIES

CHRIST CHURCH GUIDED TOURS   TOUR

(www.christchurchcathedral.ie; Christ Church Pl; adult/family €4/10; ⊙11.30am & 1.15pm Sat, 1.15pm Sun; 50, 50A, 56A from Aston Quay, 54, 54A from Burgh Quay) With its hilltop location and eye-catching flying buttresses, Christ Church Cathedral is the most photogenic of Dublin's cathedrals. Guided tours include the belfry, where a campanologist explains the art of bell-ringing and you can even have a go.

DUBLIN MUSICAL PUB CRAWL   WALKING TOUR

Map p240 (☑01-478 0193; www.discoverdublin.ie; 58-59 Fleet St; adult/student €13/11; ⊙7.30pm daily Apr-Oct, 7.30pm Thu-Sat Nov-Mar; all city centre) The story of Irish traditional music and its influence on contemporary styles is explained and demonstrated by two expert musicians in a number of Temple Bar pubs over 2½ hours. Tours meet upstairs in the Oliver St John Gogarty (p106) pub and are highly recommended.

MELT   HEALTH & FITNESS

Map p240 (☑01-679 8786; www.meltonline.com; 2 Temple Lane; full body massage 1hr/90min €55/95; ⊙9am-7pm Mon-Sat; all city centre) A full range of massage techniques – from Swedish to shiatsu and many more in between – are doled out by expert practitioners at Melt, aka the Temple Bar Healing Centre. Also available are a host of other left-of-centre healing techniques, including acupuncture, reiki and polarity therapy. Melt has also set up shop in the Westin (p182).

TEMPLE BAR ACTIVITIES

Kilmainham & the Liberties

Neighborhood Top Five

1 Kilmainham Gaol (p118) Taking a trip through Ireland's troubled history at this foreboding 18th-century prison, which housed many an Irish rebel.

2 Guinness Storehouse (p112) Sampling a pint of the black stuff at the factory where it all began in 1759 – and continues to this day.

3 Teeling Distillery (p120) Getting familiar with Irish whiskey at the first distillery to open in Dublin for more than a century.

4 St Patrick's Cathedral (p115) Visiting Jonathan Swift's tomb in the cathedral where he served as dean for more than 30 years.

5 Irish Museum of Modern Art (p119) Admiring modern art in exquisite surroundings at a former hospital for wounded soldiers.

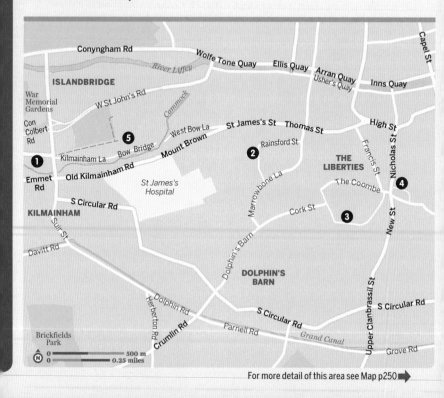

For more detail of this area see Map p250 ➡

Explore Kilmainham & the Liberties

Stretching westward along the Liffey from the city centre, you'll need a little bit of planning to get the most out of these two historic neighbourhoods. Coming from the heart of the city centre, you'll first stumble into the Liberties, on the edge of which is St Patrick's Cathedral and, behind the cathedral, the wonderful Marsh's Library. This largely working-class enclave has been beset by myriad social problems in the last couple of centuries, but in recent years the creeping influence of gentrification has turned its fortunes around, as aspiring young Dubs look to combine authenticity with affordable rents. Right in the heart of it is the new Teeling Distillery, next to one of the best food markets in the city.

The Liberties' western edge is where you'll find the Guinness brewery at St James' Gate, even if the only bit you can visit is the old grain storehouse, now the city's most visited museum. Further west again, just as the Liffey becomes more of a pastoral river in the riverside burg of Kilmainham, you'll come across the country's greatest modern-art museum and Kilmainham Gaol, which has played a key role in the tormented history of a country's slow struggle to gain its freedom. Both are well worth the westward trek (which can be made easier by bus). This is strictly day-trip territory – there's almost nothing in the way of accommodation and just a couple of decent eating options.

Local Life

→**Garden Walks** The Italianate garden at the Irish Museum of Modern Art (p119) is beautiful for a gentle amble, but one of the city's best-kept open secrets are the War Memorial Gardens (p120) in Kilmainham, which run along the Liffey.

→**Markets** The Dublin Food Co-op (p125) in Newmarket is one of the city's best, and an excellent example of socially responsible retailing; it thrives thanks to the dedication of its many customers.

→**Hang-out** The Fumbally (p121) is bringing cafe life to the Liberties.

Getting There & Away

→**Bus** Nos 50, 50A or 56A from Aston Quay and the 55 or 54A serve the cathedrals and the Liberties; for Kilmainham (including Irish Museum of Modern Art) use bus nos 51, 51D, 51X, 69, 78 or 79 from Aston Quay or the Luas to Heuston, from which it's a short walk.

→**On Foot** A 1.5km walk to the Guinness Storehouse from city centre; about 3km to IMMA and Kilmainham Gaol.

Lonely Planet's Top Tip

The most convenient way to explore the area is as part of a hop-on, hop-off bus tour, all of which stop at the Guinness Storehouse, Irish Museum of Modern Art and Kilmainham Gaol. When your visit is done you can hop back on and get back to the city centre without hassle.

Best Places to Drink

→ Fallon's (p122)
→ Old Royal Oak (p122)
→ Gravity Bar (p112)

For reviews, see p122➡

Best Places to Eat

→ 'The Dead' Dinner Experience (p122)
→ Fumbally (p121)
→ Union8 (p121)

For reviews, see p121➡

Best Places to Shop

→ Martin Fennelly Antiques (p125)
→ Dublin Food Co-op (p125)
→ Irish Museum of Modern Art Gift Shop (p125)

For reviews, see p125➡

KILMAINHAM & THE LIBERTIES

TOP SIGHT
GUINNESS STOREHOUSE

More than any beer produced anywhere in the world, Guinness has transcended its own brand and is not just the best-known symbol of the city but a substance with near spiritual qualities, according to its legions of devotees the world over. A visit to the factory museum where it's made is therefore something of a pilgrimage for many of its fans.

Mythology

The mythology of Guinness is remarkably durable: it doesn't travel well; its distinctive flavour comes from Liffey water; it is good for you – not to mention the generally held belief that you will never understand the Irish until you develop a taste for the black stuff. All absolutely true, of course, so it should be no surprise that the Guinness Storehouse, in the heart of the St James's Gate Brewery, is the city's most visited tourist attraction, an all-singing, all-dancing extravaganza that combines sophisticated exhibits, spectacular design and a thick, creamy head of marketing hype.

The Beginnings of World Domination

In the 1770s, while other Dublin brewers fretted about the popularity of a new English beer known as porter – which was first created when a London brewer accidentally burnt his hops – Arthur Guinness started making his own version. By 1799 he decided to concentrate all his efforts on this single brew. He died four years later, aged 83, but the foundations for world domination were already in place.

At one time a Grand Canal tributary was cut into the brewery to enable special Guinness barges to carry consignments out onto the Irish canal system or to the Dublin

DON'T MISS

→ A drink of Guinness
→ Gravity Bar view
→ Advertising exhibit

PRACTICALITIES

→ Map p250, E3
→ www.guinness-store house.com
→ St James's Gate, South Market St
→ adult/student/child €18/16/6.50, connoisseur experience €48
→ ⏰9.30am-5pm Sep-Jun, to 7pm Jul & Aug
→ 🛜
→ 🚌21A, 51B, 78, 78A, 123 from Fleet St, 🚆James's

LITTLENY / GETTY IMAGES ©

port. When the brewery extensions reached the Liffey in 1872, the fleet of Guinness barges became a familiar sight. Pretty soon Guinness was being exported as far afield as Africa and the West Indies. As the barges chugged their way along the Liffey towards the port, boys used to lean over the wall and shout 'bring us back a parrot'. Old school Dubliners still say the same thing to each other when they're going off on holiday.

The Essential Ingredients

One link with the past that hasn't been broken is the yeast used to make Guinness, essentially the same living organism that has been used since 1770. Another vital ingredient is a hop by the name of fuggles, which used to be grown exclusively around Dublin but is now imported from Britain, the US and Australia (everyone take a bow).

Guinness Storehouse

The brewery is far more than just a place where beer is manufactured. It is an intrinsic part of Dublin's history and a key element of the city's identity. Accordingly, the quasi-mythical stature of Guinness is the central theme of the brewery's museum, the Guinness Storehouse, which opened in 2000 and is the only part of the brewery open to visitors.

While inevitably overpriced and over-hyped, this paean to the black gold is done exceptionally well. It occupies the old Fermentation House, built in 1904. As it's a listed building, the designers could only adapt and add to the structure without taking anything away. The result is a stunning central atrium that rises seven storeys and takes the shape of a pint of Guinness. The head is represented by the glassed Gravity Bar, which provides panoramic views of Dublin to savour with your complimentary half-pint.

Before you race up to the top, however, you might want to check out the **museum** for which you've paid so handsomely. Actually, it's designed as more of an 'experience' than a museum. It has nearly 1.5 hectares of floor space, featuring a dazzling array of audiovisual and interactive exhibits, which cover most aspects of the brewery's story and explain the brewing process in overwhelming detail.

On the ground floor, a copy of Arthur Guinness' original lease lies embedded beneath a pane of glass in the floor. Wandering up through the various exhibits, including 70-odd years of advertising, you can't help feeling that the now wholly foreign-owned company has hijacked the mythology

ST PATRICK'S TOWER

St Patrick's Tower, the large smock windmill on the extensive factory grounds, was originally built as part of the Roe Distillery, which once occupied 7 hectares on the north side of James's St and was Europe's largest producer of whiskey. The Roe distillery stopped producing whiskey in 1926 and was taken over by Guinness in 1949.

Real aficionados can opt for the Connoisseur Experience, where you sample the four different kinds of Guinness – Draught, Original, Foreign Extra Stout and Black Lager – while hearing their story from your designated bartender.

THE BEST DEAL IN TOWN

When Arthur started brewing in Dublin in 1759, he couldn't have had any idea that his name would become synonymous with Dublin around the world. Or could he? Showing extraordinary foresight, he had just signed a lease for a small disused brewery under the terms that he would pay just £45 annually for the next 9000 years, with the additional condition that he'd never have to pay for the water used.

Dubliners attached to the drink, and it has all become more about marketing and manipulation than mingling and magic.

Gravity Bar

Whatever reservations you may have, however, can be more than dispelled at the top of the building in the circular **Gravity Bar**, where you get a complimentary glass of Guinness. The views from the bar are superb, but the Guinness itself is as near-perfect as a beer can be.

Real aficionados can opt for the **Connoisseur Experience**, where you sample the four different kinds of Guinness – Draught, Original, Foreign Extra Stout and Black Lager – while hearing their story from your designated bartender.

DAVID SOANES PHOTOGRAPHY / GETTY IMAGES ©

 TOP SIGHT
ST PATRICK'S CATHEDRAL

Situated on the very spot that St Paddy supposedly rolled up his sleeves and dunked the heathen Irish into a well and thereby gave them a fair to middling shot at salvation, this is one of Dublin's earliest Christian sites and a most hallowed chunk of real estate.

History

Although a church has stood here since the 5th century, this building dates from the turn of the 12th century and has been altered several times, most notably in 1864 when it was saved from ruin and, some might say, over-enthusiastically restored. The interior is as calm and soothing as the exterior is sombre. The picturesque St Patrick's Park, adjoining, was a crowded slum until it was cleared in the early 20th century.

It's likely that St Patrick's was intended to replace Christ Church as the city's cathedral but the older church's stubborn refusal to be usurped resulted in the two cathedrals being virtually a stone's throw from one another. Separated only by the city walls (with St Patrick's outside), each possessed the rights of cathedral of the diocese. While St Pat's isn't as photogenic as its neighbour, it probably one-ups its sexier-looking rival in historical terms.

Baptistry & Swift's Tomb

Fittingly, the first Guinness to show an interest in preserving the church, Benjamin, is commemorated with a **statue** at the main entrance. Inside to your left is the oldest part of the building, the **baptistry**, which was probably the entrance to the original building. It contains the original **12th-century floor tiles** and **medieval stone font**, which is still

DON'T MISS

➡ Swift's Tomb
➡ Black James' Door
➡ Boyle Monument

PRACTICALITIES

➡ Map p250, H3
➡ www.stpatricks
cathedral.ie
➡ St Patrick's Close
➡ adult/student/child
€6/5/free
➡ ⊘9.30am-5pm
Mon-Fri, 9am-6pm Sat,
9-10.30am & 12.30-
2.30pm Sun
➡ ▢50, 50A, 56A from
Aston Quay, 54, 54A from
Burgh Quay

DOOR OF RECONCILIATION

Towards the north transept is a door that has become a symbol of peace and reconciliation since it helped resolve a scrap between the earls of Kildare and Ormond in 1492. After a feud, supporters of the squabbling nobles ended up in a pitched battle inside the cathedral, during which Ormond's nephew – one Black James – barricaded himself in the chapterhouse. Kildare, having calmed down, cut a hole in the door between them and stuck his arm through it to either shake his opponent's hand, or lose a limb in his attempt to smooth things over. James chose mediation over amputation and took his hand. The term 'to chance your arm' entered the English lexicon and everyone lived happily ever after – except Black James, who was murdered by Kildare's son-in-law four years later.

The cathedral had been built twice by 1254 but succumbed to a series of natural disasters over the following century. Its spire was taken out in a 1316 storm, while the original tower and part of the nave were destroyed by fire in 1362.

in use. Inside the cathedral proper, you come almost immediately to the **graves of Jonathan Swift** and his long-term companion Esther Johnson, better known as Stella. The Latin epitaphs are both written by Swift, and assorted Swift memorabilia lies all over the cathedral, including a pulpit and a death mask.

Boyle Monument

You can't miss the huge **Boyle Monument**, erected in 1632 by Richard Boyle, Earl of Cork. It stood briefly beside the altar until, in 1633, Dublin's viceroy, Thomas Wentworth, Earl of Strafford, had it shifted from its prominent position because he felt he shouldn't have to kneel to a Corkman. Boyle took his revenge in later years by orchestrating Wentworth's impeachment and execution. A figure in a niche at the bottom left of the monument is the earl's son Robert, the noted scientist who discovered Boyle's Law, which determined that the pressure and volume of a gas have an inverse relationship at a constant temperature.

St Patrick's Well

In the opposite corner, there is a cross on a stone slab that once marked the position of **St Patrick's original well**, where (it's said) the patron saint of Ireland rolled up his sleeves and got to baptising the natives.

South Transept & South Aisle

Passing through the south transept, which was once the chapterhouse where the Earl of Kildare chanced his arm, you'll see magnificent **stained-glass windows** above the funerary monuments. The south aisle is lined with memorials to prominent 20th-century Irish Protestants, including Erskine Childers, who was president of Ireland from 1973 to 1974, and whose father was executed by the Free State during the Civil War. The son never spoke of the struggle for Irish independence because, on the eve of his death, his father made him promise never to do anything that might promote bitterness among the Irish people.

Living Stones

On your way around the church, you will also take in the four sections of the permanent exhibition, **Living Stones**, which explores the cathedral's history and the contribution it has made to the culture of Dublin.

ST PATRICK'S CATHEDRAL

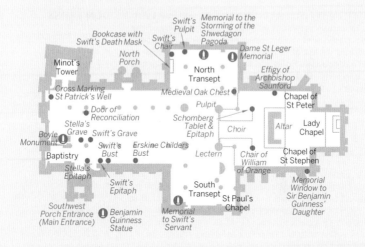

Memorial to the
Storming of the
Shwedagon
Pagoda

Swift's
Pulpit

Swift's
Chair

Bookcase with
Swift's Death Mask

Dame St Leger
Memorial

North
Porch

Minot's
Tower

North
Transept

Effigy of
Archbishop
Saunford

Cross Marking
St Patrick's Well

Medieval Oak Chest

Chapel of
St Peter

Pulpit

Door of
Reconciliation

Stella's
Grave

Schomberg
Tablet &
Epitaph

Choir

Altar

Lady
Chapel

Swift's Grave

Boyle
Monument

Swift's
Bust

Erskine Childers
Bust

Lectern

Chair of
William
of Orange

Chapel of
St Stephen

Baptistry

Stella's
Epitaph

Swift's
Epitaph

South
Transept

St Paul's
Chapel

Memorial
Window to
Sir Benjamin
Guinness'
Daughter

Southwest
Porch Entrance
(Main Entrance)

Benjamin
Guinness
Statue

Memorial
to Swift's
Servant

North Transept

The north transept contains various military memorials to Royal Irish Regiments, while the northern choir aisle has a tablet marking the **grave of the Duke of Schomberg**, a prominent casualty of the Battle of the Boyne in 1690. Swift provided the duke's epitaph, caustically noting on it that the duke's own relatives couldn't be bothered to provide a suitable memorial. On the opposite side of the choir is a chair used by William of Orange when he came to give thanks to God for his victory over the Catholic James II during the same battle.

If you have *any* interest in Irish history, you must visit this infamous prison. It was the stage for many of the most tragic and heroic episodes in Ireland's recent past, and its list of inmates reads like a who's who of Irish nationalism. Solid and sombre, its walls absorbed the hardship of British occupation and recount it in whispers to visitors.

DON'T MISS

➡ Prison Museum
➡ Stone Breakers' Yard
➡ Prison Cells

PRACTICALITIES

➡ Map p250, A3
➡ www.heritageireland.com
➡ Inchicore Rd
➡ adult/child €7/3
➡ ⊙9.30am-6pm daily Apr-Sep, 9.30am-5.30pm Mon-Sat, 10am-6pm Sun Oct-Mar
➡ 🚌26, 51X, 68, 69, 79 from city centre

History

It took four years to build, and the prison opened – or rather closed – its doors in 1796. The Irish were locked up for all sorts of misdemeanours, some more serious than others. A six-year-old boy spent a month here in 1839 because his father couldn't pay his train fare, and during the Famine it was crammed with the destitute imprisoned for stealing food and begging. But it is most famous for incarcerating 120 years of Irish nationalists, from Robert Emmet in 1803 to Éamon de Valera in 1923. All of Ireland's botched uprisings ended with the leaders' confinement here, usually before their execution.

It was the treatment of the leaders of the 1916 Easter Rising that most deeply etched the jail into the Irish consciousness. Fourteen of the rebel commanders were executed in the stone breakers' yard, including James Connolly who was so badly injured at the time of his execution that he was strapped to a chair at the opposite end of the yard, just inside the gate. The places where they were shot are marked by two simple black crosses. The executions set a previously apathetic nation on a course towards violent rebellion.

The jail's final function was as a prison for the newly formed Irish Free State, an irony best summed up with the story of Ernie O'Malley, who escaped from the jail when incarcerated by the British but was locked up again by his erstwhile comrades during the Civil War. This chapter is played down on the tour, and even the passing comment that Kilmainham's final prisoner was the future president, Éamon de Valera, doesn't reveal that he had been imprisoned by his fellow Irish citizens. The jail was decommissioned in 1924.

Guided Tour

Visits are by guided tour and start with a stirring audiovisual introduction, screened in the chapel where 1916 leader Joseph Plunkett was wed to his beloved just 10 minutes before his execution. The thought-provoking (but too crowded) tour takes you through the old and new wings of the prison, where you can see former cells of famous inmates, read graffiti on the walls and immerse yourself in the atmosphere of the execution yards.

Asgard & Museum

Incongruously sitting outside in the yard is the *Asgard*, the ship that successfully ran the British blockade to deliver arms to nationalist forces in 1914. It belonged to, and was skippered by, Erskine Childers, father of the future president of Ireland. He was executed by Michael Collins' Free State army in 1922 for carrying a revolver, which had been a gift from Collins himself. There is also an outstanding museum dedicated to Irish nationalism and prison life. On a lighter note, U2 fans will recognise the prison as the setting for the video to their 1982 single 'A Celebration'.

IMMA (Irish Museum of Modern Art) is the country's foremost gallery for contemporary Irish art, although it takes second billing to the majestic building in which it is housed: the Royal Hospital Kilmainham. The hospital (built 1680–84) served as a retirement home for veteran soldiers until 1928. It then languished for half a century before being saved in a 1980s restoration. Another refurb in 2012–13 saw the upgrade of the museum's lighting and fire-safety systems.

DON'T MISS

➡ The Madden Arnholz Collection

➡ Formal Gardens

PRACTICALITIES

➡ IMMA

➡ Map p250, C2

➡ www.imma.ie

➡ Military Rd

➡ admission free

➡ ◷11.30am-5.30pm Tue-Fri, 10am-5.30pm Sat, noon-5.30pm Sun, tours 1.15pm Wed & 2.30pm Sat & Sun

➡ ▣51, 51D, 51X, 69, 78, 79 from Aston Quay, ▣Heuston

Royal Hospital Kilmainham

The inspiration for the design came from James Butler, duke of Ormonde and Charles II's viceroy, who had been so impressed by Les Invalides on a trip to Paris that he commissioned William Robinson to knock up a Dublin version. What the architect designed was Dublin's finest 17th-century building and the highpoint of the Anglo-Dutch style of the day. It consists of an unbroken range enclosing a vast, peaceful courtyard with arcaded walks. A chapel in the centre of the northern flank has an elegant clock tower and spire. This was the first truly classical building in Dublin and was a precursor for the grand Georgian constructions of the 18th century. Christopher Wren began building London's Chelsea Royal Hospital two years after work commenced here.

The spectacularly restored hospital was unveiled in 1984, on the 300th anniversary of its construction. The next year it received the prestigious Europa Nostra award for 'distinguished contribution to the conservation of Europe's architectural heritage'.

Guided Tours

There are free guided tours of the museum's exhibits at 2.30pm on Wednesday, Friday and Sunday throughout the year, but we strongly recommend the free 50-minute seasonal heritage tour (p125) run by Heritage Ireland. It shows off some of the building's treasures, including the **Banqueting Hall**, with 22 specially commissioned portraits, and the stunning **baroque chapel**, with papier-mâché ceilings and a set of exquisite Queen Anne gates. Also worth seeing are the fully restored **formal gardens**.

Irish Museum of Modern Art

In 1991 the hospital became home to IMMA and the best of modern and contemporary Irish art. The blend of old and new is wonderful, and you'll find Irish artists such as Louis le Brocquy, Sean Scully, Kathy Prendergast and Dorothy Cross featured here, as well as a film installation by Neil Jordan. The permanent exhibition also features paintings from heavy-hitters Pablo Picasso and Joan Miró, and is topped up by regular temporary exhibitions. There's a good cafe and bookshop (p125) on the grounds.

◉ SIGHTS

GUINNESS STOREHOUSE   BREWERY, MUSEUM
See p112.

ST PATRICK'S CATHEDRAL   CATHEDRAL
See p115.

KILMAINHAM GAOL   MUSEUM
See p118.

IRISH MUSEUM OF MODERN ART   MUSEUM
See p119.

★ TEELING DISTILLERY   DISTILLERY
Map p250 (www.teelingwhiskey.com; 13-17 New-market; ⊙9.30am-5.30pm Mon-Fri; ☐27, 77A & 151 from city centre) **FREE** The first new distillery in Dublin for 125 years, it only began production in 2015 and it will be several years before any of the distillate can be called whiskey. In the meantime, you can explore the visitor centre and taste (and buy) whiskeys from the family's other distillery on the Cooley Peninsula.

You'll get a taste of whiskey at the end of the tour, but to try the really good stuff you'll have to upgrade to one of the organised tastings, which range from the Teeling Tasting (€14) to the Single Malt Reserve Tasting (€30), where you'll indulge in three special whiskeys, including the exceptional 21-year-old Reserve Single Malt, voted the world's best at the Whiskey Awards in 2014. There's also an excellent cafe on the premises.

★ MARSH'S LIBRARY   LIBRARY
Map p250 (www.marshlibrary.ie; St Patrick's Close; adult/child €3/free; ⊙9.30am-5pm Mon & Wed-Fri, 10am-5pm Sat; ☐50, 50A, 56A from Aston Quay, 54, 54A from Burgh Quay) This magnificently preserved scholars' library, virtually unchanged in three centuries, is one of Dublin's most beautiful open secrets and an absolute highlight of any visit. Atop its ancient stairs are beautiful, dark-oak bookcases, each topped with elaborately carved and gilded gables, and crammed with books, manuscripts and maps dating back to the 15th century.

Founded in 1701 by Archbishop Narcissus Marsh (1638–1713) and opened in 1707, the library was designed by Sir William Robinson, the man also responsible for the Royal Hospital Kilmainham (p119). It's the oldest public library in the country, and contains 25,000 books dating from the 16th to the early 18th century, as well as maps, manuscripts (including one in Latin dating back to 1400) and a collection of incunabula (books printed before 1500).

JAMES JOYCE
HOUSE OF THE DEAD   HISTORIC BUILDING
Map p250 (☎086-054 8880; www.jamesjoyce house.ie; 15 Usher's Island; adult/child €12/4; ⊙by appointment only; ☐25X, 26, 46A, 78, 79, 90, 92) The young Joyce spent Christmases with his aunts in this house, which he later used as the setting for 'The Dead', the last story in *Dubliners* (made into a 1997 film by John Huston). The partially restored house is only open by appointment; there's also the opportunity to book a meal (p122) like that enjoyed in the story.

WAR MEMORIAL GARDENS   PARK
(www.heritageireland.ie; South Circular Rd, Is-landbridge; ⊙8am-dusk Mon-Fri, 10am-dusk Sat & Sun; ☐26, 51X, 68, 69, 79 from city centre) **FREE** Hardly anyone ever ventures this far west, but they're missing a lovely bit of landscaping in the shape of the War Memorial Gardens – by our reckoning as pleasant a patch of greenery as any you'll find in the heart of the Georgian centre. Designed by Sir Edwin Lutyens, the memorial commemorates the 49,400 Irish soldiers who died during WWI – their names are inscribed in the two huge granite bookrooms that stand at one end.

ST AUDOEN'S
CHURCH OF IRELAND   CHURCH
Map p250 (www.heritageireland.ie; Corn Market, High St; ⊙9.30am-4.45pm May-Oct; ☐50, 50A, 56A from Aston Quay, 54, 54A from Burgh Quay) Two churches, side-by-side, each bearing the same name, a tribute to St Audoen, the 7th-century bishop of Rouen (aka Ouen) and patron saint of the Normans. They built the older of the two, the Church of Ireland, between 1181 and 1212, and today it is the only medieval church in Dublin still in use. A free 30-minute guided tour departs every 30 minutes from 9.30am to 4.45pm. Attached to it is the newer, bigger, 19th-century Catholic St Audoen's.

Through the Norman church's heavily moulded Romanesque Norman door you can touch the 9th-century 'lucky stone' that was believed to bring good luck to business, and check out the 9th-century slab in the porch that suggests it was built on an even older church. As part of the tour

EVENSONG AT THE CATHEDRALS

In a rare coming together, the choirs of St Patrick's Cathedral and Christ Church Cathedral both participated in the first-ever performance of Handel's *Messiah* in nearby Fishamble St in 1742, conducted by the great composer himself. Both houses of worship carry on their proud choral traditions, and visits to the cathedrals during evensong will provide enchanting and atmospheric memories. The choir performs evensong in St Patrick's at 5.45pm Monday to Friday (not on Wednesday in July and August), while the Christ Church choir performs at 5.30pm on Sunday, 6pm on Wednesday and Thursday, and 5pm Saturday. If you're going to be in Dublin around Christmas, do not miss the carols at St Patrick's; call ahead for the hard-to-get tickets on ☑01-453 9472.

you can explore the ruins as well as the present church, which has funerary monuments that were beheaded by Cromwell's purists. Its tower and door date from the 12th century and the aisle from the 15th century, but the church today is mainly a product of a 19th-century restoration.

St Anne's Chapel, the visitor centre, houses a number of tombstones of leading members of Dublin society from the 16th to 18th centuries. At the top of the chapel is the tower, which holds the three oldest bells in Ireland, dating from 1423. Although the church's exhibits are hardly spectacular, the building itself is beautiful and a genuine slice of medieval Dublin.

The church is entered from the south off High St through **St Audoen's Arch**, which was built in 1240 and is the only surviving reminder of the city gates. The adjoining park is pretty but attracts many unsavoury characters, particularly at night.

ST AUDOEN'S CATHOLIC CHURCH CHURCH
Map p250 (www.heritageireland.ie; Corn Market, High St; ⊗9.30am-4.45pm May-Oct; ☐50, 50A, 56A from Aston Quay, 54, 54A from Burgh Quay) **FREE** Attached to the medieval St Audoen's Church of Ireland is the bigger 19th-century Catholic St Audoen's, which in 2006 was handed over to the Polish chaplaincy.

 EATING

⭐**FUMBALLY** CAFE **$**
Map p250 (☑01-529 8732; www.thefumbally.ie; Fumbally Lane; mains €5-8; ⊗8am-5pm Tue-Fri, 10am-5pm Sat, also 7-9.30pm Wed; ☐49, 54A, 77X from city centre) A bright, airy warehouse cafe favoured by hipsters, who come for the healthy breakfasts, salads and sandwiches –

and the guitarist strumming away in the corner. In 2016 it introduced Wednesday Dinner (mains €15), where a single organic, locally sourced dish (and its vegetarian variant) is served in a communal dining experience; advance bookings suggested.

PUPP CAFE CAFE **$**
Map p250 (www.pupp.ie; 37 Lower Clanbrassil St; mains €4-10; ⊗8am-4pm Mon & Wed-Fri, 10am-5pm Sat-Sun; ☐49, 54A, 77X from city centre) Taking their lead from a California trend, this is the first cafe to cater specifically to dog lovers and the objects of their affection, which means treats and trinkets for the four-legged guests and a decent coffee and snacks for those looking to take paws. The ex-Google owners have also installed an online shop.

LEO BURDOCK'S FISH & CHIPS **$**
Map p250 (2 Werburgh St; cod & chips €9.25; ⊗noon-midnight Mon-Sat, 4pm-midnight Sun; ☐all city centre) The fresh cod and chips served these days in Dublin's most famous fish 'n' chip shop is no better than that found in most other chippers, but the deep-fried fumes of Burdock's reputation still count for something, judging by the longish queues for a 'Dubliner's caviar'.

ITSA@IMMA CAFE **$**
Map p250 (www.imma.ie; Irish Museum of Modern Art, Military Rd; mains €6-8; ⊗11.30am-5.30pm Tue-Fri, 10am-5.30pm Sat, noon-5.30pm Sun; ☐51, 51D, 51X, 69, 78, 79 from Aston Quay, ☐Heuston) Freshly made gourmet sandwiches and healthy salads and soups are the mainstay of the museum cafe at the Irish Museum of Modern Art.

UNION8 MODERN IRISH **$$**
Map p250 (☑01-677 8707; www.union8.ie; 740 South Circular Rd; mains €16-27; ⊗10am-9pm

KILMAINHAM & THE LIBERTIES EATING

Sun-Tue, to 9.30pm Wed, 10am-10pm Thu-Sat; 🔊) Kilmainham's newest (only?) restaurant of note serves contemporary Irish cuisine (beautifully presented fish dishes, succulent lamb, tasty pork belly and the like) to an appreciative local clientele who previously would have had to traipse into the city centre for a good meal. No more.

'THE DEAD'
DINNER EXPERIENCE   IRISH $$$

Map p250 (www.jamesjoycehouse.ie; 15 Usher's Island; dinner €70-150; ⊘by appointment only; 🚌25X, 26, 46A, 78, 79, 90, 92) A unique Dublin dining experience is the chance to feast on 'fat brown goose', 'a great ham', 'parallel lines of side-dishes' and lots of other dishes so meticulously described by Joyce in 'The Dead', his 1914 story from *Dubliners*, in the very room in which it's set. Chef Rory Morahan prepares the meal for groups of between 10 and 14 who've booked in advance.

🍷 DRINKING & NIGHTLIFE

FALLON'S   PUB

Map p250 (📞01-454 2801; 129 The Coombe; ⊘10.30am-11.30pm Mon-Thu, to 12.30am Fri & Sat, noon-11pm Sun; 🚌123, 206, 51B from city centre) Just west of the city centre, in the heart of medieval Dublin, this is a fabulously old-fashioned bar that has been serving a great pint of Guinness since the end of the 17th century. Prize fighter Dan Donnelly, the only boxer ever to be knighted, was head bartender here in 1818. It's a genuine Irish bar filled with Dubs.

OLD ROYAL OAK   PUB

Map p250 (11 Kilmainham Lane; ⊘10.30am-11.30pm Mon-Thu, to 12.30am Fri & Sat, noon-11pm Sun; 🚌68, 69, 79 from city centre) Locals are fiercely protective of this gorgeous traditional pub, which opened in 1845 to serve the patrons and staff of the Royal Hospital (now the Irish Museum of Modern Art). The clientele has changed, but everything else has remained the same, which makes this one of the nicest pubs in the city in which to enjoy a few pints.

BRAZEN HEAD   PUB

Map p250 (📞01-679 5186; www.brazenhead.com; 20 Lower Bridge St; ⊘10am-midnight

🏃 Neighbourhood Walk
Viking & Medieval Dublin

START ESSEX GATE, PARLIAMENT ST
END DUBLIN CASTLE
LENGTH 2.5KM; TWO HOURS

Begin your walk in Temple Bar, at the corner of Parliament St and Essex Gate, once a main entrance gate to the city. A **❶ bronze plaque** on a pillar marks the spot where the gate once stood. Further along, you can see the original foundations of the 13th-century **❷ Isolde's Tower**, once part of the city walls, through a grill in the pavement, in front of the pub of the same name. It is thought the original tower was between 12m and 15m high, but was demolished in the 17th century to make way for Georgian houses (also now demolished!).

Head west down Essex Gate and West Essex St until you reach Fishamble St; turn right towards the quays and left into Wood Quay. Cross Winetavern St and proceed along Merchant's Quay. To your left you'll see the **❸ Church of the Immaculate Conception**, otherwise known as Adam & Eve's, after a tavern through which worshippers gained access to a secret chapel during Penal Law times during the 17th and 18th centuries. To make matters even more confusing, it is also known as the Church of St Francis (after whom it was originally dedicated).

Further down Merchant's Quay you'll spot the **❹ Father Mathew Bridge**, built in 1818 on the spot of the fordable crossing that gave Dublin its Irish name, Baile Átha Cliath (Town of the Hurdle Ford) and named after temperance reformer Theobold Mathew (1790–1856), whose singular contribution to Irish life is 'the Pledge', a commitment to abstain from alcohol that most Irish Catholics took when they were confirmed (around age 12) and then abandoned when they were of age to drink (or earlier). Take a left onto Bridge St and stop for said indulgence at Dublin's oldest pub, the **❺ Brazen Head** (p122), dating from 1198 (although the present building dates from a positively youthful 1668).

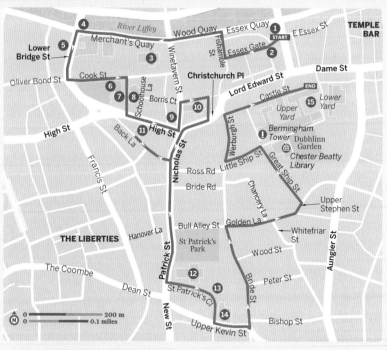

Take the next left onto Cook St, where you'll find ⑥ **St Audoen's Arch**, one of the only remaining gates of the 32 that were built into the medieval city walls, dating from 1240. Climb through the arch up to the ramparts to see one of the city's oldest existing churches, ⑦ **St Audoen's Church of Ireland** (p120). It was built around 1190, and is the only medieval church in the city that is still in use. Next door is the much newer (and larger) ⑧ **St Audoen's Catholic Church** (p121), which was known for the speedy sermons of Father 'Flash' Kavanagh, keen to ensure that he and his parishioners were out in time for the Sunday game of Gaelic football.

Leave the little park, join High St and head east until you reach the first corner. Here on your left is the former Synod Hall, now ⑨ **Dublinia** (p103), where medieval Dublin has been interactively recreated. Turn left and walk under the Synod Hall Bridge, which links Dublinia to one of the city's most important landmarks – ⑩ **Christ Church Cathedral** (p100) – and, in medieval times, the most important church inside the city walls.

Exit the cathedral onto Christ Church Pl, cross over onto Nicholas St and turn right

onto Back Lane. Proceed to ⑪ **Tailor's Hall**, Dublin's oldest surviving guild hall, built between 1703 and 1707 (though it says 1770 on the plaque) for the Tailors Guild. It's now the headquarters of An Taisce, the National Trust for Ireland.

Do an about-turn, head back along the lane and turn right into Nicholas St, which becomes Patrick St. To your left you'll see ⑫ **St Patrick's** (p115), Dublin's most important cathedral, which stood outside the city walls. Along St Patrick's Close, beyond the bend on the left, is the stunningly beautiful ⑬ **Marsh's Library** (p120), named after Archbishop Narcissus Marsh, dean of St Patrick's. Further along again on your left is the ⑭ **Dublin Metropolitan Police** building, once the Episcopal Palace of St Sepulchre.

Finally, follow our route up Bride St, Golden Lane and Great Ship St, and finish up with a long wander around ⑮ **Dublin Castle**. Be sure not to miss the striking powder-blue Bermingham Tower and the nearby Chester Beatty Library, south of the castle, which houses one of the city's most fascinating collections of rare books and manuscripts, and is well worth a visit.

POURING THE PERFECT GUINNESS

Like the Japanese Tea Ceremony, pouring a pint of Guinness is part ritual, part theatre and part logic. It's a six-step process that every decent Dublin bartender will use to serve the perfect pint.

The Glass

A dry, clean 20oz (568mL) tulip pint glass is used because the shape allows the nitrogen bubbles to flow down the side, and the contour 'bump' about halfway down pushes the bubbles into the centre of the pint on their way up.

The Angle

The glass is held beneath the tap at a 45-degree angle – and the tap faucet shouldn't touch the sides of the glass.

The Pour

A smooth pour should fill the glass to about three-quarters full, after which it is put on the counter 'to settle'.

The Head

As the beer flows into the glass its passes through a restrictor plate at high speed that creates nitrogen bubbles. In the glass, the agitated bubbles flow down the sides of the glass and – thanks to the contour bump – back up through the middle, settling at the top in a nice, creamy head. This should take a couple of minutes to complete.

The Top-Off

Once the pint is 'settled', the bartender will top it off, creating a domed effect across the top of the glass with the head sitting comfortably just above the rim. Now it's the perfect pint.

Where to Find It?

Most Dublin pubs know how to serve a decent pint of Guinness. But for something really special, you'll need the expertise of an experienced bartender and the appropriate atmosphere in which to savour their creations. Everyone has their favourites: we recommend Kehoe's, the Stag's Head and John Mulligan's on the south side; and Walshe's on the north side.

Mon-Thu, 10am-12.30am Fri & Sat, 11am-midnight Sun; 🚌51B, 78A, 123 from city centre) Reputedly Dublin's oldest pub, the Brazen Head has been serving thirsty patrons since 1198 when it set up as a Norman tavern. It's a bit away from the city centre, and the clientele consists of foreign language students, tourists and some grizzly auld locals.

Though its history is uncertain, the sunken level of the courtyard indicates how much street levels have altered since its construction. Robert Emmet was believed to have been a regular visitor, while in *Ulysses,* James Joyce reckoned 'you get a decent enough do in the Brazen Head'.

 ENTERTAINMENT

VICAR STREET   LIVE MUSIC

Map p250 (✆01-454 5533; www.vicarstreet.com; 58-59 Thomas St; tickets €25-60; ⏰7pm-midnight; 🚌13, 49, 54A, 56A from city centre) Vicar Street is a mid-sized venue with a capacity of around 1000, spread between the table-serviced group seating downstairs and a theatre-style balcony. It offers a varied program of performers, from comedians to soul, jazz, folk and foreign music.

TIVOLI THEATRE   THEATRE

Map p250 (✆01-454 4472; 135-136 Francis St; adult/child & student €20/15; 🚌51B, 51C, 78A, 123 from city centre) This commercial theatre offers a little bit of everything, from a good play with terrific actors to absolute nonsense with questionable comedic value.

SHOPPING

MARTIN FENNELLY ANTIQUES ANTIQUES
Map p250 (www.fennelly.net; 60 Francis St; ◉9.30am-6pm Mon-Sat, 2-4.30pm Sun; ☐123, 206, 51B from city centre) One of the best known antique dealers on Francis St is Martin Fennelly, who specialises in household items ranging from candlesticks and tea caddies to jewellery boxes and French and English porcelain. He also has an excellent collection of exquisite Irish furniture.

DUBLIN FOOD CO-OP MARKET
Map p250 (www.dublinfoodcoop.com; 12 Newmarket; ◉noon-8pm Wed-Fri, 9.30am-4.30pm Sat, 11am-5pm Sun; ☐49, 54A, 77X from city centre) From dog food to detergent, everything in this market hall is organic and/or ecofriendly. Thursday has a limited selection of local and imported fair-trade products, but Saturday is when it's all on display – Dubliners from all over drop in for their responsible weekly shop. There's an on-the-premises baker and even baby-changing facilities.

OXFAM HOME HOMEWARES
Map p250 (☑01-402 0555; 86 Francis St; ◉9.30am-5.30pm Mon-Sat; ☐123, 206, 51B from city centre) They say charity begins at home, so get rummaging among the veneer cast-offs in this furniture branch of the charity chain where you might stumble across the odd 1960s Subbuteo table or art-deco dresser. Esoteric vinyl from the '80s is another speciality of the house.

FRANCIS STREET ANTIQUES
Map p250 Some of the most interesting – and wackiest – shopping is done along Francis St in the Liberties, the home of antiquarians and, in recent years, art dealers of every hue. Although you mightn't fancy transporting the hand luggage, you can have that original Edwardian fireplace you've always wanted shipped to you by the shop.

IRISH MUSEUM OF MODERN ART GIFT SHOP BOOKS
Map p250 (Military Rd; ◉11.30am-5.30pm Tue-Fri, 10am-5.30pm Sat, noon-5.30pm Sun; ⓗHeuston) Offers a comprehensive selection of coffee-table books on Irish contemporary art.

FLEURY ANTIQUES ANTIQUES
Map p250 (☑01-473 0878; 57 Francis St; ◉9.30am-6pm Mon-Sat; ☐123, 206, 51B from city centre) This blue-fronted antiques shop does a steady connoisseur's trade in all manner of oil paintings (there's something for virtually every taste), vases, candelabras, silverware, porcelain and decorative pieces from the 18th century right up to the 1930s.

O'SULLIVAN ANTIQUES ANTIQUES
Map p250 (☑01-454 1143; osullivanantiques. com; 43-44 Francis St; ◉10am-6pm Mon-Sat; ☐123, 206, 51B from city centre) Fine furniture and furnishings from the Georgian, Victorian and Edwardian eras are the speciality of this respected antiques shop (which also has a branch in New York), where a rummage might also reveal some distinctive bits of ceramic and crystal, not to mention medals and uniforms from a bygone era that will win you first prize at the costume ball.

ACTIVITIES

ROYAL HOSPITAL KILMAINHAM TOUR TOUR
(☑01-612 9000; www.heritageireland.ie; ◉Wed-Sun Jul-Sep) **FREE** Shows off some of the building's treasures, including the Banqueting Hall, with 22 specially commissioned portraits, and the stunning baroque chapel, with papier-mâché ceilings and a set of exquisite Queen Anne gates.

DOUG MCKINLAY / GETTY IMAGES ©

CSFOTOIMAGES / GETTY IMAGES ©

1. Marsh's Library (p120)
Founded in 1701, Ireland's oldest public library is a highlight of any Dublin visit.

2. Temple Bar Food Market (p107)
Dublin's best open-air food market teems with gourmet and organic goods and produce.

3. Temple Bar pub (p106)
A traditional Dublin pub with perhaps the city's most photographed facade.

4. Irish Museum of Modern Art (p119)
Housed in the majestic Royal Hospital Kilmainham, the IMMA is Ireland's foremost contemporary art gallery.

HOLGER LEUE / GETTY IMAGES ©

North of the Liffey

Neighborhood Top Five

1 **Dublin City Gallery – Hugh Lane** (p133) Nodding sagely at the exquisite collection of modern and contemporary art.

2 **Old Jameson Distillery** (p134) Sampling a snifter of the hard stuff – that's whiskey to you and me – after discovering how it's made in this converted distillery museum.

3 **Abbey Theatre** (p144) Spending a night at the spiritual home of Irish theatre, being entertained by plays both old and new by the great dramatists as well as emerging talent.

4 **National Museum of Ireland – Decorative Arts & History** (p134) Wandering about the glorious yard of Collins Barracks, without

forgetting the collection itself – which includes fascinating exhibits on Ireland's struggle for independence as well as the history of design.

5 **Tantalising your taste-buds** (p141) Eating in the north side's new breed of restaurants, like Cotto or Fish Shop.

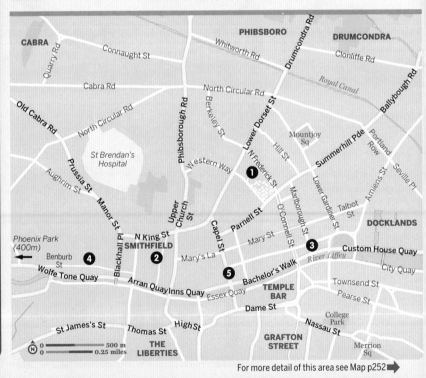

For more detail of this area see Map p252 ➡

Explore North of the Liffey

With the biggest geographical spread of any neighbourhood, a little planning and a bit of transport will be required to fully explore Dublin north of the Liffey. O'Connell St and its attractions are pretty straightforward and can be explored with ease on foot, with the biggest demand on your time being the fabulous collection at the Hugh Lane gallery and the collection at Collins Barracks. The north side's other attractions are to the west, and the best way to get to them is by Luas, which will reduce your journey to mere minutes. The Old Jameson Distillery and Collins Barracks are within walking distance of each other, on either side of Smithfield, but you'll be under your own steam to explore Europe's largest enclosed city park, home to the president, the US Ambassador, the zoo and a herd of red deer, not to mention visiting Dubliners when the weather is good.

Beyond the Royal Canal, which encloses the northern edge of the city centre, are a bunch of attractions that are well worth the effort: you could devote the guts of half a day each visiting the Croke Park museum, Glasnevin cemetery and the National Botanic Gardens; an excursion to Marino to see the famous Casino is also worthwhile, and you can get there via the DART suburban train.

Local Life

→**Hang-out** Go to Brother Hubbard (p141) on Capel St for great coffee and an easy-going atmosphere; equally good is Third Space in Smithfield.

→**Food** The northside's culinary credentials are elevated by the likes of Oxmantown (p141), Cotto (p141) and Fish Shop (p141) – but don't ignore stalwarts such as 101 Talbot (p141) either!

→**Park Life** Do as Dubliners do on a fine day and take in the massive expanse of Phoenix Park (p130), where you can run, cycle, play, walk or just lie down, depending on your fancy.

Getting There & Away

→**Bus** All city centre buses stop on O'Connell St or the nearby quays. City buses serve Glasnevin and Croke Park, while national bus services, operated by Bus Eireann, arrive and depart from the Busáras (p217) depot on Store St.

→**Tram** The Luas runs east to west parallel to the Liffey from The Point to Heuston Station.

→**Train** The DART runs from Connolly Station northeast to Clontarf Rd, which is handy for the Casino at Marino. Mainline trains for the north and northwest go from Connolly Station (p217).

Lonely Planet's Top Tip

The area between the northern end of O'Connell St and Gardiner St to the east as far up as Dorset St is best avoided late at night, as the potential for drug- or alcohol-fuelled trouble is heightened in a neighbourhood beset by the ills of urban deprivation.

Best Places to Eat

→ M&L (p141)
→ Chapter One (p142)
→ 101 Talbot (p141)
→ Oxmantown (p141)
→ Fish Shop (p141)

For reviews, see p141➡

Best Places to Drink

→ Walshe's (p143)
→ Dice Bar (p143)
→ Pantibar (p143)

For reviews, see p143➡

Best Places to Shop

→ Arnott's (p145)
→ Winding Stair (p145)
→ Jervis Centre (p145)

For reviews, see p145➡

NORTH OF THE LIFFEY

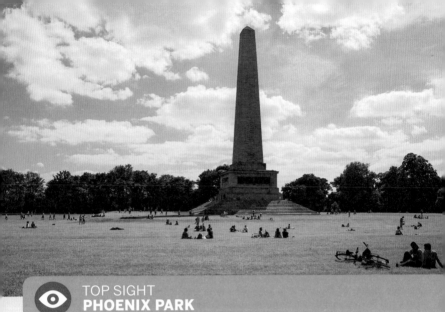

DAVID SOANES PHOTOGRAPHY / GETTY IMAGES ©

TOP SIGHT
PHOENIX PARK

The hugely impressive 709 hectares that comprise Phoenix Park are not just a magnificent playground for all kinds of sport from running to polo, but are also home to the president of Ireland, the American ambassador, a shy herd of fallow deer and also where you'll find Europe's oldest zoo. How's that for a place to stretch your legs?

The Park

Chesterfield Ave runs northwest through the length of the park from the Parkgate St entrance to the Castleknock Gate. Near the Parkgate St entrance is the 63m-high **Wellington Monument** obelisk (pictured above), which was completed in 1861. Nearby is the **People's Garden**, dating from 1864, and the bandstand in the Hollow. Across Chesterfield Ave from the Áras an Uachtaráin – and easily visible from the road – is the massive **Papal Cross**, which marks the site where Pope John Paul II preached to 1.25 million people in 1979. In the centre of the park the **Phoenix Monument**, erected by Lord Chesterfield in 1747, looks so unlike a phoenix that it's often referred to as the Eagle Monument.

Dublin Zoo

Established in 1831, the 28-hectare **Dublin Zoo** (www.dublinzoo.ie; Phoenix Park; adult/child/family €17/12/48; ⊙9.30am-6pm Mar-Sep, to dusk Oct-Feb; 🚌10 from O'Connell St, 25 & 26 from Middle Abbey St) just north of the Hollow is one of the oldest in the world. It is well known for its lion-breeding program, which dates back to 1857, and includes among its offspring the lion that roars at the start of MGM films. You'll see these tough cats, from a distance, on the 'African Savanna', just one of several habitats created since 2005.

DON'T MISS

➡ Wellington Monument
➡ Tour of Áras an Uachtaráin
➡ Dublin Zoo

PRACTICALITIES

➡ www.phoenixpark.ie
➡ admission free
➡ ⊙24hr
➡ 🚌10 from O'Connell St, 25 & 26 from Middle Abbey St

The zoo is home to roughly 400 animals from 100 different species, and you can visit all of them across the eight different habitats that range from an Asian jungle to a family farm, where kids get to meet the inhabitants up close and even milk a (model) cow. There are restaurants, cafes and even a train to get you round.

Áras an Uachtaráin

The residence of the Irish president is a Palladian **lodge** (www.president.ie; Phoenix Park; ☺guided tours hourly 10am-4pm Sat; 🚌10 from O'Connell St, 25 & 26 from Middle Abbey St) **FREE** that was built in 1751 and enlarged a couple of times since, most recently in 1816. It was home to the British viceroys from 1782 to 1922, and then to the governors general until Ireland cut ties with the British Crown and created the office of president in 1937. Queen Victoria stayed here during her visit in 1849, when she appeared not to even notice the Famine. The candle burning in the window is an old Irish tradition, to guide 'the Irish diaspora' home.

Tickets for the free one-hour **tours** can be collected from the **Phoenix Park Visitor Centre** (www.phoenixpark.ie; Phoenix Park; ☺10am-6pm Apr-Dec, 9.30am-5.30pm Jan-Mar; 🚌10 from O'Connell St, 25 & 26 from Middle Abbey St), the converted former stables of the papal nunciate, where you'll see a 10-minute introductory video before being shuttled to the Áras itself to inspect five state rooms and the president's study. If you can't make it on a Saturday, just become elected president of your own country or become a Nobel laureate or something, and then wrangle a personal invite.

Ashtown Castle

Next door to Áras an Uachtaráin is the restored four-storey Ashtown Castle, a 17th-century tower house 'discovered' inside the 18th-century nuncio's mansion when the latter was demolished in 1986 due to dry rot. You can visit the castle only on a guided tour from the visitor centre.

Elsewhere in the Park

The southern part of the park has many **football** and **hurling pitches**; although they actually occupy about 80 hectares (200 acres), the area is known as the **Fifteen Acres**. To the west, the rural-looking **Glen Pond** corner of the park is extremely attractive.

At the northwestern end of the park near the White's Gate entrance are the offices of **Ordnance Survey Ireland**, the government mapping department. This building was originally built in 1728

DID YOU KNOW?

At 709 hectares, Phoenix Park is big – but when it was first developed it was even larger, as it stretched across the Liffey to the south. Part of the original park was on the site of a Viking burial ground (in the Islandbridge/Kilmainham area) that was the biggest Viking cemetery outside of Scandinavia.

At weekends the football pitches at the Fifteen Acres are used by local league teams that can be fun to watch.

Although the park is open 24 hours a day, it is not advised to hang around after dark.

FARMLEIGH HOUSE

Situated in the northwest corner of Phoenix Park, opulent **Farmleigh House** (🖋01-815 5900; www.farmleigh.ie; Phoenix Park, Castleknock; ☺10am-5pm Sat & Sun; guided tours hourly 10.15am-4.15pm; 🚌37 from city centre) **FREE** can only be visited by joining one of the 30-minute house tours. However, the real highlight of the 32-hectare estate is the garden, where regular shows are held. There is also an extensive program of events in summer, from food fairs to classical concerts.

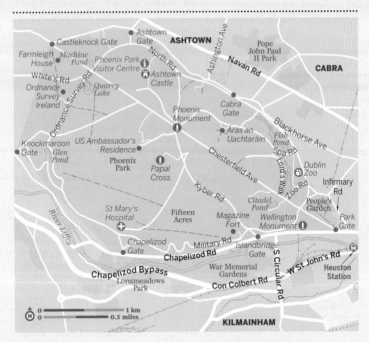

by Luke Gardiner, who was responsible for the architecture in O'Connell St and Mountjoy Sq in north Dublin.

Back towards the Parkgate St entrance is the **Magazine Fort** (closed to the public) on Thomas's Hill. The fort was no quick construction, the process taking from 1734 to 1801. It provided useful target practice during the 1916 Easter Rising, and was raided by the Irish Republican Army (IRA) in 1940 when the entire ammunition reserve of the Irish army was nabbed, but recovered a few weeks later.

Whatever reputation Dublin may have as a repository of top-class art is in large part due to the collection at this magnificent gallery, home to Impressionist masterpieces, the best of modern Irish work from 1950 onward, and the actual studio of Francis Bacon.

The Gallery

Founded in 1908, the gallery's home since 1933 has been the stunning **Charlemont House**, designed by Georgian superstar architect William Chambers in 1763. A modernist extension, which opened in 2006, has seen the addition of 13 bright galleries spread across three floors.

Hugh Lane

The gallery owes its origins to one Sir Hugh Lane (1875–1915). Born in County Cork, Lane worked in London art galleries before setting up his own gallery in Dublin. He had a connoisseur's eye and a good nose for the directions of the market, which enabled him to build up a superb collection, particularly strong in Impressionists.

Unfortunately, neither his talents nor his collection were much appreciated. Irish rejection led him to rewrite his will and bequeath some of the finest works in his collection to the National Gallery in London. Later he relented and added a rider to his will leaving the collection to Dublin but failed to have it witnessed, causing a long legal squabble over which gallery had rightful ownership.

The Hugh Lane Bequest

The collection (known as the Hugh Lane Bequest 1917) was split in a 1959 settlement that sees the eight masterpieces divided into two groups and alternated between Dublin and London every six years. Currently on display are works by Renoir, Manet, Morisot and Pissarro.

Francis Bacon Studio

Impressionist masterpieces notwithstanding, the gallery's most popular exhibit is the Francis Bacon Studio, which was painstakingly moved, in all its shambolic mess, from 7 Reece Mews, South Kensington, London, where the Dublin-born artist (1909–92) lived for 31 years. The display features some 80,000 items strewn about the place, including slashed canvases, the last painting he was working on, tables piled with materials, walls daubed with colour samples, portraits with heads cut out, bits of furniture and many assorted piles of crap. It's a teasing, tantalising, riveting, ridiculous masterpiece that provides no real sense of the artist himself. More revealing is the 10-minute profile of him with Melvyn Bragg and the photographs of Bacon's immaculately tidy bachelor pad, which suggest a deep, personal loneliness.

Elsewhere in the Gallery

Just by the main reception desk is the **Stained Glass gallery**, whose highlight is Harry Clarke's wonderful *The Eve of St Agnes* (1924). His masterpiece is made up of 22 separate panels, each a depiction of a stanza of John Keats's eponymous poem about the doomed love between Madeline and Porphyro, who cannot meet because their families are sworn enemies.

The gallery's newest wing (opened 2006) is a two-storey extension with – on the ground floor – a gallery dedicated to seven abstract paintings by Irish-born **Sean Scully**, probably Ireland's most famous painter. Elsewhere in the new wing is work by contemporary Irish artists including Dorothy Cross, Brian Maguire and Norah McGuinness.

DON'T MISS

→ The Hugh Lane Bequest 1917 paintings
→ The Francis Bacon Studio
→ The Sean Scully collection

PRACTICALITIES

→ Map p252, E3
→ ☏01-222 5550
→ www.hughlane.ie
→ 22 N Parnell Sq
→ admission free
→ ⊙10am-6pm Tue-Thu, to 5pm Fri & Sat, 11am-5pm Sun
→ ▣3, 7, 10, 11, 13, 16, 19, 46A, 123

⊙ SIGHTS

**DUBLIN CITY
GALLERY – THE HUGH LANE** GALLERY

See p133.

★ **NATIONAL MUSEUM OF IRELAND –
DECORATIVE ARTS & HISTORY** MUSEUM

Map p252 (www.museum.ie; Benburb St; ⊙10am-5pm Tue-Sat, 2-5pm Sun; ☐25, 66, 67, 90 from city centre, ☐Museum) FREE Once the world's largest military barracks, this splendid early neoclassical grey-stone building on the Liffey's northern banks was completed in 1704 according to the design of Thomas Burgh, whose CV also includes the Old Library in Trinity College and St Michan's Church. It is now home to the Decorative Arts & History collection of the National Museum of Ireland.

The building's central square held six entire regiments and is a truly awesome space, surrounded by arcaded colonnades and blocks linked by walking bridges. Following the handover to the new Irish government in 1922, the barracks was renamed to honour Michael Collins, a hero of the struggle for independence, who was killed that year in the Civil War; to this day most Dubliners refer to the museum as the **Collins Barracks**. Indeed, the army coat he wore on the day of his death (there's still mud on the sleeve) is part of the **Soldiers and Chiefs** exhibit, which covers the history of Irish soldiery at home and abroad from 1550 to the 21st century.

The museum's exhibits include a treasure trove of artefacts ranging from silver, ceramics and glassware to weaponry, furniture and folk-life displays – and an exquisite exhibition dedicated to iconic Irish designer **Eileen Gray** (1878–1976). The fascinating **Way We Wore** exhibit displays Irish clothing and jewellery from the past 250 years. An intriguing sociocultural study, it highlights the symbolism jewellery and clothing had in bestowing messages of mourning, love and identity. An exhibition chronicling Ireland's **1916 Easter Rising** is on the ground floor. Visceral memorabilia, such as first-hand accounts of the violence of the Black and Tans and post-Rising hunger strikes, the handwritten death certificates of the Republican prisoners and their postcards from Holloway prison, bring to life this poignant period of Irish history. Some of the best pieces are gathered in the **Curator's Choice** exhibition, which is a collection of 25 objects hand-picked by different curators, and displayed alongside an account of why they were chosen.

OLD JAMESON DISTILLERY MUSEUM

Map p252 (www.jamesonwhiskey.com; Bow St; adult/student/child €15/12/8; ⊙9am-6pm Mon-Sat, 10am-6pm Sun; ☐25, 66, 67, 90 from city centre, ☐Smithfield) Smithfield's biggest draw is devoted to *uisce beatha* (ish-kuh ba-ha, 'the water of life'); that's Irish for whiskey. To its more serious devotees, that is precisely what whiskey is, although they may be put off by the slickness of the museum (occupying part of the old distillery that stopped production in 1971), which shepherds visitors through a compulsory tour of the recreated factory (the tasting at the end is a lot of fun) and into the ubiquitous gift shop.

If you're buying whiskey, go for the stuff you can't buy at home, such as the excellent Red Breast or the superexclusive Midleton, a very limited reserve that is appropriately expensive.

GENERAL POST OFFICE HISTORIC BUILDING

Map p252 (☐01-705 7000; www.anpost.ie; Lower O'Connell St; ⊙8am-8pm Mon-Sat; ☐all city centre, ☐Abbey) Not just the country's main post office, or an eye-catching neoclassical building: the General Post Office is at the heart of Ireland's struggle for independence as it served as command HQ for the rebels during the Easter Rising of 1916. As a result it has become the focal point for all kinds of protests, parades and remembrances.

The building – a neoclassical masterpiece designed by Francis Johnston in 1818 – was burnt out in the siege that resulted from the rising, but that wasn't the end of it. There was bitter fighting in and around the building during the Civil War of 1922; you can still see the pockmarks of the struggle in the Doric columns. Since its reopening in 1929 it has lived through quieter times, although its role in Irish history is commemorated inside with a series of communist noble worker–style paintings depicting scenes from the Easter Rising.

DUBLIN WRITERS MUSEUM MUSEUM

Map p252 (www.writersmuseum.com; 18 N Parnell Sq; adult/child €8/5; ⊙10am-5pm Mon-Sat, 11am-5pm Sun; ☐3, 7, 10, 11, 13, 16, 19, 46A, 123) Memorabilia aplenty and lots of literary ephemera line the walls and display cabinets of this elegant museum devoted to preserving the city's rich literary tradition up to 1970. The building, comprising two 18th-century houses, is worth exploring on its own; Dublin stuccodore Michael Stapleton decorated the upstairs gallery.

However, the curious decision to omit living writers limits its appeal, and no account at all is given to contemporary writers, who would arguably be more popular with today's readers.

Although the busts and portraits of the greats in the gallery upstairs warrant more than a cursory peek, the real draws are the ground-floor displays, which include Samuel Beckett's phone (with a button for excluding incoming calls, of course), a letter from the 'tenement aristocrat' Brendan Behan to his brother, and a first edition of Bram Stoker's *Dracula*.

The **Gorham Library** next door is worth a visit, and there's also a calming Zen garden. The basement restaurant, Chapter One (p142), is one of the city's best.

While the museum focuses on the dearly departed, the **Irish Writers Centre** (Map p252; ☑01-872 1302; irishwriterscentre.ie; 19 N Parnell Sq; ⊗10am-10pm; 🚌3, 7, 10, 11, 13, 16, 19, 46A, 123) next door provides a meeting and working place for their living successors.

SPIRE   MONUMENT
Map p252 (O'Connell St; 🚌all city centre, 🚊Abbey) The city's most visible landmark soars over O'Connell St and is an impressive bit of architectural engineering that was erected in 2001: from a base only 3m in diameter, it soars more than 120m into the sky and tapers into a 15cm-wide beam of light...it's tall and shiny and it does the trick rather nicely.

The brainchild of London-based architect Ian Ritchie, it is apparently the highest sculpture in the world, but much like the Parisian reaction to the construction of the Eiffel Tower, Dubliners are divided as to its aesthetic value and have regularly made fun of it. Among other names, we like 'the erection in the intersection', the 'stiletto in the ghetto', and the altogether brilliant 'eyeful tower'.

JAMES JOYCE
CULTURAL CENTRE   CULTURAL CENTRE
Map p252 (www.jamesjoyce.ie; 35 N Great George's St; adult/student/child €5/4/free; ⊗10am-5pm Tue-Sat; 🚌3, 10, 11, 11A, 13, 16, 16A, 19, 19A, 22 from city centre) Denis Maginni, the exuberant, flamboyant dance instructor and 'confirmed bachelor' immortalised by James Joyce in *Ulysses,* taught the finer

points of dance out of this beautifully restored Georgian house, now a centre devoted to promoting and preserving the Joycean heritage. Inside are a handful of exhibits that will pique the interest of a Joyce enthusiast.

The exhibits include some of the furniture from Joyce's Paris apartment; a life-size recreation of a typical Edwardian bedroom (not Joyce's, but one similar to what James and Nora would have used); and the original door of 7 Eccles St, the home of Leopold and Molly Bloom in *Ulysses,* which was demolished in real life to make way for a private hospital.

It's not much, but the absence of period stuff is more than made up for by the superb interactive displays, which include three short documentary films on various aspects of Joyce's life and work, and – the highlight of the whole place – computers that allow you to explore the content of *Ulysses* episode by episode and trace Joyce's life year by year. It's enough to demolish the myth that Joyce's works are an impenetrable mystery and render him as he should be to the contemporary reader: a writer of enormous talent who sought to challenge and entertain his audience with his breathtaking wit and use of language.

While here, you can also admire the fine plastered ceilings, some of which are restored originals while others are meticulous reproductions of Dublin stuccodore Michael Stapleton's designs. The street has also been given a facelift and now boasts some of the finest Georgian doorways and fanlights in the city.

ST MICHAN'S CHURCH   CHURCH
Map p252 (☑01-872 4154; Lower Church St; adult/child €5/3.50; ⊗10am-12.45pm & 2-4.45pm Mon-Fri, 10am-12.45pm Sat; 🚉Smithfield) Macabre remains are the main attraction at this church, which was founded by the Danes in 1095 and named after one of their saints. Among the 'attractions' is an 800-year-old Norman crusader who was so tall that his feet were lopped off so he could fit in a coffin. Visits are by guided tour only.

St Michan's was the north side's only church until 1686, a year after it was almost completely rebuilt (it was remodelled in 1825 and again after the Civil War), leaving only the 15th-century battlement tower as its oldest bit. The courtroom-like interior hasn't changed much since the 19th century: still in place is the organ from 1724,

WORTH A DETOUR

BEYOND THE ROYAL CANAL

The Royal Canal, constructed from 1790, marks the traditional boundary of the city centre's northern edge, and beyond it, amid the semi-detached suburban dwellings, are a handful of sights that are well worth a visit.

Croke Park Experience

The Gaelic Athletic Association (GAA) considers itself not just the governing body of a bunch of Irish games but also the stout defender of a cultural identity that is ingrained in Ireland's sense of self. To get an idea of just how important the GAA is, a visit to the **Croke Park Experience** (www.crokepark.ie; Clonliffe Rd, New Stand, Croke Park; adult/child/student museum €6.50/4.50/5.50, museum & tour €13/8.50/10; ⊙9.30am-6pm Mon-Sat, to 5pm Sun Jun-Aug, 9.30am-5pm Mon-Sat, 10.30am-5pm Sun Sep-May; ▣3, 11, 11A, 16, 16A, 123 from O'Connell St) is a must. The twice-daily tours (except match days) of the impressive Croke Park stadium are excellent, and well worth the cost. The stadium's newest attraction is the **Skyline** (www.skylinecrokepark.ie; Croke Park; adult/student/child €20/18/12; ⊙11.30am & 2.30pm Mon-Fri May-Sep, hourly 10.30am-2.30pm Sat, 11.30am-2.30pm Sun; ▣3, 11, 11A, 16, 16A, 123 from O'Connell St), a guided tour around the stadium roof.

Glasnevin Cemetery

The tombstones at Ireland's largest and most historically important **burial site** (Prospect Cemetery; www.glasnevintrust.ie; Finglas Rd; ⊙10am-5pm; ▣40, 40A, 40B from Parnell St) **FREE** read like a 'who's who' of Irish history, as most of the leading names of the last 150 years are buried here.

A modern replica of a round tower acts as a handy landmark for locating the tomb of Daniel O'Connell, who died in 1847. Charles Stewart Parnell's tomb is topped with a large granite rock, on which only his name is inscribed – a remarkably simple tribute to a figure of such historical importance. Other notable people buried here include Sir Roger Casement, Republican leader Michael Collins, docker and trade unionist Jim Larkin, and poet Gerard Manley Hopkins.

The history of the cemetery is told in wonderful, award-winning detail in the **museum** (www.glasnevintrust.ie; Finglas Rd; museum €6, museum & tour €8; ⊙10am-5pm Mon-Fri, 11am-6pm Sat & Sun; ▣40, 40A, 40B from Parnell St), which tells the social and political story of Ireland through the lives of the people known and unknown that are buried here. The best way to visit the cemetery is to take one of the daily **tours** (11.30am, 12.30pm and 2.30pm).

National Botanic Gardens

Founded in 1795, the 19.5-hectare **botanic gardens** (Botanic Rd; ⊙9am-6pm Mon-Sat, 11am-6pm Sun Apr-Oct, 10am-4.30pm Mon-Sat, 11am-4.30pm Sun Nov-Mar; ▣13, 13A, 19 from O'Connell St, bus 34, 34A from Middle Abbey St) **FREE** are home to a series of curvilinear glasshouses, dating from 1843 to 1869, created by Richard Turner. Within these Victorian masterpieces you will find the latest in botanical technology, including a series of computer-controlled climates reproducing environments of different parts of the world. Among the pioneering botanical work conducted here was the first attempt to raise orchids from seed, back in 1844.

Casino at Marino

It's not the roulette-wheel kind of casino but the original Italian kind, the one that means 'summer home', and this particular **casino** (www.heritageireland.ie; Malahide Rd; adult/child/senior €4/2/3; ⊙10am-5pm Mar-May & Oct, to 6pm Jun-Sep; ▣20A, 20B, 27, 27B, 42, 42C, 123 from city centre) is one of the most enchanting constructions in all of Ireland. It was built in the mid-18th century for the Earl of Charlemont, who returned from his grand tour of Europe with more art than he could store in his own home, Marino House. He also came home with a big love of the Palladian style – hence the architecture of this wonderful folly.

Entrance is by guided tour only. The exterior of the building, with a huge entrance doorway, and 12 Tuscan columns forming a templelike facade, creates the expectation that its interior will be a single open space. Instead, it is an extravagant maze. A variety of statuary adorns the outside but it's the amusing fakes that are most enjoyable.

which Handel may have played for the first-ever performance of his *Messiah*. The organ case is distinguished by the fine oak carving of 17 entwined musical instruments on its front. A skull on the floor on one side of the altar is said to represent Oliver Cromwell. On the opposite side is the Stool of Repentance, where 'open and notoriously naughty livers' did public penance.

The tours of the underground vaults are the real draw, however. The bodies within are aged between 400 and 800 years, and have been preserved by a combination of methane gas coming from rotting vegetation beneath the church, the magnesium limestone of the masonry (which absorbs moisture from the air), and the perfectly constant temperature. Although there are caskets strewn about the place, the main attractions are 'the big four' – mummified bodies labelled The Unknown (a female about whom nothing is known), The Thief (his hands and feet are missing; some say as punishment for his crimes), The Nun and The Crusader: if he is indeed 800 years old then he may have participated in the piratical free-for-all crusades of the 13th century that resulted in the sack of Constantinople but weren't sanctioned by the church. Also in the crypt are the bodies of two brothers executed following the Rising of 1798 and – it is claimed – the remains of Robert Emmett, the fallen leader of the 1803 rebellion. Bram Stoker is said to have visited the crypt, which may have inspired him to write a story about a certain vampire who slept in a coffin....

FOUR COURTS HISTORIC BUILDING

Map p252 (Inns Quay; ⊘9am-5pm Mon-Fri; ☐25, 66, 67, 90 from city centre, ⓐFour Courts) **FREE**
This masterpiece of James Gandon (1743–1823) is a mammoth complex stretching 130m along Inns Quay, as fine an example of Georgian public architecture as there is in Dublin. Despite the construction of a brand-new criminal courts building further west along the Liffey, the Four Courts is still the enduring symbol of Irish law going about its daily business. Visitors are allowed to wander through the building, but not to enter courts or other restricted areas.

The Corinthian-columned central block, connected to flanking wings with enclosed quadrangles, was begun in 1786 and not completed until 1802. The original four courts (Exchequer, Common Pleas, King's Bench and Chancery) all branch off the central rotunda. In the lobby of the central rotunda you'll see bewigged barristers conferring and police officers handcuffed to their charges.

ARBOUR HILL CEMETERY CEMETERY

Map p252 (⊘01-821 3021; www.heritageireland. ie; Arbour Hill; ⊘8am-4pm Mon-Fri, 11am-4pm Sat, 9.30am-4pm Sun; ☐25, 25A, 37, 38, 39, 66, 67, 90, 134 from city centre, ⓐMuseum) **FREE**
Just north of Collins Barracks, this small cemetery is the final resting place of all 14 of the executed leaders of the 1916 Easter Rising. The burial ground is plain, with the 14 names inscribed in stone. Beside the graves is a cenotaph bearing the Easter Proclamation, a focal point for official and national commemorations.

The front of the cemetery incongruously, but poignantly, contains the graves of British personnel killed in the War of Independence. Here, in the oldest part of the cemetery, as the gravestones toppled, they were lined up against the boundary walls where they still stand solemnly today.

BELVEDERE HOUSE HISTORIC BUILDING

Map p252 (6 Great Denmark St; ⊘closed to public; ☐3, 10, 11, 13, 16, 19, 22 from city centre)
The home of Jesuit Belvedere College since 1841. James Joyce studied here between 1893 and 1898 (and described his experiences in *A Portrait of the Artist as a Young Man*), and we can only wonder if he ever took a moment to admire the magnificent plasterwork by master stuccodore Michael Stapleton in between catechism classes and arithmetic homework?

LIBERTY HALL LANDMARK

Map p252 (Eden Quay; ⊘closed to the public)
Dublin's third-tallest storied building is either a modernist masterpiece or an unconscionable eyesore, depending on how you see modern architecture. It was built between 1961 and 1965 to replace the original Liberty Hall, which had been a hotel before it was taken over by James Connolly's Irish Citizen Army in 1913. It also served as the HQ for Jim Larkin's Irish Transport & General Workers Union, and so played a role in both the Dublin Lockout and the Easter Rising.

The original building was demolished in the 1950s and replaced by this tired-looking structure. It was originally fitted with non-reflective windows, but they were damaged by an Ulster Volunteer Force (UVF) car bomb in 1972 and replaced with the current reflective glass windows. The car bomb also put paid to the viewing platform, which had just opened but has remained closed ever since. Today it's the headquarters of the Services, Industrial, Professional and Technical Union (SIPTU), Ireland's largest trade union, who've long wanted to demolish it and replace it with something new, but so far they've been denied planning permission on account of the building's 'architectural significance'.

ROTUNDA HOSPITAL HOSPITAL

Map p252 (✆01-873 0700; Parnell Sq; ⊙visiting hours 6-8pm; ☐3, 10, 11, 13, 16, 19, 22 from city centre) Irish public hospitals aren't usually attractions, but this one – founded in 1748 as the first maternity hospital in the British Isles – makes for an interesting walk-by or an unofficial wander inside if you're interested in Victorian plasterwork. It shares its basic design with Leinster House (p90) because the architect of both, Richard Cassels, used the same floor plan to economise.

The hospital was established by Dr Bartholomew Mosse and was for a time the world's largest hospital devoted to maternity care – at a time when the burgeoning urban population was enduring shocking infant mortality rates. To the main building Cassels added a three-storey tower, which Mosse intended to use for fundraising purposes (charging visitors an entry fee). He also laid out pleasure gardens, which were fashionable among Dublin's high society for a time, and built the Rotunda Assembly Hall to raise money. The hall is now occupied by the Ambassador Theatre (p145), and the Supper Rooms house the Gate Theatre (p144).

Inside, the public rooms and staircases give some idea of how beautiful the hospital once was, and they lead to one of Dublin's largely hidden gems, the sumptuous **Rotunda Chapel**, built in 1758, and featuring superb coloured plasterwork by German stuccodore Bartholomew Cramillion. The Italian artist Giovanni Battista Cipriani was supposed to supplement the work but his paintings were never installed, which is probably just as well because you can't imagine how this little space would have looked with even more decoration. If you intend visiting, you have to bear in mind that this is still a functioning hospital and you must be very quiet when coming to see the chapel. It's not terribly well signposted inside and is often locked outside visiting hours (although if you ask kindly or look like you're in desperate need of a prayer, somebody will let you in).

GARDEN OF REMEMBRANCE PARK

Map p252 (Parnell Sq; ⊙8.30am-6pm Apr-Sep, 9.30am-4pm Oct-Mar; ☐3, 10, 11, 13, 16, 19, 22 from city centre) This rather austere little park was opened by President Éamon de Valera in 1966 for the 50th anniversary of the Easter Rising. The most interesting feature in the garden is a bronze statue of the **Children of Lir** (Map p252; Parnell Sq; ⊙8.30am-6pm Apr-Sep, 9.30am-4pm Oct-Mar; ☐3, 10, 11, 13, 16, 19, 22 from city centre) by Oisín Kelly; according to Irish legend the children were turned into swans by their wicked stepmother.

The park is still known to some Dubs as the 'Garden of Mature Recollection', mocking the linguistic gymnastics employed by former favourite-for-president Brian Lenihan, who was caught out lying in a minor political scandal and used the phrase to try and wiggle his way out of it.

ST MARY'S PRO-CATHEDRAL CHURCH

Map p252 (Marlborough St; ⊙8am-6.30pm; ☐all city centre, ☐Abbey) FREE Dublin's most important Catholic church is not quite the showcase you'd expect. It's in the wrong place for starters. The large neoclassical building, built between 1816 to 1825, was intended to stand where the GPO is, but Protestant objections resulted in its location on a cramped street that was then at the heart of Monto, the red-light district.

In fact, it's so cramped for space around here that you'd hardly notice the church's six Doric columns, which were modelled on the Temple of Theseus in Athens, much less be able to admire them. The interior is fairly functional, and its few highlights include a carved altar by Peter Turnerelli and the high relief representation of the Ascension by John Smyth. The best time to visit is 11am on Sunday when the Latin Mass is sung by the Palestrina Choir, with whom Ireland's most celebrated tenor, John McCormack, began his career in 1904.

KING'S INNS HISTORIC BUILDING

Map p252 (www.kingsinns.ie; Henrietta St; ⊙closed to the public; ☐25, 25A, 66, 67, 90, 134 from city centre, ☐Four Courts) Home to Dublin's legal profession (and where barristers are still trained), King's Inns occupies a

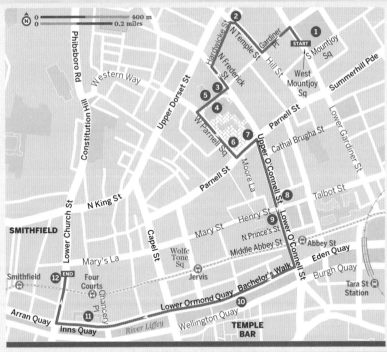

🏃 Neighbourhood Walk
A Walk on the Northside

START MOUNTJOY SQ
END ST MICHAN'S CHURCH
LENGTH 2.5KM; TWO HOURS

From ❶ **Mountjoy Square**, take a left at the northwestern corner and walk down Gardiner Pl, turning right onto North Temple St. Up ahead is the fine but now deconsecrated Georgian ❷ **St George's Church** (p140), designed by architect Francis Johnston.

Take a left onto Hardwicke St and left again onto North Frederick St. On your right you'll spot the distinctive ❸ **Abbey Presbyterian Church**, built in 1864.

The northern slice of Parnell Sq houses the ❹ **Garden of Remembrance** (p138), opened in 1966 for the 50th anniversary of the 1916 Easter Rising. North of the square is the excellent ❺ **Dublin City Gallery – Hugh Lane** (p133), home to some of the best modern art in Europe.

In the southern part of Parnell Sq is the ❻ **Rotunda Hospital** (p138), a wonderful example of public architecture in the Georgian style and now one of the city's three

main maternity hospitals. The southeastern corner of the square has the ❼ **Gate Theatre** (p144), one of the city's most important theatres – and where Orson Welles began his acting career in 1931 as a 16-year-old.

Head south down O'Connell St, passing by the 120m-high ❽ **Spire** (p135). Erected in 2001, it has become an iconic symbol of the city. On the western side of O'Connell St, the neoclassical ❾ **General Post Office** (p134) towers over the street – this was the operational HQ for the Easter Rising of 1916: you can still see bullet holes in the columns.

When you hit the river, turn right and walk along the boardwalk until you reach the city's most distinctive crossing point, the ❿ **Ha'Penny Bridge** (named for the charge levied on those who used it).

Continue west along Ormond Quay to one of James Gandon's Georgian masterpieces, the ⓫ **Four Courts** (p137), home to the most important law courts in Ireland. Finally take a right onto Church St to admire ⓬ **St Michan's Church** (p135), a beautiful Georgian construction with grisly vaults populated by the remains of the departed.

THE EVOLUTION OF A GEORGIAN STREET

Dublin's first example of Georgian urban design was **Henrietta Street** (p140), laid out in the 1720s at the behest of Luke Gardiner, who was to become the city's pre-eminent Georgian developer. Wider than most 18th-century streets, it was lined with a series of large, red-bricked Palladian mansions. Gardiner himself lived at No 10, in a house designed by Richard Cassels. The street was originally known as Primate's Hill, as the Archbishop of Armagh owned one of the houses; it was later demolished (along with two others) to make way for the Law Library of **King's Inns** (p138; still there at the street's western end). The name Henrietta was inspired by either the wife of Charles FitzRoy, the Duke of Grafton, or the wife of Charles Paulet, the 2nd Duke of Bolton (after whom nearby Bolton St is named).

The street was Dublin's most fashionable address until the Act of Union in 1801, after which it fell into disrepair. For most of the 20th century it was a tenement street, with each house crammed with as many as 70 residents. Recent restorations have restored the 13 remaining houses to something approaching their elegant best, and the cul-de-sac remains a wonderful insight into the evolution of Georgian residential architecture.

classical building built by James Gandon between 1795 and 1817 on Constitution Hill, with Francis Johnston chipping in with the cupola. A fine example of Georgian public architecture, the building itself is, alas, only open to members and their guests.

HENRIETTA STREET   STREET
Map p252 (🚌25, 25A, 37, 38, 39, 66, 67, 90, 134 from city centre, 🚊Four Courts) Henrietta St dates from the 1720s and was the first project of Dublin's pre-eminent Georgian developer, Luke Gardiner. It was designed as an enclave of prestigious addresses (Gardiner himself lived at No 10), and remained one of Dublin's most fashionable streets until the Act of Union (1801). Some of the residences are in disrepair, yet it's still a wonderful insight into the evolution of Georgian residential architecture, and features mansions of varying size and style.

ST GEORGE'S CHURCH   CHURCH
Map p252 (Hardwicke Pl; ⊘closed to the public; 🚌11, 16, 41 from city centre) One of Dublin's most beautiful buildings is this deconsecrated church, built by Francis Johnston between 1802 and 1813 in Greek Ionic style. It is topped by an eye-catching, 60m-high steeple modelled on that of St Martin-in-the-Fields in London. Alas, it has fallen into serious disrepair and has been shrouded in scaffolding for more than a decade.

Although this was one of Johnston's finest works, and the Duke of Wellington was married here, the building's neglect is largely due to the fact that it's Church of Ireland and not Roman Catholic – the Protestant (and largely moneyed) community for whom it was built has shrunk to the point of disappearance. The bells that Leopold Bloom heard in *Ulysses* were removed, the ornate pulpit was carved up and used to decorate a pub, and the spire is in danger of crumbling, which has resulted in the scaffolding.

NATIONAL
LEPRECHAUN MUSEUM   MUSEUM
Map p252 (www.leprechaunmuseum.ie; Twilfit House, Jervis St; adult/child €14/10; ⊘9.30am-6.30pm Mon-Sat, 10.30am-6.30pm Sun; 🚌all city centre, 🚊Jervis) Ostensibly designed as a child-friendly museum of Irish folklore, this is really a romper-room for kids sprinkled with bits of fairy tale. Which is no bad thing, even if the picture of the leprechaun painted here is more Lucky Charms and Walt Disney than sinister creature of pre-Christian mythology.

There's the optical illusion tunnel (which makes you appear smaller to those at the other end), the room full of oversized furniture, the wishing wells and, inevitably, the pot of gold; all of which is strictly for the kids. But if Walt Disney himself went on a leprechaun hunt when visiting Ireland during the filming of *Darby O'Gill and the Little People* in 1948, what the hell do we know?

EATING

★ M&L
CHINESE $

Map p252 (13/14 Cathedral St; mains €9-13; ⊘11.30am-10pm Mon-Sat, noon-10pm Sun; ☐all city centre) Beyond the plain frontage and the cheap-looking decor is Dublin's best Chinese restaurant...by some distance. It's usually full of Chinese people, who come for the authentic Szechuan-style cuisine – spicier than Cantonese and with none of the concessions usually made to Western palates (no prawn crackers or curry chips).

★ OXMANTOWN
CAFE $

Map p252 (16 Mary's Abbey, City Markets; sandwiches €5.50-6.90; ⊘7.30am-4pm Mon-Fri; ☐Four Courts, Jervis) Delicious breakfasts and excellent sandwiches make this relatively new cafe one of the standout places for daytime eating on the north side of the Liffey. Locally baked bread, coffee supplied by Cloud Nine (Dublin's only micro-roastery) and meats sourced from Irish farms are the ingredients, but it's the way it's all put together that makes it so worthwhile.

COTTO
MEDITERRANEAN $

Map p252 (46 Manor St; mains €9-12; ☐25, 25A, 66, 67 from city centre) In the daytime, this new place serves brunch with flavours from all over the Mediterranean (and Mexico); in the evenings, it's all about delicious pizzas. It's run by the same folks behind Oxmantown (who also provide the sandwiches), so the everything-local philosophy is very much in force.

THIRD SPACE
CAFE $

Map p252 (www.thirdspace.ie; Unit 14, Block C, Smithfield Market; sandwiches €6; ⊘8am-7pm Mon, Tue & Fri, 8am-9.30pm Wed & Thu, 9.30am-5pm Sat; ☐Smithfield) One of the most welcoming cafes in town is this wonderful spot in Smithfield, which serves gorgeous sandwiches, wraps and baps, as well as a tart of the day and wines by the glass. Sit in the window, take out a book and just relax. The staff is fabulous.

SOUP DRAGON
FAST FOOD $

Map p252 (☏01-872 3277; www.soupdragon.com; 168 Capel St; mains €5-8; ⊘8am-5pm Mon-Fri; ☏; ☐all city centre, ☐Jervis) Queues are a regular feature outside this fabulous spot which specialises in soups on the go – but it also does excellent stews, sandwiches, bagels and salads. The all-day breakfast options are excellent – we especially like the mini breakfast quiche of sausage, egg and bacon. Bowls come in two sizes and prices include fresh bread and a piece of fruit.

BROTHER HUBBARD
CAFE $

Map p252 (☏01-441 6595; 153 Capel St; dishes €7-11; ⊘7.30am-5.30pm Mon & Tue, 7.30am-10pm Wed-Fri, 9.30am-10pm Sat; ☐all city centre, ☐Jervis) Anchored by its excellent baristas (beans by coffee experts 3FE), this cafe with a small garden at the back also does a nice menu of sandwiches, flatbreads and salads. It's recently introduced the evening Middle East Feast, a sharing experience made up of a variety of small plates. Reservations for evenings are recommended.

PANEM
CAFE $

Map p252 (21 Lower Ormond Quay; mains €7-10; ⊘9am-5pm Mon-Sat; ☐all city centre) Pasta, focaccia and salads are the standard fare at this diminutive quayside cafe, but the specialities are wickedly sweet and savoury pastries, which are all made on-site. The croissants and brioche – filled with Belgian chocolate, almond cream or hazelnut *amaretti* – are the perfect snack for a holiday stroll along the Liffey Boardwalk. Lunchtimes are chaotic.

★ 101 TALBOT
MODERN IRISH $$

Map p252 (www.101talbot.ie; 100-102 Talbot St; mains €17-24; ⊘noon-3pm & 5-11pm Tue-Sat; ☐all city centre) This Dublin classic has expertly resisted every trendy wave and has been a stalwart of good Irish cooking since opening more than two decades ago. Its speciality is traditional meat-and-two-veg dinners, but with vague Mediterranean and even Middle Eastern influences: roast Wicklow venison with sweet potato, lentil and bacon cassoulet and a sensational Morccocan-style lamb tagine. Superb.

FISH SHOP
SEAFOOD $$

Map p252 (www.fish-shop.ie; 6 Queen St; mains €14-19; ⊘noon-2.30pm & 5-10pm Wed-Fri, 5-10pm Tue & Sat; ☐25, 25A, 66, 67 from city centre, ☐Museum) The menu changes daily at this tiny restaurant (it only has 16 seats) to reflect what's good and fresh, and the options aren't huge, usually about five different choices. One day you might fancy line-caught mackerel with a green sauce, another day slip sole with caper butter. Maybe the best seafood restaurant in town. It doesn't take bookings.

L MULLIGAN GROCER
MODERN IRISH **$$**

Map p252 (🖉01-670 9889; www.lmulligangrocer.com; 18 Stoneybatter; mains €16-27; ⊙4-10pm Mon-Fri, 12.30-10pm Sat & Sun; 🚋25, 25A, 66, 67 from city centre, 🚋Museum) 🏷 It's a great traditional pub, but the main reason to come here is for the food, all sourced locally and made by expert hands. The menu includes dishes like slow-cooked free-range pork belly and herb-crumbed haddock, as well as particularly tasty lamb burger. There are about a dozen craft beers on draught and as many again in a bottle.

MUSASHI NOODLES
& SUSHI BAR
JAPANESE **$$**

Map p252 (🖉01-532 8057; www.musashidublin.com; 15 Capel St; mains €13-17; ⊙noon-10pm; 🚋all city centre, 🚋Jervis) One of the best Japanese restaurants in town is this low-lit spot that serves freshly crafted sushi and other Japanese specialities if you don't fancy raw fish. The lunch bento deals are a steal. It's BYOB (corkage charged), and evening bookings are recommended. There's another branch (p153) in the IFSC.

YAMAMORI SUSHI
JAPANESE **$$**

Map p252 (www.yamamorinoodles.ie; 38-39 Lower Ormond Quay; sushi €4-4.50, mains €17-35; ⊙noon-10.30pm; 🚋all city centre) A sibling of the long-established Yamamori on South Great George's Street (p70), this large restaurant – spread across two converted Georgian houses and including a bamboo garden – does Japanese with great aplomb, serving up all kinds of favourites from steaming bowls of ramen to a delicious *nami moriawase* (sushi platter).

WUFF
INTERNATIONAL **$$**

Map p252 (23 Benburb St; mains €18-24; ⊙7.30am-4pm Mon-Wed, 7.30am-10pm Thu & Fri, 10am-10pm Sat, 10am-4pm Sun; 🚋25, 25A, 66, 67 from city centre, 🚋Museum) This neighbourhood bistro does excellent breakfasts and brunches – the truffle-infused poached eggs with Gruyère on toast are divine – as well as fine dinner mains that feature fish, duck, beef and a couple of veggie options.

WOOLLEN MILLS
MODERN IRISH **$$**

Map p252 (www.thewoollenmills.com; 42 Lower Ormond Quay; sandwiches €10-11, mains €15-25; ⊙9am-11pm Mon-Fri, 9am-4pm & 5-11pm Sat, noon-4pm & 5-10.30pm Sun; 🚋all city centre) Styling itself as a modern Irish brasserie, this newish restaurant spread over two floors serves a spruced-up version of Irish farmhouse cooking, from tasty sandwiches to dishes such as smoked pork belly. For over a century the building was a much-loved knitwear shop (James Joyce worked here for a time), so you're dining in a piece of local history.

HOT STOVE
MODERN IRISH **$$**

Map p252 (www.thehotstove.ie; 38-39 W Parnell Sq; mains €16-30; ⊙noon-2.30pm & 5-9.30pm Tue-Fri, 5.30-10pm Sat; 🚋3, 10, 11, 13, 16, 19, 22 from city centre) This elegant restaurant serves locally sourced, beautifully prepared Irish dishes including pork belly, a changing selection of fish dishes and the ubiquitous steak. The wine list is excellent and the service is right on point.

ENOTECA DELLE LANGHE
ITALIAN **$$**

Map p252 (Bloom's Lane; mains €14-20; ⊙12.30pm-midnight; 🚋Jervis) Developer, Italophile and, latterly, outspoken parliamentarian Mick Wallace's Italian Quarter – as the lane between Ormond Quay and Great Strand St is known – has a trio of eateries that serve simple pastas, antipasti and cheeses. It also has an excellent selection of Piedmontese wines.

★CHAPTER ONE
MODERN IRISH **$$$**

Map p252 (🖉01-873 2266; www.chapterone restaurant.com; 18 N Parnell Sq; 2-course lunch €50, 4-course dinner €85; ⊙12.30-2pm Tue-Fri, 7.30-10.30pm Tue-Sat; 🚋3, 10, 11, 13, 16, 19, 22 from city centre) Flawless haute cuisine and a relaxed, welcoming atmosphere make this Michelin-starred restaurant in the basement of the Dublin Writers Museum our choice for best dinner experience in town. The food is French-inspired contemporary Irish, the menus change regularly and the service is top-notch. The three-course pretheatre menu (€37.50) is great if you're going to the Gate (p144) around the corner.

MORRISON GRILL
INTERNATIONAL **$$$**

Map p252 (🖉01-878 2999; www.morrisonhotel.ie; Morrison Hotel, Lower Ormond Quay; mains €18-31; ⊙noon-10pm; 🚋all city centre) The main eatery of the newly refurbished Morrison Hotel is really a very fancy grill whose specialities are meats cooked in Ireland's only Josper indoor barbecue oven. If you don't fancy steaks, burgers or grilled fish, there's a selection of other main courses, but the real treat here is food cooked at over 260°C.

WINDING STAIR
MODERN IRISH $$$

Map p252 (✆01-873 7320; www.winding-stair. com; 40 Lower Ormond Quay; 2-course lunch €20, mains €21-28; ⊙noon-5pm & 5.30-10.30pm; ☐all city centre) In a beautiful Georgian building that once housed the city's most beloved bookshop (the ground floor still is one), the Winding Stair's conversion to elegant restaurant has been faultless. The wonderful Irish menu – creamy fish pie, bacon and organic cabbage, steamed mussels, and Irish farmyard cheeses – coupled with an excellent wine list makes for a memorable meal.

🍷 DRINKING & 🍸 NIGHTLIFE

WALSHE'S
PUB

Map p252 (6 Stoneybatter; ⊙10.30am-11.30pm Mon-Thu, to 12.30am Fri & Sat, noon-11pm Sun; ☐25, 25A, 66, 67 from city centre, ☐Museum) If the snug is free, a drink in Walshe's is about as pure a traditional experience as you'll have in any pub in the city; if it isn't, you'll have to make do with the old-fashioned bar, where the friendly staff and brilliant clientele (a mix of locals and hipster imports) are a treat. A proper Dublin pub.

COBBLESTONE
PUB

Map p252 (N King St; ⊙4.30-11.30pm Mon-Thu, to 12.30am Fri & Sat, from 1.30pm Sat & Sun; ☐Smithfield) This pub in the heart of Smithfield has a great atmosphere in its cosy back room, where there are superb nightly music sessions performed by traditional musicians (especially Thursday) and up-and-coming folk acts.

DICE BAR
BAR

Map p252 (✆01-674 6710; www.dicebar.com; 79 Queen St; ⊙4pm-midnight Mon-Wed, 4pm-1am Fri & Sat, 5-11.30pm Sun; ☐25, 25A, 66, 67 from city centre, ☐Museum) Co-owned by Huey from the Fun Lovin' Criminals, the Dice Bar looks like something you might find on New York's Lower East Side. Its dodgy locale, black-and-red painted interior, dripping candles and stressed seating, combined with rocking DJs most nights, make it a magnet for Dublin hipsters. It has Guinness and local microbrews.

PANTIBAR
GAY & LESBIAN

Map p252 (www.pantibar.com; 7-8 Capel St; ⊙5-11.30pm Mon, Wed & Sun, to 2am Tue, to 2.30am

LOCAL KNOWLEDGE

ONE FOOT IN THE GRAVE
A contender for best pub in Dublin is **John Kavanagh's** (Gravediggers; ✆01-830 7978; 1 Prospect Sq; ☐13, 19, 19A from O'Connell St) of Glasnevin, more commonly known as the Gravediggers because the employees from the adjacent cemetery had a secret serving hatch so that they could drink on the job. Founded in 1833, it is reputedly Dublin's oldest family-owned pub: the current owners are the sixth generation of Kavanaghs to be in charge. Inside, it's as traditional a boozer as you could hope: stone floors, lacquered wooden wall panels and all. In summer time the green of the square is full of drinkers basking in the sun, while inside the hardened locals ensure that ne'er a hint of sunshine disturbs some of the best Guinness in town. An absolute classic.

Thu-Sat; ☐all city centre) A raucous, fun gay bar owned by Rory O'Neill, aka Panti, star of 2015's acclaimed documentary *The Queen of Ireland,* about the struggle for equality that climaxes in the historic marriage referendum of May 2015. The bar has become a place of LGBT pilgrimage – and no holds-barred enjoyment.

WIGWAM
BAR

Map p252 (www.wigwamdublin.com; 54 Middle Abbey St; ⊙11am-11.30pm Mon-Thu, to 2.30am Fri & Sat; ☐all city centre, ☐Abbey) The latest venture by the Bodytonic crew, this excellent new bar serves 50 types of craft beer on the ground floor and excellent music in the basement bar, where top-notch DJs play regularly.

HUGHES' BAR
PUB

Map p252 (19 Chancery St; ⊙10.30am-11.30pm Mon-Thu, to 12.30am Fri & Sat, noon-11pm Sun; ☐25, 66, 67, 90 from city centre, ☐Four Courts) Traditional purists love the nightly music sessions at this pub, which by day caters to barristers, solicitors and their clients from the nearby Four Courts – all of whom probably need a pint, but for different reasons! Although the playing is very good, the atmosphere is a little lacking and the sessions can be a bit dead.

FLOWING TIDE PUB

Map p252 (9 Lower Abbey St; ◷10.30am-12.30am Mon-Sat, to 11pm Sun; ⊟all city centre, ⊡Abbey) This longtime stalwart of Dublin's theatre-going community – the Abbey (p144) is directly across the street – has been given a spit shine in recent years, but who says that chrome and polished wood isn't conducive to a post-theatre drink and natter?

GRAND SOCIAL BAR

Map p252 (☑01-874 0076; www.thegrandso cial.ie; 35 Lower Liffey St; ◷4pm-2.30am Thu-Sat, to 11.30pm Sun-Wed; ⊟all city centre, ⊡Jervis) This multipurpose venue hosts club nights, comedy and live-music gigs, and is a decent bar for a drink. It's spread across three floors, each of which has a different theme: the Parlour downstairs is a cosy, old-fashioned bar; the midlevel Ballroom is where the dancing is; and the upstairs Loft hosts a variety of events.

OVAL PUB

Map p252 (☑01-872 1259; 78 Middle Abbey St; ⊟all city centre, ⊡Abbey) This is a great little pub, where young and old come together in conversation and rich, creamy pints go down a treat. The Tardis effect is evident once you walk through the door: it is much bigger than it looks from the outside, spreading over three floors.

SACKVILLE LOUNGE PUB

Map p252 (Sackville Pl; ◷11am-11.30pm Mon-Thu, to 12.30am Fri & Sat, noon-11pm Sun; ⊟all city centre, ⊡Abbey) This tiny 19th-century, one-room, wood-panelled bar lies just off O'Connell St and is popular with actors from the nearby Abbey Theatre (p144), as well as a disproportionate number of

elderly drinkers. It's a good pub for a solitary pint.

QUAY 14 BAR

Map p252 (☑01-878 2999; Morrison Hotel, Upper Ormond Quay; ◷9am-11pm Sun-Thu, to 12.30am Fri & Sat; ⊟all city centre, ⊡Jervis) Sleek and contemporary, the Morrison Hotel's main bar is perfectly adequate if you fancy an evening in a bar that is indistinguishable from a fancy hotel bar found in any city pretty much anywhere.

☆ ENTERTAINMENT

ABBEY THEATRE THEATRE

Map p252 (☑01-878 7222; www.abbeytheatre. ie; Lower Abbey St; performances 8pm Mon-Sat, matinees 2.30pm Sat; ⊟all city centre, ⊡Abbey) Ireland's national theatre was founded by WB Yeats in 1904 and was a central player in the development of a consciously native cultural identity. Its relevance has waned dramatically in recent decades but it still provides a mix of Irish classics (Synge, O'Casey etc), established international names (Shepard, Mamet) and contemporary talent (O'Rowe, Carr et al).

Debate over the theatre's home – an ugly, purpose-built box from 1966 – has been silenced by economic realities, and so the city's theatregoers have had to make do with an acoustic makeover that has improved the experience of going to a play. Monday performances are cheaper.

GATE THEATRE THEATRE

Map p252 (☑01-874 4045; www.gatetheatre. ie; 1 Cavendish Row; ◷performances 7.30pm Mon-Sat, matinees 2.30pm Wed; ⊟all city centre)

DA NORT'SOYID & THE SOUTHSYDE

It is commonly assumed that the southside is totally posh and the northside is a derelict slum – it makes the jokes easier to make and the prejudices easier to maintain. But the truth is a little more complex. The 'southside' generally refers to Dublin 4 and the fancy suburbs immediately west and south – conveniently ignoring the traditionally working-class neighbourhoods in southwestern Dublin like Bluebell and Tallaght. North Dublin is huge, but the northside tag is usually applied to the inner suburbs, where incomes are lower, accents are more pronouncedly Dublin and – most recently – the influx of foreign nationals is more in evidence. All Dubliners are familiar with the posh twit stereotype born and raised on the southside, but there's another kind of Dubliner, usually from the middle-class districts of northern Dublin, who affects a salt-of-the-earth accent while talking about the 'gee-gees' and says things like 'tis far from sushi we was rared' while tucking into a *maki* roll.

The city's most elegant theatre, housed in a late-18th-century building, features a generally unflappable repertory of classic Irish, American and European plays. Orson Welles and James Mason played here early in their careers. Even today it is the only theatre in town where you might see established international movie stars work on their credibility with a theatre run.

LIGHTHOUSE CINEMA CINEMA

Map p252 (☑01-8797601; www.lighthousecinema.ie; Smithfield Plaza; ☑all city centre, ☑Smithfield) The most impressive cinema in town is this snazzy four-screener in a stylish building just off Smithfield Plaza. The menu is strictly art house, and the cafe-bar on the ground floor is perfect for discussing the merits of German Expressionism.

ACADEMY LIVE MUSIC

Map p252 (☑01-877 9999; www.theacademydublin.com; 57 Middle Abbey St; ☑all city centre, ☑Abbey) A terrific midsized venue, the Academy's stage has been graced by an impressive list of performers, from Nick Cave's Bad Seeds to '80s superstar Nik Kershaw. It's also the place to hear those unknown names who stand a better-than-even chance of making it somewhere.

LAUGHTER LOUNGE COMEDY

Map p252 (☑1800 266 339; www.laughterlounge.com; 4-8 Eden Quay; from €20; ☑doors open 7.30pm; ☑all city centre) Dublin's only specially designated comedy theatre is where you'll find those comics too famous for the smaller pub stages but not famous enough to sell out the city's bigger venues. Think comedians on the way up (or on the way down).

AMBASSADOR THEATRE THEATRE

Map p252 (☑1890 925 100; http://ambassadordublin.com; S Parnell Sq; ☑all city centre) The Ambassador started life as a theatre and then became a cinema. It's now primarily an exhibition and performance space, hosting everything from contemporary science exhibits to live action performances. Not much has changed inside; if you get the opportunity to do so, it's worth checking out the retro interior.

CINEWORLD MULTIPLEX CINEMA

Map p252 (☑0818 304 204; www.cineworld.ie; Parnell Centre, Parnell St; ☑all city centre) This 17-screen cinema shows only commercial

releases. The seats are comfy, the concession stand is huge and the selection of pick 'n' mix could induce a sugar seizure. It lacks the charm of the older-style cinemas, but we like it anyway.

SAVOY CINEMA

Map p252 (☑01-874 6000; Upper O'Connell St; ☑from 2pm; ☑all city centre) The Savoy is a five-screen, first-run cinema, and has late-night shows at weekends. Savoy Cinema 1 is the largest in the country and its enormous screen is the perfect way to view really spectacular blockbuster movies.

 # SHOPPING

WINDING STAIR BOOKS

Map p252 (☑01-872 6576; www.winding-stair.com/bookshop; 40 Lower Ormond Quay; ☑10am-6pm Mon-Wed & Fri, to 7pm Thu & Sat, noon-6pm Sun; ☑all city centre) There was a public outcry when this creaky old place closed a few years ago, but it soon reopened and Dublin's bohemians, students and literati can once more thumb the fine selection of new and secondhand books crammed into heaving bookcases. After browsing, head up the winding stairs to the excellent restaurant (p143).

ARNOTT'S DEPARTMENT STORE

Map p252 (☑01-805 0400; 12 Henry St; ☑10am-6pm Mon-Wed, Fri & Sat, to 7pm Thu, noon-6pm Sun; ☑all city centre) Occupying a huge block with entrances on Henry, Liffey and Abbey Sts, this is our favourite of Dublin's department stores. It stocks virtually everything, from garden furniture to high fashion, and it's all relatively affordable.

DUBLIN CITY GALLERY – HUGH LANE SHOP ARTS & CRAFTS

Map p252 (N Parnell Sq, Charlemont House, Northside; ☑10am-6pm Tue-Thu, to 5pm Fri & Sat, 11am-5pm Sun) A cultural playground for adults, where you can dig out cubist fridge magnets, huge po-mo hanging mobiles, masterpiece colour-by-number prints, cloth puppets, unusual wooden toys and beautiful art and pop culture hardbacks.

JERVIS CENTRE SHOPPING CENTRE

Map p252 (☑01-878 1323; Jervis St; ☑9am-6.30pm Mon-Wed, Fri & Sat, to 7pm Thu, 11am-6.30pm Sun; ☑all city centre) This modern, domed mall is a veritable shrine to the British chain store. Boots, Topshop, Debenhams, Argos, Dixons, M&S and Miss Selfridge all get a look-in.

PENNEY'S   DEPARTMENT STORE
Map p252 (☎01-888 0500; www.primark.co.uk; 47 Mary St; ◷8.30am-8pm Mon-Wed, to 9pm Thu & Fri, to 7pm Sat, 10.30am-7pm Sun; ▣all city centre) Ireland's cheapest department

O'CONNELL STREET

The grand dame of Dublin thoroughfares is the imperially wide O'Connell St, a street that has played a central role in key episodes of Dublin's – and the nation's – history. None more so than the 1916 Easter Rising, when the proclamation announcing Ireland's independence was read out to a slightly bemused crowd from the steps of the **General Post Office** (p134).

History

The street owes its existence to the efforts of Luke Gardiner, Dublin's premier Georgian developer, who laid out plans for a grand boulevard to reflect the exalted status of the neighbourhood. The whole project was completed in 1794 – just seven short years before the Act of Union closed the doors on an independent Irish parliament and led many of the city's aristocrats to leave Dublin for good. For much of the next two centuries Sackville St (as it was called until 1924) fell into decline. Its handsome residences were partly converted into slum dwellings for the city's burgeoning poor.

The destruction of 1916 didn't do the street any favours, but the real damage to O'Connell St occurred in the decades after WWII, when the street fell into the care of fast-food outlets, ugly shops and amusement arcades. A huge program of redevelopment has seen the street restored to something approaching its former grandeur, including the construction of new, pedestrian-friendly pavements, a central mall and refurbished shopfronts.

Statuary

O'Connell St is lined with statues of Irish history's good and great. The big daddy of them all is the 'Liberator' himself, **Daniel O'Connell** (1775–1847; Map p252; Lower O'Connell St; ▣all city centre, ▣Abbey), completed in 1880, whose massive bronze bulk soars above the street at the bridge end. The four winged figures at his feet represent O'Connell's supposed virtues: patriotism, courage, fidelity and eloquence. Dubs began to refer to the street as O'Connell St soon after the monument was erected; its name was officially changed after independence.

Heading away from the river, past a monument to **William Smith O'Brien** (1803–64), leader of the Young Irelanders, is a statue that easily rivals O'Connell's for drama: just outside the GPO is the spread-armed figure of trade-union leader **Jim Larkin** (1876–1947; Map p252; Lower O'Connell St; ▣all city centre, ▣Abbey). His finest moment came when he helped organise the general strike in 1913 – the pose catches him in full flow, urging workers to rise up for their rights. We're with you, comrade.

Next up and difficult to miss is the **Spire** (p135), but just below it, on pedestrianised North Earl St, is the detached figure of **James Joyce** (Map p252; N Earl St; ▣all city centre, ▣Abbey), looking on the fast and shiny version of 21st-century O'Connell St with a bemused air. Dubs have lovingly dubbed him the 'prick with the stick' and we're sure Joyce would have loved the vulgar rhyme.

Further on is **Father Theobald Mathew** (1790–1856; Map p252; Upper O'Connell St; ▣all city centre, ▣Abbey), the 'apostle of temperance'. There can't have been a tougher gig in Ireland, but he led a spirited campaign against 'the demon drink' in the 1840s and converted hundreds of thousands to teetotalism.

The top of the street is completed by the imposing statue of **Charles Stewart Parnell** (1846–91; Map p252; Upper O'Connell St; ▣all city centre, ▣Abbey), the 'uncrowned king of Ireland', who was an advocate of Home Rule and became a political victim of Irish intolerance.

store is a northside favourite, a place to find all kinds of everything without paying a fortune for it – it's the best place in town for men's socks and jocks. True, the stuff you'll find here isn't guaranteed to last, but at prices like these, why quibble over quality?

MOORE STREET MARKET   MARKET

Map p252 (Moore St; ⏱8am-4pm Mon-Sat; ▣all city centre) An open-air, steadfastly 'Old Dublin' market, with fruit, fish and flowers. Traditional vendors hawk cheap cigarettes, tobacco and chocolate among the new wave of Chinese and Nigerians selling phonecards and hair extensions. Don't try to buy just one banana though – if it says 10 for €1, that's what it is.

EASON'S   BOOKS

Map p252 (☏01-873 3811; www.easons.ie; 40 Lower O'Connell St; ⏱10am-6pm Mon-Wed, Fri & Sat, to 7pm Thu, noon-6pm Sun; ▣all city centre) The biggest selection of magazines and foreign newspapers in the whole country can be found on the ground floor of this huge bookshop near the GPO, along with literally dozens of browsers leafing through mags with ne'er a thought of purchasing one.

ACTIVITIES

CITY SIGHTSEEING   BUS TOUR

Map p252 (www.citysightseeingdublin.ie; 14 Upper O'Connell St; adult/student €19/17; ▣all city centre, ▣Abbey) A typical hop-on, hop-off tour should last around 1½ hours and lead you up and down O'Connell St, past Trinity College and St Stephen's Green, before heading up to the Guinness Storehouse and back around the north quays, via the main entrance to Phoenix Park. Tours run every eight to 15 minutes, from 9am to 6pm.

JAMES JOYCE WALKING TOUR   WALKING TOUR

Map p252 (☏01-878 8547; www.jamesjoyce.ie; 35 N Great George's St; adult/student €10/8; ⏱2pm Tue, Thu & Sat; ▣3, 10, 11, 11A, 13, 16, 16A, 19, 19A, 22 from city centre) Joyce lived, schooled and lost his virginity on the north side – and he put it all down on paper with cartographic precision from his self-imposed continental exile. You can explore all of the northside attractions associated with the bespectacled one on a 1¼-hour tour run by the James Joyce Cultural Centre (p135).

DUBLIN BUS TOURS   BUS TOUR

Map p252 (www.dublinsightseeing.ie; 59 Upper O'Connell St; €22-27; ⏱daily; ▣all city centre, ▣Abbey) Offers a variety of tours, including the hop-on, hop-off Dublin City Tour, Ghost Bus Tour, Coast and Castles Tour, and South Coast and Gardens Tour.

1. Samuel Beckett Bridge (p214)
Named for the legendary playwright, this bridge over the River Liffey blends Docklands' modern architecture with Dublin's literary heritage.

2. Phoenix Park (p130)
This 709-hectare park houses a herd of fallow deer, along with the Irish president, the American ambassador and Europe's oldest zoo.

3. Old Jameson Distillery (p134)
Finish your tour with a tasting at this recreated factory and museum.

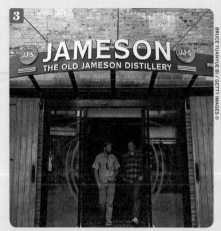

CEZARY ZAREBSKI PHOTOGRPAHY / GETTY IMAGES ©

Docklands & the Grand Canal

Neighborhood Top Five

❶ Jeanie Johnston (p152) Visting this working replica of a 19th-century 'coffin' ship, as the barques transporting emigrants during the Famine were known.

❷ Famine Memorial (p152) Contemplating the Famine while walking gently among Rowan Gillespie's thought-provoking bronze statues.

❸ Bord Gáis Energy Theatre (p155) Attending a gig at this spectacular theatre designed by Daniel Libeskind.

❹ Poolbeg Lighthouse (p153) Enjoying the stunning views of the bay and city with a late-afternoon stroll down the south wall to this elegant lighthouse.

❺ Sea Safaris (p156) Getting the historical tour of Dublin and its port, from the watery perspective of a sea-and-river cruise.

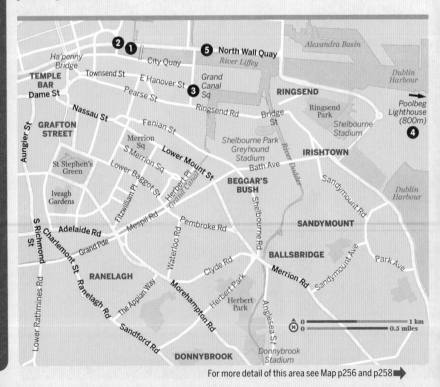

For more detail of this area see Map p256 and p258 ➡

Explore Docklands & the Grand Canal

Although much of the Docklands development that transformed the eastern end of the Liffey towards Dublin Port is given over to office and apartment blocks, there are parts of 'Canary Dwarf' (as it's jokingly named, after London's Canary Wharf) that are worth exploring at ground level. The aesthetic of the area is the 10,000-sq-metre Grand Canal Sq, designed by American landscape architect Martha Schwartz. Flanking its northwestern side is the magnificent Bord Gáis Energy Theatre (2010), designed by Daniel Libeskind and named after its primary sponsor, one of Ireland's leading energy providers. Stretching across the square from its entrance is a red 'carpet' – a series of red, resin-glass angled sticks that glow – and a green one – made up of polygon-shaped planters filled with marshlike vegetation.

On the north banks of the Liffey, the standout buildings are the snazzy National Convention Centre (2010), designed by Kevin Roche; the Custom House (1781–91), a colossal Georgian building topped by a copper dome; and the city's premier indoor venue, the O2, which is the main attraction in the Point Village, a development that also includes a cinema and a hotel.

Local Life

→**Sustenance** For proper Neapolitan-style pizza, Paulie's Pizza (p153) is one of the best in town; just around the corner (and owned by the same two brothers) is the equally popular Juniors (p153), which attracts the trendy crowd with its version of a Brooklyn eatery.

→**Imbibe** If you want to celebrate (or commiserate) with fans after a game at the Aviva Stadium, you'll find plenty of company in the Chophouse (p155) and across the street in the more traditional Slattery's (p155). Closer to the city centre, John Mulligan's (p155) is one of Dublin's most famous traditional pubs.

→**Explore** Irish emigration is a major theme in the Docklands – aboard the Jeanie Johnston (p152), wandering among Rowan Gillespie's haunting statues (p152), and exploring the hands-on, interactive exhibits of the new Epic Ireland (p152) museum, devoted to the Irish diaspora.

Getting There & Away

→**Bus** The most convenient public transport option is the bus – Nos 1, 47, 56A and 77A go from Dame St to the edge of Grand Canal Sq. For the north side, bus 151 goes from Bachelor's Walk to the Docklands. **Bus 44** (Map p256) goes to Powerscourt.

→**Tram** The Luas Red Line terminus is at the Point Village.

→**Train** The DART stops at Grand Canal Quay.

Lonely Planet's Top Tip

To quell your hunger or quench your thirst, head southwest of the Grand Canal Dock to the junction of Haddington Rd, Upper Grand Canal St and Bath Ave, where you'll find a handful of terrific restaurants and popular pubs.

Best Places to Eat

→ Juniors (p153)
→ Paulie's Pizza (p153)
→ Mourne Seafood Bar (p153)
→ Workshop Gastropub (p153)

For reviews, see p153➡

Best Places to Drink

→ Beggar's Bush (p155)
→ Slattery's (p155)
→ John Mulligan's (p155)

For reviews, see p155➡

Best For Modern Architecture

→ National Convention Centre
→ Bord Gáis Energy Theatre (p155)
→ Marker (p188)

For reviews, see p155➡

◉ SIGHTS

CUSTOM HOUSE
MUSEUM

Map p256 (Custom House Quay; ⊘10am-5pm Mon-Fri, 2-5pm Sat & Sun; ☐all city centre) Georgian genius James Gandon (1743–1823) announced his arrival on the Dublin scene with this magnificent building (1781–91), constructed just past Eden Quay at a wide stretch in the River Liffey. It's a colossal, neoclassical pile that stretches for 114m topped by a copper dome, beneath which the visitor centre (p153) features a small museum on Gandon and the history of the building.

Best appreciated from the south side of the Liffey, its fine detail deserves closer inspection. Below the frieze are heads representing the gods of Ireland's 13 principal rivers; the sole female head, above the main door, represents the River Liffey. The cattle heads honour Dublin's beef trade, and the statues behind the building represent Africa, America, Asia and Europe. Set into the dome are four clocks and, above that, a 5m-high statue of Hope.

JEANIE JOHNSTON
MUSEUM

Map p256 (www.jeaniejohnston.ie; Custom House Quay; adult/child €9.50/5; ⊘tours hourly 11am-3pm; ☐all city centre, ☐George's Dock) One of the city's most original tourist attractions is an exact working replica of a 19th-century 'coffin ship', as the sailing boats that transported starving emigrants away from Ireland during the Famine were gruesomely known. A small on-board museum details the harrowing plight of a typical journey, which usually took around 47 days.

This particular ship, a three-masted barque originally built in Quebec in 1847, made 16 transatlantic voyages, carrying more than 2500 people, and never suffered a single death. The ship also operates as a Sail Training vessel, with journeys taking place from May to September. If you are visiting during these times, check the website for details of when it will be in dock.

EPIC IRELAND
MUSEUM

Map p256 (☑01-531 3688; epicirelandchq.com; CHQ Bldg, Custom House Quay; adult/child €16/8; ⊘9am-7pm; ☐George's Dock) Dublin's newest museum is a high-tech, interactive exploration of emigration and its effect on Ireland and the 70 million or so people spread throughout the world that claim Irish ancestry. Start your visit with a 'passport' and

proceed through 21 galleries examining why they left, where they went and how they maintained their relationship with their ancestral home.

NATIONAL PRINT MUSEUM
MUSEUM

Map p258 (☑01-660 3770; www.nationalprint museum.ie; Haddington Rd, Garrison Chapel, Beggar's Bush; adult/concession €3.50/2; ⊘9am-5pm Mon-Fri, 2-5pm Sat & Sun, tours 11.30am & 2.30pm; ☐7, 8 or 45 from city centre, ☐DART to Grand Canal Dock) You don't have to be into printing to enjoy this quirky little museum, where personalised guided tours are offered in a delightfully casual and compelling way. A video looks at the history of printing in Ireland and then you wander through the various (still working) antique presses amid the smell of ink and metal.

The guides are excellent and can tailor the tours to suit your special interests – for example, anyone interested in history can get a detailed account of the difficulties encountered by the rebels of 1916 when they tried to have the proclamation printed. Upstairs there are lots of old newspaper pages recording important episodes in Irish history over the last century.

GRAND CANAL SQUARE
SQUARE

Map p256 (☐Grand Canal Dock) The square was designed by American landscape artist Martha Schwartz and opened in 2008. Its most distinctive feature is the red 'carpet' made of bright red resin-glass paving covered with red glowing angled light sticks.

FAMINE MEMORIAL
MEMORIAL

Map p256 (Custom House Quay; ☐all city centre) Just east of Custom House is one of Dublin's most thought-provoking examples of public art: the set of life-size bronze figures (1997) by Rowan Gillespie known simply as 'Famine'. Designed to commemorate the ravages of the Great Hunger (1845–51), their haunted, harrowed look testifies to a journey that was both hazardous and unwelcome.

The location of the sculptures is also telling, for it was from this very point in 1846 that one of the first 'coffin ships' (as they quickly came to be called) set sail for the US. Steerage fare on the *Perseverance* was £3 and 210 passengers made that first journey, landing in New York on 18 May 1846, with all passengers and crew intact.

In June 2007 a second series of Famine sculptures by Rowan Gillespie was unveiled on the quayside in Toronto's Ireland Park

WORTH A DETOUR

POOLBEG LIGHTHOUSE

One of the city's most rewarding walks is a stroll along the Great South Wall to the Poolbeg Lighthouse (that red tower visible in the middle of Dublin Bay). The lighthouse dates from 1768, but it was redesigned and rebuilt in 1820. To get there, you'll have to make your own way from Ringsend (which is reachable by bus 1, 47, 56A, 77A or 84N from the city centre), past the power station to the start of the wall (it's about 1km). It's not an especially long walk – about 800m or so – but it will give you a stunning view of the bay and the city behind you, a view best enjoyed just before sunset on a summer's evening.

by Irish president Mary McAleese to commemorate the arrival of Famine refugees in the New World.

CUSTOM HOUSE VISITOR CENTRE MUSEUM
Map p256 (Custom House Quay; admission €1.50; ⊗10am-12.30pm Mon-Fri, 2-5pm Sat & Sun mid-Mar–Oct, closed Mon, Tue & Sat Nov–mid-Mar; ⬛ all city centre) Beneath the Custom House's copper dome, this visitor centre features a small museum on the building's history, and on its architect, James Gandon.

WATERWAYS VISITOR CENTRE MUSEUM
Map p256 (☑01-677 7510; www.waterwaysireland visitorcentre.org; Grand Canal Quay; adult/child €8/4; ⊗10am-6pm Wed-Sun May-Sep, to 5pm Mon-Fri Oct-Apr; ⬛Grand Canal Dock) The 'box in the docks' is a snazzy centre documenting the history of Ireland's waterways and where visitors can 'drive' a barge. It also runs excellent walking tours (p156) of the Grand Canal Docks during the summer months.

 EATING

★**JUNIORS DELI & CAFE** ITALIAN $$
Map p258 (☑01-664 3648; www.juniors.ie; 2 Bath Ave; mains €17-26; ⊗8.30am-2.30pm & 5.30-10pm Mon-Fri, 11am-3pm & 5.30-10.30pm Sat, 11am-3.30pm Sun; ⬛3 from city centre, ⬛Grand Canal Dock) Cramped and easily mistaken for any old cafe, Juniors is anything but ordinary. Designed to imitate a New York deli, the food (Italian-influenced, all locally sourced produce) is delicious, the atmosphere always buzzing (it's often hard to get a table) and the ethos top-notch, which is down to the two brothers who run the place.

WORKSHOP GASTROPUB MODERN IRISH $$
Map p256 (Kennedy's; ☑01-677 0626; 10 George's Quay; lunch mains €7-9, dinner mains €10-24; ⊗noon-3pm Mon-Fri plus 5-9pm Mon-Sat; ☑; ⬛ all city centre, ⬛Tara St) Take a traditional pub and introduce a chef with a vision: hey presto you've got a gastropub (surprisingly one of the few in the city) serving burgers, moules frites and sandwiches for lunch, and classic dishes such as spring lamb and beer-battered fish and chips for dinner. There are excellent vegetarian options too.

MOURNE SEAFOOD BAR SEAFOOD $$
Map p256 (www.mourneseafood.com; Millennium Tower, Charlotte Quay; mains €19-22; ⊗5-9pm Mon-Thu & Sat, noon-3pm & 5-10pm Fri; ⬛Grand Canal Dock) The dining room is a glass shell, with 360-degree views of the Grand Canal Dock. The seafood is plentiful and fresh – appetisers range from oysters to salt-and-chilli squid, main courses include whole fish like sea bream and trout, pasta dishes with scallops and more international flavours like a Thai fish curry or moules frites in a Provençale sauce.

PAULIE'S PIZZA ITALIAN $$
Map p258 (www.juniors.ie; 58 Upper Grand Canal St; pizzas €12-17; ⊗6-10pm; ☑; ⬛3 from city centre, ⬛Grand Canal Dock) At the heart of this lovely, occasionally boisterous restaurant is a Neapolitan pizza oven, used to create some of the best pizzas in town. Margheritas, *biancas* (no tomato sauce), calzoni and other Neapolitan specialities are the real treat, but there's also room for a classic New York slice and a few local creations.

MUSASHI IFSC JAPANESE $$
Map p256 (☑01-555 73 73; www.musashidublin.com; Unit 2, Burton Hall, Custom House Sq; mains €12-17; ⊗noon-10pm Sun-Thu, to 11pm Fri & Sat; ⬛George's Dock) Freshly made sushi and sashimi and other Japanese specialities, including a particularly tasty *tatsuta* chicken, served to an appreciative lunchtime and after-work crowd. It is the sister restaurant to Musashi Noodles & Sushi Bar (p142) on Capel St.

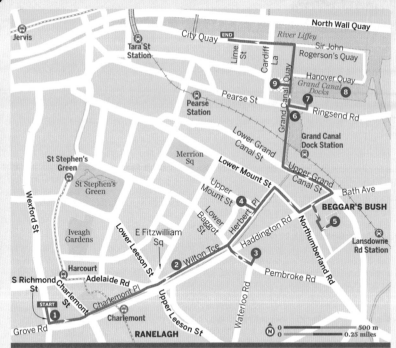

🏃 Neighbourhood Walk
Portobello Pub to City Quay

START PORTOBELLO PUB, SOUTH RICH-MOND ST
END CITY QUAY
LENGTH 5KM; 2½ HOURS

Begin at the ❶ **Portobello Pub**, a popular watering hole built to service the solid hunger of workers building the canal.

Turn left at the Grand Canal and begin your stroll along the towpath. About 300m past Leeson St Bridge is the ❷ **Patrick Kavanagh statue**, relaxing on a bench. The Monaghan-born poet is immortalised in the spot he loved most in Dublin – where he couldn't be barred.

When you get to Baggot St Bridge take a right onto Baggot St and refuel at ❸ **Searson's** (42–44 Upper Baggot St), a popular bar. Return to the canal and continue eastwards, diverting left at Upper Mount St for ❹ **St Stephen's Church**, a Greek Revival structure known as the 'pepper canister' on account of its curious shape.

Back on the towpath, turn right at North-umberland Rd and left onto Haddington Rd

for one of Dublin's secret little treasures (the vast majority of Dubliners don't even know about it): the ❺ **National Print Museum** (p152). Housed in the old Beggar's Bush barracks, this is a surprisingly interesting museum, especially if you're a fan of old books and the printing process in general.

Turn left onto Upper Grand Canal St, then right into Grand Canal Quay for the ❻ **Waterways Visitor Centre** (p153), where you can find out everything you could possibly want to know about the construction of the country's canals and waterways. The ❼ **Mourne Seafood Bar** (p153) is a great spot for a bit of lunch if you're feeling hungry, but there are options around the whole of the dock.

Before heading back to the city, take a stroll around Grand Canal Sq – you can try some wakeboarding at ❽ **Wakedock** (p156) if you like – and then sit outside and take in Daniel Libeskind's ❾ **Bord Gáis Energy Theatre** (p155).

Walk north to Sir John Rogerson's Quay and walk west along City Quay.

HERBSTREET
FUSION **$$**

Map p256 (www.herbstreet.ie; Hanover Quay; mains €13-19; ⊘8.30am-10pm Mon-Fri, 10am-4pm Sat & Sun; ⊠Grand Canal Dock) ✒ Low-power hand driers, one-watt LED bulbs, second-hand furniture and strictly European wines: this eatery is taking its green responsibilities seriously. Most of the food is sourced locally, but what really makes this place a hit is the terrific brunch menu – pancakes, Irish breakfasts, Mexican-style eggs…it's all good.

ELY BAR & BRASSERIE
FUSION **$$**

Map p256 (www.elywinebar.ie; Custom House Quay; mains €16-29; ⊘noon-11pm Mon-Fri, 4pm-midnight Sat; ⊠George's Dock) ✒ Scrummy homemade burgers, bangers and mash, and wild smoked salmon salad are some of the meals served in this converted tobacco warehouse in the International Financial Services Centre (IFSC). Dishes are prepared with organic and free-range produce from the owner's family farm in County Clare, so you can be assured of the quality.

QUAY 16
FUSION **$$$**

Map p256 (☑01-817 8760; www.mvcillairne.com; MV Cill Airne, North Wall Quay; bar food €4-12, mains €19-32; ⊘noon-3pm Mon-Fri, plus 6-10pm Mon-Sat; ⊠Spencer Dock) The MV *Cill Airne,* commissioned in 1961 as a passenger liner tender, is now permanently docked along the north quays, where it serves the public as a bar, a bistro and a fine restaurant. Dishes such as Himalayan salt–aged fillet steak and pan-roasted sea bass are expertly prepared and served alongside an excellent variety of wines.

🍺 DRINKING & NIGHTLIFE

★ JOHN MULLIGAN'S
PUB

Map p256 (8 Poolbeg St; ⊘10.30am-11.30pm Mon-Thu, to 12.30am Fri & Sat, noon-11pm Sun; ⊠all city centre) This brilliant old boozer has barely changed since its establishment in 1782. It has one of the finest pints of Guinness in Dublin and a colourful crew of regulars. It's just off Fleet St, outside the eastern boundary of Temple Bar.

BEGGAR'S BUSH
PUB

Map p258 (Jack Ryan's; 115 Haddington Rd; ⊘11am-11pm; ⊠4, 7, 8, 120 from city centre, ⊠Grand Canal Dock) A staunch defender of the traditional pub aesthetic, Ryan's (as it's referred to by its older clientele) has adjusted to the modern age by adding an outside patio for good weather. Everything else, though, has remained the same, which is precisely why it's so popular with flat-capped pensioners and employees from nearby Google.

SLATTERY'S
PUB

Map p258 (☑01-668 5481; www.slatterysd4.ie; 62 Upper Grand Canal St; ⊘1-11.30pm Mon-Thu, noon-12.30am Fri & Sat, noon-11pm Sun; ⊠4, 7, 8, 120 from city centre) A decent boozer that is a favourite with rugby fans who didn't get tickets to the match – they congregate around the TVs and ebb and flow with each passage of the game. It's also popular on Friday and Saturday nights.

CHOPHOUSE
BAR

Map p258 (2 Shelbourne Rd; ⊘11am-11pm; ⊠4, 7, 8, 120 from city centre) A big sprawling bar with a variety of lounges that get packed when there's something on at Aviva Stadium.

LONG STONE
PUB

Map p256 (☑01-671 8102; 10-11 Townsend St; ⊘noon-midnight Sun-Thu, to 1am Fri & Sat; ⊠all city centre, ⊠Tara St) This is too big a boozer to be an 'old man pub', but it was established in 1754, the flagstone floors are original and the pint it serves is a good one. But this is a favourite with students from Trinity College and is usually packed with revellers on a good night out.

☆ ENTERTAINMENT

BORD GÁIS ENERGY THEATRE
THEATRE

Map p256 (☑01-677 7999; www.grandcanaltheatre.ie; Grand Canal Sq; ⊠Grand Canal Dock) Forget the uninviting sponsored name: Daniel Libeskind's masterful design is a three-tiered, 2100-capacity auditorium where you're as likely to be entertained by the Bolshoi or a touring state opera as you are to see *Disney on Ice* or Barbra Streisand. It's a magnificent venue – designed for classical, paid for by the classics.

ODEON CINEMA
CINEMA

Map p256 (www.odeoncinemas.ie; Point Village; ⊠The Point) A six-screen multiplex showing all the latest releases.

SPAR EXPRESS
BOOKING SERVICE

Map p258 (54-56 Donnybrook Rd; ⊘6am-10pm Mon-Fri & Sun, from 7am Sat) Tickets for Leinster games.

SHELBOURNE PARK
GREYHOUND STADIUM   SPECTATOR SPORT
Map p258 (✆01-668 3502, on race nights 01-202 6601; www.igb.ie; Bridge Town Rd, Ringsend; adult/child €10/6; ☻7-10.30pm Wed-Sat; 🚌3, 7, 7A, 8, 45, 84 from city centre) A top-class dog track with terrific vantage points from the glassed-in restaurant, where you can eat, bet and watch without leaving your seat.

AVIVA STADIUM   STADIUM
Map p258 (✆01-238 2300; www.avivastadium.ie; 11-12 Lansdowne Rd; 🚆Lansdowne Rd) Gleaming 50,000-capacity ground with an eye-catching curvilinear stand in the swanky neighbourhood of Donnybrook. Home to Irish rugby and football internationals.

3 ARENA   LIVE MUSIC
Map p256 (✆01-819 8888; www.3arena.ie; East Link Bridge, North Wall Quay; tickets €30-90; ☻6.30-11pm; 🚆The Point) The premier indoor venue in the city has a capacity of 23,000 and plays host to the brightest touring stars in the firmament. Bryan Adams, Dixie Chicks, Neil Young and Adele performed here in 2016.

ROYAL DUBLIN
SOCIETY SHOWGROUND   SPECTATOR SPORT
Map p258 (RDS Showground; ✆01-668 9878; Merrion Rd, Ballsbridge; 🚌7 from Trinity College) The impressive, Victorian-era showground is used for various exhibitions throughout the year. The most important annual event here is the late July **Dublin Horse Show**, which includes an international showjumping contest. Leinster rugby also plays its home matches in the 35,000-capacity arena. Ask at the tourist office for other events.

The Royal Dublin Society Showground was founded in 1731 and has had its headquarters in a number of well-known Dublin buildings, including Leinster House from 1814 to 1925. The society was involved in the foundation of the National Museum, National Library, National Gallery and National Botanic Gardens.

🛍 SHOPPING

DESIGN TOWER   ARTS & CRAFTS
Map p256 (✆01-677 5655; www.thedesigntower.com; Pearse St; ☻9am-5pm Mon-Fri; 🚆Grand Canal Dock) Housed in a 19th-century warehouse that was Dublin's first iron-structured building, this seven-storey design centre houses studios for around 20 local craftspeople, producing everything from Celtic-inspired jewellery to wall hangings and leather bags.

Some studios are open by appointment only; check the website for details.

🏃 ACTIVITIES

SEA SAFARIS   BOAT TOUR
Map p256 (✆01-668 9802; www.seasafari.ie; National Convention Centre; adult/child €20/12.50; 🚆Mayor's Square NCI) Historical tour of the River Liffey and Dublin Port, departing from outside the Convention Centre.

GRAND CANAL DOCKS
WALKING TOURS   WALKING TOUR
Map p256 (✆01-677 7510; www.waterwaysireland visitorcentre.org; Grand Canal Dock; adult/concession €8/4; ☻11.30am & 2.30pm Wed-Sun Apr-Sep; 🚆Grand Canal Quay) Hour-long walking tours of the Grand Canal Docks run by enthusiastic and highly informed guides.

WAKEDOCK   ADVENTURE SPORTS
Map p256 (www.wakedock.ie; Grand Canal Dock; 30min tuition adult/student €60/45; ☻noon-8pm Tue-Fri, 10am-8pm Sat-Sun; 🚆Grand Canal Dock) Try the relatively new sport of cable wakeboarding – waterskiing by holding on to a fixed overhead cable instead of a motorboat. The sport is shortlisted for the 2020 Olympics. You can also rent wetsuits (€2).

1916 EASTER RISING COACH TOUR   BUS TOUR
Map p256 (www.1916easter risingcoachtour.ie; Custom House Quay; adult/child €15/10) A 90-minute tour of the sites that played a part in the 1916 Easter Rising. Buy your tickets online or at the Dublin Tourism office in Suffolk St.

MARKIEVICZ
LEISURE CENTRE   HEALTH & FITNESS
Map p256 (✆01-672 9121; www.dublincity.ie; Townsend St; adult/child €6.50/3.50; ☻7am-9.45pm Mon-Thu, 7am-8.45pm Fri, 9am-5.45pm Sat, 10am-3.45pm Sun; 🚌all city centre, 🚆Tara St) This excellent fitness centre has a swimming pool, a workout room (with plenty of gym machines) and a sauna. You can swim for as long as you please, but children are only allowed at off-peak times (10am to 5.30pm Monday to Saturday).

DONNYBROOK STADIUM   STADIUM
Map p258 (www.leinsterrugby.ie; Donnybrook Rd; 🚌10, 46A from city centre) The former home of Leinster Rugby, this purpose-built, 6000-capacity arena still hosts some Leinster friendlies as well as the home matches of the Irish women's rugby team and local club sides Old Wesley and Bective Rangers.

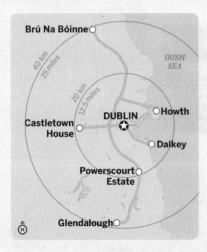

Day Trips from Dublin

Brú Na Bóinne p158
Neolithic passage tombs that are a highlight of any visit to Ireland.

Glendalough p163
The remains of an early Christian monastic settlement nestled in a beautiful glacial valley.

Howth p168
Seaside village with terrific restaurants at the foot of a bulbous head with fine walks.

Enniskerry & Powerscourt Estate p170
A Palladian mansion with a stunning garden and even better views of the surrounding countryside.

Castletown House & Around p174
Ireland's largest Palladian home, built for the 18th century's richest man.

Dalkey p175
Compact village by the sea with a nice harbour and coastal walks.

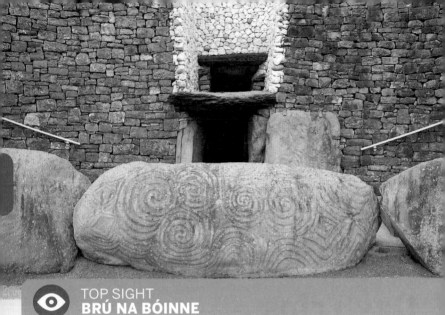

STEPHAN HOEROLD / GETTY IMAGES ©

TOP SIGHT
BRÚ NA BÓINNE

The vast Neolithic necropolis known as Brú na Bóinne (the Boyne Palace) is one of the most extraordinary sites in Europe. A thousand years older than Stonehenge, it's a powerful testament to the mind-boggling achievements of prehistoric humankind.

The complex was built to house the remains of those who were at the top of the social heap and its tombs were the largest artificial structures in Ireland until the construction of the Anglo-Norman castles 4000 years later. The area consists of many different sites; the three principal ones are Newgrange, Knowth and Dowth.

Over the centuries the tombs decayed, were covered by grass and trees, and were plundered by everybody from Vikings to Victorian treasure hunters, whose carved initials can be seen on the great stones of Newgrange. The countryside around the tombs is home to countless other ancient tumuli (burial mounds) and standing stones.

Visitor Centre

The superb interpretive centre, whose spiral design echoes that of Newgrange, features an excellent series of interactive exhibits on all aspects of pre-Celtic history, including a full-scale replica of the burial chamber at Newgrange. There's a good film introducing the complex, a decent **cafe** (dishes €4.50-12; ⊘breakfast & lunch; 🐾) and a bookshop.

Newgrange

A startling 80m in diameter and 13m high, Newgrange's white round stone walls, topped by a grass dome, look eerily futuristic. Underneath lies the finest Stone Age passage tomb in Ireland – one of the most remarkable prehistoric sites in Europe. Dating from around

DON'T MISS

➡ Newgrange
➡ Brú Na Bóinne Visitor Centre

PRACTICALITIES

➡ ☑041-988 0300
➡ www.heritageireland.ie
➡ Donore
➡ adult/child visitor centre €3/2, visitor centre & Newgrange €6/3, visitor centre & Knowth €5/3, all 3 sites €11/6
➡ ⊘9am-6.30pm May-Sep, to 5pm Nov-Jan, 9.30am-5.30pm Feb-Apr & Oct

3200 BC, it predates Egypt's pyramids by some six centuries.

The tomb's precise alignment with the sun at the time of the winter solstice suggests it was also designed to act as a calendar.

No one is quite sure of its original purpose, however – the most common theories are that it was a burial place for kings or a centre for ritual.

Newgrange's name derives from 'New Granary' (the tomb did in fact serve as a repository for wheat and grain at one stage), although a more popular belief is that it comes from the Irish for 'Cave of Gráinne', a reference to a popular Celtic myth. The Pursuit of Diarmuid and Gráinne tells of the illicit love between the woman betrothed to Fionn McCumhaill (or Finn McCool), leader of the Fianna, and Diarmuid, one of his most trusted lieutenants. When Diarmuid was fatally wounded, his body was brought to Newgrange by the god Aengus in a vain attempt to save him, and the despairing Gráinne followed him into the cave, where she remained long after he died. This suspiciously Arthurian tale (substitute Lancelot and Guinevere for Diarmuid and Gráinne) is undoubtedly a myth, but it's still a pretty good story. Newgrange also plays another role in Celtic mythology as the site where the hero Cúchulainn was conceived.

Over time, Newgrange, like Dowth and Knowth, deteriorated and at one stage was even used as a quarry. The site was extensively restored in 1962 and again in 1975.

A superbly carved **kerbstone** (picture left) with double and triple spirals guards the tomb's main entrance, but the area has been reconstructed so that visitors don't have to clamber in over it. Above the entrance is a slit, or roof-box, which lets light in. Another beautifully decorated kerbstone stands at the exact opposite side of the mound. Some experts say that a **ring of standing stones** encircled the mound, forming a great circle about 100m in diameter, but only 12 of these stones remain, with traces of others below ground level.

Holding the whole structure together are the 97 boulders of the **kerb ring**, designed to stop the mound from collapsing outwards. Eleven of these are decorated with motifs similar to those on the main entrance stone, although only three have extensive carvings.

The white quartzite that encases the tomb was originally obtained from Wicklow, 70km south – in an age before horse and wheel, it was transported by sea and then up the River Boyne. More than 200,000 tonnes of earth and stone also went into the mound.

TOP TIPS:

All visits to Brú na Bóinne start at the **Brú na Bóinne Visitor Centre** from where there's a shuttle bus to the tombs. If you turn up at either Newgrange or Knowth first, you'll be sent to the visitor centre, 4km from either site. Walking is discouraged, as the lanes are narrow and dangerous due to passing tour buses.

Allow plenty of time: an hour for the visitor centre alone, two hours to include a trip to Newgrange or Knowth, and half a day to see all three.

In summer, particularly at weekends, Brú na Bóinne gets very crowded; on peak days more than 2000 people can show up. As there are only 750 tour slots, you may not be guaranteed a visit to either of the passage tombs. Tickets are sold on a first-come, first-served basis (no advance booking). Arrive early in the morning or visit midweek and be prepared to wait. Alternatively, visiting as part of an organised tour guarantees a spot.

Tours are primarily outdoors with no shelter so bring rain gear, just in case.

Brú na Bóinne

All visits start at the **visitor centre** ❶, which has a terrific exhibit that includes a short context-setting film. From here, you board a shuttle bus that takes you to **Newgrange** ❷, where you'll go past the **kerbstone** ❸ into the **main passage** ❹ and the **burial chamber** ❺. If you're not a lucky lottery winner for the solstice, fear not – there's an artificial illumination ceremony that replicates it. If you're continuing on to tour **Knowth** ❻, you'll need to go back to the visitor centre and get on another bus; otherwise, you can drive directly to **Dowth** ❼ and visit, but only from outside (the information panels will tell you what you're looking at).

Newgrange interior passage
The passage is lined with 43 orthostats, or standing stones, averaging 1.5m in height: 22 on the left (western) side, 21 on the right (eastern) side.

Newgrange

Knowth
Roughly one third of all megalithic art in Western Europe is contained within the Knowth complex, including more than 200 decorated stones. Alongside typical motifs like spirals, lozenges and concentric circles are rare crescent shapes.

TOP TIP
Best time to visit is early morning mid-week during summer, when there are fewer tourists and no school tours.

Newgrange entrance kerbstone
Newgrange is surrounded by 97 kerbstones (24 of which are still buried), numbered sequentially from K1, the beautifully decorated entrance stone.

Dowth

Like Newgrange, Dowth's passage grave is designed to allow for a solar alignment during the winter solstice. The crater at the top was due to a clumsy attempt at excavation in 1847.

WIEDTMEDIA / GETTY IMAGES ©

FACT FILE

The winter solstice event is witnessed by a maximum of 50 people selected by lottery and their guests (one each). In 2015, 30,475 people applied.

⑦

Newgrange burial chamber
The corbelled roof of the chamber has remained intact since its construction, and is considered one of the finest of its kind in Europe.

①

BRÚ NA BÓINNE VISITOR CENTRE ©

Brú na Bóinne Visitor Centre
Opened in 1997, the modern visitor centre was heavily criticised at first as being unsuitable, but then gained plaudits for the way it was integrated into the landscape.

You can walk down the narrow 19m passage, lined with 43 stone uprights (some of them engraved), which leads into the **tomb chamber** about one third of the way into the colossal mound. The chamber has three recesses, and in these are large **basin stones** that held cremated human bones. As well as the remains, the basins would have held funeral offerings of beads and pendants, but these were stolen long before the archaeologists arrived.

Above, the massive stones support a 6m-high **corbel-vaulted roof**. A complex drainage system means that not a drop of water has penetrated the interior in 40 centuries.

Knowth

Northwest of Newgrange, the burial mound of **Knowth** was built around the same time. It has the greatest collection of passage-grave art ever uncovered in Western Europe, and has been under intermittent excavation since 1962 (you may see archaeologists at work when you visit).

Early excavations soon cleared a **passage** leading to the central chamber which, at 34m, is much longer than the one at Newgrange. In 1968 a 40m passage was unearthed on the opposite side of the mound.

Also in the mound are the remains of six early-Christian **souterrains** (underground chambers) built into the side. Some 300 **carved slabs** and 17 **satellite graves** surround the main mound.

Human activity at Knowth continued for thousands of years after its construction, which accounts for the site's complexity. The Beaker folk, so called because they buried their dead with drinking vessels, occupied the site in the Early Bronze Age (c 1800 BC), as did the Celts in the Iron Age (c 500 BC). Remnants of bronze and iron workings from these periods have been discovered. Around AD 800 to 900, it was turned into a *ráth* (earthen ring fort), a stronghold of the very powerful O'Neill clan. In 965 it was the seat of Cormac MacMaelmithic, later Ireland's high king for nine years, and in the 12th century the Normans built a motte and bailey (a raised mound with a walled keep) here. The site was finally abandoned around 1400.

Dowth

The circular mound at Dowth is similar in size to Newgrange – about 63m in diameter – but is slightly taller at 14m high. Due to safety issues, Dowth's tombs are closed to visitors, though you can visit the mound (and its resident grazing sheep) from the L1607 road between Newgrange and Drogheda.

North of the tumulus are the ruins of **Dowth Castle** and **Dowth House**.

Dowth has two entrance passages leading to separate chambers (both sealed), and a 24m early-Christian underground passage at either end, which connect with the western passage. This 8m-long passage leads into a small cruciform chamber, in which a recess acts as an entrance to an additional series of small compartments, a feature unique to Dowth. To the southwest is the entrance to a shorter passage and smaller chamber.

It has suffered badly at the hands of everyone from road builders and treasure hunters to amateur archaeologists, who scooped out the centre of the tumulus in the 19th century. For a time, Dowth even had a tearoom ignobly perched on its summit.

PETER ZELEI IMAGES / GETTY IMAGES ©

TOP SIGHT
GLENDALOUGH

If you've come to Wicklow, chances are that a visit to Glendalough (Gleann dá Loch, 'Valley of the Two Lakes') is one of your main reasons for being here. And you're not wrong, for this is one of the most beautiful corners of the whole country and the epitome of the kind of rugged, romantic Ireland that probably drew you to the island in the first place.

The substantial remains of this important monastic settlement are certainly impressive, but the real draw is the splendid setting: two dark and mysterious lakes tucked into a deep valley covered in forest. It is, despite its immense popularity, a deeply tranquil and spiritual place, and you will have little difficulty in understanding why those solitude-seeking monks came here in the first place.

St Kevin

In AD 498 a young monk named Kevin arrived in the valley looking for somewhere to kick back, meditate and be at one with nature. He pitched up in what had been a Bronze Age tomb on the southern side of the Upper Lake and for the next seven years slept on stones, wore animal skins, maintained a near-starvation diet and – according to the legend – became bosom buddies with the birds and animals. Kevin's ecofriendly lifestyle soon attracted a bunch of disciples, all seemingly unaware of the irony that they were flocking to hang out with a hermit who wanted to live as far away from other people as possible. Over the next couple of centuries his one-man operation mushroomed into a proper settlement and by the 9th century Glendalough rivalled Clonmacnoise as the island's premier monastic city.

DON'T MISS

➡ Round Tower
➡ St Kevin's Church
➡ St Kevin's Bed

PRACTICALITIES

➡ 25km south of Dublin

➡ To drive, take the N11 south to Kilmacanogue, then R755 west through Roundwood, Annamoe and Laragh.

➡ **St Kevin's Bus** (www.glendaloughbus. com; one-way/return €13/20) departs from outside the Mansion House on Dawson St in Dublin at 11.30am & 6pm Mon-Sat, and 11.30am & 7pm Sun (1½ hours). It returns at 7.15am & 4.30pm Mon-Sat.

GUIDED TOURS

The award-winning **Wild Wicklow Tour** (☑01-280 1899; www. wildwicklow.ie; adult €28, student & child €25; ☺departs 9am) of Glendalough, Avoca and the Sally Gap never fails to generate rave reviews for atmosphere and all-round fun. The first pick-up is at the Shelbourne and then the tourist office (p221), but there are a variety of pick-up points throughout Dublin; check the point nearest you when booking. The tour returns to Dublin about 5.30pm. Alternatively, **Bus Éireann** (☑01-836 6111; www.buseireann. ie; 59 Upper O'Connell St; adult/child/student €28.80/18/25.20; ☺10am mid-Mar–Oct) runs good but slightly impersonal whole-day tours of Glendalough and the Powerscourt Estate, which return to Dublin at about 5.45pm.

Thousands of students studied and lived in a thriving community that was spread over a considerable area.

Inevitably, Glendalough's success made it a key target for Viking raiders, who sacked the monastery at least four times between 775 and 1071. The final blow came in 1398, when English forces from Dublin almost destroyed it. Efforts were made to rebuild and some life lingered on here as late as the 17th century when, under renewed repression, the monastery finally died.

Upper Lake

The original site of St Kevin's settlement, **Teampall na Skellig** is at the base of the cliffs towering over the southern side of the Upper Lake and is accessible only by boat; unfortunately, there's no boat service to the site and you'll have to settle for looking at it across the lake. The terraced shelf has the reconstructed ruins of a church and early graveyard. Rough wattle huts once stood on the raised ground nearby. Scattered around are some early grave slabs and simple stone crosses.

Just east of here and 10m above the lake waters is the 2m-deep artificial cave called **St Kevin's Bed**, said to be where Kevin lived. The earliest human habitation of the cave was long before St Kevin's era – there's evidence that people lived in the valley for thousands of years before the monks arrived. In the green area just south of the car park is a large circular wall thought to be the remains of an early Christian **stone fort** (caher).

Follow the lakeshore path southwest of the car park until you come to the considerable remains of **Reefert Church** above the tiny River Poulanass. It's a small, plain, 11th-century Romanesque nave-and-chancel church with some reassembled arches and walls. Traditionally, Reefert (literally 'Royal Burial Place') was the burial site of the chiefs of the local O'Toole family. The surrounding graveyard contains a number of rough stone crosses and slabs, most made of shiny mica schist.

Climb the steps at the back of the churchyard and follow the path to the west and you'll find, at the top of a rise overlooking the lake, the scant remains of **St Kevin's Cell**, a small beehive hut.

Lower Lake

While the Upper Lake has the best scenery, the most fascinating buildings lie in the lower part of the valley east of the Lower Lake (pictured p163), huddled together in the heart of the ancient **monastic site**.

Around the bend from the Glendalough Hotel is the stone arch of the **monastery gatehouse**, the only surviving example of a monastic entranceway in the country.

Beyond that lies a **graveyard**, which is still in use. The 10th-century **round tower** is 33m tall and 16m in circumference at the base. The upper storeys and conical roof were reconstructed in 1876. Near the tower, to the southeast, lies the **Cathedral of St Peter and St Paul**, with a 10th-century nave. The chancel and sacristy both date from the 12th century.

At the centre of the graveyard, to the south of the round tower, is the **Priest's House**, dating from 1170 but heavily reconstructed. During the 18th century it became a burial site for local priests – hence the name. The 10th-century **St Mary's Church**, 140m southwest of the round tower, probably stood outside the walls of the monastery and belonged to local nuns. A little to the east are the scant remains of **St Kieran's Church**, the smallest at Glendalough.

Glendalough's trademark is **St Kevin's Church** – or Kitchen – at the southern edge of the enclosure. With its miniature belfry, protruding sacristy and steep stone roof, it's a masterpiece. It was thought that the bell tower was the chimney to the kitchen (hence its name) but no food was ever cooked there. The oldest parts of the building date from the 11th century – the structure has been remodelled since but it's still a classic early Irish church.

At the junction with Green Rd is the **Deer Stone**, in the middle of a group of rocks. Legend claims that when St Kevin needed milk for two orphaned babies, a doe stood here waiting to be milked. The stone is actually a **bullaun**, used as a grinding stone for medicines or food.

The road heading away to the east leads to **St Saviour's Church**, with its detailed Romanesque carvings. To the west, a nice woodland trail leads up the valley past the Lower Lake to the Upper Lake.

Glendalough

WALKING TOUR

A visit to Glendalough is a trip through ancient history and a refreshing hike in the hills. The ancient monastic settlement founded by St Kevin in the 5th century grew to be quite powerful by the 9th century, but it started falling into ruin from 1398 onwards. Still, you won't find more evocative clumps of stones anywhere.

Start at the **Main Gateway** ❶ to the monastic city, where you will find a cluster of important ruins, including the (nearly perfect) 10th-century **Round Tower** ❷, the **Cathedral** ❸ dedicated to Sts Peter and Paul, and **St Kevin's Kitchen** ❹, which is really a church. Cross the stream past the famous **Deer Stone** ❺, where Kevin was supposed to have milked a doe, and turn west along the path. It's a 1.5km walk to the **Upper Lake** ❻. On the lake's southern shore is another cluster of sites, including the **Reefert Church** ❼, a plain 11th-century Romanesque church where the powerful O'Toole family buried their kin, and **St Kevin's Cell** ❽, the remains of a beehive hut where Kevin is said to have lived.

ST KEVIN

St Kevin came to the valley as a young monk in AD 498, in search of a peaceful retreat. He was reportedly led by an angel to a Bronze Age tomb now known as St Kevin's Bed. For seven years he slept on stones, wore animal skins, survived on nettles and herbs and – according to legend – developed an affinity with the birds and animals. One legend has it that, when Kevin needed milk for two orphaned babies, a doe stood waiting at the Deer Stone to be milked.

Kevin soon attracted a group of disciples and the monastic settlement grew, until by the 9th century Glendalough rivalled Clonmacnoise as Ireland's premier monastic city. According to legend, Kevin lived to the age of 120. He was canonised in 1903.

Round Tower
Glendalough's most famous landmark is the 33m-high Round Tower, which is exactly as it was when it was built a thousand years ago except for the roof; this was replaced in 1876 after a lightning strike.

OLOS / SHUTTERSTOCK ©

Deer Stone
The spot where St Kevin is said to have truly become one with the animals is really just a large mortar called a *bullaun*, used for grinding food and medicine.

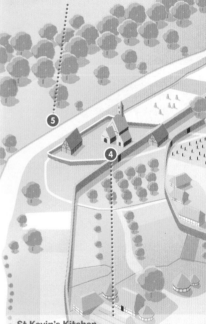

St Kevin's Kitchen
This small church is unusual in that it has a round tower sticking out of the roof – it looks like a chimney, hence the church's nickname.

SIR FRANCIS CANNER PHOTOGRAPHY / GETTY IMAGES ©

St Kevin's Cell
This beehive hut is reputedly where St Kevin would go for prayer and meditation; not to be confused with St Kevin's Bed, a cave where he used to sleep.

Reefert Church
Its name derives from the Irish *righ fearta*, which means 'burial place of the kings'. Seven princes of the powerful O'Toole family are buried in this simple structure.

Upper Lake
The site of St Kevin's original settlement is on the banks of the Upper Lake, one of the two lakes that give Glendalough its name – the 'Valley of the Lakes'.

8

7

6

2

3

1

← NORTH

INFORMATION
At the eastern end of the Upper Lake is the National Park Information Point, which has leaflets and maps on the site, local walks etc. The grassy spot in front of the office is a popular picnic spot in summer.

Cathedral of Sts Peter & Paul
The largest of Glendalough's seven churches, the cathedral was built gradually between the 10th and 13th centuries. The earliest part is the nave, where you can still see the *antae* (slightly projecting column at the end of the wall) used for supporting a wooden roof.

Main Gateway
The only surviving entrance to the ecclesiastical settlement is a double arch; notice that the inner arch rises higher than the outer one in order to compensate for the upward slope of the causeway.

Howth

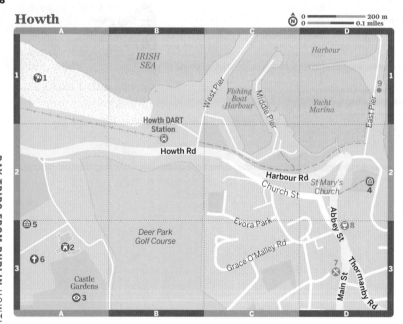

Howth

Explore

Tidily positioned at the foot of a bulbous peninsula, the pretty port village of Howth (the name rhymes with 'both') is a major fishing centre, yachting harbour and one of the most sought-after addresses in town.

Howth is divided between the upper headland – where the best properties are, discreetly spread atop the gorse-rich hill where there are some fine walks and spectacular views of Dublin Bay – and the busy port town, where all the restaurants are (as well as an excellent weekend farmers market).

The Best...

➡ **Sight** Howth Summit (p169)

➡ **Place to Eat** House (Map p168; ☑ 01-839 6388; www.thehouse-howth.ie; 4 Main St; mains €17-24; ⊙ 8.45am-4pm Mon, to 9.30pm Tue-Fri, 10am-10pm Sat & Sun; ☐ 31, 31A from Beresford Pl, ☐ Howth)

➡ **Place to Drink** Abbey Tavern (p169)

Getting There & Away

➡ **DART** The 20-minute train ride from the city centre to Howth Village cost €3.25.

➡ **Bus** Nos 31 and 31A from Beresford Pl near Busáras run up to Howth Summit for €2.70.

Need to Know

➡ **Area Code** ☑ 01
➡ **Population** 8256
➡ **Location** 15km northeast of Dublin

◉ SIGHTS

HOWTH CASTLE   CASTLE
Map p168 (☐ 31, 31A from Beresford Pl, ☐ Howth)
FREE Most of Howth backs onto the extensive grounds of Howth Castle, built in 1564 but much changed over the years, most recently in 1910 when Sir Edwin Lutyens gave it a modernist makeover. Today the castle is divided into four very posh and private residences (the grounds are open to the public).

The original estate was acquired in 1177 by the Norman noble Sir Almeric Tristram, who changed his surname to St Lawrence after winning a battle at the behest (or so he believed) of his favourite saint. The family has owned the land ever since, though the unbroken chain of male succession came to an end in 1909.

On the grounds are the ruins of the 16th-century Corr Castle and an ancient dolmen

Howth

(tomb chamber or portal tomb made of vertical stones topped by a huge capstone) known as Aideen's Grave. Legend has it that Aideen died of a broken heart after her husband was killed at the Battle of Gavra near Tara in AD 184, but the legend is rubbish because the dolmen is at least 300 years older than that.

HOWTH SUMMIT   VIEWPOINT
(⊡31, 31A from Beresford Pl, ⊠Howth) Howth Summit (171m) has excellent views across Dublin Bay right down to County Wicklow. From the top of Howth hill you can walk to the top of the Ben of Howth, a headland near the village, which has a cairn said to mark a 2000-year-old Celtic **royal grave**. The 1814 **Baily Lighthouse**, at the southeastern corner, is on the site of an old stone fort and can be reached by a dramatic clifftop **walk**.

HOWTH CASTLE GARDENS   GARDENS
Map p168 (⊘24hr; ⊡31, 31A from Beresford Pl, ⊠Howth) FREE The castle gardens are worth a visit; they're noted for their rhododendrons (which bloom in May and June), for their azaleas and for the long, 10m-high beech hedge planted in 1710.

ST MARY'S ABBEY   CHURCH
Map p168 (Abbey St; ⊡31, 31A from Beresford Pl, ⊠Howth) FREE Within the Howth Castle grounds are the ruins of St Mary's Abbey, originally founded in 1042 by the Viking King Sitric, who also founded the original church on the site of Christ Church Cathedral. See the caretaker or read the instructions on the gate for opening times.

The abbey was amalgamated with the monastery on Ireland's Eye in 1235. Some parts of the ruins date from that time, but most are from the 15th and 16th centuries. The tomb of Christopher St Lawrence (Lord Howth), in the southeastern corner, dates from around 1470.

HURDY GURDY
MUSEUM OF VINTAGE RADIO   MUSEUM
Map p168 (https://hurdygurdyradiomuseum.word press.com; €3; ⊘11am-4pm May-Oct, Sat-Sun only Nov-Apr; ⊡31, 31A from Beresford Pl, ⊠Howth) Housed in the old Martello tower overlooking the harbour is this museum of wonderful curiosities collected by Pat Herbert. Inside you'll find artefacts related to all forms of communication, from radio to gramophones and early TVs. The name derives from a comment made by former Taoiseach (prime minister) Sean Lemass who asked a radio controller in the 1950s, 'How's the hurdy gurdy?' (A hurdy gurdy is a type of string instrument.)

CLAREMONT BEACH   BEACH
Map p168 (⊡31, 31A from Beresford Pl, ⊠Howth) Howth's 'hidden' beach is Claremont. On the other side of the railway, it's a lovely sandy strand, with perfect views of Ireland's Eye directly in front. To get here, go past the semi-industrial area by the West Pier.

NATIONAL TRANSPORT MUSEUM   MUSEUM
Map p168 (⊘01-832 0427; www.nationaltransport museum.org; Howth Castle; adult €3, child & student €1.50; ⊘2-5pm Sat & Sun; ⊡31, 31A from Beresford Pl, ⊠Howth) A more recent addition is the rather ramshackle National Transport Museum, which has a range of exhibits including double-decker buses, a bakery van, fire engines and trams – most notably a Hill of Howth electric that operated from 1901 to 1959. To reach the museum, go through the castle gates and turn right just before the castle.

☕ DRINKING & NIGHTLIFE

ABBEY TAVERN   PUB
Map p168 (28 Abbey St; ⊘noon-11.30pm Mon-Sat, 12.30-11pm Sun; ⊡31, 31A from Beresford Pl, ⊠Howth) At the front is an old-style tavern frequented by a mix of locals and visitors; at the back is the venue for a nightly **traditional**

WORTH A DETOUR

IRELAND'S EYE
....

A short distance offshore from Howth is **Ireland's Eye** (☎01-831 4200), a rocky seabird sanctuary with the ruins of a 6th-century monastery.

Ireland's Eye is really only worth exploring if you're interested in birds, although the boat trip out here affords some lovely views of Dublin Bay.

Irish music and dance show (from 7.30pm), which also includes a four-course meal. A bit of fun, but strictly for tourists!

 ## ACTIVITIES

DOYLE & SONS
BOAT TOUR

Map p168 (☎01-831 4200; www.howth-boats.com; return €20; ☒31, 31A from Beresford Pl, ☒Howth) Doyle & Sons takes boats out to Ireland's Eye island from the East Pier of Howth Harbour. It also conducts half- and full-day angling trips.

HOWTH SUMMIT WALK
WALKING

(Howth DART station; ☒31, 31A from Beresford Pl, ☒Howth) A 6km looped walk around the headlands begins at Howth DART station – follow the green arrow along the promenade and then turn right onto the cliff path. The walk takes you up to the summit before looping back down again. There are other, longer, walks marked by blue, red and purple arrows (which partially overlap the green route).

Enniskerry & Powerscourt Estate
....

Explore
At the top of the '21 Bends', as the winding R117 from Dublin is known, the handsome village of Enniskerry is home to art galleries and the kind of all-organic gourmet cafes that would treat you as a criminal if you admitted to eating battery eggs. Such preening self-regard is a far cry from the village's

origins, when Richard Wingfield, Earl of nearby Powerscourt, commissioned a row of terraced cottages for his labourers in 1760. These days, you'd want to have laboured pretty successfully to get your hands on one of them.
....

The Best
➡**Sight** Formal Gardens (p171)
➡**Place to Eat** Johnnie Fox (p171)
➡**Place to Stay** Powerscourt Hotel & Spa (p174)
....

Top Tip
You can visit Powerscourt and Glendalough together as part of a **Bus Éireann Tour** (☎01-836 6111; www.buseireann.ie; Busáras; adult/child/student €27.50/19/25.50; ⏱10am mid-Mar–Oct), which departs from the **Dublin Discover Ireland Centre** (14 Upper O'Connell St; ⏱9am-5pm Mon-Sat; ☒all city centre). Dublin Bus Tours (p220) includes a visit in its four-hour 'South Coast & Gardens' tour, which takes in the stretch of coastline between Dun Laoghaire and Killiney before turning inland to Wicklow and on to Enniskerry. Admission to the gardens is included.
....

Getting There & Away
Enniskerry is 18km south of Dublin, just 3km west of the M11 along the R117. From here, getting to Powerscourt House on foot is not a problem (it's 500m from the town), but getting to the waterfall is a longer hike.
....

Need to Know
➡**Area Code** ☎01
➡**Location** 18km south of Dublin
➡**Dublin Discover Ireland Centre**

SIGHTS

POWERSCOURT ESTATE
HOUSE, GARDENS

(www.powerscourt.ie; near Enniskerry; admission to house free, gardens adult/child €8.50/5; ☉9.30am-5.30pm Mar-Oct, to dusk Nov-Feb) Wicklow's most visited attraction is this magnificent 64-sq-km estate, whose main entrance is 500m south of Enniskerry town. At the heart of it is a 68-room Palladian mansion, but the real draw are the formal gardens and the stunning views that accompany them. The upper floors of the house are closed, but there's a fine cafe and craft shop on the ground floor, while the grounds are home to two golf courses and the best hotel in Wicklow.

The estate has existed more or less since 1300, when the LePoer (later anglicised to Power) family built themselves a castle here. The property changed Anglo-Norman hands a few times before coming into the possession of Richard Wingfield, newly appointed Marshall of Ireland, in 1603. His descendants were to live here for the next 350 years. In 1730 the Georgian wunderkind Richard Cassels (or Castle) was given the job of building a 68-room Palladian-style mansion around the core of the old castle. He finished the job in 1741, but an extra storey was added in 1787 and other alterations were made in the 19th century.

The Wingfields left during the 1950s, after which the house had a massive restoration. Then, on the eve of its opening to the public in 1974, a fire gutted the whole building. The estate was eventually bought by the Slazenger sporting-goods family who have overseen a second restoration as well as the addition of all the amenities the estate now has to offer, including the two golf courses and the fabulous hotel, now part of Marriott's Autograph collection.

The star of the show is the 20-hectare **garden**, originally laid out in the 1740s but redesigned in the 19th century by gardener Daniel Robinson. Robinson was one of the foremost horticulturalists of his day, and his passion for growing things was matched only by his love of booze: the story goes that by a certain point in the day he was too drunk to stand and so insisted on being wheeled around the estate in a barrow.

Perhaps this influenced his largely informal style, which resulted in a magnificent blend of landscaped gardens, sweeping terraces, statuary, ornamental lakes, secret hollows, rambling walks and walled enclosures replete with more than 200 types of trees and shrubs, all beneath the stunning natural backdrop of the Great Sugarloaf Mountain to the southeast. Tickets come with a map laying out 40-minute and hour-long tours of the gardens. Don't miss the exquisite Japanese Gardens or the Pepperpot Tower, modelled on a three-inch actual pepper pot owned by Lady Wingfield. Our own favourite, however, is the **animal cemetery**, final resting place of the Wingfield pets and even some of the family's favourite milking cows. Some of the epitaphs are astonishingly personal.

The house itself is every bit as grand, but the ongoing renovation means there's not much to see beyond the bustle of the ground-floor Avoca cafe and craft shop. The sole exception is the **Museum of Childhood** (Tara's Palace; www.taraspalace.ie; Powerscourt Estate, near Enniskerry; adult/child/family €5/3/12; ☉10am-5pm Mon-Sat, noon-5pm Sun; 🚹), full of period miniature dolls and dolls' houses, including Tara's Palace, a 22-room house designed to one-twelfth scale and inspired by the Palladian piles of Castletown House, Leinster House and Carton House. Each of the rooms is decorated in exquisite, hand-crafted miniatures.

A 7km walk to a separate part of the estate takes you to the 130m **Powerscourt Waterfall** (near Enniskerry; adult/child €5.50/3.50; ☉9.30am-7pm May-Aug, 10.30am-5.30pm Mar-Apr, Sep & Oct, to 4.30pm Nov-Jan). It's the highest waterfall in the British Isles, and is most impressive after heavy rain. You can also get to the falls by road, following the signs from the estate. A nature trail has been laid out around the base of the waterfall, taking you past giant redwoods, ancient oaks, beech, birch and rowan trees. There are plenty of birds in the vicinity, including the chaffinch, cuckoo, chiffchaff, raven and willow warbler.

EATING

JOHNNIE FOX
SEAFOOD $$

(☎01-295 5647; www.jfp.ie; Glencullen; mains €12-20; ☉noon-10pm) Busloads of tourists fill this place nightly throughout the summer, mostly for the knees-up, faux-Irish Hooley Show of music and dancing. But there's nothing contrived about the seafood, which is so damn good we'd happily sit through yet another chorus of *Danny Boy* and even

PM78 / GETTY IMAGES ©

JIM FOLEY / GETTY IMAGES ©

1. Glendalough (p163)

This monastic settlement established by St Kevin in AD 496 has become the epitome of Ireland's rugged, romantic beauty.

2. Powerscourt Estate (p171)

The gardens of this stately home, originally laid out in the 1740s, blend landscaping, statuary and horticulture to magnificent effect.

3. Knowth (p162)

The enormous neolithic burial mound of Knowth, part of the Brú na Bóinne necropolis, is home to Western Europe's largest collection of passage-grave art.

4. Howth (p168)

Howth's Baily Lightouse sits on the site of an old stone fort and offers stunning views over Dublin Bay.

NIALL DUNNE / SHUTTERSTOCK ©

consider joining in the jig. The pub is 3km northwest of Enniskerry in Glencullen.

🛏 SLEEPING

★ POWERSCOURT HOTEL & SPA HOTEL $$$

(☑01-274 8888; www.powerscourthotel.com; Powerscourt Estate, Enniskerry; r from €170) Wicklow's most luxurious hotel is this 200-room stunner on the grounds of the Powerscourt Estate. Inside this Marriott-managed property all is OTT luxury, and the decor is a thoroughly contemporary version of the estate's Georgian style. The rooms are massive. Downstairs there's a decent restaurant and a superb spa.

Castletown House & Around

Explore

In a country full of elegant Palladian mansions, it is no mean feat to be considered the grandest of the lot, but Castletown House simply has no peer. It is Ireland's largest and most imposing Georgian estate, and a testament to the vast wealth enjoyed by the Anglo-Irish gentry during the 18th century.

The Best

➡ **Sight** Wonderful Barn (p174)

➡ **Place to Stay** Carton House (☑01-505 2000; www.cartonhouse.com; r from €140; P @ 🛜 ☰)

Top Tip

Be sure to take the guided tour of the house; informative and full of detail about its construction and its larger-than-life owners and inhabitants.

Getting There & Away

➡ **Bus** 67 runs from Dublin to Celbridge (€3.50, about one hour, hourly)

➡ **Car** Take the N4 to Celbridge

Need to Know

➡ **Area Code** ☑01
➡ **Location** 21km west of Dublin
➡ **Dublin Discover Ireland Centre** (p170)

◉ SIGHTS

CASTLETOWN HOUSE HISTORIC BUILDING

(☑01-628 8252; www.castletown.ie; Celbridge; adult/child €7/3; ⊙10am-6pm mid-Mar–Oct) The magnificent Castletown House simply has no peer. It is Ireland's largest and most imposing Georgian estate, and a testament to the vast wealth enjoyed by the Anglo-Irish gentry during the 18th century. The hour-long guided tour gives you an insight into how the one per cent made out in the 18th century, what furniture they liked and how they enjoyed a fine oil painting.

The house was built between the years 1722 and 1732 for William Conolly (1662–1729), speaker of the Irish House of Commons and, at the time, Ireland's richest man. Born into relatively humble circumstances in Ballyshannon, County Donegal, Conolly made his fortune through land transactions in the uncertain aftermath of the Battle of the Boyne (1690).

The job of building a palace fit for a prince was entrusted to Sir Edward Lovett Pearce (1699–1733) – hence the colonnades and terminating pavilions. Lovett's design was an extension of a pre-existing 16th-century Italian palazzo-style building, created by Italian architect Alessandro Galilei (1691–1737) in 1718, but Conolly wanted something even grander, hence Lovett's appearance on the job in 1724. A highlight of the opulent interior is the Long Gallery, replete with family portraits and exquisite stucco work by the Francini brothers.

Conolly didn't live to see the completion of his wonder-palace. His widow, Katherine, continued to live at the unfinished house after his death in 1729, and instigated many improvements. Her main architectural contribution was the curious 42.6m obelisk, known locally as the Conolly Folly. Her other offering is the Heath Robinson–esque (or Rube Goldberg–esque, if you prefer) **Wonderful Barn** (☑01-624 5448; Leixlip; ⊙closed to the public), six teetering storeys wrapped by an exterior spiral staircase, on private property just outside Leixlip.

Castletown House remained in the family's hands until 1965, when it was purchased by Desmond Guinness, who restored the house to its original splendour. His investment was continued from 1979 by the Castletown Foundation. In 1994 Castletown House was transferred to state care and today it is managed by the Heritage Service.

Dalkey

Explore

Dublin's most important medieval port has long been settled into its role as an elegant dormitory village, but there are some revealing vestiges of its illustrious past, most notably the remains of three of the eight castles that once lorded over the area.

The waters around the island are popular with scuba divers; qualified divers can rent gear in Dun Laoghaire, further north, from Ocean Divers (p176).

The Best...

- **Sight** Dalkey Castle & Heritage Centre (p175)
- **Place to Eat** Select Stores (p175)
- **Place to Drink** Finnegan's (p176)

Top Tip

To the south there are good views from the small park at Sorrento Point and from Killiney Hill. A number of rocky swimming pools are also found along the Dalkey coast.

Getting There & Away

- **DART** Best way to get to Dalkey is by train from Pearse or Connolly stations – one way ticket costs €3.25.
- **Bus** No 7 takes a slow route from Mountjoy Sq through the city centre to Dalkey – fare is €3.25.

Need to Know

- **Area Code** ☎01
- **Location** 8km south of Dublin
- **Dublin Discover Ireland Centre** (p170)

SIGHTS

DALKEY CASTLE & HERITAGE CENTRE HERITAGE CENTRE
(☎01-285 8366; www.dalkeycastle.com; Castle St, Dalkey; adult/child €8.50/6.50; ⏰10am-5.30pm Mon-Fri, from 11am Sat & Sun Jun-Aug, closed Tue Sep-May; 🚆Dalkey) Spread across Goat Castle and St Begnet's Church, this heritage centre has models, displays and exhibitions on Dalkey's history; a Living History tour in the format of a theatre performance; and a Writers' Gallery, covering the town's rich literary heritage – from Samuel Beckett (who was born here) to Joseph O'Connor (who lives here). The centre also organises walking tours.

BULLOCK CASTLE RUIN
(Bullock Harbour; 🚆Dalkey) These are the ruins of a castle built by the monks of St Mary's Abbey in Dublin around 1150.

ST BEGNET'S HOLY WELL CHRISTIAN SITE
(boat from Coliemore Harbour per hr €20-30; 🚆Dalkey) FREE A few hundred metres offshore is Dalkey Island, home to St Begnet's Holy Well, the most important of Dalkey's so-called holy wells. This one is reputed to cure rheumatism, making the island a popular destination for tourists and the faithful alike. The island is easily accessible by boat from Coliemore Harbour; you can't book a boat, so just show up.

EATING

SELECT STORES HEALTH FOOD $
(www.selectstores.ie; 1 Railway Rd; mains €4-10; ⏰8am-6pm, closed Sun Oct-Apr; 🚆Dalkey) This long-established food emporium has been transformed into a one-stop shop for all things good for you: the award-winning kitchen rolls out veggie burgers, fresh juices, salads and, in the mornings, a range of healthy breakfasts. Bono is a fan, apparently.

GUINEA PIG SEAFOOD $$
(☎01-285 9055; www.guineapig.dalkey.net; 17 Railway Rd, Dalkey; mains €19-30; ⏰5.30-10pm; 🚆Dalkey) Despite the name, is this the best seafood restaurant in Dublin? Many a food critic seems to think so.

DAY TRIPS FROM DUBLIN DALKEY

WORTH A DETOUR

JAMES JOYCE MUSEUM & FORTY FOOT

About 1km north of Dalkey is the residential suburb of Sandycove, a pretty little beach with a Martello tower – built by British forces as a lookout for signs of a Napoleonic invasion – now home to the **James Joyce Museum** (☎01-280 9265; www.jamesjoyce tower.com; Joyce Tower; ☺10am-4pm) **FREE**. This tower is where the action begins in Joyce's epic novel *Ulysses*. The museum was opened in 1962 by Sylvia Beach, the Paris-based publisher who first dared to put *Ulysses* into print, and has photographs, letters, documents, various editions of Joyce's work and two death masks of Joyce on display.

Below it, the **Forty Foot Pool** (Sandycove) is an open-air, sea-water bathing pool that took its name from the army regiment, the Fortieth Foot, that was stationed at the tower until the regiment was disbanded in 1904. At the close of the first chapter of *Ulysses*, Buck Mulligan heads off to the Forty Foot Pool for a morning swim. A morning wake-up here is still a local tradition, in summer and winter: the Christmas Day Dip is one of Dublin's most enduring traditions.

MAGPIE INN PUB FOOD **$$**

(☎01-202 3909; www.magpieinn.ie; 115-116 Coliemore Rd; mains €10-25; ☺noon-11.30pm; ☒Dalkey) The excellent menu's main strength is, obviously, seafood, including a range of mouth-watering lunch options like fresh Sligo mussels marinière with toasted sourdough bread and more substantial dinner mains like a seafood skillet of pan-fried salmon, cod, langoustine, mussels, tomatoes, potatoes, onions and garlic in a white wine sauce. Wash it all down with a choice of craft beer.

🍷 DRINKING & NIGHTLIFE

FINNEGAN'S PUB

(1 Sorrento Rd; ☺noon-11.30pm Mon-Thu, to 12.30am Fri & Sat, noon-11pm Sun; ☒Dalkey) There's a fabulous local atmosphere in this lovely traditional pub.

MAGPIE INN PUB

(☎01-202 3909; www.magpieinn.ie; 115-116 Coliemore Rd; ☺noon-11.30pm; ☒Dalkey) Two

dozen or so craft beers complement the usual selection of brewery beers; add to it the excellent lunch and dinner menu and you've got one of the best gastropubs in the whole county.

ACTIVITIES

OCEAN DIVERS DIVING

(www.oceandivers.ie; The Boat Yard, Dun Laoghaire Harbour, Dun Laoghaire; boat dive €35-55; ☺9.30am-5pm Tue-Sat; ☒Dalkey) A PADI diving school operating out of Dun Laoghaire Harbour, Ocean Divers offers boat diving from its RIBs around Dalkey Island, site of two wrecks: the MV *Leinster* (sank in 1918) and the *Bolivar,* which sank in 1947.

GUIDED TOURS TOUR

(€8.50; ☺11am & noon Wed & Fri Jun-Aug) Historical and literary tours of Dalkey, including a Maeve Binchy–themed walk (the writer lived here) and a Joyce-themed one.

Sleeping

Prices soar and room sizes diminish the closer your accommodation is to the city centre. There are good midrange options north of the Liffey, but the biggest spread of accommodation is south of the river, from midrange Georgian townhouses to the city's top hotels. Excellent options also sprinkle the suburbs immediately south of the city centre. Prices soar during summer and festivals.

Accommodation Styles

Top-end and deluxe hotels fall into two categories – period Georgian elegance and cool, minimalist chic. No matter what the decor, you can expect luxurious surrounds, king-sized beds, satellite TV, full room service, wi-fi and discreet, professional pampering. While the luxury of the best places is undeniable, their inevitable affiliation to the world's most celebrated hotel chains has introduced the whiff of corporate homogeneity into the carefully ventilated air.

Dublin's midrange accommodation is more of a mixed bag, ranging from no-nonsense but soulless chains to small B&Bs in old Georgian townhouses. These days, hotel connoisseurs the world over have discovered the intimate, but luxurious, boutique hotel, where the personal touch is maintained through fewer rooms, each of which is given lavish attention. Dublin's townhouses and guesthouses – usually beautiful Georgian homes converted into lodgings – are this city's version of the boutique hotel, and there are some truly outstanding ones to choose from.

These are beautifully decked out and extremely comfortable, while at the lower end, rooms are simple, a little worn and often rather overbearingly decorated. Here you can look forward to kitsch knick-knacks, chintzy curtains, lace doilies and clashing floral fabrics so loud they'll burn your retinas. Breakfast can range from home-baked breads, fruit and farmhouse cheeses to a traditional, fat-laden fry-up.

Budget options are few and far between in a city that has undergone a dramatic tourist revolution, so if you want to stay anywhere close to the city centre, you'll have to settle for a hostel. Thankfully, most of these maintain a pretty high standard of hygiene and comfort. Many offer various sleeping arrangements, from a bed in a dorm to a four-bed room or a double. There are plenty to choose from, but they tend to fill up very quickly and stay full.

There are also central self-catering apartments for groups, families or those on extended stays who may prefer to do their own thing.

The accommodation-sharing giant Airbnb has a substantial presence in Dublin, even if you don't consider that their European headquarters are here. There are in excess of 300 rental options in the city, ranging from a basic room in an apartment to fully furnished Georgian homes. Gay-friendly Misterbnb (www.misterbnb.com) also has some Dublin listings.

Bookings

Getting the hotel of your choice without a reservation can be tricky in high season (May to September), so always book your room in advance.

In 2016 room rates once again reached the peak levels of the Celtic Tiger, as visitor numbers increased and the economy is once again in decent shape.

You can book directly with the hotel, or through Dublin Tourism's online booking service (www.visitdublin.com).

There are also great savings if you book online. These rates are generally available year-round, but are tougher to find during high season. Be sure to book ahead and ask for a pre-booking rate.

SLEEPING

NEED TO KNOW

Prices

The below categories indicate the cost per night of a standard double room in high season.

€	under €100
€€	€100–€200
€€€	over €200

Websites

Advance internet bookings are your best bet for deals. These are just a handful of services that will get you a competitive rate.

All Dublin Hotels (www. irelandhotels.com/hotels)

Dublin City Centre Hotels (http://dublin. city-centre-hotels.com)

Dublin Hotels (www. dublinhotels.com)

Dublin Tourism (www. visitdublin.com)

Hotels.com (www. hotels.com)

Hostel Dublin (www. hosteldublin.com)

Discounted Rates

In these uncertain times it's unlikely you will ever have to pay the quoted rate, but you'll need flexibility to get the best deals, usually midweek specials outside the high season.

Check-In & Check-Out Times

Check-out at most establishments is noon, but some of the smaller guesthouses and B&Bs require that you check out a little earlier, usually around 11am. Check-in times are usually between noon and 2pm.

Lonely Planet's Top Choices

Merrion (p183) The city's best hotel.

Aberdeen Lodge (p187) A wonderful hidden gem.

Radisson Blu Royal Hotel (p182) Excellent business hotel.

Isaacs Hostel (p185) Best bunks in town.

Shelbourne (p183) Historic and very elegant.

Best by Budget

€

Trinity Lodge (p180) Comfy and central B&B.

Isaacs Hostel (p185) Best bunks in the city.

€€

Radisson Blu Royal Hotel (p182) Swanky spot for business.

Cliff Townhouse (p182) Terrific boutique bolthole.

Aberdeen Lodge (p187) Hospitality at its best.

€€€

Merrion (p183) Sophisticated, elegant and central.

Fitzwilliam Hotel (p182) Modern and very tasteful.

Best Hotel Bars

Central Hotel (p181) The Library Bar is discreet and elegant.

Radisson Blu Royal Hotel (p182) Bangkok-style bar.

Westbury Hotel (p182) I recognise him/her/them!

Best Comfy Pillows

Brooks Hotel (p180) Everyone needs a pillow menu.

Merrion (p183) Nestle your head in luxury.

Aberdeen Lodge (p187) Sublime sleeps.

Westin Dublin (p182) The beds are heavenly.

Best Afternoon Tea

Merrion (p183) The most decadent petit fours.

Shelbourne (p183) A timeless experience.

Best Boutique Beds

Cliff Townhouse (p182) Ten magnificent rooms.

Irish Landmark Trust (p184) A unique sleeping experience.

Number 31 (p183) Architect-designed marvel.

Where to Stay

Neighbourhood	For	Against
Grafton Street & Around	Close to sights, nightlife and pretty much everything; a good choice of midrange and top-end hotels.	Generally more expensive than elsewhere; not always good value for money and rooms tend to be smaller.
Merrion Square & Around	Lovely neighbourhood, elegant hotels and townhouse accommodation; some of the best restaurants in town are also in the area.	Not a lot of choice; virtually no budget accommodation. Also relatively quiet after dark.
Temple Bar	In the heart of the action; close to everything, especially the party.	Noisy and touristy; not especially good value for money; rooms are very small and often less than pristine.
Kilmainham & the Liberties	Close to the old city and the sights of west Dublin.	No good accommodation; only a small selection of restaurants.
North of the Liffey	Good range of choices; within walking distance of sights and nightlife.	Budget accommodation not always good quality; some locations not especially comfortable after dark.
Docklands & the Grand Canal	Excellent contemporary hotels with good service, including some top-end choices.	Isolated in neighbourhood that doesn't have a lot of life after dark; reliant on taxis or public transport to get to city centre.

🛏 Grafton Street & Around

Grafton St itself has only one hotel – one of the city's best – but you'll find a host of choices in the area surrounding it. Not surprisingly, being so close to the choicest street in town comes at a premium, but the competition for business is fierce, which ensures quality is top rate.

AVALON HOUSE HOSTEL $

Map p244 (☎01-475 0001; www.avalon-house. ie; 55 Aungier St; dm/s/d from €19/34/54; @ 🛜; ⛟ all city centre, 🚇 St Stephen's Green) One of the city's most popular hostels, welcoming Avalon House has pine floors, high ceilings and large, open fireplaces that create the ambience for a good spot of meet-the-backpacker lounging. Some of the cleverly designed rooms have mezzanine levels, which are great for families. Book well in advance.

DEAN HOTEL $$

Map p242 (☎01-607 8110; www.deanhoteldublin. ie; 33 Harcourt St; r/ste from €155/425; P @ 🛜; ⛟ 10, 11, 13, 14 or 15A, 🚇 St Stephen's Green) Every room at this newish designer hotel comes with earplugs, vodka, wine and barocca – so you know what to expect. Take your pick from well-appointed and elegant Mod Pods (single bed on a couch), Punk Bunks (yup, bunkbeds) or deluxe doubles (SupeRooms or Hi-Fis) and suites. The more expensive rooms come with Netflix and a turntable.

The hotel deliberately advertises as an upmarket party hotel that borrows its ethos (if not its look) from the Ace Hotel in New York and the Hoxton in London: sandwiched between two of the most popular nightclubs in town the rooms can get very noisy indeed, especially those on the 1st floor. The top floor is home to Sophie's (p69), a brasserie that turns into a popular bar after 11pm. It has discounted parking arrangements with a car park that is a five-minute walk away.

BUSWELL'S HOTEL HOTEL $$

Map p244 (☎01-614 6500; www.buswells.ie; 23-27 Molesworth St; s/d from €170/190; P ✳ @; ⛟ all cross-city, 🚇 St Stephen's Green) This Dublin institution, open since 1882, has a long association with politicians, who wander across the road from Dáil Éireann to wet

their beaks at the hotel bar. The 69 bedrooms have all been given the once-over, but have kept their Georgian charm intact.

KELLY'S HOTEL BOUTIQUE HOTEL $$

Map p244 (www.kellysdublin.com; 36 S Great George's St; r from €180; ✳ @ 🛜; ⛟ all city centre) A trendy boutique hotel in an original Victorian redbrick, the interiors are thoroughly modern – rooms are small, but tastefully decorated with polished wooden floors and elegant minimalist furnishings. It's part of a complex that includes two bars – Hogan's (p73) below and the Bar With No Name (p72) – with L'Gueuleton (p71) next door. Thankfully, the thick walls keep out the noise.

TRINITY LODGE GUESTHOUSE $$

Map p244 (☎01-617 0900; www.trinitylodge. com; 12 S Frederick St; r from €150; 🛜; ⛟ all city centre, 🚇 St Stephen's Green) Martin Sheen's grin greets you upon entering this award-winning guesthouse, which he declared his favourite spot for an Irish stay. Marty's not the only one: this place is so popular they've added a second town house across the road, which has also been kitted out to the highest standards. Room 2 of the original house has a lovely bay window.

TRINITY COLLEGE APARTMENT $$

Map p244 (☎01-896 1177; www.tcd.ie; Accommodations Office, Trinity College; s/d from €76/124; ⊙ May-Sep; P @ 🛜; ⛟ all cross-city) The closest thing to living like a student at this stunningly beautiful university is crashing in their rooms when they're on holidays. Rooms and two-bed apartments in the newer block have their own bathrooms; those in the older blocks share facilities, though there are private sinks. Breakfast is included.

BROOKS HOTEL HOTEL $$

Map p244 (☎01-670 4000; www.brookshotel. ie; 59-62 Drury St; r from €160; P ✳ @ 🛜; ⛟ all cross-city, 🚇 St Stephen's Green) About 120m west of Grafton St, this small, plush place has an emphasis on familial, friendly service. The decor is nouveau classic with high-veneer-panelled walls, decorative bookcases and old-fashioned sofas, while bedrooms are extremely comfortable and come fitted out in subtly coloured furnishings. The clincher though, is the king- and superking-size beds in all rooms, complete with…a pillow menu.

CENTRAL HOTEL   HOTEL **$$**

Map p244 (☑01-679 7302; www.centralhoteldub
lin.com; 1-5 Exchequer St; r from €120; @ 🛜; 🖳all
city centre, 🚇St Stephen's Green) The rooms
are a modern – if miniaturised – version of
Edwardian luxury. Heavy velvet curtains
and custom-made Irish furnishings (in-
cluding beds with draped backboards) fit
a little too snugly into the space afforded
them, but they do lend a touch of class. Note
that street-facing rooms can get a little
noisy. Location-wise, the name says it all.

DAWSON   BOUTIQUE HOTEL **$$**

Map p244 (☑01-612 7900; www.thedawson.ie;
35 Dawson St; r from €140; @ 🛜; 🖳all city centre, 🚇St Stephen's Green) A boutique hotel
with a range of elegant rooms designed in
a variety of styles, from classical French to
more exotic Moroccan. Crisp white sheets
throughout, and Gilchrist & Soames amenities in the bathrooms. There's also a fancy
spa and the trendy Sam's Bar below.

CAMDEN COURT HOTEL   HOTEL **$$**

Map p242 (☑01-475 9666; www.camdencourtho
tel.com; Camden St; r from €170; 🅿❄@🛜🏊;
🖳all cross-city, 🚇Harcourt) Big and bland
ain't such a bad thing this close to St Ste-
phen's Green, especially if the mainstay
of your clientele is the business crowd.
They like the standardised rooms but *love*
the amenities, which include a 16m pool,
health club (with Jacuzzi, sauna and steam
room) and fully equipped gym.

**O'CALLAGHAN
STEPHEN'S GREEN**   HOTEL **$$**

Map p242 (☑01-607 3600; www.stephens
greenhotel.ie; 1-5 Harcourt St; r from €120;
🅿@🛜; 🖳all cross-city, 🚇St Stephen's Green)
Past the glass-fronted lobby are 75 thoroughly modern rooms that make full use
of the visual impact of primary colours,
most notably red and blue. This is a business hotel *par excellence:* everything
here is what you'd expect from a top international hotel (including a gym and a
business centre). There are extraordinary
online deals available.

GRAFTON HOUSE   B&B **$$**

Map p244 (☑01-648 0010; www.graftonguest
house.com; 26-27 S Great George's St; s/d from
€90/140; @🛜; 🖳all city centre, 🚇St Stephen's
Green) This slightly offbeat guesthouse in
a Gothic-style building gets the nod in all
three key categories: location, price and

style. Just next to George's St Arcade, the
Grafton offers the traditional friendly
features of a B&B (breakfast is served in
L'Gueuleton (p71)), coupled with a funky,
if somewhat dated, design. You check in at
Kelly's Hotel (p180), a few doors away.

HARRINGTON HALL   GUESTHOUSE **$$**

Map p242 (☑01-475 3497; www.harringtonhall.
com; 69-70 Harcourt St; s/d from €99/129; @🛜;
🚇Harcourt) Want to fluff up the pillows in
the home of a former Lord Mayor of Dublin?
The traditional Georgian style of Timothy
Charles Harrington's home – he wore the
gold chain from 1901 to 1903 – has thankfully been retained and this smart guesthouse
stands out for its understated elegance. The
1st- and 2nd-floor rooms have their original
fireplaces and ornamental ceilings.

GRAFTON CAPITAL HOTEL   HOTEL **$$**

Map p244 (☑01-648 1221; www.graftoncapi
talhotel.com; Lower Stephen's St; r from €100;
🅿❄@🛜; 🖳all cross-city) It's hardly recog-
nisable as such today, but this hotel just off
Grafton St is actually a couple of converted
Georgian townhouses. Its 75 modern rooms
are designed along the lines of function be-
fore form, ideal for the weekend visitor who
wants to bed down somewhere central and
still keep some credit-card space for a good
night out. Breakfast is included.

HILTON   HOTEL **$$**

Map p242 (☑01-402 9988; www.dublin.hilton.
com; Charlemont Pl; r from €160; 🅿@🛜;
🚇Charlemont) Hilton is synonymous with
modern, well-appointed rooms with all
mod cons, and this canalside property delivers just that. Rooms are bright and comfortable; there's a decent restaurant and a
good gym; and the hotel is close to a Luas
stop so it's an easy commute into the city
centre. As this is a business hotel, rooms are
dramatically more expensive midweek.

There's parking arrangements (€15) with
a nearby car park.

STAUNTON'S ON THE GREEN   HOTEL **$$**

Map p242 (☑01-478 2300; www.stauntonsonthe
green.ie; 83 St Stephen's Green S; r from €125;
@🛜; 🖳all cross-city, 🚇St Stephen's Green) A
perfect location on St Stephen's Green (next
door to the Department of Foreign Affairs),
this handsome Georgian house has clean
rooms that are just a mite careworn. The
front-facing rooms have floor-to-ceiling

windows overlooking the Green. Any closer and you're sleeping with the Lord Mayor.

★**FITZWILLIAM HOTEL**   HOTEL **$$$**
Map p244 (☑️01-478 7000; www.fitzwilliam hotel.com; St Stephen's Green W; r from €220; 🅿️✳️@🛜; 🚇all cross-city, 🚇Stephen's Green) You couldn't pick a more prestigious spot on the Dublin Monopoly board than this minimalist Terence Conrad–designed number overlooking the Green. Ask for a corner room on the 5th floor (502 or 508), with balmy balcony and a view. The hotel is also home to one of the city's best restaurants, Thornton's (p71). It's contemporary elegance at its very best.

WESTBURY HOTEL   HOTEL **$$$**
Map p244 (☑️01-679 1122; www.doylecollection. com; Grafton St; r/ste from €240/360; 🅿️@🛜; 🚇all city centre) Tucked away just off Grafton St is one of the most elegant hotels in town, although you'll need to upgrade to a suite to really feel the luxury. The standard rooms are perfectly comfortable but not really of the same theme as the luxurious public space – the upstairs lobby is a great spot for afternoon tea or a drink.

RADISSON BLU ROYAL HOTEL   HOTEL **$$$**
Map p242 (☑️01-898 2900; www.radissonblu. ie/royalhotel-dublin; Golden Lane; r from €160; 🅿️✳️@🛜; 🚇all city centre, 🚇St Stephen's Green) A business hotel that is an excellent example of how sleek lines and muted colours combine beautifully with luxury,

ensuring a memorable night's stay. From hugely impressive public areas to sophisticated bedrooms – each with a flat-screen digital TV embedded in the wall to go along with all the other little touches – this hotel will not disappoint.

CLIFF TOWNHOUSE   BOUTIQUE HOTEL **$$$**
Map p242 (☑️01-638 3939; www.theclifftown house.com; 22 St Stephen's Green N; r from €200; @🛜; 🚇all city centre, 🚇St Stephen's Green) As pieds-à-terre go, this is a doozy: there are 10 exquisitely appointed bedrooms spread across a wonderful Georgian property whose best views overlook St Stephen's Green. Downstairs is Sean Smith's superb restaurant Cliff Townhouse (p71).

WESTIN DUBLIN   HOTEL **$$$**
Map p244 (☑️01-645 1000; www.thewestindublin. com; Westmoreland St; r from €200; 🅿️@🛜; 🚇all city centre) Once a fancy bank branch, now a fancier hotel: rooms are decorated in elegant mahogany and soft colours that are reminiscent of the USA's finest. You will sleep on 10 layers of the Westin's own trademark Heavenly Bed, which is damn comfortable indeed. The old bank vault is now the basement bar.

🛏️ Merrion Square & Around

It's the most sought-after real estate in town, so it's hardly surprising that it's home

---

HOME AWAY FROM HOME

Self-catering apartments are a good option for visitors staying a few days, for groups of friends, or for families with kids. Apartments range from one-room studios to two-bedroom flats with lounge areas, and include bathrooms and kitchenettes. A decent two-bedroom apartment will cost about €100 to €150 per night. Good, central places include the following:

➡ **Clarion Stephen's Hall** (Map p248; ☑️01-638 1111; www.premgroup.com; 14-17 Lower Leeson St; s/d €150/250; 🅿️✳️@; 🚇all city centre) Deluxe studios and suites, with all mod cons; akin to an elegant hotel room.

➡ **Home From Home Apartments** (Map p256; ☑️01-678 1166; www.yourhomefrom home.com; The Moorings, Fitzwilliam Quay; apt €100-180; 🚇Grand Canal Dock) Deluxe one- to three-bedroom apartments in the south-side city centre. Minimum two-night stay in high season.

➡ **Latchfords** (p183) Studios and two-bedroom flats in a Georgian townhouse.

➡ **Oliver St John Gogarty's Penthouse Apartments** (Map p240; ☑️01-671 1822; www.gogartys.ie; 18-21 Anglesea St; 2 bed €99-199; 🚇all city centre) Perched high atop the pub of the same name, these one- to three-bedroom places have views of Temple Bar.

to the lion's share of the city's top hotels. But although you'll pay for the privilege of bedding down in luxury, there are some excellent deals available at many of these well-located properties, which are within a gentle stroll of the best restaurants, bars and attractions the city has to offer.

DAVENPORT HOTEL   HOTEL $$

Map p248 (☏01-607 3500; www.davenporthotel. ie; N Merrion Sq; r from €130; P@🛜; ☐all city centre) Housed within the old Merrion Hall, which was built in 1863 for the Plymouth Brethren, this is a solid business hotel with large rooms equipped with orthopaedic beds and big bathrooms. It's popular with both business and leisure visitors.

LATCHFORDS   APARTMENT $$

Map p248 (☏01-676 0784; www.latchfords.ie; 99-100 Lower Baggot St; studio/2-bedroom apt from €90/130) Studios and two-bedroom flats in a Georgian townhouse.

★MERRION   HOTEL $$$

Map p248 (☏01-603 0600; www.merrionhotel. com; Upper Merrion St; r/ste from €295/715; P@🛜🏊; ☐all city centre) This resplendent five-star hotel, in a terrace of beautifully restored Georgian townhouses, opened in 1988 but looks like it's been around a lot longer. Try to get a room in the old house (with the largest private art collection in the city), rather than the newer wing, to sample its truly elegant comforts.

Located opposite Government Buildings, its marble corridors are patronised by politicos, visiting dignitaries and the odd celeb. Even if you don't stay, book a table for the superb Art Afternoon Tea (€85 for two), with endless cups of tea served out of silver pots by a raging fire.

★NUMBER 31   GUESTHOUSE $$$

Map p248 (☏01-676 5011; www.number31.ie; 31 Leeson Close; s/d €200/240; P🛜; ☐all city centre) The city's most distinctive property is the former home of modernist architect Sam Stephenson, who successfully fused '60s style with 18th-century grace. Its 21 bedrooms are split between the retro coach house, with its coolly modern rooms, and the more elegant Georgian house, where rooms are individually furnished with tasteful French antiques and big comfortable beds. Breakfast included.

Gourmet breakfasts with kippers, home-made breads and granola are served in the conservatory.

SHELBOURNE   HOTEL $$$

Map p248 (☏01-676 6471; www.theshelbourne. ie; 27 St Stephen's Green N; r from €460; P@🛜; ☐all city centre, ☐St Stephen's Green) Dublin's most famous hotel was founded in 1824 and has been the preferred halting post of the powerful and wealthy ever since. Several owners and refurbs later it is now part of Marriott's Renaissance portfolio, and while it has a couple of rivals in the luxury stakes, it cannot be beaten for heritage.

Guests are staying in a slice of history: it was here that the Irish Constitution was drafted in 1921, and this is the hotel in Elizabeth Bowen's eponymous novel. Afternoon tea in the refurbished Lord Mayor's Lounge remains one of the best experiences in town.

CONRAD DUBLIN
INTERNATIONAL   HOTEL $$$

Map p248 (☏01-602 8900; www.conradhotels. com; Earlsfort Tce; r €280; P@🛜; ☐all city centre) Dublin's first truly modern international business hotel has not just kept up with the pace of change but has set the standard for other newer hotels in its class. The king-size rooms are spotless and well equipped, the public areas elegant and the staff absolutely top-notch.

There's a dizzying array of special discount rates – at the last minute, room prices are often slashed by half – for both business and leisure travellers. Weekend rates are cheaper.

🛏 Temple Bar

If you're here for a weekend of wild abandon and can't fathom anything more than a quick stumble into bed, then Temple Bar's choice of hotels and hostels will suit you perfectly. Generally speaking the rooms are small, the prices are large and you must be able to handle the late-night symphonies of diehard revellers.

BARNACLES   HOSTEL $

Map p240 (☏01-671 6277; www.barnacles.ie; 19 Lower Temple Lane; dm/tw from €18/60; P🛜; ☐all city centre) If you're here for a good time, not a long time, then this bustling Temple Bar hostel is the ideal spot to meet fellow

SLEEPING TEMPLE BAR

revellers, and tap up the helpful and knowledgeable staff for the best places to cause mischief. Rooms are quieter at the back.

DUBLIN CITI HOTEL
HOTEL **$**

Map p240 (☑01-679 4455; www.dublincitihotel.com; 46-49 Dame St; s/d from €49/59; @; ☐all city centre) An unusual turreted 19th-century building right next to the Central Bank is home to this midrange hotel. Rooms aren't huge, are simply furnished and have fresh white quilts. It's only a stagger (literally) from the heart of Temple Bar, hic.

GOGARTY'S TEMPLE BAR HOSTEL
HOSTEL **$**

Map p240 (☑01-671 1822; www.gogartys.ie/hostel; 58-59 Fleet St; dm/d €12/55; P☎; ☐all city centre) Sleeping isn't really the activity of choice for anyone staying in this compact, decent hostel in the middle of Temple Bar, next to the pub of the same name. It tends to get booked up with stag and hen parties so, depending on your mood, bring either your earplugs or bunny ears. Six self-catering apartments are also available.

KINLAY HOUSE
HOSTEL **$**

Map p240 (☑01-679 6644; www.kinlaydublin.ie; 2-12 Lord Edward St; dm/d from €17/54; ☎; ☐all city centre) This former boarding house for boys has massive, mixed dormitories (for up to 24), and smaller rooms, including doubles. It's in Temple Bar, so it's occasionally raucous. Staff are friendly, and there are cooking facilities and a cafe. Breakfast is included.

ASHFIELD HOUSE
HOSTEL **$**

Map p240 (☑01-679 7734; www.ashfieldhostel.com; 19-20 D'Olier St; dm/tw from €18/73; @☎; ☐all city centre) A stone's throw from Temple Bar and O'Connell Bridge, this modern hostel in a converted church has a selection of tidy four- and six-bed rooms, one large dorm and 25 rooms with private bathroom. It's more like a small hotel, but without the price tag. A continental-style breakfast is included – a rare beast indeed for hostels. Maximum stay is six nights.

PARAMOUNT HOTEL
HOTEL **$$**

Map p240 (☑01-417 9900; www.paramounthotel.ie; cnr Parliament St & Essex Gate; d/tr €140/170; P@☎; ☐all city centre) Behind the Victorian facade, the lobby is a faithful recreation of a 1930s hotel, complete with dark-wood floors, deep-red leather Chesterfield couches and

heavy velvet drapes. The 70-odd rooms don't quite bring *The Maltese Falcon* to mind, but they're handsomely furnished and very comfortable. Downstairs is the **Turk's Head** (Map p240; ☑01-679 9701; 27-30 Parliament St; ⊙11.30am-3am; ☐all city centre), one of the area's most popular bars.

ELIZA LODGE
GUESTHOUSE **$$**

Map p240 (☑01-671 8044; www.elizalodge.com; 23-24 Wellington Quay; d from €120; ✱; ☐all city centre) It's priced like a hotel, looks like a hotel, but it's still a guesthouse. The 18 rooms are comfortable, spacious and – due to its position right over the Millennium Bridge – come with great views of the Liffey. It has discounted parking rates with a nearby car park.

MORGAN HOTEL
BOUTIQUE HOTEL **$$**

Map p240 (☑01-643 7000; www.themorgan.com; 10 Fleet St; r from €150; @☎; ☐all city centre) It was built to attract the Spice Girls, now it just caters to girls (and guys) on a spicy weekend in Dublin. No bad thing, of course, especially as the hotel has stood up well to the ravages of recession. It's a little less resilient in the face of noise: if you're looking for quiet, you might consider elsewhere.

★IRISH LANDMARK TRUST
HERITAGE HOTEL **$$$**

Map p240 (☑01-670 4733; www.irishlandmark.com; 25 Eustace St; 2 nights for 7 people €930; ☐all city centre) This 18th-century heritage house has been gloriously restored to the highest standard by the Irish Landmark Trust. Furnished with tasteful antiques and authentic furniture and fittings (including a grand piano in the drawing room), it sleeps up to seven in its three bedrooms, which must be booked for a minimum of two nights.

The house was built in 1720 and was variously home to a wealthy wool merchant and later to author and historian Standish O'Grady (1846–1928), whom WB Yeats called the 'Father of the Irish Revival' for works like *The Story of Ireland* (1894; written while he lived in the house), despite being a Protestant and a staunch unionist!

CLARENCE HOTEL
HOTEL **$$$**

Map p240 (☑01-407 0800; www.theclarence.ie; 6-8 Wellington Quay; r/ste from €199/390; P@☎; ☐all city centre) Bono and the Edge's handsome boutique hotel was once the hottest bed in town, but now it's just another elegant Dublin four-star designed to reflect

CAMPUS ACCOMMODATION

During the summer months, visitors can opt to stay in campus accommodation, which is both convenient and comfortable.

➡ **Trinity College** (p180) The closest thing to living like a student at this stunningly beautiful university is crashing in their rooms when they're on holidays. Rooms and two-bed apartments in the newer block have their own bathrooms; those in the older blocks share facilities, though there are private sinks. Breakfast is included.

➡ **Dublin City University** (DCU; ☑01-700 5736; www.summeraccommodation.dcu. ie; Larkfield Apartments, Campus Residences, Dublin City University; s/d from €60/100; ☺mid-Jun–mid-Sep; ☐11, 11A, 11B, 13, 13A, 19, 19A from city centre) This accommodation is proof that students slum it in relative luxury. The modern rooms have plenty of amenities at hand, including a kitchen, common room and a fully equipped health centre. The Glasnevin campus is only 15 minutes by bus or car from the city centre.

the aesthetic of a 1930s gentlemen's club, complete with Shaker oak beds draped in Irish linen, an excellent bar and a fine restaurant.

Its owners have been involved in a long-running legal wrangle over plans to demolish part of the building as part of a €150m expansion, but so far Dublin City Council has proven stubbornly resistant.

🛏 North of the Liffey

There are scattering of good midrange options between O'Connell St and Smithfield. Gardiner St, to the east of O'Connell St, is the traditional B&B district of town, but you're better off sticking to the southern end of the street where the properties are better and the street is safer.

★ISAACS HOSTEL   HOSTEL $

Map p252 (☑01-855 6215; www.isaacs.ie; 2-5 Frenchman's Lane; dm/tw from €10/54; @☂; ☐all city centre, ☒Connolly) The north side's best hostel – hell, for atmosphere alone it's the best in town – is in a 200-year-old wine vault just around the corner from the main bus station. With summer barbecues, live music in the lounge, internet access and colourful dorms, this terrific place generates consistently good reviews from backpackers and other travellers.

★GENERATOR HOSTEL   HOSTEL $

Map p252 (☑01-901 0222; www.generator hostels.com; Smithfield Sq; dm/tw from €16/70; @☂) This European chain brings its own brand of funky, fun design to Dublin's hostel scene, with bright colours, comfortable

dorms (including women-only) and a lively social scene. It even has a screening room for movies. Good location right on Smithfield Sq, next to the Old Jameson Distillery.

JACOB'S INN   HOSTEL $

Map p252 (☑01-855 5660; www.jacobsinn.com; 21-28 Talbot Pl; dm/d from €12/70; ☂; ☐all city centre, ☒Connolly) Sister hostel to Isaacs around the corner, this clean and modern hostel offers spacious accommodation with private bathrooms and outstanding facilities, including some wheelchair-accessible rooms, a bureau de change, bike storage and a self-catering kitchen.

MEC HOSTEL   HOSTEL $

Map p252 (☑01-873 0826; www.mechostel. com; 42 N Great George's St; dm/d from €16/72; ☂; ☐36, 36A) A Georgian classic on one of Dublin's most beautiful streets, this popular hostel has a host of dorms and doubles, all with private bathroom. Facilities include a full kitchen, two lounges and a bureau de change. Breakfast is only €2 and there's decent wi-fi throughout.

ABBEY COURT HOSTEL   HOSTEL $

Map p252 (☑01-878 0700; www.abbey-court. com; 29 Bachelor's Walk; dm/d from €16/78; ☂; ☐all city centre) Spread over two buildings, this large, well-run hostel has 33 clean dorm beds with good storage. Its excellent facilities include a dining hall, a conservatory and a barbecue area. Doubles with bathrooms are in the newer building where a light breakfast is provided in the adjacent cafe. Not surprisingly, this is a popular spot; reservations are advised.

SLEEPING NORTH OF THE LIFFEY

CLIFDEN GUESTHOUSE
GUESTHOUSE **$$**

Map p252 (☎01-874 6364; www.clifdenhouse. com; 32 Gardiner Pl; r from €140; ⓟ🐾; 🚌36, 36A) The Clifden is a very nicely refurbished Georgian house with 14 tastefully decorated rooms. They all come with bathroom, and are immaculately clean and extremely comfortable. It offers a 50% discount on nearby parking.

MY PLACE DUBLIN
HOTEL **$$**

Map p252 (☎01-855 0034; www.myplacedublin. ie; 80-90 Lower Gardiner St; s/d €70/100; ⓟ🐾; 🚇Connolly Station) My Place's 37 rooms are nothing fancy, just tidy, comfortable and colourfully decorated. It's especially popular with groups of friends who fill up the triples and quads. The free wi-fi only works in the public areas. It offers a discounted rate to a nearby car park.

ANCHOR HOUSE
B&B **$$**

Map p252 (☎01-878 6913; www.anchorhousedub lin.com; 49 Lower Gardiner St; s/d from €100/120; ⓟ🐾; 🚌all city centre, 🚇Connolly) While most B&Bs round these parts offer pretty much the same stuff – TV, half-decent shower, tea- and coffee-making facilities and wi-fi – the Anchor does all of that with a certain (frayed) elegance, and also has a friendliness the others can't easily match.

MALDRON HOTEL SMITHFIELD
HOTEL **$$**

Map p252 (☎01-485 0900; www.maldronhotels. com; Smithfield Village; r/ste €140/180; 🐾; 🚌25, 25A, 25B, 66, 66A, 66B, 67, 90, 151 to Upper Ormond Quay, 🚇Smithfield) With big bedrooms and plenty of earth tones to soften the contemporary edges, this functionally modern hotel is your best bet in this part of town. We love the floor-to-ceiling windows: great for checking out what's going on below in the square.

CASTLE HOTEL
HOTEL **$$**

Map p252 (☎01-874 6949; www.castle-hotel.ie; 3-4 Great Denmark St; r from €100; ⓟ🐾; 🚌all city centre, 🚇Connolly) In business since 1809, the Castle Hotel may be slightly rough around the edges but it's one of the most pleasant hotels this side of the Liffey. The fabulous palazzo-style grand staircase leads to the 50-odd bedrooms, whose furnishings are traditional and a tad antiquated, but perfectly good throughout – check out the original Georgian cornicing around the high ceilings.

JURY'S INN PARNELL ST
HOTEL **$$**

Map p252 (☎01-878 4900; www.jurysinns.com; Moore St Plaza, Parnell St; r from €149; ❄@🐾; 🚌36, 36A) Jury's hotels are nothing if not reliable, and this edition of Ireland's most popular hotel chain is no exception. What do you care that the furnishings were massproduced and flat-packed and that the decor was created to be utterly inoffensive to everything save good taste? The location – just off Upper O'Connell St – is terrific.

ACADEMY PLAZA HOTEL
HOTEL **$$**

Map p252 (☎01-878 0666; www.academyplaza hotel.ie; Findlater Pl; r from €100; ⓟ🐾; 🚌all city centre) Only a few steps from O'Connell St, this solidly three-star hotel is part of the Best Western group and as such offers the kind of comfortable, if unmemorable, night's sleep associated with the brand. The deluxe suites come with free wi-fi and flat-screen digital TVs. There's discounted parking (€4.50) at the covered car park next door.

MORRISON HOTEL
HOTEL **$$$**

Map p252 (☎01-887 2400; www.morrisonhotel. ie; Lower Ormond Quay; r from €250; ⓟ@🐾; 🚌all city centre, 🚇Jervis) Space-age funky design is the template at this hip hotel, recently taken over by the Hilton Doubletree group. King-size beds (with Serta mattresses), 40in LCD TVs, free wi-fi and Crabtree & Evelyn toiletries are just some of the hotel's offerings. Easily the northside's most luxurious address.

GRESHAM HOTEL
HOTEL **$$$**

Map p252 (☎01-874 6881; www.greshamhotels.com; Upper O'Connell St; r from €200; ⓟ❄@🐾; 🚌all city centre) A landmark hotel with a bright, modern appearance and a fabulous open-plan foyer, all of which pleases its loyal clientele – elderly groups on shopping breaks to the capital and wellheeled Americans. Rooms are spacious and well serviced.

🛏 Docklands & the Grand Canal

Staying in the Docklands area means you'll be relying on public transport or taxis to get you in and out of the city centre.

★ ABERDEEN LODGE — GUESTHOUSE $$

Map p258 (📋01-283 8155; www.aberdeen-lodge.
com; 53-55 Park Ave; r from €180; 🅿 @🛜; 🚇2,
3, 🚋Sydney Parade) Not only is this absolutely one of Dublin's best guesthouses, but
it's also a carefully guarded secret, known
only to those who dare stay a short train
ride from the city centre. Their reward is a
luxurious house with a level of personalised
service as good as you'll find in one of the
city's top hotels.

Most of the stunning rooms have either
a four-poster, a half-tester or a brass bed
to complement the authentic Edwardian
furniture and tasteful art on the walls. The
suites even have fully working Adams fireplaces. As there is one member of staff for
every two rooms, the service is exceptional,
not to mention totally hands-on and very
courteous.

CLAYTON HOTEL CARDIFF LANE — HOTEL $$

Map p256 (📋01-643 9500; www.claytonhotel
cardifflane.com; Cardiff Lane; r/ste €170/220;
@🛜🏊; 🚋Grand Canal Dock) A good midrange
hotel with excellent amenities (two restaurants, a bar and a fitness centre), this hotel
suffers only because of its location, on an
isolated street far from the city-centre action. Its saving grace is the nearby Grand
Canal Dock and its selection of bars and
restaurants.

SCHOOLHOUSE HOTEL — BOUTIQUE HOTEL $$

Map p258 (📋01-667 5014; www.schoolhouse
hotel.com; 2-8 Northumberland Rd; r from €130;
🅿🛜🛗; 🚇5, 7, 7A, 8, 18, 27X or 44 from city centre) A Victorian schoolhouse dating from
1861, this beautiful building has been

successfully converted into an exquisite
boutique hotel that is (ahem) ahead of its
class. Its 31 cosy bedrooms, named after famous Irish people, all have king-sized beds,
big white quilts and loudly patterned head-
boards. The Canteen bar and patio bustles
with local businessfolk in summer.

HERBERT PARK HOTEL — HOTEL $$

Map p258 (📋01-667 2200; www.herbertpark
hotel.ie; Merrion Rd; r from €165; 🚇5, 7, 7A, 8,
18, 45 from Trinity College) A bright, modernist foyer that opens onto two buzzing bars,
spacious comfortable rooms, designed with
chichi New York in mind and with huge
windows and balconies overlooking gorgeous 19-hectare Herbert Park. Rooms also
come with PlayStations. The Royal Dublin
Society Showground (p156) is 100m away.

WATERLOO HOUSE — INN $$

Map p258 (📋01-660 1888; www.waterloohouse.
ie; 8-10 Waterloo Rd; s/d €139/159; 🅿🛜; 🚇5, 7,
7A, 8, 18 or 45 from city centre) Within walking
distance of St Stephen's Green, this lovely
guesthouse is spread over two ivy-clad
Georgian houses off Baggot St. Rooms are
tastefully decorated with high-quality furnishings in authentic Farrow & Ball Georgian colours, and all have cable TV and
kettles. Home-cooked breakfast is served
in the conservatory or in the garden on
sunny days.

PEMBROKE TOWNHOUSE — INN $$

Map p258 (📋01-660 0277; www.pembroke
townhouse.ie; 90 Pembroke Rd; r from €150;
🅿🛜🛗; 🚇5, 7, 7A, 8, 18 or 45 from city centre) This once elegant boutique hotel in a

SLEEPING DOCKLANDS & THE GRAND CANAL

BEDS BEYOND THE ROYAL CANAL

Just beyond the Royal Canal, about 3km east of Upper O'Connell St in the suburb of
Drumcondra, are rows of late-Victorian and Edwardian houses, some of which offer
comfortable B&B rooms: the attraction is that they're on the road to the airport and
are served by all of the airport buses.

➡ **Griffith House** (📋01-837 5030; www.griffithhouse.com; 125 Griffith Ave; s/d €40/60;
🅿; 🚇41, 41B, 16A from city centre) Suburban elegance should never be underestimated,
especially not if it comes in the shape of this handsome Victorian home with four
elegant rooms, three of which are en suite. It's a simple, traditional place that puts the
emphasis on a warm welcome, a good night's sleep and a filling breakfast.

➡ **Croke Park Hotel** (📋01-607 0000; www.doylecollection.com; Croke Park, Jones's Rd;
r from €125; 🛜; 🚇3, 11, 11A, 16, 16A, 123 from O'Connell St) Just across the street from
the cathedral of Gaelic sports, this branch of the Jury's chain targets fans up for
the match. The rooms are big, clean and characterless – but what does that matter
when you're celebrating...or commiserating?

handsome Georgian townhouse has shown signs of age in recent years, and a spruce-up is long overdue. Nevertheless, it is still a comfortable place to stay and its location – on a leafy street near the bustling Baggot St – is excellent.

SPENCER HOTEL
HOTEL **$$**

Map p256 (✆01-433 8800; www.thespencer hotel.com; Custom House Quay; r/ste from €140/200; ⓟ@⟩⎙) This swanky business hotel in the heart of the Irish Financial Services Centre has beautiful rooms decorated with contemporary light oak furnishings, Respa beds and rainforest power showers. Guests have free use of the health club.

ARIEL HOUSE
INN **$$**

Map p258 (✆01-668 5512; www.ariel-house.net; 52 Lansdowne Rd; s/d from €99/139; ⓟ⟩; ⎕5, 7, 7A, 8, 18 or 45 from city centre) Somewhere between a boutique hotel and a luxury B&B, this highly rated Victorian-era property has 28 rooms with private bathrooms, all individually decorated in period furniture, which lends the place an air of genuine luxury. A far better choice than most hotels.

★MARKER
HOTEL **$$$**

Map p256 (✆01-687 5100; www.themarker hoteldublin.com; Grand Canal Sq; r from €220; ⓟ@⟩; ⧉Grand Canal Dock) Behind the eye-catching chequerboard facade created by Manuel Aires Mateus are 187 swanky rooms and suites decked out in a wintry palette (washed out citruses and cobalts) and starkly elegant furnishings, which give them an atmosphere of cool sophistication. The public areas are a little wilder and the rooftop bar is a summer favourite with the 'in' crowd.

DYLAN
HOTEL **$$$**

Map p258 (✆01-660 3001; www.dylan.ie; Eastmoreland Pl; r from €225; ✱@⟩; ⎕5, 7, 7A, 8, 18, 27X or 44 from city centre) The Dylan's baroque-meets-Scandinavian-sleek designer look has stood the test of time, despite opening when Celtic Tiger's brash-is-beautiful attitude was in full voice. These days the Dylan is just a stylishly elegant hotel, with wonderfully appointed rooms adorned in crisp Frette linen and a buzzy bar where the beautiful people still gather in force.

GIBSON HOTEL
HOTEL **$$$**

Map p256 (✆01-618 5000; www.thegibson hotel.ie; Point Village; r from €200; ⓟ@⟩; ⎕151 from city centre, ⧉The Point) Built for business travellers and out-of-towners taking in a gig at the 3 Arena (p156) next door, the Gibson is impressive: 250-odd ultramodern rooms decked out in Respa beds, flat-screen TVs and internet work stations. You might catch last night's star act having breakfast the next morning in the snazzy restaurant area.

Understand Dublin

Dublin Today

The last few years have been pretty tumultuous for Dublin. It has yo-yoed in and – largely – out of the biggest recession in Irish history, witnessed a landmark shift in social attitudes and still managed to prepare for the mother of all commemorations, the centenary of the 1916 Easter Rising. A general election brought a new government but little change, at least in the eyes of Dubliners who've grown increasingly disillusioned with the political process.

Best on Film

The Commitments (Alan Parker, 1994) Roddy Doyle's novel about a soul band in Dublin made into a terrific film by Alan Parker.

What Richard Did (Lenny Abrahamson, 2012) The story of what happens when a privileged youth assaults a romantic who dies of his injuries; loosely based on real events that occurred in 2000.

The Dead (John Huston, 1987) Stunning rendition of James Joyce's story from *Dubliners* starring Donal McCann and Angelica Huston.

Best in Print

Dubliners (James Joyce, 1914) Fifteen poignant and powerful tales of Dubliners and the moments that define their lives. Even if you never visit, read this book.

Strumpet City (James Plunkett, 1969) Epic novel set in Dublin between 1907 and 1914, especially the Lockout of 1913.

The Barrytown Trilogy (Roddy Doyle) *The Commitments* (1987), *The Snapper* (1990) and *The Van* (1991) – yes, they've all been made into films, but the books are still better.

Political (R)evolution

In February 2016 the Fine Gael/Labour government was given the heave-ho by an electorate sick of austerity and government insistence that they were doing the very best for the country. Seventy days later, a new government was formed – made up of Fine Gael and a motley collection of independents, while opposition party Fianna Fáil waits in the wings for the collapse that everyone assumes will happen long before the government's term is up.

Water Reaches Boiling Point

The single issue that sent many Dubliners over the edge and destroyed their confidence in the government was water, or rather the government's establishment of a new utility company that would collect water charges for the first time. The argument in favour was that the water utility needed serious upgrading and, anyway, most European countries paid water charges. The argument against was that this was a financial burden too heavy on a country already hit hard by the rigours of austerity, where key social services were slashed or eliminated altogether between 2009 and 2013 and wages fell by an average of 15%.

Protests against water charges got pretty heated: in one incident deputy prime minister Joan Burton was forced to remain in her car for several hours while angry protestors surrounded it. The water charges were implemented in 2014 but a year later nearly 40% of the citizenry had not paid their water bill, forcing the government into a series of embarrassing climbdowns on the issue of how much the charges would be and when they would be collected.

Marriage for All

Far less controversial than the water charges was the campaign for marriage equality, which resulted in the measure being overwhelmingly approved by universal plebiscite on 22 May 2015. When the results were announced in the grounds of Dublin Castle, the city exploded in rainbow-coloured joy: the motion had passed by 62% nationally, and by a whopping majority of 70% in Dublin. The city hadn't witnessed this level of celebration since the summer of 1990, when the Irish football team reached the quarter-finals of the World Cup in Italy. The party went on long into the night: for once, the reasoning went, Ireland was making headlines for all the right reasons.

But the result was about more than just the majority attitude to LGBT rights. It was about Generation Y turning its back once and for all on traditional Ireland, where the Catholic Church (who adopted a largely dignified opposition to the motion) was the final arbiter on all matters related to morality and social justice.

But it also showed that Dublin – for so long considered (and, in some quarters, condemned) as being liberally out of touch with the rest of the country – wasn't all that different to the rest of Ireland, and that the traditional urban-rural divide wasn't as pronounced as it was in decades past.

An Uncertain Future

The immediate political future is uncertain. The parliamentary stalemate will most likely provoke another general election by the end of 2016, which may result in the nearly miraculous rehabilitation of Fianna Fáil, the party that less than a decade ago was held accountable for the financial collapse. The water charges issue hasn't gone away, and Dubliners await a resolution one way or the other.

Marriage equality was the feel-good story of 2015, but the next big social issue is the future of abortion, as campaigners step up their efforts to force the government to hold a referendum on repealing the constitutional ban on abortion. Although the two main political parties, Fine Gael and Fianna Fáil, have shown little appetite for the issue and treat it as the third rail of Irish politics, polls demonstrate a huge shift in general attitudes, with 64% favouring allowing abortion in specific cases like fatal foetal abnormality or rape, with 25% against any kind of repeal.

Away from the big sociopolitical issues, Dubliners have more immediate concerns, namely a runaway rental market that has made renting even more expensive than it was during the Celtic Tiger; and the ongoing roadworks for the expansion of the Luas light rail system that have turned the city centre into a construction site: Dubliners are united in their hope that works finish soon so they can get their city back.

if Dublin were 100 people

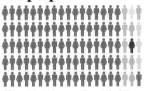

85 would be Irish
5 would be EU
1 would be British
1 would be American
1 would be Other European
3 would be Asian
3 would be African
1 would be Other

age of Dubliners
(% of population)

0-4 years old   5-12

13-18   18-65   65 and over

population per sq km

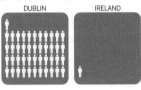

DUBLIN   IRELAND

≈ 65 people

History

Until a couple of decades ago, if you'd asked your average Dubliner the key to the city's complex history, they'd most likely give you a version of the past punctuated with '800 years'. This refers to the duration of the English (or British) occupation, the sine qua non of everything that happened to this city. No more. 'Eight hundred years' is now a historical anachronism, rendered irrelevant by contemporary concerns focused on where the city is going, not where it's been.

Early Footprints & Celtic Highways

Celtic society was ruled by Brehon Law, the tenets of which still form the basis of Ireland's ethical code today.

Stone Age farmers who arrived in Ireland between 10,000 and 8000 BC provided the country's genetic stock and lay the foundations of its agricultural economy. During the following Bronze Age, in addition to discovering and crafting metals to stock the future National Museum, they also found time to refine their farming techniques and raise livestock.

Iron Age warriors from Eastern Europe, who were known as the Celts, arrived in the country around 500 BC and divided Ireland into provinces and myriad districts ruled by chieftains. Roads connecting these provinces converged at a ford over the River Liffey called Átha Cliath (Ford of the Hurdles) and the settlement that grew up at this junction during the 9th century was to give Dublin its Irish name, Baile Átha Cliath (Town of the Hurdle Ford).

The Coming of Christianity

St Patrick founded the See of Dublin sometime in the mid-5th century and went about the business of conversion in present-day Wicklow and Malahide, before laying hands on Leoghaire, the King of Ireland, using water from a well next to St Patrick's Cathedral. Or so the story goes. Irrespective of the details, Patrick and his monk buddies were successful because they managed to fuse the strong tradition of druidism and pagan ritual with the new Christian teaching, which created an exciting hybrid known as Celtic, or Insular, Christianity.

TIMELINE	10,000 BC	500 BC	AD 431–432
	Human beings arrive in Ireland during the mesolithic era, originally crossing a land bridge between Scotland and Ireland and later the sea in hide-covered boats.	Iron Age warriors from Eastern Europe, known as the Celts, divide Ireland into provinces and myriad districts ruled by chieftains.	Pope Celestine I sends Bishop Palladius to Ireland to minister to those 'already believing in Christ'; St Patrick arrives the following year to continue the mission.

Compared to new hot spots like Clonmacnoise in County Offaly and Glendalough in County Wicklow, Dublin was a rural backwater and didn't really figure in the Golden Age, when Irish Christian scholars excelled in the study of Latin and Greek learning and Christian theology. They studied in the monasteries that were, in essence, Europe's most important universities, producing brilliant students, magnificent illuminated books such as the *Book of Kells* (now housed in Trinity College), ornate jewellery and the many carved stone crosses that dot the island 'of saints and scholars'.

The nature of Christianity in Ireland was one of marked independence from Rome, especially in the areas of monastic rule and penitential practice, which emphasised private confession to a priest followed by penances levied by the priest in reparation – which is the spirit and letter of the practice of confession that exists to this day.

St Patrick showed a remarkable understanding of Celtic power structures by working to convert chieftains rather than ordinary Celts, who inevitably followed their leaders into adopting the new religion.

The Vikings

Raids by marauding Vikings had been a fact of Irish life for quite some time, before a group of them decided to take a break from their hell-raising to build a harbour (or *longphort,* in Irish) on the banks of the Liffey in 837. Although a Celtic army forced them out some 65 years later, they returned in 917 with a massive fleet, established a stronghold by the black pool at Wood Quay, just behind Christ Church Cathedral, and dug their heels in. They went back to plundering the countryside but also laid down guidelines on plot sizes and town boundaries for their town of 'Dyflinn' (derived from the Irish for 'black pool', *'dubh linn'*), which became the most prominent trading centre in the Viking world.

But their good times came to an end in 1014 when an alliance of Irish clans led by Brian Ború decisively whipped them (and the Irish clans that *didn't* side with Brian Ború) at the Battle of Clontarf, forever breaking the Scandinavian grip on the eastern seaboard. However, rather than abandoning the place in defeat, the Vikings enjoyed Dublin so much that they decided to stay there and integrate.

Strongbow & the Normans

The next wave of invaders came in 1169, when an army of Cambro-Norman knights led by Richard de Clare (better known as Strongbow) landed in Wexford at the urging of Dermot MacMurrough, ousted King of Leinster, who needed help to regain his throne. As a gesture of thanks, MacMurrough made Strongbow his heir and gave him Aoife, his daughter, as a wife. Strongbow and his knights then took Dublin in 1170 and decided to make it their new capital.

Best Books

Dublin: The Making of a Capital City (2014) David Dickson

Come Here to Me: Dublin's Other History (2013) Donal Fallon, Sam McGrath and Ciaran Murray

Dublin: A Cultural & Literary History (2005) Siobhán Kilfeather

Stones of Dublin: A History of Dublin in Ten Buildings (2014) Lisa Marie Griffith

A Short History of Dublin (2010) Richard Killeen

917	988	1169	1170
Plundering Vikings establish a new settlement at the mouth of the harbour and call it 'Dyfflin', which soon becomes a centre of economic power.	High King Mael Seachlainn II leads the permanent Irish conquest of Dyfflin, giving the settlement its modern name in Irish – Baile Átha Cliath, meaning 'Town of the Hurdle Ford'.	Henry II's Welsh and Norman barons capture Waterford and Wexford with the help of Dermot MacMurrough, beginning a 750-year occupation of Ireland by Britain.	Strongbow captures Dublin and then takes Aoife, MacMurrough's daughter, as his wife before being crowned King of Leinster.

During the 12th century Dublin became a pilgrimage city, in part because it housed the Bacall Íosa (staff of Jesus), St Patrick's legendary crozier.

Christ Church Cathedral (p100)

For all their might, the Anglo-Normans' dominance was limited to a walled area surrounding what today is loosely Greater Dublin, and was then called 'the Pale'. Beyond the Pale – a phrase that entered the English language to mean 'beyond convention' – Ireland remained unbowed and unconquered.

Meanwhile, King Henry II of England, concerned that the Normans might set up a rival power base in Ireland, organised his own invading force, and landed his army in 1171 – with the blessing of Pope Adrian IV, who wanted Henry to make Ireland's renegade monks toe the Roman line.

The Normans declared their fealty to the English throne and set about reconstructing and fortifying their new capital. In 1172 construction began on Christ Church Cathedral, and 20 years later work began on St Patrick's Cathedral, a few hundred metres to the south.

Henry II's son, King John, commissioned the construction of Dublin Castle in 1204 'for the safe custody of our treasure...and the defence of the city'. As capital of the English 'colony' in Ireland, Dublin expanded. Trade was organised and craft guilds developed, although membership was limited to those of 'English name and blood'.

1172	1297	1315	1317
King Henry II of England invades Ireland, forcing the Cambro-Norman warlords and some of the Gaelic Irish kings to accept him as their overlord.	Dublin becomes the main seat of the Parliament of Ireland, comprised of merchants and landowners.	A Scottish army led by Edward de Bruce attacks the city; waning English interest in defending Dublin forces the Earls of Kildare to become the city's main protector.	Ireland's worst famine of the Middle Ages kills off thousands and reduces some to cannibalism.

As Dublin grew bigger so did its problems, and over the next few centuries misery seemed to pile upon mishap. In 1317 Ireland's worst famine of the Middle Ages killed off thousands and reduced some to cannibalism. In 1348 the country was decimated by the Black Death, the devastating recurrence of which over the following century indicates the terrible squalor of medieval Dublin.

In the 15th century the English extended their influence beyond the Pale by throwing their weight behind the dominant Irish lords. The atmosphere was becoming markedly cosier as the Anglo-Norman occupiers began to follow previous invaders by integrating into Irish culture.

The Tudors & the Protestant Ascendancy

Ireland presented a particular challenge to Henry VIII (r 1509–47), in part due to the Anglo-Norman lords' more or less unfettered power over the country, which didn't sit well with Henry's belief in strong monarchical rule. He decreed absolute royal power over Ireland, but the Irish lords weren't going to take it lying down.

In 1534 the most powerful of Leinster's Anglo-Normans, 'Silken' Thomas Fitzgerald, renounced his allegiance to the king, and Henry came at him ferociously: within a year Fitzgerald was dead and all his lands confiscated. Henry ordered the surrender of all lands to the English Crown and, three years later, after his spat with Rome, he dissolved the monasteries and all Church lands passed to the newly constituted Anglican Church. Dublin was declared an Anglican city and relics such as the Bacall Íosa (Staff of Jesus) were destroyed.

Elizabeth I (r 1558–1603) came to the throne with the same uncompromising attitude to Ireland as her father. Ulster was the most hostile to her, with the Irish fighting doggedly under the command of Hugh O'Neill, the Earl of Tyrone, but they too were finally defeated in 1603.

O'Neill's defeat signalled the end of Gaelic Ireland and the renewed colonisation of the country through plantation. Loyal Protestants from England and Scotland were awarded the rich agricultural, confiscated lands of Ulster, sowing the bitter seeds of division that blight the province to this day. Unlike previous arrivals, these new colonists kept very much apart from the native Irish, who were left disenfranchised, landless and reduced to a state of near misery.

All the while, Dublin prospered as the bulwark of English domination and became a bastion of Protestantism. A chasm developed between the 'English' city and the 'Irish' countryside, where there was continuing unrest and growing resentment. After winning the English Civil War (1641–51), Oliver Cromwell came to Ireland to personally reassert English control and, while Protestant Dublin was left untouched (save the

Hugh O'Neill achieved something of a pyrrhic victory in 1603 when he refused to surrender until after he heard of Elizabeth I's death. He and his fellow earls then fled the country in what become known as the Flight of the Earls.

1348	1350–1530	1487	1487
Roughly half of the city's population of 30,000 succumbs to the Black Death; victims were buried in mass graves in an area of the Liberties still known as the 'Blackpitts'.	The Anglo-Norman barons establish power bases independent of the English crown. English control gradually extends to an area around Dublin known as 'the Pale'.	Gerard Mór Fitzgerald, Earl of Kildare, occupies Dublin with help of troops from Burgundy, in direct defiance of King Henry VII.	Fitzgerald supports claims of Yorkist pretender Lambert Simnel, a 10-year-old who is crowned King Edward VI in Christ Church Cathedral.

use of St Patrick's Cathedral as a stable for English horses), his troops were uncompromising in their dealing with rebellion up and down the eastern coast.

Georgian Dublin & the Golden Age

Following the Restoration of 1660 and the coronation of Charles II (r 1660–85), Dublin embarked upon a century of unparalleled development and essentially waved two fingers at the rest of Ireland, which was being brought to its knees. In 1690 the rest of Ireland backed the losing side when it took up arms for the Catholic king of England, James II (r 1685–88), who was ultimately defeated by the Protestant William of Orange at the Battle of the Boyne, not far from Dublin, in 1690.

William's victory ushered in the punitive Penal Code, which stripped Catholics of most basic rights in a single, sweeping legislative blow. Again, however, the country's misfortune proved the capital's gain as the city was flooded with landless refugees willing to work for a pittance.

With plenty of cash to go around and an eagerness to live in a city that reflected their new-found wealth, the Protestant nobility overhauled Dublin during the reigns of the four Georges (1714–1830). Speculators bought up swathes of land and commissioned substantial projects of urban renewal, including the creation of new streets, the laying out of city parks and the construction of magnificent new buildings and residences.

It was impossible to build in the heart of the medieval city, so the nouveau riche moved north across the river, creating a new Dublin of stately squares surrounded by fine Georgian mansions. The elegantly made-over Dublin became the second city in the British Empire and the fifth largest in Europe.

Dublin's teeming, mostly Catholic, slums soon spread north in pursuit of the rich, who turned back south to grand new homes around Merrion Sq, St Stephen's Green and Fitzwilliam Sq.

The end of the 17th century saw an influx of Huguenot weavers, who settled in Dublin after fleeing anti-Protestant legislation in France and established a successful cloth industry, largely in the Liberties, that helped fuel the city's growth.

Dublin Declines, Catholicism Rises

Constant migration from the countryside into Dublin meant that, by the end of the 18th century, the capital had a Catholic majority, most of whom lived in terrible conditions in ever-worsening slums. Inspired by the Enlightenment and the principles of the French Revolution of 1789, many leading Irish figures (nearly all of whom were Protestant) began to question the quality and legitimacy of British rule.

Rebellion was in the air by the turn of the century, starting with the abortive French invasion at the urging of Dubliner Wolfe Tone (1763–98)

1537	1584	1592	1594–1603
'Silken' Thomas Fitzgerald, son of the Earl of Kildare, storms Dublin and its English garrisons. The rebellion is squashed; Thomas and his followers are executed.	Mayoress Margaret Ball dies following imprisonment for her Catholic sympathies. Archbishop Dermot O'Hurley is hanged for his support of a rebellion against the English crown.	Trinity College is founded on the grounds of a former monastery, on the basis of a charter granted by Elizabeth I to 'stop Ireland being infected by popery'.	Nine Years' War between English and Irish chieftains led by Hugh O'Neill brings English troops to Dublin, who force citizenry to house them.

and his United Irishmen in 1798. The 'Year of the French' resulted in defeat for the invaders and the death of Tone, but in 1803 the United Irishmen tried again, this time under the leadership of Robert Emmet (1778–1803), which also resulted in failure and Emmet's execution on Thomas St, near the Guinness brewery.

It was only a matter of time before Dublin's bubble burst, and the pin came in the form of the 1801 Act of Union, which dissolved the Irish parliament (originally established in 1297) and reintroduced direct rule from Westminster. Many of the upper classes fled to London, the dramatic growth that had characterised Dublin in the previous century came to an almost immediate halt, and the city fell into a steady decline.

While Dublin was licking its wounds, a Kerry lawyer called Daniel O'Connell (1775–1847) launched his campaign to recover basic rights for Catholics, achieving much with the Catholic Emancipation Act of 1829. The 'Liberator', as he came to be known, became the first Catholic lord mayor of Dublin, in 1841.

In 1745 when James Fitzgerald, the Earl of Kildare, started construction of Leinster House he was mocked for his move into the wilds. 'Where I go society will follow', he confidently predicted. He was right; today Leinster House is the seat of Irish parliament and is in modern Dublin's centre.

A Nation's Soup Kitchen

Rural Ireland had become overwhelmingly dependent on the easily grown potato. Blight – a disease that rots tubers – had always been an occasional hazard, but when three successive crops failed between 1845 and 1847, it spelt disaster. The human cost was cataclysmic: up to one million people died from disease and starvation, while more again fled the country for Britain and the United States. The damage was compounded by the British government's adoption of a laissez-faire economic policy, which opposed food aid for famine occurring within the Empire. In Ireland, landowners refused to countenance any forbearance on rents, all the while exporting crops to foreign markets. Defaulters – starving or not – were penalised with incarceration in workhouses or prison.

The British government's uncompromising stance hardened the steel of opposition. The deaths and mass exodus caused by the Famine had a profound social and cultural effect on Ireland and left a scar on the Irish psyche that cannot be overestimated. Urban Dublin escaped the worst ravages, but desperate migrants flooded into the city looking for relief – soup kitchens were set up all over the city, including in the bucolic Merrion Sq, where presumably its affluent residents bore direct witness to the tragedy.

The horrors of the Famine and its impact on Dublin's centre saw the wealthy abandon the city for a new set of salubrious suburbs south of Dublin along the coast, now accessible via Ireland's first railway

1597	1603	1640s–1682	1680
An accidental explosion in a gunpowder store in Winetavern St kills 200 civilians.	Hugh O'Neill and the Irish fighting under his command in Ulster are defeated by Elizabeth I's forces. He and his fellow earls flee the country in what is known as the Flight of the Earls.	Dublin's resurgence begins as the city's population grows from 10,000 in the mid-1640s to nearly 60,000 in 1682.	The architectural style known as Anglo-Dutch results in the construction of notable buildings such as the Royal Hospital, Kilmainham, now the Irish Museum of Modern Art.

line, built in 1834 to connect the city to Kingstown (present-day Dun Laoghaire). The flight from the city continued for the next 70 years and many of the fine Georgian residences became slum dwellings. With such squalor came a host of social ills, including alcohol, which had always been a source of solace but now became a chronic problem.

The Blossoming of National Pride

In the second half of the 19th century, Dublin was staunchly divided along sectarian lines and, although Catholics were still partly second-class citizens, a burgeoning Catholic middle class provided the impetus for Ireland's march towards independence.

Charles Stewart Parnell suffered a swift fall from grace after it was made public that he had been having an affair with a married woman, Kitty O'Shea. He was ditched as leader of his own Irish Parliamentary Party in 1890 and died a broken man the following year. More than 200,000 people attended his funeral at Glasnevin Cemetery.

It was the dashing figure of Protestant landlord Charles Stewart Parnell (1846–91), from County Wicklow, that first harnessed the broad public support for Home Rule. Elected to Westminster in 1875, the 'Uncrowned King of Ireland' campaigned tirelessly for land reform and a Dublin parliament.

He appeared to have an ally in the British prime minister, William Gladstone, who lightened the burden on tenants by passing Land Acts enabling them to buy property. He was also converted to the cause of Home Rule, for both principled reasons and practical ones: the granting of some form of self-government would at least have the effect of reconciling Irish nationalism to the British state.

In the twilight of the 19th century there was a move to preserve all things Irish. The Gaelic Athletic Association (GAA) was set up in 1884 to promote Irish sports, while Douglas Hyde and Eoin McNeill formed the Gaelic League in 1893 to encourage Irish arts and language. The success of the Gaelic League paved the way for the Celtic Revival Movement, spearheaded by WB Yeats and Lady Gregory, who founded the Abbey Theatre in 1904.

The Struggle for Independence

Although Irish culture was thriving at the start of the 20th century, the country's peaceful efforts to free itself from British rule were thwarted at every juncture. Dublin's slums were the worst in Europe, and the emergence of militant trade unionism introduced a socialist agenda to the struggle for self-determination.

In 1905 Arthur Griffith (1871–1922) founded a new political movement called Sinn Féin ('Ourselves Alone'), which sought to achieve Home Rule through passive resistance rather than political lobbying. It urged the Irish to withhold taxes and its MPs to form an Irish government in Dublin.

1695	1757	1759	1801
Penal Laws prohibit Catholics from owning a horse, marrying outside their religion and from buying or inheriting property; within 100 years Catholics will own only 5% of Irish land.	The Wide Street Commission is set up to design the framework of a modern city: new parks are laid out, streets widened and new public buildings commissioned.	Arthur Guinness buys a disused brewery on a plot of land opposite St James's Gate. Initially he brews only ale, but in the 1770s turns his expertise to a new beer called porter.	The Act of Union unites Ireland politically with Britain. The Irish Parliament votes itself out of existence following an intensive campaign of bribery.

CAUSE OF LABOUR IS THE CAUSE OF IRELAND   THE CAUSE OF IRELAND IS THE CAUSE OF LABO

JAMES
CONNOLLY
1868 – 1916

Statue of James Connolly, near Liberty Hall (p137)

By 1910 it was reckoned that 20,000 Dublin families each occupied a single room.

Meanwhile, trade union leaders Jim Larkin and James Connolly agitated against low wages and corporate greed, culminating in the Dublin Lockout of 1913, where 300 employers 'locked out' 20,000 workers for five months. During this time Connolly established the Irish Citizen Army (ICA) to defend striking workers from the police. Things were heating up.

Home Rule was finally passed by Westminster in 1914, but its provisions were suspended for the duration of WWI. Bowing to pressure from Protestant-dominated Ulster, where 140,000 members of the newly formed Ulster Volunteer Force (UVF) swore to resist any attempts to weaken British rule in Ireland, the bill also made provisions for the 'temporary' exclusion of the North from the workings of the future act. How temporary was 'temporary' was anybody's guess – and

British prime minister William Gladstone introduced Home Rule bills three times into the House of Commons between 1886 and 1895, but the House of Lords voted them down on each occasion.

1839	1840	1841	1845–51
Following a powerful campaign by Daniel O'Connell, the 'Liberator', the Catholic Emancipation Act is passed, repealing the remaining Penal Laws.	The Corporation Act allows Catholics to vote in local elections for the first time since the 1690s, giving them a two-to-one majority.	Daniel O'Connell is elected the first Catholic mayor of Dublin in 150 years; one of his first acts is to found a multidenominational cemetery in Glasnevin.	A mould called phytophthora ravages the potato harvest. The Great Famine is the single greatest catastrophe in Irish history, with the deaths of up to one million people.

When WWI ended in 1918, 50,000 Irish citizens had lost their lives.

it was in such political fudging that the seeds of trouble were sown. To counter the potential threat from the UVF, Irish nationalists formed the Irish Volunteer Force (IVF), but a stand-off was avoided when the vast majority of them enlisted in the British Army: if Britain was going to war 'in defence of small nations', then loyalty to the Allied cause would help Ireland's long-term aspirations.

The Easter Rising

The more radical factions within Sinn Féin, the IVF and the ICA saw Britain's difficulty as Ireland's opportunity, and planned to rise up against the Crown on Easter Sunday, 1916. In typical fashion, the rhetoric of the rebellion outweighed the quality of the planning. When the head of the IVF, Eoin McNeill, got wind of the plans, he published an advertisement in the newspaper cancelling the planned 'manoeuvres'. The leaders rescheduled the revolution for the following day but word never spread beyond the capital, where a motley band of about a thousand rebels assembled and seized strategic buildings. The main garrison was the General Post Office, outside which the poet and school teacher Pádraig Pearse read out the 'Proclamation of the Republic'.

Many Dubliners were appalled at the sentences received by the leaders of the Rising, especially the fate suffered by 18-year-old Willie Pearse, whose main offence was that he was Pádraig's brother. James Connolly, the hero of the Dublin working classes, was severely injured during the Rising, so was strapped to a chair and shot.

The British Army didn't take the insurgence seriously at first but after a few soldiers were killed, they sent a gunboat down the Liffey to rain shells on the rebels. After six days of fighting the city centre was ravaged and the death toll stood at 300 civilians, 130 British troops (many of whom were Irish) and 60 rebels.

The rebels, prompted by Pearse's fear of further civilian casualties, surrendered and were arrested. Crowds gathered to mock and jeer them as they were led away. Initially, Dubliners resented them for the damage they had caused in their futile rising, but their attitudes began to change following the executions of the leaders in Kilmainham Gaol. The hostility shown to the rebels turned to outright sympathy and support.

The War of Independence

In the 1918 general election, the more radical Sinn Féin party won three quarters of the Irish seats. In May 1919 they declared independence and established the first Dáil Éireann (Irish Assembly) in Dublin's Mansion House, led by Éamon de Valera. This was effectively a declaration of war.

Mindful that they could never match the British on the battlefield, Sinn Féin's military wing – made up of Irish Volunteers now renamed the Irish Republican Army (IRA) – began attacking arms dumps and barracks in guerrilla strikes. The British countered by strengthening

1867	1882	1905	1913
Several thousand supporters of the Irish Republican Brotherhood (IRB) fight the police in Tallaght; they disperse and some 200 agitators are arrested.	An offshoot of the IRB, known as the Invincibles, assassinate the Chief Secretary and his assistant in Phoenix Park.	Journalist Arthur Griffiths founds a new movement whose aim is independence under a dual monarchy; he names the movement Sinn Féin, meaning 'Ourselves Alone'.	The largest labour dispute in Irish history sees 20,000 Dublin workers 'locked out' for five months by defiant employers.

the Royal Irish Constabulary (RIC) and introducing a tough auxiliary force made up of returning WWI servicemen known as the Black and Tans (after the colour of their uniforms).

They met their match in Michael Collins, the IRA's commander and a master of guerrilla warfare. Although the British knew his name, Collins masterfully concealed his identity and throughout the war was able to freewheel around the city on his bicycle like he didn't have a care in the world.

On 10 November 1920, Collins learned that 14 undercover British intelligence operatives known as the 'Cairo Gang' had just arrived in Dublin. The following morning he had his own crack squad ('the Apostles') assassinate each one of them as they lay in their beds. That afternoon, British troops retaliated by opening fire on the crowd at a hurling match in Croke Park, resulting in the death of 10 spectators and one player, Michael Hogan, whose death was later commemorated when the main stand at the stadium was named after him. The events of 'Bloody Sunday' galvanised both sides in the conflict and served to quash any moral doubts over what was becoming an increasingly brutal struggle.

Brutalities notwithstanding, the war resulted in relatively few casualties – 2014 in total – and by mid-1921 had ground to a kind of stalemate. Both sides were under pressure to end it: the international community was urging Britain to resolve the issue one way or another, while, unbeknownst to the British, the IRA was on the verge of collapse. A truce was signed on 11 July 1921.

Éamon de Valera, the leader of the first Dáil Éireann (Irish Assembly), was spared the firing squad in 1916 because of his US birth; killing him would have been a public-relations disaster.

Civil War

The terms of – and the circumstances surrounding – the Treaty that ended the War of Independence make up the single most divisive episode in Irish politics, one that still breeds prejudice, inflames passions and shapes the political landscape in parts of the country.

After months of argument and facing the threat of, in the words of British Prime Minister Lloyd George, an 'immediate and terrible war', the Irish negotiating team, led by Michael Collins, signed the Anglo-Irish Treaty on 6 December 1921. Instead of establishing the Irish Republic for which the IRA had fought, it created an Irish Free State, effectively a British dominion, in which members of the newly constituted parliament would have to swear allegiance to the British Crown before they could participate in government. The six counties comprising Northern Ireland were given the choice of becoming part of the Free State or remaining in the United Kingdom; they chose the latter, sowing the seeds of discontent that would lead to further rounds of the

The 1922 Civil War began when anti-Treaty IRA forces occupied Dublin's Four Courts and were shelled by pro-Treaty forces, led by Michael Collins. Dublin, which escaped any real damage during the War of Independence, became a primary theatre of the Civil War, which cost the lives of 250 Dubliners.

1916	1919–21	1921–22	1948
Republicans take the GPO in Dublin and announce the formation of an Irish Republic. After less than a week of fighting, the rebels surrender and are summarily executed.	The Irish War of Independence begins in January 1919. Two years (and 2014 casualties) later, the war ends in a truce on 11 July 1921, leading to peace talks.	The Anglo-Irish Treaty is signed on 6 December. It gives 26 counties of Ireland independence and six Ulster counties the choice of opting out. The Irish Free State is founded in 1922.	Fine Gael, in coalition with the new Republican Clann na Poblachta, wins the 1948 general election and declares the Free State a republic.

General Post Office (p134)

Author and treaty negotiator Robert Erskine Childers was executed by the government on 24 November 1922. Childers ended up on the anti-Treaty side during the Civil War, but was arrested for possessing a gun given to him by (the now pro-Treaty) Michael Collins and sentenced to death.

Troubles in the North. Although Collins was dissatisfied with the deal, he hoped it would be the 'first real step' in the journey towards an Irish republic. Nevertheless, he also foresaw trouble and remarked prophetically that 'I've just signed my own death warrant'.

De Valera vehemently opposed the Treaty and the two erstwhile comrades were pitted against one another into pro-Treaty and anti-Treaty camps. Although the Dáil narrowly ratified the Treaty and the electorate accepted it by a large majority, Ireland slid into civil war during June 1922.

Ironically, the Civil War was more brutal than the struggle that preceded it. In 11 months roughly 3000 Irish died – including 77 state executions – but the vindictive nature of the fighting left indelible scars that have yet to be fully healed. The assassination of Michael

1949	1960s	1969	1972
Ireland leaves the British Commonwealth, and the South cut its links to the North.	A construction boom sees the growth of new suburbs north and south of the city in an effort to re-house Dubliners removed from dangerous city-centre tenements.	Marches in Derry are disrupted by Loyalist attacks and heavy-handed police action, culminating in the 'Battle of the Bogside' (12–14 August). It marks the beginning of the 'Troubles'.	Angry demonstrators burn the British Embassy in Dublin in response to the killing of 13 civilians in Derry by British paratroopers.

Collins in his home county of Cork on 22 August 1922 rocked the country; 500,000 people (almost one-fifth of the population) attended his funeral. The last few months of fighting were especially ugly, with both sides engaging in tit-for-tat atrocities. On 24 May 1923, de Valera ordered the anti-Treaty forces to drop their arms.

The Irish Republic

Ireland finally entered a phase of peace. Without an armed struggle to pursue – at least not one pursued by the majority – the IRA became a marginalised force in independent Ireland and Sinn Féin fell apart. In 1926 de Valera created a new party, Fianna Fáil (Soldiers of Destiny), which has been the dominant force in Irish politics ever since. Over the following decades Fianna Fáil gradually eliminated most of the clauses of the Treaty with which it had disagreed (including the oath of allegiance).

In 1932 a freshly painted Dublin hosted the 31st Eucharistic Congress, which drew visitors from around the world. The Catholic Church began to wield disproportionate control over the affairs of the state; contraception was made illegal in the 1930s and the age of consent was raised from 16 to 17.

In 1936, when the IRA refused to disarm, de Valera had it banned. The following year the Civil War–tainted moniker 'Free State' was dropped in favour of Eire as the country's official name in a rewrite of the constitution.

Despite having done much of the groundwork, Fianna Fáil lost out to its rivals Fine Gael, descendants of the original pro-Treaty Free State government, on declaring the 26 counties a republic in 1949.

The Stroll to Modernisation

Sean Lemass succeeded de Valera as Taoiseach (prime minister) in 1959 and set about fixing the Irish economy, which he did so effectively that the rate of emigration soon halved. While neighbouring London was swinging in the '60s, Dublin was definitely swaying. Youngsters from rural communities poured into the expanding city and it seemed like the good times were never going to end. But, almost inevitably, the economy slid back into recession.

On the 50th anniversary of the 1916 Easter Rising, Nelson's Pillar on O'Connell St was partially blown up by the IRA and crowds cheered as the remainder was removed the following week. Republicanism was still prevalent and a new round of the 'Troubles' were about to flair up in the North.

Although Ireland remained neutral during WWII – as a way of pushing its independence – Dublin's North Strand was hit by a 227kg German bomb on 31 May 1941, killing more than 30 and injuring 90.

1974	1988	1990s	1993
Simultaneous bombings in Monaghan and Dublin on 17 May leave 33 dead and 300 injured, the biggest loss of life in any single day during the Troubles.	Dublin celebrates its millennium, even though the town was established long before 988.	Low corporate tax, decades of investment in higher education, transfer payments from the EU and a low-cost labour market lead to the 'Celtic Tiger' boom.	20,000 demonstrators call for an end to IRA violence as a result of the bomb that killed two children in Warrington, England.

The visit of Pope John Paul II in 1979 – the first time for a pontiff – saw more than one million people flock to Phoenix Park to hear him say Mass.

Ireland joined the European Economic Community (EEC), a forerunner to the European Union (EU), in 1973 and got a significant leg-up from the organisation's coffers over the following decades. But the tides of change were once again on the rise. Political instability and an international recession did little to help hopes of economic recovery, and by the early '80s emigration was once again a major issue. But Ireland – and Dublin in particular – was growing increasingly liberal, and was straining at the shackles imposed on its social and moral mores by a largely conservative Catholic Church. Politicians too were seen in a new light as stories of corruption and cronyism became increasingly commonplace.

Dublin was hardly touched by the sectarian tensions that would pull Northern Ireland asunder, although 25 people died after three Loyalist car bombs exploded in the city in 1974.

From Celtic Tiger...

In the early 1990s European funds helped kick-start economic growth. Huge sums of money were invested in education and physical infrastructure, while the policy of low corporate tax rates coupled with attractive incentives made Ireland very attractive to high-tech businesses looking for a door into EU markets. In less than a decade, Ireland went from being one of the poorest countries in Europe to one of the wealthiest: unemployment fell from 18% to 3.5%, the average industrial wage somersaulted to the top of the European league, and the dramatic rise in GDP meant that the country laid claim to an economic model of success that was the envy of the entire world. Ireland became synonymous with the term 'Celtic Tiger'.

...To Rescue Cat

From 2002 the Irish economy was kept buoyant by a gigantic construction boom that was completely out of step with any measure of responsible growth forecasting. The out-of-control international derivatives market flooded Irish banks with cheap money, and they lent it freely.

Then Lehman Bros and the credit crunch happened. The Irish banks nearly went to the wall, but were bailed out at the last minute, and before Ireland could draw breath, the International Monetary Fund (IMF) and the EU held the chits of the country's mid-term economic future. Ireland found itself yet again confronting the familiar demons of high unemployment and emigration, but a deep-cutting program of austerity saw the corner turned by the end of 2014.

2007	2008	2009	2011
The IRA ends its campaign of violence on 28 July, ordering its units to assist 'the development of purely political and democratic programs through exclusively peaceful means'.	The global financial crisis triggers the collapse of the Irish banking system and the property boom; Ireland's economy goes into financial free-fall.	The publication of the Murphy Report reveals a vast network of secrecy and cover-up of widespread crimes of sexual abuse by serving priests within the Dublin diocese.	National elections result in a coalition between Fine Gael and Labour; for the first time Fianna Fáil fail to win any seats in Dublin.

Literary Dublin

Dubliners know a thing or two about the written word. No other city of comparable size can claim four Nobel Prize winners for Literature, but the city's impact on the English-reading world extends far beyond the fab four of Shaw, Yeats, Beckett and Heaney...one name, folks: James Joyce.

Literary Capital

Before Dublin was even a glint in a Viking's eye, Ireland was the land of saints and scholars, thanks to the monastic universities that sprang up around the country to foster the spread of Christianity and the education of Europe's privileged elite. But for our purposes, we need to fast-forward 1000 years to the 18th century and the glory days of Georgian Dublin, when the Irish and English languages began to cross-fertilise. Experimenting with English, using turns of phrase and expressions translated directly from Gaeilge, and combining these with a uniquely Irish perspective on life, Irish writers have dazzled and delighted readers for centuries. British theatre critic Kenneth Tynan summed it up in the *Observer* thus: 'The English hoard words like misers: the Irish spend them like sailors.'

Dublin has as many would-be sailors as Hollywood has frustrated waitresses, and it often seems like a bottomless well of creativity. The section given over to Irish writers is often the largest and busiest in any local bookstore, reflecting not only a rich literary tradition and thriving contemporary scene, but also an appreciative, knowledgeable and hungry local audience that attends readings and poetry recitals like rock fans at a gig.

Indeed, Dublin has produced so many writers, and has been written about so much, that you could easily plan a Dublin literary holiday. *A Literary Guide to Dublin*, by Vivien Igoe, includes detailed route maps, a guide to cemeteries and an eight-page section on literary and historical pubs. A Norman Jeffares' *Irish Writers: From Swift to Heaney* also has detailed and accessible summaries of writers and their work.

Old Literary Dublin

Modern Irish literature begins with Jonathan Swift (1667–1745), the master satirist, social commentator, dean of St Patrick's Cathedral and author of *Gulliver's Travels*. Fast-forward a couple of centuries and you're in the company of acclaimed dramatist Oscar Wilde (1854–1900); *Dracula* creator Bram Stoker (1847–1912) – some have claimed that the name of the count may have come from the Irish *droch fhola* (bad blood); and playwright and essayist George Bernard Shaw (1856–1950), author of *Pygmalion* (which was later turned into *My Fair Lady*), who hailed from Synge St near the Grand Canal.

Towering above all of them – in reputation if not popularity – is James Joyce (1882–1941), whose name and books elicit enormous pride in Ireland. The majority of Joyce's literary output came when he had left Ireland for the artistic hotbed that was Paris, which was also true

If you want to see Beckett's phone, Behan's union card and a first edition of *Dracula* all under the one roof, the Dublin Writers' Museum has extensive collections of the city's most famous (dead) writers.

for another great experimenter of language and style, Samuel Beckett (1906–89). Beckett's work centres on fundamental existential questions about the human condition and the nature of self. He is probably best known for his play *Waiting for Godot,* but his unassailable reputation is based on a series of stark novels and plays.

Of the dozens of 20th-century Irish authors to have achieved published renown, some names to look out for include playwright and novelist Brendan Behan (1923–64), who wove tragedy, wit and a turbulent life into his best works, including *Borstal Boy, The Quare Fellow* and *The Hostage,* before dying young of alcoholism. A collection of his newspaper columns was published under the title *Hold Your Hour and Have Another.*

The Contemporary Scene

'I love James Joyce. Never read him, but he's a true genius.' And while this is certainly true of Dublin's greatest literary son, most Dubliners feel more or less the same about the other literary giants of yesteryear. Ask them for their favourite contemporary authors, though, and you'd kick off a knowledgeable debate peppered with dozens of worthy names.

They might mention Roddy Doyle (1958–), whose mega-successful Barrytown quartet – *The Commitments, The Snapper, The Van* and *Paddy Clarke, Ha Ha Ha* – have all been made into films; his latest book, *The Guts* (2013), saw the return of *The Commitments* protagonist Jimmy Rabbitte – older, wiser and battling illness.

Sebastian Barry (1955–) has been shortlisted twice for the Man Booker Prize, for his WWI drama *A Long Long Way* (2005) and the absolutely compelling *The Secret Scripture* (2008), about a 100-year-old inmate of a mental hospital called Roseanne who decides to write an autobiography. His latest novel, *The Temporary Gentleman* (2014), tells the story of Roseanne's brother-in-law, Jack McNulty, an ex-British Army officer posted to Africa during WWII but unable to return home to Ireland because of personal and professional guilt.

Anne Enright (1962–) did nab the Booker for *The Gathering* (2007), a zeitgeist tale of alcoholism and abuse – she described it as 'the intellectual equivalent of a Hollywood weepie'. Her latest novel, *The Green Road* (2015), continues to mine the murky waters of the Irish family. Another Booker Prize winner is heavyweight John Banville (1945–), who won it for *The Sea* (2005); we also recommend either *The Book of Evidence* (1989) or the masterful roman-à-clef *The Untouchable* (1997), based loosely on the secret-agent life of art historian Anthony Blunt. Banville's literary alter-ego is Benjamin Black, author of a series of seven hard-boiled detective thrillers set in the 1950s starring a troubled pathologist called Quirke – the latest book is *Even the Dead* (2015). Another big hitter is Wexford-born Colm Tóibín (1955–), author of nine novels including *Brooklyn* (2009; made into an Oscar-nominated film in 2015 starring Saoirse Ronan) and, most recently, *Nora Webster* (2014), a powerful study of widowhood.

Emma Donoghue (1969–) followed the award-winning *Room* (2010; the 2015 film picked up an Oscar for best actress) with *Frog Music* (2014), about the real-life shooting of cross-dressing gamine Jenny Bonnet in late 19th-century San Francisco. John Boyne (1971–) made his name with Holocaust novel *The Boy in the Striped Pyjamas* (2006; the film version came out in 2008); his latest novel, *A History of Loneliness* (2014), explores the thorny issue of child abuse and the Catholic Church.

Dubliner Colum McCann (1965–) left Ireland in 1986, eventually settling in New York, where his sixth novel, the post–September 11 *Let the*

Dublin's Nobel Laureates

William Butler Yeats (1923)

George Bernard Shaw (1925)

Samuel Beckett (1969)

Seamus Heaney (1995)

JAMES JOYCE

Uppermost among Dublin writers is James Joyce, author of *Ulysses*, the greatest book of the 20th century – although we've yet to meet five people who've actually finished it. Still, Dubliners are immensely proud of the writer once castigated as a literary pornographer by locals and luminaries alike – even George Bernard Shaw dismissed him as vulgar. Joyce was so unappreciated that he left the city, never to reside in it again, though he continued to live here through his imagination and literature.

His Life

Born in Rathgar in 1882, the young Joyce had three short stories published in an Irish farmers' magazine under the pen name Stephen Dedalus in 1904. The same year he fled town with the love of his life, Nora Barnacle (when Joyce's father heard her name he commented that she would surely stick to him). He spent most of the next 10 years in Trieste, now part of Italy, where he wrote prolifically but struggled to get published. His career was further hampered by recurrent eye problems and he had 25 operations for glaucoma, cataracts and other conditions.

The first major prose he finally had published was *Dubliners* (1914), a collection of short stories set in the city, including the three stories he had written in Ireland. Publishers began to take notice and his autobiographical *A Portrait of the Artist as a Young Man* (1916) followed. In 1918 the US magazine *Little Review* started to publish extracts from *Ulysses* but notoriety was already pursuing his epic work and the censors prevented publication of further episodes after 1920.

Passing through Paris on a rare visit to Dublin, he was persuaded by Ezra Pound to stay a while in the French capital. What he intended to be a brief visit turned into a 20-year stay. It was a good move for the struggling writer for, in 1922, he met Sylvia Beach of the Paris bookshop Shakespeare & Co, who finally managed to put *Ulysses* (1922) into print. The publicity from its earlier censorship ensured instant success.

Buoyed by the success of the inventive *Ulysses,* Joyce went for broke with *Finnegans Wake* (1939), 'set' in the dreamscape of a Dublin publican. Perhaps not one to read at the airport, the book is a daunting and often obscure tome about eternal recurrence. It is even more complex than *Ulysses* and took the author 17 years to write.

In 1940 WWII drove the Joyce family back to Zürich, Switzerland, where the author died the following year.

Ulysses

Ulysses is the ultimate chronicle of the city in which, Joyce once said, he intended to 'give a picture of Dublin so complete that if the city suddenly one day disappeared from the earth it could be reconstructed out of my book'. It is set here on 16 June 1904 – the day of Joyce's first date with Nora Barnacle – and follows its characters as their journeys around town parallel the voyage of Homer's *Odyssey*.

The experimental literary style makes it difficult to read, but there's much for even the slightly bemused literary reader to relish. It ends with Molly Bloom's famous stream of consciousness discourse, a chapter of eight huge, unpunctuated paragraphs. Because of its sexual explicitness, the book was banned in the US and the UK until 1933 and 1937 respectively.

In testament to the book's enduring relevance and extraordinary innovation, it has inspired writers of every generation since. Joyce admirers from around the world descend on Dublin every year on 16 June to celebrate Bloomsday and retrace the steps of its central character, Leopold Bloom. It is a slightly gimmicky and touristy phenomenon that appeals almost exclusively to Joyce fanatics and tourists, but it's plenty of fun and a great way to lay the groundwork for actually reading the book.

Great World Spin (2009), catapulted him to the top of the literary tree and won him the National Book Award for fiction as well as the International IMPAC Dublin Literary Award. His next novel, *TransAtlantic* (2013), weaves three separate stories together: the flight of Alcock and

WOMEN WRITERS

The last few years have seen an important bit of literary revisionism, as scholars and editors seek to redress the imbalance that saw women chronically under-represented in the Irish literary canon. One notable effort has been *The Long Gaze Back* (ed Sinead Gleeson), an anthology of 30 short stories by women writers, including eight by luminaries such as Elizabeth Bowen and Maria Edgeworth and 22 stories by contemporary writers such as Anne Enright and Niamh Boyce.

Brown, the visit of Frederick Douglass to Ireland in 1845 and the story of the Northern Irish peace process of the late 1990s.

Paul Murray's (1975–) second novel, *Skippy Dies* (2010), about a group of privileged students at an all-boys secondary school, won him lots of critical praise (and an upcoming movie version directed by Neil Jordan) but his follow-up, *The Mark and the Void* (2015), which is set against the backdrop of the financial crisis, met with far more lukewarm praise. Not so Shane Hegarty (1976–), who published the first volume of *Darkmouth* in 2015, a YA novel set in a fictional Irish town (Darkmouth) where young Finn is learning about girls and fighting monsters.

Other names to look out for include Kevin Curran, whose first novel, *Beatsploitation* (2013), tackled racism in Ireland; his follow-up, *Citizens* (2016), is set during the Easter Rising of 1916. Caitriona Lally's debut novel, *Eggshells* (2015), is a feast of wordplay and double-meaning as it follows eccentric Vivian on her journey in Celtic Tiger Dublin. The excesses of the Celtic Tiger is the subject of Claire Kilroy's savage satire, *The Devil I Know* (2012), the fourth novel by the Dublin author.

The boom in post-crash literature is evidenced in the work of Cork-born Lisa McInerney, author of *The Glorious Heresies* (2015), and Colin Barrett, who won the Guardian First Book Award for *Young Skins* (2014).

The Stinging Fly (www.stingingfly. org) is one of the best literary magazines for discovering and promoting new authors. It is published quarterly.

Musical Dublin

Dublin's literary tradition may have the intellectuals nodding sagely, but it's the city's musical credentials that have the rest of us bopping, for it's no cliché to say that music is as intrinsic to the local lifestyle as a good night out. Even the streets – well, Grafton St and Temple Bar – are alive with the sounds of music, and you can hardly get around without stubbing your toe on the next international superstar busking their way to a record contract.

Traditional & Folk

Irish music – commonly referred to as 'traditional' or simply 'trad' – has retained a vibrancy not found in other traditional European forms. This is probably because, although Irish music has retained many of its traditional aspects, it has itself influenced many forms of music, most notably US country and western – a fusion of Mississippi Delta blues and Irish traditional tunes that, combined with other influences like Gospel, is at the root of rock and roll. Other reasons for its current success include the willingness of its exponents to update the way it's played (in ensembles rather than the customary *céilidh* – communal dance – bands) and the habit of pub sessions, introduced by returning migrants.

The pub session is still the best way to hear the music at its rich, lively best – and thanks largely to the tourist demand there are some terrific sessions in pubs throughout the city. Thankfully, though, the best musicians have also gone into the recording studio. If you want to hear musical skill that will both tear out your heart and restore your faith in humanity, go no further than the fiddle-playing of Tommy Peoples on *The Quiet Glen* (1998), the beauty of Paddy Keenan's uillean pipes on his eponymous 1975 album, or the stunning guitar playing of Andy Irvine on albums like *Compendium: The Best of Patrick Street* (2000).

The most famous traditional band is the Chieftains, who spend most of their time these days playing in the US and marked their 50th anniversary in 2012 with the ambitious *Voice of Ages*, a collaboration with the likes of Bon Iver and Paolo Nutini. More folksy than traditional were the Dubliners, founded in O'Donoghue's on Merrion Row the same year as the Chieftains. Most of the original members, including the utterly brilliant Luke Kelly and front-man Ronnie Drew, have died, but the group still plays the odd nostalgia gig. In 2006 it released *Live at Vicar St,* which captures some of its brilliance.

Another band whose career has been stitched into the fabric of Dublin life is the Fureys, comprising four brothers originally from the travelling community (no, not like the Wilburys) along with guitarist Davey Arthur. And if it's rousing renditions of Irish rebel songs you're after, you can't go past the Wolfe Tones. Ireland is packed with traditional talent and we strongly recommend that you spend some time in a specialised traditional shop such as Claddagh Records.

Since the 1970s various bands have tried to blend traditional with more progressive genres with mixed success. The first band to pull it

Traditional Playlist

....

Compendium: The Best of Patrick Street (2001) Patrick Street

....

Old Hag You Have Killed Me (1976) The Bothy Band

Paddy Keenan (1975) Paddy Keenan

Dublin Songs

....

'Lay Me Down' (2001) The Frames

....

'One' (1991) U2

....

'Raglan Road' (1972) Luke Kelly & the Dubliners

....

'Still in Love with You' (1978) Thin Lizzy

off was Moving Hearts, led by Christy Moore, who went on to become an important folk musician in his own right.

Popular Music

From the 1960s onwards, Dublin became a hotbed of rock and pop; most of the artists have now faded into obscurity. Notable exceptions are Thin Lizzy, led by Phil Lynott (1949–86), and Bob Geldof's proto-punk/New Wave Boomtown Rats, who didn't like Mondays or much else either.

But they all paled in comparison to the supernova that is U2, formed in 1976 in North Dublin and in the late 1980s one of the world's most successful rock bands. What else can we say about them that hasn't already been said? After 13 studio albums, 22 Grammy awards and 150 million album sales they have nothing to prove to anyone – and not even their minor faux pas in 2014, when Apple 'gave' copies of their latest release, *Songs of Innocence,* to iTunes subscribers whether they wanted it or not, has managed to dampen their popularity. Their iNNOCENCE + eXPERIENCE tour (note the typographic ode to Apple), which ran until the end of 2015, was a massive success.

Of all the Irish acts that followed in U2's wake during the 1980s and early 1990s, a few managed to comfortably avoid being tarred with 'the next U2' burden. The Pogues' mix of punk and Irish folk kept everyone going for a while, but the real story there was the empathetic song-writing of Shane MacGowan, whose genius has been overshadowed by his heavy drinking – but he still managed to pen Ireland's favourite song, 'A Fairytale of New York', sung with emotional fervour by everyone around Christmas. Sinéad O'Connor thrived by acting like a U2 antidote – whatever they were into she was not – and by having a damn fine voice; the raw emotion on *The Lion and the Cobra* (1987) makes it a great offering. And then there were My Bloody Valentine, the pioneers of late 1980s guitar-distorted shoegazer rock: *Loveless* (1991) is one of the best Dublin albums of all time.

The 1990s were largely dominated by DJs, dance music and a whole new spin on an old notion, the boy band. Behind Ireland's most successful groups (Boyzone and Westlife) is the Svengali of Saccharine,

---

Never one to shy away from difficult issues, U2 has been subject to intense criticism in Ireland for its 2006 decision to establish the Netherlands as a base for some of its business interests, thereby minimising the amount of tax it pays in its home country.

LUKE KELLY: THE ORIGINAL DUBLINER

With a halo of wiry ginger hair and a voice like hardened honey, Luke Kelly (1940–84) was perhaps the greatest Irish folk singer of the 20th century, a performer who used his voice in the manner of the American blues singers he admired so much, to express the anguish of being 'lonely and afraid in a world they never made' (to paraphrase AE Housman).

He was a founding member of the Dubliners, along with Ronnie Drew (1934–2008), Barney McKenna (1939–2012) and Ciaran Burke (1935–88), but he treated Dublin's most famous folk group as more of a temporary cooperative enterprise. He shared the singing duties with Drew, lending his distinctive voice to classic drinking ditties like *Dirty Old Town* and rousing rebel songs like *A Nation Once Again,* but it was his mastery of the more reflective ballad that made him peerless. His rendition of *On Raglan Road,* from a poem by Patrick Kavanagh that the poet himself insisted he sing, is the most beautiful song about Dublin we've ever heard; but it is his version of Phil Coulter's *Scorn Not His Simplicity* that grants him his place among the immortals. Coulter wrote the song following the birth of a son with Down's syndrome and even though it became one of Kelly's best-loved songs, he had such respect for it that he only sang it a handful of times, and only in the most respectful of settings.

Luke Kelly: The Collection is recommended listening.

impresario Louis Walsh, whose musical sensibilities seem mired in '60s showband schmaltz. In the last decade, Walsh, who then became a judge on *The X Factor* in the UK, unleashed Jedward on the world – identical twins who couldn't sing a note but endeared themselves to everyone with their wacky antics.

The Contemporary Scene

If Boyzone and Westlife were big, their success pales in comparison to that of One Direction, another product of the X Factory. We mention them here because one of their members, Niall Horan, is from Mullingar, County Westmeath – about an hour west of Dublin – which inevitably means that when One Direction plays Dublin's Croke Park it's treated as a homecoming.

The established crop of more serious artists include Damien Rice, who came out of self-imposed seclusion in 2014 with a new album called *My Favourite Faded Fantasy*; alt-rockers Kodaline, whose second album *Coming Up For Air* (2015) cemented its position as one of the best Irish bands going; and Bray-born blues-influenced Hozier, whose eponymous debut album in 2015 garnered a huge amount of critical acclaim but inevitably couldn't match the global success of his 2013 single 'Take Me to Church'. Although he spends a lot of his time in New York these days, Glen Hansard (of *Once* fame) is still a major presence in Ireland, and occasionally goes on the road with his old band, the Frames.

Hugely successful Dublin trio the Script pack out the stadiums and sell millions of records (the latest is *No Sound Without Silence*, released in 2014) with their melodic pop-rock, which has also found its way onto a host of TV programs from *90210* to *Made in Chelsea*. They mightn't sell nearly as many records, but Villagers, fronted by Conor O'Brien, have earned kudos from every Irish critic for their brand of indie-folk rock – their third album, *Darling Arithmetic,* was released in 2015. And if you like your rock tinged with electronica, then look no further than Jape – the hypnotic sound of their 2015 album *This Chemical Sea* was very well received.

Dublin Albums

Boy (U2)

I Do Not Want What I Haven't Got (Sinéad O'Connor)

Music in Mouth (Bell X1)

Loveless (My Bloody Valentine)

Becoming a Jackal (Villagers)

MUSICAL DUBLIN THE CONTEMPORARY SCENE

Architecture

Dublin's skyline is a clue to its age, with visible peaks of its architectural history dating back to the Middle Ages. Of course, Dublin is older still, but there's no traces left of its Viking origins and you'll have to begin your architectural exploration in the 12th century, with the construction of the city's castle and two cathedrals. Its finest buildings, however, date from much later – built during the golden century that came to be known as the Georgian period.

Medieval Dublin

Viking Dublin was largely built of not-so-durable wood, of which there's virtually no trace left. The Norman footprint is a little deeper, but even its most impressive structures have been heavily reconstructed. The imposing Dublin Castle – or the complex of buildings that are known as Dublin Castle – bears little resemblance to the fortress that was erected by the Anglo-Normans at the beginning of the 13th century and more to the neoclassical style of the 17th century. However, there are some fascinating glimpses of the lower reaches of the original, which you can visit on a tour.

Although the 12th-century cathedrals of Christ Church and St Patrick's were heavily rebuilt in Victorian times, there are some original features, including the crypt in Christ Church, which has a 12th-century Romanesque door. The older of the two St Audoen's Churches dates from 1190 and it too has a few Norman features, including a late 12th-century doorway.

Anglo-Dutch Period

After the restoration of Charles II in 1660, Dublin embarked upon almost a century and a half of unparalleled growth as the city raced to become the second most important in the British Empire. The most impressive examples of the style are the Royal Hospital Kilmainham (1680), designed by William Robinson and now home to the Irish Museum of Modern Art; and the Royal Barracks (Collins Barracks; 1701) built by Thomas Burgh and now home to a branch of the National Museum of Ireland.

Georgian Dublin

Dublin's architectural apogee can roughly be placed in the period spanning the rule of the four English Georges, between the accession of George I in 1714 and the death of George IV in 1830. The greatest influence on the shape of modern Dublin throughout this period was the Wide Street Commissioners, appointed in 1757 and responsible for designing civic spaces and the framework of the modern city. Their efforts were complemented by Dublin's Anglo-Irish Protestant gentry who, flush with unprecedented wealth, dedicated themselves wholeheartedly towards improving their city.

Their inspiration was the work of the Italian architect Andrea Palladio (1508–80), who revived the symmetry and harmony of classical architecture. When the Palladian style reached these shores in the 1720s, the architects of the time tweaked it and introduced a number of, let's call them, 'refinements'. Most obvious were the elegant brick exteriors

Archéire (www.archiseek.com) is a comprehensive website covering all things to do with Irish architecture and design. If you want something in book form, look no further than Christine Casey's superb The Buildings of Ireland: Dublin (2005; Yale University Press), which goes through the city literally street by street.

GEORGIAN PLASTERERS

The handsome exteriors of Dublin's finest Georgian houses are often matched by superbly crafted plasterwork within. The fine work of Michael Stapleton (1770–1803) can be seen in Trinity College, Ely House near St Stephen's Green, and Belvedere House in north Dublin. The LaFranchini brothers, Paolo (1695–1776) and Filippo (1702–79), are responsible for the outstanding decoration in Newman House on St Stephen's Green. But perhaps Dublin's most famous plastered surfaces are in the chapel at the heart of the Rotunda Hospital. Although hospitals are never the most pleasant places to visit, it's worth it for the German stuccodore, Bartholomew Cramillion's fantastic rococo plasterwork.

and decorative touches, such as coloured doors, fanlights and ironwork, which broke the sometimes austere uniformity of the fashion. Consequently, Dublin came to be known for its 'Georgian style'.

Sir Edward Lovett Pearce

The architect credited with the introduction of the Georgian style to Dublin's cityscape was Sir Edward Lovett Pearce (1699–1733), who first arrived in Dublin in 1725 and turned heads with the building of Parliament House (Bank of Ireland; 1728–39). It was the first two-chamber debating house in the world and the main chamber, the House of Commons, is topped by a massive pantheon-style dome.

Pearce also created the blueprint for the city's Georgian townhouses, the most distinguishing architectural feature of Dublin. The local version typically consists of four storeys, including the basement, with symmetrically arranged windows and an imposing, often brightly painted front door. Granite steps lead up to the door, which is often further embellished with a delicate leaded fanlight. The most celebrated examples are on the south side of the city, particularly around Merrion and Fitzwilliam Sqs, but the north side also has some magnificent streets, including North Great George's and Henrietta Sts. The latter features two of Pearce's originals (at Nos 9 and 10) and is still Dublin's most unified Georgian street. Mountjoy Sq, the most elegant address in 18th-century Dublin, is currently being renewed after a century of neglect.

Richard Cassels

German architect Richard Cassels (Richard Castle; 1690–1751) hit town in 1728. While his most impressive country houses are outside Dublin, he did design Nos 85 and 86 St Stephen's Green (1738), which were combined in the 19th century and renamed Newman House, and No 80 (1736), which was later joined with No 81 to create Iveagh House, now the Department of Foreign Affairs; you can visit the peaceful gardens there still. The Rotunda Hospital (1748), which closes off the top of O'Connell St, is also one of Cassels' works. As splendid as these buildings are, it seems he was only warming up for Leinster House (1745–48), the magnificent country residence built on what was then the countryside, but is now the centre of government.

Sir William Chambers

Dublin's boom attracted such notable architects as the Swedish-born Sir William Chambers (1723–96), who designed some of Dublin's most impressive buildings, though he never actually bothered to visit the city. It was the north side of the Liffey that benefited most from Chambers' genius: the chaste and elegant Charlemont House (Hugh Lane Gallery; 1763) lords over Parnell Sq, while the Casino at Marino (1755–79) is his most stunning and bewitching work.

Sir William Chambers designed the Examination Hall (1779–91) and the Chapel (1798) that flank the elegant 18th-century quadrangle of Trinity College, known as Parliament Sq. However, Trinity College's most magnificent feature, the Old Library Building, with its breathtaking Long Room (1712), was designed by Thomas Burgh.

James Gandon & Thomas Cooley

It was towards the end of the 18th century that Dublin's developers really kicked into gear, when the power and confidence of the Anglo-Irish Ascendancy seemed boundless. Of several great architects of the time, James Gandon (1743–1823) stood out, and he built two of Dublin's most enduring and elegant neoclassical landmarks: Custom House (1781–91) and the Four Courts (1786–1802). They were both built on the quays to afford plenty of space in which to admire them.

James Gandon's greatest rival was Thomas Cooley (1740–84), who died too young to reach his full potential. His greatest building, the Royal Exchange (City Hall; 1779), was butchered to provide office space in the mid-19th century, but returned to its breathtaking splendour in a stunning 2000 restoration.

Regency & Victorian

The Act of Union (1801) turned Dublin from glorious capital to Empire backwater, which resulted in precious little construction for much of the 19th century. Exceptions include the General Post Office (GPO; 1814), designed by Francis Johnston, and the stunning series of curvilinear glasshouses in the National Botanic Gardens, which were created mid-century by the Dublin iron-master Richard Turner (1798–1881).

After Catholic Emancipation in 1829, there was a wave of church building, and later the two great Protestant cathedrals of Christ Church and St Patrick's were reconstructed. One especially beautiful example is the splendidly ornate and incongruous Newman University Church (1856), built in a Byzantine style by John Hungerford Pollen (1820–1902) because Cardinal Newman was none too keen on the Gothic style that was all the rage at the time.

Modern Architecture

Without any blank slate like a mass demolition or an architecturally convenient fire (like Chicago suffered in 1871), the architecture of modern Dublin has largely been squeezed in between other periods and has been low on avant-garde examples of international movements.

Exceptions include modernist buildings like Busáras (1953) and Liberty Hall (1965), which have divided critics; less so Paul Koralek's bold and brazen Berkeley Library (1967) in the grounds of Trinity College.

It wasn't until the explosive growth of the 1990s that the city's modern landscape really began to improve, even if some of the early constructions – such as the Irish Financial Services Centre (IFSC; 1987) and the Waterways Visitor Centre (1994) – don't seem as impressive now as they did when they first opened.

The most stunning makeover has occurred in the Docklands, which has been transformed from quasi-wasteland to a fine example of contemporary urban design. You'll find the best examples on Grand Canal Sq, dominated by Daniel Libeskind's elegant Bord Gáis Energy Theatre (2010) and Manuel Aires Mateus' Marker Hotel (2011), but the plaza itself, designed by American landscape artist Martha Schwartz in 2008, is equally eye-catching.

Modern Bridges

Over the last few years the Liffey has been spanned by a handful of new bridges that are all pretty good examples of modern design. Santiago Calatrava's James Joyce Bridge (2003) at Ussher's Island gave the city its first piece of design with the imprimatur of a starchitect, and he outdid himself again in 2009 with the harp-like Samuel Beckett Bridge at Spencer Dock. In between them is the award-winning pedestrian Sean O'Casey Bridge (2005), designed by Cyril O'Neill, while the latest addition is the Rosie Hackett Bridge, joining Hawkins St and Marlborough St. It opened in 2014 and is the only bridge named after a woman; Hackett was a prominent trade unionist and participated in the Easter Rising of 1916.

Survival Guide

Transport

ARRIVING IN DUBLIN

Ireland's capital and biggest city is the most important point of entry and departure for the country – the overwhelming majority of airlines fly in and out of Dublin Airport. The city has two ferry ports: the Dun Laoghaire ferry terminal and the Dublin Port terminal. Ferries from France arrive in the southern port of Rosslare. Dublin is also the nation's primary rail hub. Flights, cars and tours can be booked online at lonelyplanet.com.

Dublin Airport

Located 13km north of the city centre, **Dublin Airport** (🗹01-814 1111; www.dublinairport.com) has two terminals: most international flights (including all US flights) use Terminal 2; Ryanair and select others use Terminal 1. Both terminals have the usual selection of pubs, restaurants, shops, ATMs and car-hire desks.

There are direct flights to Dublin from all major European centres (including a dizzying array of options from the UK) and from Atlanta, Boston, Charlotte, Chicago, Los Angeles, New York, Orlando, Philadelphia, San Francisco and Washington, DC in the USA. Flights from further afield (Australasia or Africa) are usually routed through another European hub such as London.

Most airlines have walk-up counters at Dublin airport; those that don't have their ticketing handled by other airlines.

There is no train service from the airport to the city centre.

Bus

It takes about 45 minutes to get into the city by bus.

Aircoach (🗹01-844 7118; www.aircoach.ie; one-way/return €7/12) Private coach service with two routes from the airport to 18 destinations throughout the city, including the main streets of the city centre. Coaches run every 10 to 15 minutes between 6am and midnight, then hourly from midnight until 6am.

Airlink Express Coach (🗹01-873 4222; www.dublinbus.ie; one-way/return €10/6) Bus 747 runs every 10 to 20 minutes from 5.45am to 11.30pm between the airport, the central bus station (Busáras) and the Dublin Bus office on Upper O'Connell St. Bus 748 runs every 15 to 30 minutes from 6.50am to 10.05pm between the airport, and Heuston and Connolly train stations.

Dublin Bus (Map p252; 🗹01-873 4222; www.dublinbus.ie; 59 Upper O'Connell St; ⏰9am-5.30pm Mon-Fri, to 2pm Sat; 🚌all city centre) A number of buses serve the airport from various points in Dublin, including buses 16A (Rathfarnham), 746 (Dun Laoghaire) and 230 (Portmarnock); all cross the city centre on their way to the airport.

Taxi

There is a taxi rank directly outside the arrivals concourse. It should take about 45 minutes to get into the city centre by taxi and cost around €25, including a supplementary charge of €3 (not applied when going to the airport). Make sure the meter is switched on.

ONLINE BOOKING AGENCIES

➡ www.bestfares.com
➡ www.cheapflights.com
➡ www.ebookers.com
➡ www.expedia.com
➡ www.ferrybooker.com
➡ www.flycheap.com
➡ www.opodo.com
➡ www.priceline.com
➡ www.statravel.com
➡ www.travelocity.com

TRANSPORT GETTING AROUND

CLIMATE CHANGE & TRAVEL

Every form of transport that relies on carbon-based fuel generates CO_2, the main cause of human-induced climate change. Modern travel is dependent on aeroplanes, which might use less fuel per kilometre per person than most cars but travel much greater distances. The altitude at which aircraft emit gases (including CO_2) and particles also contributes to their climate change impact. Many websites offer 'carbon calculators' that allow people to estimate the carbon emissions generated by their journey and, for those who wish to do so, to offset the impact of the greenhouse gases emitted with contributions to portfolios of climate-friendly initiatives throughout the world. Lonely Planet offsets the carbon footprint of all staff and author travel.

Dublin Port Terminal

The **Dublin Port terminal** (☑01-855 2222; Alexandra Rd) is 3km northeast of the city centre.

Operators serve the following routes:

Irish Ferries (☑0818 300 400; www.irishferries.com; Ferryport, Terminal Rd South) Holyhead in Wales; three hours

P&O Irish Sea (☑01-407 3434; www.poferries.com; Terminal 3) Liverpool; 8½ hours or four hours on fast boat

Isle of Man Steam Packet Company/Sea Cat (Map p256; ☑01-836 4019; www.steam-packet.com; Maritime House, North Wall) Isle of Man; 1½ hours

Bus

Buses from Busáras are timed to coincide with arrivals and departures from the Dublin Port terminal. For the 9.45am ferry departure from Dublin, buses leave Busáras at 8.30am; for the 1am sailing to Liverpool, the bus departs from Busáras at 11.45pm. All buses cost adult/child €3/1.50.

Dun Laoghaire Ferry Terminal

The **Dun Laoghaire ferry terminal** (☑01-280 1905; Dun Laoghaire; ☑7A or 8 from Burgh Quay, 46A from Trinity College, ☑Dun Laoghaire), 13km southeast of the city, receives **Stena Line** (☑01-204 7777; www.stenaline.com; Ferry Terminal, Dun Laoghaire) ferries to/from Holyhead in Wales. The crossing takes just over three hours and costs around €30 for foot passengers or €110 for a medium-sized car with two passengers. The fast-boat service from Holyhead to Dun Laoghaire takes a little over 1½ hours and costs €40 or €130 for the same.

Bus

To get into Dublin by bus, take bus 46A to St Stephen's Green, or bus 7, 7A or 8 to Burgh Quay.

Train

To travel between the Dun Laoghaire ferry terminal and Dublin, take the DART to Pearse Station (for south Dublin) or Connolly Station (for north Dublin). Trains from Dublin to Dun Laoghaire take about 15 to 20 minutes. A one-way DART ticket costs €3.25.

Busáras Terminal

Dublin's central bus station, **Busáras** (Map p252; ☑01-836 6111; www.buseireann.ie; Store St; ☑Connolly) is just north of the river behind Custom House; it has different-sized luggage lockers costing €6 to €10 per day.

It's possible to combine bus and ferry tickets from major UK centres to Dublin on the bus network. The journey between London and Dublin takes about 12 hours and costs around €34 return. For details in London, contact **Eurolines** (☑0870 514 3219; www.eurolines.com).

From here, Bus Eireann buses serve the whole national network, including buses to towns and cities in Northern Ireland.

Heuston & Connolly Stations

Dublin has two main train stations: **Heuston Station** (☑01-836 5421), on the western side of town near the Liffey; and **Connolly Station** (☑01-836 3333), a short walk northeast of Busáras, behind the Custom House.

Connolly Station is a stop on the DART line into town; the Luas Red Line serves both Connolly and Heuston stations.

GETTING AROUND

Bicycle

Despite the intermittent presence of rust-red cycle lanes throughout the city centre, getting around by bike can be something of an obstacle course as cyclists have to share roads with buses and indifferent motorists. Bike theft is a major problem, so be sure to park your bike on busier streets, preferably at one of the myriad U-shaped parking bars, and lock it securely. Never leave your bike on the street overnight or it may just be gone in the morning. Dublin City Cycling (www.cycledublin.ie) is an excellent online resource.

Bikes are only allowed on suburban trains (not the DART), either stowed in the guard's van or in a special compartment at the opposite end of the train from the engine. There's a flat €4 charge for transporting a bicycle up to 56km.

Dublinbikes

One of the most popular ways to get around the city is with the blue bikes of Dublinbikes (www.dublinbikes.ie), a pay-as-you-go service similar to the Parisian Vélib system: cyclists purchase a €10 smart card (as well as pay a credit-card deposit of €150) – either online or at any of the 40 stations throughout the city centre – before 'freeing' a bike for use, which is then free of charge for the first 30 minutes and €0.50 for each half-hour thereafter.

Hire, Purchase & Repair

Bike rental has become tougher due to the Dublinbikes scheme. Typical rental for a hybrid or touring bike is around €25 a day or €140 per week.

Cycleways (www.cycleways.com; 185-186 Parnell St; ⏲8.30am-6.30pm Mon-Wed & Fri, to 8pm Thu, 9.30am-6pm Sat) An excellent bike shop that rents hybrids and touring bikes during the summer months (May to September).

Eurocycles & Eurobaby (57 S William St; ⏲10am-6pm Mon, Tue & Sat, to 8pm Wed, Thu & Fri, noon-6pm Sun) New bikes, all the gear you could possibly need and a decent repair service; but be sure to book an appointment as they are generally quite busy.

MacDonald Cycles (☎01-475 2586; www.macdonaldcycles.ie; 38 Wexford St) Does repairs, and will have your bike back to you within a day or so (barring serious damage).

Bus

The **Dublin Bus Office** (Map p252; ☎01-873 4222; www.dublinbus.ie; 59 Upper O'Connell St; ⏲9am-5.30pm Mon-Fri, to 2pm Sat; ▣all city centre) has free single-route timetables for all its services. Buses run from around 6am (some start at 5.30am) to about 11.30pm.

Bus Fares

Fares are calculated according to stages:

➡ 1–3 stages: €2
➡ 4–13 stages: €2.70
➡ Over 13 stages: €3.30

If you're travelling within the designated bus corridor zone (roughly between Parnell Sq to the north and St Stephen's Green to the south) you can use the €0.75 special City Centre fare. You must tender exact change when boarding; anything more and you will be given a receipt for reimbursement, only possible at the Dublin Bus main office.

Avoid this by getting a **Leap Card** (www.leapcard.ie), a plastic smart card available in most newsagents. Once you register it online, you can top it up with whatever amount you need. When you board a bus, Luas or suburban train, just swipe your card and the fare – usually 20% less than a cash fare – is automatically deducted.

Fare-Saver Passes

Fare saver passes include the following:

Freedom Ticket (adult/child €33/14) Three-day unlimited travel on all bus services, including Airlink and Dublin Bus Hop-On, Hop-Off tours.

Luas Flexi Ticket (one/seven/30 days €6.80/24.90/98) Unlimited travel on all Luas services.

Rambler Pass (five/30 days €30.60/153) Valid for unlimited travel on all Dublin Bus and Airlink services, except Nitelink.

Visitor Leap Card (three days €19.50) Unlimited travel on bus, Luas and DART, including Airlink, Nitelink and Xpresso DART.

Nitelink

Nitelink late-night buses run from the College, Westmoreland and D'Olier Sts triangle. On Fridays and Saturdays, departures are at 12.30am, then every 20 minutes until 4.30am on the more popular routes, and until 3.30am on the less frequented ones; there are no services Sunday to Thursday. Fares are €6.50 (€5.20 with Leap card). See www.dublinbus.ie for route details.

Car & Motorcycle

Driving

Traffic in Dublin is a nightmare and parking is an expensive headache. There are no free spots to park anywhere in the city centre during business hours (7am to 7pm Monday to Saturday), but there are plenty of parking meters, 'pay & display' spots (€3 to €6 per hour) and over a dozen sheltered and supervised car parks (around €5 per hour).

Clamping of illegally parked cars is thoroughly enforced, and there is an €80 charge for removal. Parking is free after 7pm Monday to Saturday, and all day Sunday, in most metered spots and on single yellow lines.

Car theft and break-ins are a problem, and the police advise visitors to park in a supervised car park. Cars with foreign number plates are prime targets; never leave your valuables behind. When you're booking accommodation, check on parking facilities.

The **Automobile Association of Ireland** (AA; ☑01-617 9999, breakdown 1800 667 788; www.aaireland.ie; 56 Drury St; 🚶all city centre) is located in the city centre.

Hire

All the main agencies are represented in Dublin. Book in advance for the best fares, especially at weekends and during summer months, when demand is highest.

Motorbikes and mopeds are not available for rent. People aged under 21 are not allowed to hire a car; for the majority of rental companies you have to be at least 23 and have had a valid driving licence for a minimum of one year. Many rental agencies will not rent to people over 70 or 75.

The following rental agencies have several branches across the capital and at the airport:

Avis Rent-a-Car (☑01-605 7500; www.avis.ie; 35 Old Kilmainham Rd; ⏲8.30am-5.45pm Mon-Fri, 8.30am-2.30pm Sat-Sun; 🚌23, 25, 25A, 26, 68, 69 from city centre)

Budget Rent-a-Car (☑01-837 9611; www.budget.ie; 151 Lower Drumcondra Rd; ⏲9am-6pm; 🚌41 from O'Connell St)

Europcar (☑01-812 2800; www.europcar.ie; 1 Mark St;

⏲8am-6pm Mon-Fri, 8.30am-3pm Sat-Sun; 🚶all city centre)

Hertz Rent-a-Car (☑01-709 3060; www.hertz.com; 151 South Circular Rd; ⏲8.30am-5.30pm Mon-Fri, 9am-4.30pm Sat, 9am-3.30pm Sun; 🚌9, 16, 77, 79 from city centre)

Thrifty (☑01-844 1944; www.thrifty.ie; 26 Lombard St E; ⏲8am-6pm Mon-Fri, to 3pm Sat-Sun; 🚶all city centre)

Taxi

All taxi fares begin with a flagfall of €3.60 (€4 from 10pm to 8am), followed by €1.10 per kilometre thereafter (€1.40 from 10pm to 8am). In addition to these there are a number of extra charges – €1 for each extra passenger and €2 for telephone bookings. There is no charge for luggage.

Taxis can be hailed on the street and found at taxi ranks around the city, including on the corner of Abbey and O'Connell Sts; College Green, in front of Trinity College; and St Stephen's Green at the end of Grafton St.

Numerous taxi companies, such as **National Radio Cabs** (☑01-677 2222; www.nrc.ie), dispatch taxis by radio.

You can also try Lynk (www.lynk.ie), a taxi app.

Train

The **Dublin Area Rapid Transport** (DART; ☑01-836 6222; www.irishrail.ie) provides quick train access to the coast as far north as Howth (about 30 minutes) and as far south as Greystones in County Wicklow. Pearse Station is convenient for central Dublin south of the Liffey, and Connolly Station for north of the Liffey. There are services every 10 to 20 minutes, sometimes even more frequently, from around 6.30am to midnight Monday to Saturday. Services are less frequent on Sunday. A one-way DART ticket from Dublin to Dun Laoghaire or Howth costs €3.25.

There are also suburban rail services north as far as Dundalk, inland to Mullingar and south past Bray to Arklow.

Train Passes

DART passes include the following:

Adult All Day Rail (one/three days €11.40/26.50) Valid for unlimited travel on DART and suburban rail travel.

ROAD SAFETY RULES IN DUBLIN

➡ Drive on the left, overtake to the right.

➡ Seat belts must be worn by the driver and all passengers.

➡ Children aged under 12 are not allowed to sit in front seats.

➡ Motorcyclists and their passengers must wear helmets.

➡ When entering a roundabout, give way to the right.

➡ Speed limits are 50km/h or as signposted in the city, 100km/h on all roads outside city limits and 120km/h on motorways (marked in blue).

➡ The legal alcohol limit is 50mg of alcohol per 100mL of blood, or 22mg on the breath (roughly one unit of alcohol for a man and less than that for a woman).

Family All Day Rail (€20)
Valid for travel for one day for a family of two adults and two children aged under 16 on rail services.

Tram

The Luas (www.luas.ie) light-rail system has two lines: the green line (running every five to 15 minutes) connects St Stephen's Green with Sandyford in south Dublin via Ranelagh and Dundrum; the red line (every 20 minutes) runs from the Point Village to Tallaght via the north quays and Heuston Station.

There are ticket machines at every stop or you can use a tap-on, tap-off Leap Card, which is available from most newsagents. A typical short-hop fare (around four stops) is €2.30. Services run from 5.30am to 12.30am Monday to Friday, from 6.30am to 12.30am Saturday and from 7am to 11.30pm Sunday.

TOURS

Dublin isn't that big, so a straightforward sightseeing tour is only really necessary if you're looking to cram in the sights or avoid blistered feet. What is worth considering, however, is a specialised guided tour, especially for those of a musical, historical or literary bent.

Boat Tours

Dublin Discovered Boat Tours (Map p252; ☎01-473 4082; www.dublindiscovered. ie; Bachelor's Walk; adult/ student/child €14/12/8; ⊙9am-5.30pm Mar-Oct; 🚌all city centre, 🚆Abbey) 'See the sights without the traffic' is the pitch; you get to hear the history of Dublin from a watery point of view aboard an (all-important) all-weather cruiser.

Sea Safaris (Map p256; ☎01-

668 9802; www.seasafari.ie; National Convention Centre; adult/child €20/12.50; 🚌Mayor's Square NCI) Historical tour of the River Liffey and Dublin Port, departing from outside the Convention Centre.

Viking Splash Tours (Map p244; ☎01-707 6000; www. vikingsplash.ie; St Stephen's Green N; adult/child €22/12; ⊙every 30-90min 10am-3pm; 🚌all city centre, 🚆St Stephen's Green) Go on, what's the big deal? You stick a plastic Viking's helmet on your head and yell 'yay' at the urging of your guide, but the upshot is you'll get a 1¼-hour semiamphibious tour that ends up in the Grand Canal Dock. 'Strictly for tourists' seems so...superfluous.

Bus Tours
Dublin Bus Tours

Dublin Bus (Map p244; ☎01-872 0000; www.dublin-sightseeing.ie; adult €22-28), the city's bus company, runs a variety of tours, all of which can be booked at its office, or at the Bus Éireann counter at the **Visit Dublin Centre** (Map p244; www.visitdublin. com; 25 Suffolk St; ⊙9am-5.30pm Mon-Sat, 10.30am-3pm Sun; 🚌all city centre). Tours include the following:

➡ **City Sightseeing** (Map p252; www.citysightseeingdublin.ie; 14 Upper O'Connell St; adult/ student €19/17; 🚌all city centre, 🚆Abbey) A typical hop-on-hop-off tour should last around 1½ hours and lead you up and down O'Connell St, past Trinity College and St Stephen's Green, before heading up to the Guinness Storehouse and back around the north quays, via the main entrance to Phoenix Park. Tours run every eight to 15 minutes, from 9am to 6pm.

➡ **Ghost Bus Tour** (adult

€28; ⊙8pm Mon-Thu, 8pm & 8.30pm Fri, 7pm & 9.30pm Sat & Sun) Popular two-hour tour of graveyards and 'haunted' places (not suitable for under-14s).

➡ **South Coast & Gardens Tour** (adult/child €24/12; ⊙11am) A 4½-hour tour running along the stretch of coastline between Dun Laoghaire and Killiney before turning inland into Wicklow and on to Powerscourt Estate (admission included).

Other Bus Tours

1916 Easter Rising Coach Tour (Map p256; www.1916easter risingcoach-tour.ie; Custom House Quay; adult/child €15/10) A 90-minute tour of the sites that played a part in the 1916 Easter Rising. Buy your tickets online or at the Visit Dublin Centre on Suffolk St.

Carriage Tours

Old-style horse-and-carriage tour operators congregate at the top of Grafton St by St Stephen's Green. Each carriage takes up to five people. Half-hour tours cost up to €60, but different length trips can be negotiated: fix a price *before* the driver says giddy-up.

Walking Tours

1916 Rebellion Walking Tour (Map p244; ☎086 858 3847; www.1916rising.com; 23 Wicklow St; €13; ⊙11.30am Mon-Sat, 1pm Sun Mar-Oct; 🚌7 & 44 from city centre) Superb two-hour tour starting in the International Bar on Wicklow St. Lots of information, humour and irreverence to boot. The guides – all Trinity graduates – are uniformly excellent and will not say no to the offer of a pint back in the International at tour's end.

Dublin Literary Pub Crawl
(Map p244; ☏01-670 5602;
www.dublinpubcrawl.com; 9
Duke St; adult/student €12/10;
☽7.30pm daily Apr-Oct, 7.30pm
Thu-Sun Nov-Mar; ⌨all city centre) A tour of pubs associated
with famous Dublin writers is a
sure-fire recipe for success, and
this 2½-hour tour/performance
by two actors – which includes
them acting out the funny bits –
is a riotous laugh. There's plenty
of drink taken, which makes it all
the more popular. It leaves from
the Duke on Duke St; get there
by 7pm to reserve a spot for the
evening tour.

Dublin Musical Pub Crawl
(Map p240; ☏01-478 0193;
www.discoverdublin.ie; 58-59
Fleet St; adult/student €13/11;
☽7.30pm daily Apr-Oct,
7.30pm Thu-Sat Nov-Mar;
⌨all city centre) The story of
Irish traditional music and its
influence on contemporary
styles is explained and demonstrated by two expert musicians in a number of Temple
Bar pubs over 2½ hours. Tours
meet upstairs in the Oliver
St John Gogarty pub and are
highly recommended.

Pat Liddy Walking Tours
(Map p244; ☏01-831 1109;
www.walkingtours.ie; Visit
Dublin Centre, 25 Suffolk
St; €10-14; ⌨all city centre)
Dublin's best-known tour
guide is local historian Pat
Liddy, who leads a variety of
guided walks including Dublin
Highlights and The Best of
Dublin – The Complete Heritage Walking Tour. He is also
available for private guided
walks (check the website for
timings) and has a bunch of
podcast walks (www.visitdub-
lin.com/iwalks) available for
download.

Dublin Visitor Centre (www.
visitdublin.com; ☽8am-10pm)
The tourist office has put
together an app with four
themed walking tours covering
Dublin's history over the last
200 years. Each walk takes
approximately two hours;
the app is available for both
iPhone and Android.

Directory A–Z

Customs Regulations

Ireland has a two-tier customs system: one for goods bought duty-free outside the European Union (EU); the other for goods bought in another EU country where tax and duty is paid. There is technically no limit to the amount of goods transportable within the EU, but customs will use certain guidelines to distinguish personal use from commercial purpose.

Duty Free

For duty-free goods from outside the EU, limits include 200 cigarettes, 1L of spirits or 2L of wine, 60mL of perfume and 250mL of *eau de toilette*.

Tax & Duty Paid

Amounts that officially constitute personal use include 3200 cigarettes (or 400 cigarillos, 200 cigars or 3kg of tobacco) and either 10L of spirits, 20L of fortified wine, 60L of sparkling wine, 90L of still wine or 110L of beer.

Discount Cards

Senior citizens are entitled to discounts on public transport and museum fees. Students and under-26s also get discounts with the appropriate student or youth card. Local discount passes include the following:

Dublin Pass (adult/child one day €49/29, three day €79/49) For heavy-duty sightseeing, the Dublin Pass will save you a packet. It provides free entry to over 25 attractions (including the Guinness Storehouse), discounts at 20 others and guaranteed fast-track entry to some of the busiest sights. To avail of the free Aircoach transfer to and from the airport, order the card online so you have it when you land. Otherwise, it's available from any Discover Ireland Dublin Tourism Centre.

Heritage Card (adult/child and student €25/10) This card entitles you to free access to all sights in and around Dublin managed by the Office of Public Works (OPW). You can buy it at OPW sites or Dublin Tourism offices.

Electricity

230V/50Hz

Emergency

For emergency assistance, phone 999 or 112. This call is free and the operator

ETIQUETTE

➡ **Greetings** Shake hands with both men and women when meeting for the first time. Female friends are greeted with a single kiss on the cheek.

➡ **Queues** Dubliners can be a little lax about proper queuing etiquette, but are not shy about confronting queue skippers who jump in front of them.

➡ **Polite Requests** Dubliners often use 'sorry' instead of 'excuse me' when asking for something; they're not really apologising for anything.

will connect you with the type of assistance you specify: fire, police (gardaí), ambulance, boat or coastal rescue. There are garda stations at **Fitzgibbon St** (Fitzgibbon St), **Harcourt Tce** (☎01-676 3481; Harcourt Tce; ⏱24hr), **Pearse St** (☎01-677 8141; Pearse St; 🖿all city centre) and **Store St** (Store St).

A full list of all emergency numbers can be found in the front pages of the telephone book.

Insurance

Comprehensive travel insurance to cover theft, loss and medical problems is highly recommended. Worldwide travel insurance is available at www.lonelyplanet.com/travel-insurance. You can buy, extend and claim online anytime – even if you're already on the road.

Internet Access

Wi-fi and 3G networks are making internet cafes largely redundant (except to gamers); the few that are left will charge around €6 per hour. Most accommodations have wi-fi service, either free or for a daily charge (up to €10 per day).

Legal Matters

The possession of small quantities of marijuana attracts a fine or warning, but harder drugs are treated more seriously. Public drunkenness is illegal but commonplace – the police will usually ignore it unless you're causing trouble. If you need legal assistance, contact the **Legal Aid Board** (☎1890 615 200; 47 Upper Mount St).

PRACTICALITIES

➡ **Newspapers** Irish Independent (www.independent.ie), Irish Times (www.irishtimes.com), Irish Examiner (www.examiner.ie), The Herald (www.herald.ie).

➡ **Radio** RTE Radio 1 (88-90 MHz), RTE Radio 2 (90-92 MHz), Today FM (100-103 MHz), Newstalk 106-108 (106-108 MHz).

LGBTQI Travellers

Dublin's a pretty good place to be gay. Most people wouldn't bat an eyelid at public displays of affection between same-sex couples, or cross-dressing in the city centre, but discretion is advised in some suburbs. If you do encounter any sort of trouble or harassment, call the **Gay & Lesbian Garda Liaison Officer** (☎116006) or the **Sexual Assault Unit** (☎01-666 6000) at the Pearse St Garda station.

Resources include the following:

Gaire (www.gaire.com) Online message board and resource centre.

Gay Men's Health Project (☎01-660 2189; http://hse.ie/go/GMHS) Practical advice on men's health issues.

National Lesbian & Gay Federation (NLGF; ☎01-675 5025; www.nxf.ie; 2 Exchange St Upper, Temple Bar; 🖿all city centre) Publishers of Gay Community News.

Outhouse (☎01-873 4932; www.outhouse.ie; 105 Capel St; 🖿all city centre) Top gay, lesbian and bisexual resource centre. Great stop-off point to see what's on, check noticeboards and meet people. It publishes the free Ireland's Pink Pages, a directory of gay-centric services, which is also accessible on the website.

Money

ATMs are widespread. Credit cards (with PIN) are accepted at most restaurants, hotels and shops.

ATMs

Most banks have ATMs that are linked to international money systems such as Cirrus, Maestro or Plus. Each transaction incurs a currency conversion fee and credit cards can incur immediate and exorbitant cash-advance interest-rate charges. We strongly recommend that if you're staying in the city centre, you get your money out early on a Friday to avoid the long queues that can form after 8pm.

Changing Money

Best exchange rates are at banks, although bureaux de change and other exchange facilities usually open for more hours. There's a cluster of banks located around College Green opposite Trinity College and all have exchange facilities.

Credit Cards

Visa and MasterCard credit and debit cards are widely accepted in Dublin. Smaller businesses prefer debit cards (and will charge a fee for credit cards). Nearly all credit and debit cards use the chip-and-PIN system and an increasing number of places will not accept your card if you don't.

Tipping

You're not obliged to tip if the service or food was unsatisfactory (even if it's been automatically added to your bill as a 'service charge').

Hotels Only for bellhops who carry luggage, then €1 per bag.

Pubs Not expected unless table service is provided, then €1 for a round of drinks.

Restaurants Tip 10% for decent service, up to 15% in more expensive places.

Taxis Tip 10% or round up to the nearest euro.

Toilet attendants Tip €0.50.

Opening Hours

Standard opening hours in relatively late-rising Dublin are as follows:

Banks From 10am to 4pm Monday to Friday (to 5pm Thursday).

Cafes From 8am to 5pm Monday to Saturday.

Offices From 9am to 5pm Monday to Friday.

Post offices From 9am to 6pm Monday to Friday, 9am to 1pm Saturday.

Pubs From 10.30am to 11.30pm Monday to Thursday, 10.30am to 12.30am Friday and Saturday, noon to 11pm Sunday (30 minutes 'drinking up' time allowed). Pubs with bar extensions open to 2.30am Thursday to Saturday, pubs with theatre licences open to 3.30am; closed Christmas Day and Good Friday.

Restaurants From noon to 10pm (or midnight); food

SMOKING

It is illegal to smoke indoors everywhere except private residences and prisons.

service generally ends around 9pm. Top-end restaurants often close between 3pm and 6pm; restaurants serving brunch open around 10am.

Shops From 9.30am to 6pm Monday to Saturday (until 8pm on Thursday and sometimes Friday, to 9pm for the bigger shopping centres and supermarkets), noon to 6pm Sunday.

Post

The Irish postal service, An Post, is reliable, efficient and generally on time. Post boxes in Dublin are usually green and have two slots: one for 'Dublin only', the other for 'All Other Places'. There are a couple of post offices in the city centre including **An Post** (Map p244; ☎01-705 8206; www.anpost.ie; St Andrew's St; ⊗8.30am-5pm Mon-Fri; 🚇all city centre) and the **General Post Office** (Map p252; ☎01-705 7000; www.anpost.ie; Lower O'Connell St; ⊗8am-8pm Mon-Sat; 🚇all city centre, 🚇Abbey).

Postal Codes

Postal codes on letters and parcels in Dublin (presented as 'Dublin + number') are fairly straightforward. Their main feature is that all odd numbers refer to areas north of the Liffey and all even ones to areas south of the Liffey. They fan out numerically from the city centre, so the city centre to the north of the river is Dublin 1 and its southern equivalent is Dublin 2.

A new postcode system called Eircode was introduced in late 2015. Similar to the UK postcode system, all addresses now have a seven character alphanumeric code split into two parts, eg A65 F4E2. The new system is operational, but the majority of Dubliners still use the old system as

the new one will take some time to bed in.

Public Holidays

The only public holidays that will impact on you are Good Friday and Christmas Day, the only two days in the year when all pubs close. Otherwise, the half-dozen or so bank holidays (all of which fall on a Monday) mean just that – the banks are closed, along with about half the shops. St Patrick's Day, May Day and St Stephen's Day holidays are taken on the following Monday should they fall on a weekend.

New Year's Day 1 January

St Patrick's Day 17 March

Easter (Good Friday to Easter Monday inclusive) March/April

May Bank Holiday 1 May

June Bank Holiday First Monday in June

August Bank Holiday First Monday in August

October Bank Holiday Last Monday in October

Christmas Day 25 December

St Stephen's Day 26 December

Safe Travel

Dublin is a safe city by any standards, except maybe those set by the Swiss. Basically, act as you would at home. However, certain parts of the city are pretty dodgy due to the presence of drug addicts and other questionable types, including north and northeast of Gardiner St and along parts of Dorset St, on the north side, and west along Thomas St, on the south side.

Telephone

When calling Dublin from abroad, dial your international access code, followed by 353 and 1 (dropping the 0 that precedes it). To make international calls from Dublin, first dial 00, then the country code, followed by the local area code and number.

Country Code ⌕+353
City Code ⌕01
International Access Code ⌕00
Directory Enquiries ⌕11811 or ⌕11850
International Directory Enquiries ⌕11818

Mobile Phones

All European and Australasian phones work in Dublin; some North American (non-GSM) phones don't. Check with provider. Prepaid SIM cards cost from €10.

Time

In winter, Dublin (and the rest of Ireland) is on GMT, also known as Universal Time Coordinated (UTC); the same as Britain. In summer, the clock shifts to GMT plus one hour. When it's noon in Dublin in summer, it's 3am in Los Angeles and Vancouver, 7am in New York and Toronto, 1pm in Paris, 8pm in Singapore, and 10pm in Sydney.

Toilets

There are no on-street facilities in Dublin. All shopping centres have public toilets; if you're stranded, go into any bar or hotel.

Tourist Information

Dublin Visitor Centre (Map p244; www.visitdublin.com; 25 Suffolk St; ⊗9am-5.30pm Mon-Sat, 10.30am-3pm Sun; ▣all city centre) has general visitor information on Dublin and Ireland; also has a free accommodation booking service, a concert-booking agent, local and national bus information, rail information, and tour information and bookings.

Travellers with Disabilities

Despite the fact that many of the city's hotels, restaurants and sights are increasingly being adapted for people with disabilities, there's still a long way to go. Fáilte Ireland's annual accommodation guide, *Be Our Guest*, indicates which places are accessible by wheelchair. Public transport can be a nightmare, although a limited

number of buses are now equipped with electronic elevators for wheelchairs, and nearly all DART stations have ramps and/or elevators.

The **Citizens Information Board** (⌕0761 07 7230; www.citizensinformationboard. ie; 13A Upper O'Connell St; ⊗10am-5pm Mon, Tue, Thu & Fri, to 1.30pm Wed) provides plenty of helpful information regarding Dublin's accessibility for wheelchairs.

Another useful organisation is the **Irish Wheelchair Association** (⌕01-818 6400; www.iwa.ie; Áras Chúchulain, Blackheath Dr, Clontarf).

Visas

Not required for citizens of Australia, New Zealand, USA and Canada. Citizens of European nations that belong to the European Economic Area (EEA) don't need one either.

Women Travellers

Dublin should pose no problems for women travellers. In the unlikely event of a sexual assault, get in touch with the police and the **Rape Crisis Centre** (⌕1800 778 888, 01-661 4911; www.drcc. ie; 70 Lower Leeson St; ⊗24hr; ▣all city centre).

Behind the Scenes

SEND US YOUR FEEDBACK

We love to hear from travellers – your comments keep us on our toes and help make our books better. Our well-travelled team reads every word on what you loved or loathed about this book. Although we cannot reply individually to your submissions, we always guarantee that your feedback goes straight to the appropriate writers, in time for the next edition. Each person who sends us information is thanked in the next edition – the most useful submissions are rewarded with a selection of digital PDF chapters.

Visit **lonelyplanet.com/contact** to submit your updates and suggestions or to ask for help. Our award-winning website also features inspirational travel stories, news and discussions.

Note: We may edit, reproduce and incorporate your comments in Lonely Planet products such as guidebooks, websites and digital products, so let us know if you don't want your comments reproduced or your name acknowledged. For a copy of our privacy policy visit lonelyplanet.com/privacy.

OUR READERS

Many thanks to the travellers who used the last edition and wrote to us with helpful hints, useful advice and interesting anecdotes: Alison Tavare, Arnold Fanning, Emma King, Seán McDaid, Sinead Browne, Steven Scramuzzo.

AUTHOR THANKS
Fionn Davenport

A big thanks to everyone who assisted this wayward travel writer in his hometown. Paul, Tracy and Billy – for company, advice and meals. To everyone who answered my persistently ridiculous questions and to Miceal for his encyclopaedic knowledge of new Dublin restaurants. To James and all the editors at Lonely Planet for their forbearance as I struggled to get used to new formats and new demands. And to Laura, who always made coming home the best part of any day.

ACKNOWLEDGEMENTS

Cover photograph: Temple Bar district. Carolin Voelker/Getty ©.

Illustrations p56–7, p86–7 and p166–7 by Javier Zarracina; p160–1 by Michael Weldon.

DART Commuter Network Map © Iarnród Éireann. Dublin Transit Map © Irish Rail

THIS BOOK

This 10th edition of Lonely Planet's *Dublin* guidebook was researched and written by Fionn Davenport, who also wrote the previous edition. This guidebook was produced by the following:

Destination Editor James Smart

Product Editor Joel Cotterell

Regional Senior Cartographer Mark Griffiths

Book Designers Cam Ashley, Jessica Rose

Assisting Editors Andrea Dobbin, Victoria Harrison, Anne Mulvaney, Gabrielle Stefanos, Simon Williamson

Cover Researcher Naomi Parker

Thanks to Carolyn Boicos, Daniel Corbett, Grace Dobell, Ryan Evans, Larissa Frost, Andi Jones, Lauren Keith, Katherine Marsh, Anne Mason, Wayne Murphy, Cat Naghten, Kirsten Rawlings, Angela Tinson, Dora Whitaker

Index

Dublin Maps

Sights
- Beach
- Bird Sanctuary
- Buddhist
- Castle/Palace
- Christian
- Confucian
- Hindu
- Islamic
- Jain
- Jewish
- Monument
- Museum/Gallery/Historic Building
- Ruin
- Shinto
- Sikh
- Taoist
- Winery/Vineyard
- Zoo/Wildlife Sanctuary
- Other Sight

Activities, Courses & Tours
- Bodysurfing
- Diving
- Canoeing/Kayaking
- Course/Tour
- Sento Hot Baths/Onsen
- Skiing
- Snorkelling
- Surfing
- Swimming/Pool
- Walking
- Windsurfing
- Other Activity

Sleeping
- Sleeping
- Camping

Eating
- Eating

Drinking & Nightlife
- Drinking & Nightlife
- Cafe

Entertainment
- Entertainment

Shopping
- Shopping

Information
- Bank
- Embassy/Consulate
- Hospital/Medical
- Internet
- Police
- Post Office
- Telephone
- Toilet
- Tourist Information
- Other Information

Geographic
- Beach
- Gate
- Hut/Shelter
- Lighthouse
- Lookout
- Mountain/Volcano
- Oasis
- Park
- Pass
- Picnic Area
- Waterfall

Population
- Capital (National)
- Capital (State/Province)
- City/Large Town
- Town/Village

Transport
- Airport
- Border crossing
- Bus
- Cable car/Funicular
- Cycling
- Ferry
- Metro station
- Monorail
- Parking
- Petrol station
- Subway station
- Taxi
- Train station/Railway
- Tram
- Underground station
- Other Transport

Note: Not all symbols displayed above appear on the maps in this book

Routes
- Tollway
- Freeway
- Primary
- Secondary
- Tertiary
- Lane
- Unsealed road
- Road under construction
- Plaza/Mall
- Steps
- Tunnel
- Pedestrian overpass
- Walking Tour
- Walking Tour detour
- Path/Walking Trail

Boundaries
- International
- State/Province
- Disputed
- Regional/Suburb
- Marine Park
- Cliff
- Wall

Hydrography
- River, Creek
- Intermittent River
- Canal
- Water
- Dry/Salt/Intermittent Lake
- Reef

Areas
- Airport/Runway
- Beach/Desert
- Cemetery (Christian)
- Cemetery (Other)
- Glacier
- Mudflat
- Park/Forest
- Sight (Building)
- Sportsground
- Swamp/Mangrove

MAP INDEX

EAST WALL

NORTH WALL

RINGSEND

IRISHTOWN

SANDYMOUNT

BALLSBRIDGE

BEGGAR'S BUSH

DONNYBROOK

DOCKLANDS

MILLTOWN

Royal Canal

River Liffey

Merrion Sq

RANELAGH

Parnell Sq

St Stephen's Green

TEMPLE BAR

GRAFTON STREET

SMITHFIELD

THE LIBERTIES

St Brendan's Hospital

Grand Canal

DOLPHIN'S BARN

HAROLD'S CROSS

Phoenix Park

0   1 km
0   0.5 miles

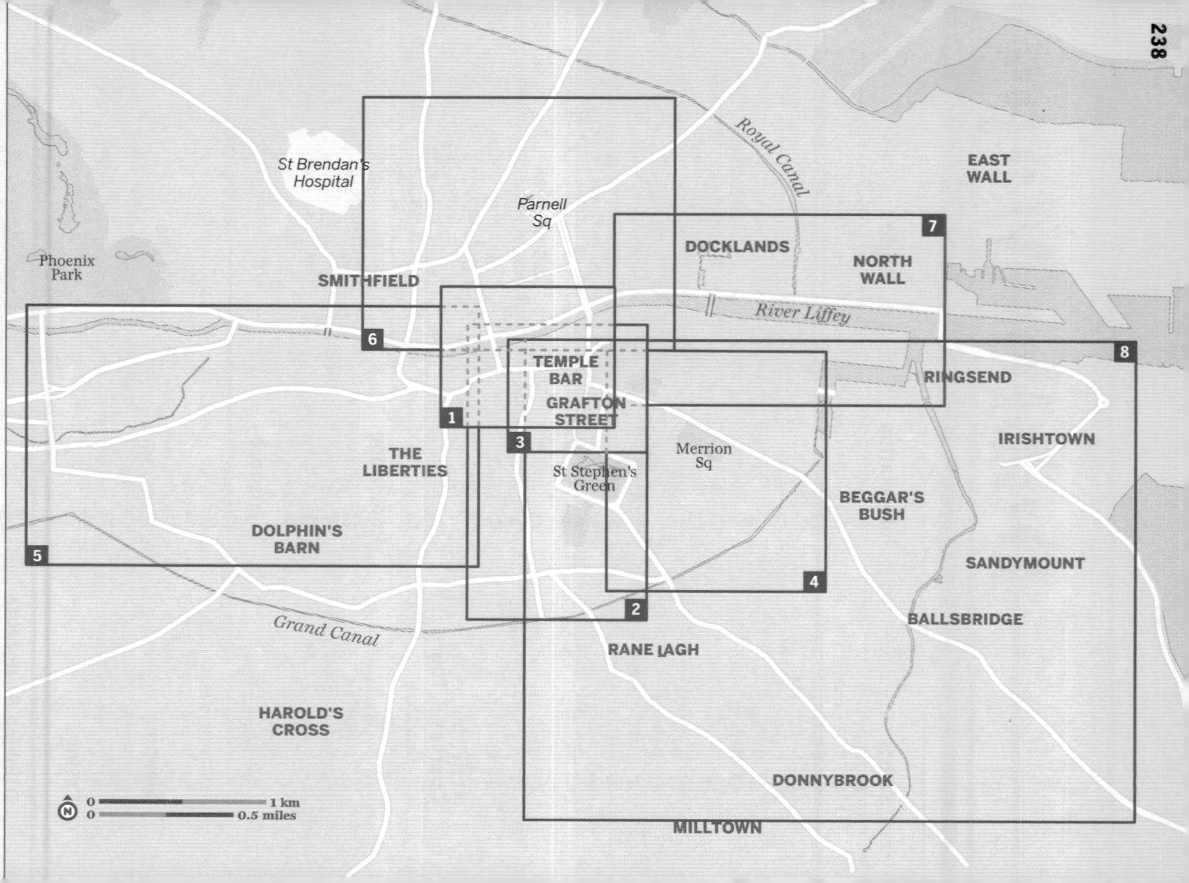

INDEX

TEMPLE BAR *Map on p240*

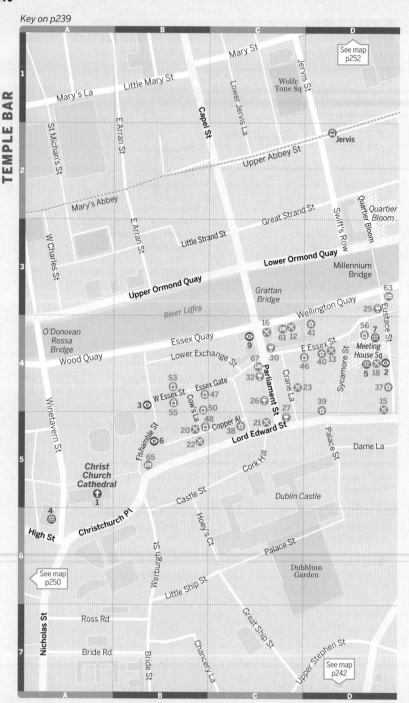

Key on p239

TEMPLE BAR

See map p252

Mary St

Little Mary St

Mary's La

Wolfe Tone Sq

Jervis St

Capel St

Lower Jervis La

St Michan's St

E Arran St

Jervis

Upper Abbey St

Mary's Abbey

Great Strand St

Swift's Row

Quartier Bloom

Quartier Bloom

W Charles St

E Arran St

Little Strand St

Lower Ormond Quay

Millennium Bridge

Upper Ormond Quay

River Liffey

Grattan Bridge

Wellington Quay

63

25

Eustace St

O'Donovan Rossa Bridge

Essex Quay

16

61 12

41

56 7

Meeting House Sq

Wood Quay

Lower Exchange St

9

67

30

E Essex St

46

40 13

5 18 2

Parliament St

32

Crane La

Sycamore St

37

53

Essex Gate

23

39

15

3

W Essex St

47

26

Winetavern St

55

Cow's La

50

27

21

Fishamble St

20

Copper Al

48

38

Lord Edward St

Palace St

Dame La

22

6

65

Cork Hill

Christ Church Cathedral

1

Castle St

Dublin Castle

4

Christchurch Pl

Hoey's Ct

Palace St

High St

See map p250

Werburgh St

Little Ship St

Dubhlinn Garden

Nicholas St

Ross Rd

Bride Rd

Bride St

Chancery La

Great Ship St

Upper Stephen St

See map p242

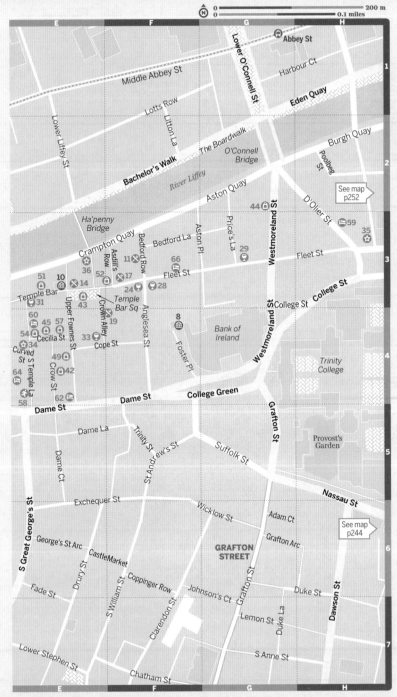

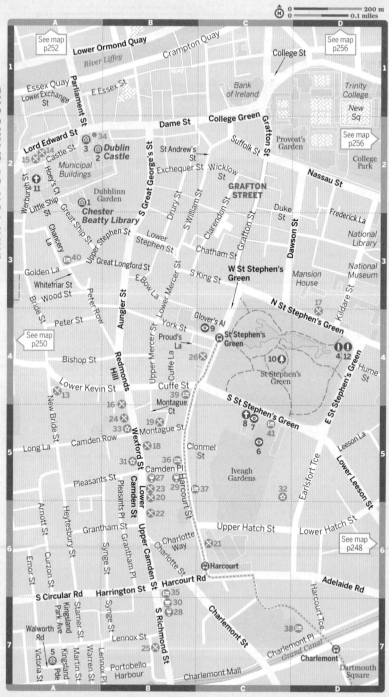

GRAFTON STREET & AROUND

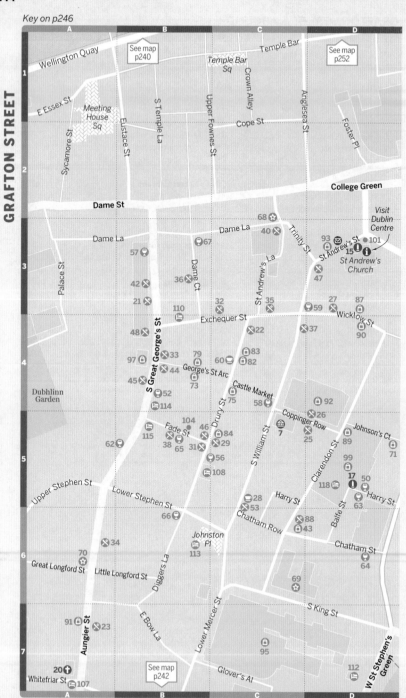

GRAFTON STREET

Key on p246

Wellington Quay

E Essex St

Sycamore St

Meeting House Sq

See map p240

S Temple La

Eustace St

Temple Bar Sq

Upper Fownes St

Crown Alley

Cope St

Temple Bar

Anglesea St

Foster Pl

See map p252

College Green

Dame St

Dame La

Palace St

Dame La

57

42

21

48

S Great George's St

110

Exchequer St

32

22

36

Dame Ct

St Andrew's La

68

40

67

Trinity St

35

59

27

87

90

Wicklow St

Visit Dublin Centre

93

101

15

St Andrew's St

St Andrew's Church

47

37

St Andrew's St

97

33

44

45

52

114

79

60

73

83

82

Drury St

Castle Market

75

58

92

26

Coppinger Row

7

25

89

Johnson's Ct

71

Dubhlinn Garden

62

115

38

Fade St

104

46

65

31

84

29

56

108

S William St

99

17

118

50

63

Clarendon St

Harry St

Upper Stephen St

Lower Stephen St

66

28

53

Harry St

Chatham Row

88

43

Balfe St

Great Longford St

34

70

Little Longford St

Diggers La

Johnston Pl

113

Chatham St

64

69

91

23

Aungler St

E Bow La

Lower Mercer St

S King St

W St Stephen's Green

20

Whitefriar St

107

See map p242

Glover's Al

95

112

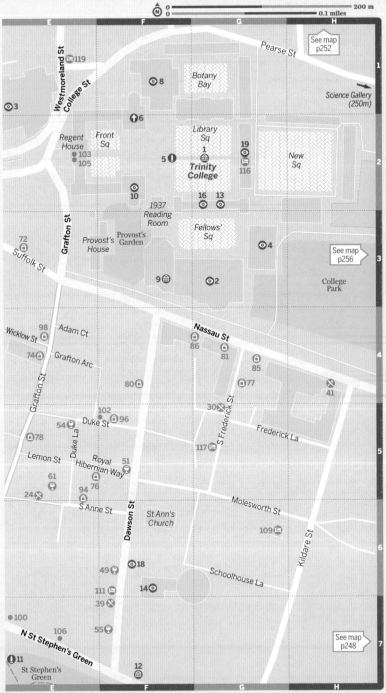

0 ___ 200 m
0 ___ 0.1 miles

E **F** **G** **H**

1

Pearse St

See map
p252

Westmoreland St
College St
119

Botany
Bay

8

Science Gallery
(250m)

3

6

Library
Sq

Regent
House
103
105

Front
Sq

5

1
**Trinity
College**

19

116

New
Sq

2

10

16 13

1937
Reading
Room

Fellows'
Sq

4

72

Grafton St

Suffolk St

Provost's
House

Provost's
Garden

9

2

See map
p256

College
Park

3

Wicklow St

98 Adam Ct

74 Grafton Arc

80

Nassau St

86

81

85

77

41

4

Grafton St

102
54 96
Duke St

Duke La

78

Lemon St

61

24 94 76
S Annie St

51

Royal
Hibernian Way

Dawson St

30

117

S Frederick St

Frederick La

Molesworth St

109

Kildare St

5

6

St Ann's
Church

49 18

111

14

39

55

100

106

N St Stephen's Green

11

St Stephen's
Green

12

Schoolhouse La

See map
p248

7

GRAFTON STREET *Map on p244*

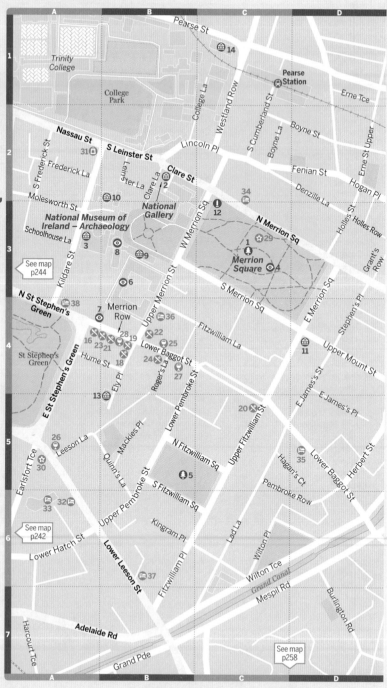

Pearse St

Trinity
College

College
Park

14

Pearse
Station

Erne Tce

Nassau St

S Leinster St

College La

Westland Row

S Cumberland St

Boyne La

Boyne St

Erne St Upper

S Frederick St

Frederick La

Lincoln Pl

Fenian St

Hogan Pl

Molesworth St

Leinster La

Clare La

Clare St

Denzille La

Holles St

Holles Row

31

10

2

34

Schoolhouse La

Kildare St

National
Gallery

National Museum of
Ireland – Archaeology

W Merrion St

12

N Merrion Sq

See map
p244

3

8

9

1

29

Grant's Row

6

Merrion
Square

4

S Merrion Sq

E Merrion Sq

Stephen's Pl

N St Stephen's
Green

38

7

Merrion
Row

Upper Merrion St

36

Fitzwilliam La

11

Upper Mount St

16 23 21

28 19

22

25

Lower Baggot St

E James's St

E James's Pl

St Stephen's
Green

Hume St

18

24

Roger's La

27

Herbert St

E St Stephen's Green

Ely Pl

Lower Pembroke St

13

Upper Fitzwilliam St

20

Hagan's Ct

35

Lower Baggot St

26

Leeson La

Mackies Pl

N Fitzwilliam Sq

5

Pembroke Row

30

Quinn's La

Upper Pembroke St

S Fitzwilliam Sq

Lad La

Wilton Pl

33

32

Wilton Tce

See map
p242

Lower Hatch St

Kingram Pl

Fitzwilliam Pl

Grand Canal

Mespil Rd

Burlington Rd

37

Lower Leeson St

Adelaide Rd

Harcourt Tce

Grand Pde

See map
p258

MERRION SQUARE & AROUND

KILMAINHAM & THE LIBERTIES

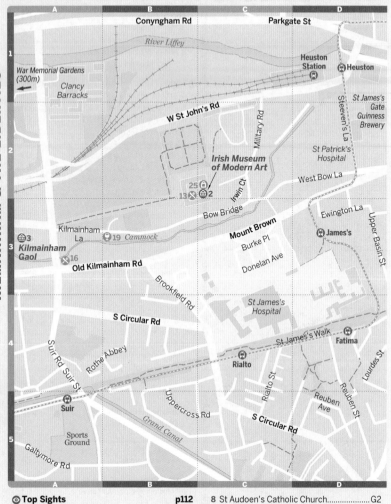

KILMAINHAM & THE LIBERTIES

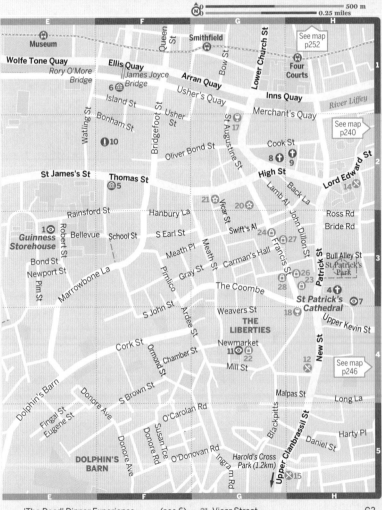

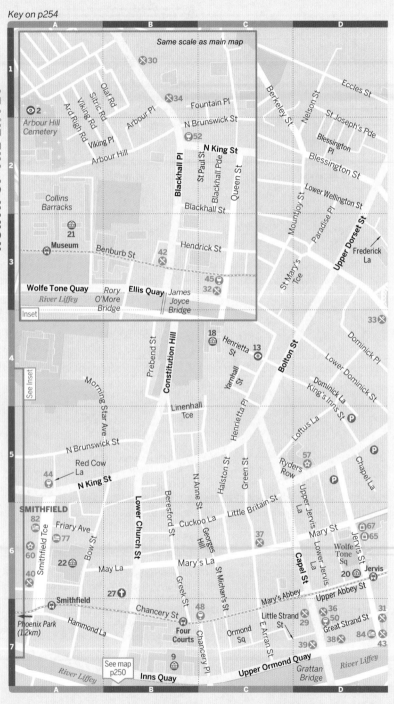

Same scale as main map

Eccles St

Olaf Rd

Stiric Rd

Viking Rd

Ard Righ Rd

Viking Pl

Arbour Pl

Arbour Hill

Fountain Pl

N Brunswick St

Berkeley St

Nelson St

St Joseph's Pde

Blessington Pl

Blessington St

⊙2

Arbour Hill
Cemetery

⊗30

⊗34

☖52

N King St

Blackhall Pl

St Paul's St

Blackhall Pde

Queen St

Lower Wellington St

Mountjoy St

Paradise Pl

Upper Dorset St

Frederick La

Collins
Barracks

Blackhall St

Blackhall St

Hendrick St

St Mary's
Tce

21
Museum

Benburb St

42⊗

Hendrick St

Wolfe Tone Quay

Rory
O'More
Bridge

Ellis Quay

James
Joyce
Bridge

45☖
32⊗

33⊗

River Liffey

Inset

See Inset

Prebend St

Constitution Hill

18
☖

Henrietta
St

13
⊙

Bolton St

Dominick Pl

Dominick St

Lower Dominick St

Dominick La

King's Inns St

Morning Star Ave

Linenhall
Tce

Yarnhall
St

Henrietta Pl

Loftus La

King's Inns St

P

N Brunswick St

Red Cow
La

N King St

44
☖

SMITHFIELD

82

60

40

Smithfield Tce

Friary Ave

77

22

Lower Church St

Beresford St

Bow St

Cuckoo La

Georges
Hill

St Michan's St

N Anne St

Halston St

Green St

Little Britain St

Mary St

57
✦

Ryders
Row

P

P

Chapel La

P

37⊗

Upper Jervis La

Lower Jervis
La

Capel St

67
65

**Wolfe
Tone
Sq**

20
Jervis

May La

27
🛈

Mary's La

Greek St

Smithfield

Chancery St

48

Four
Courts

Phoenix Park
(1.2km)

Hammond La

See map
p250

9

Inns Quay

Chancery Pl

Little Strand
St

Ormond
Sq

Mary's Abbey

E Arran St

Upper Abbey St

29

36
50

Great Strand St

39⊗

38⊗

Upper Ormond Quay

*Grattan
Bridge*

31⊗

84

43

River Liffey

River Liffey

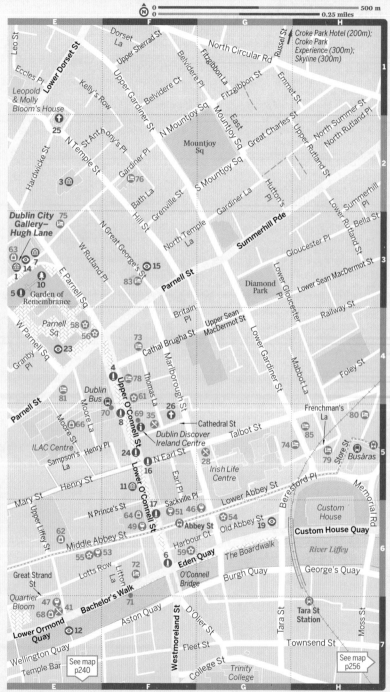

0 500 m
0 0.25 miles

Croke Park Hotel (200m);
Croke Park
Experience (300m);
Skyline (300m)

Leo St
Eccles St
Leopold
& Molly
Bloom's House
25
Lower Dorset St
Kelly's Row
N St Anthony's Pl
N Temple St
Hardwicke St
3
Dorset
La
Upper Sherrard St
Upper Gardiner St
Belvidere Ct
Belvidere Pl
Fitzgibbon Pl
Fitzgibbon St
North Circular Rd
Russel St
Emmet St
North Summer St
North Rutland Pl
East
Mountjoy Sq
N Mountjoy Sq
Mountjoy
Sq
S Mountjoy Sq
Gardiner Pl
Gardiner La
Great Charles St
Upper Rutland St
North Rutland St
Hutton's
Summerhill
Pl
Lower Rutland St
Bella St

Dublin City
Gallery–
Hugh Lane
75
Bath La
Grenville St
Hill St
North Temple
La
Summerhill Pde
Gloucester Pl
63
7
14
1
10
5
Garden of
Remembrance
N Great George's St
W Rutland Pl
E Parnell Sq
15
83
Parnell St
Diamond
Park
Lower Gloucester
Pl
Lower Sean MacDermot St
Railway St

Parnell
Sq
58
56
23
W Parnell Sq
Granby
Pl
73
Cathal Brugha St
Britain
Pl
Upper Sean
MacDermot St
Lower Gardiner St
Mabbot La
Foley St

Parnell St
81
Dublin
Bus
4
78
61
Thomas La
Marlborough St
26
Cathedral St
Talbot St
Frenchman's
La
80
85
Store St
Busáras
66
70
8
69
35
24
N Earl St
28
Irish Life
Centre
74
79
Moore La
Moore St
Henry Pl
ILAC Centre
Sampson's
La
Henry St
16
Earl Pl
Dublin Discover
Ireland Centre

Mary St
Upper Liffey St
11
62
Middle Abbey St
N Prince's St
17
Sackville Pl
64
46
51
Abbey St
49
54
Old Abbey St
19
Lower Abbey St
Beresford Pl
Custom
House
Custom House Quay
Memorial Rd

55
53
72
6
Eden Quay
The Boardwalk
River Liffey
George's Quay

Great Strand
St
Quartier
Bloom
47
41
68
Lower Ormond
Quay
12
Lotts Row
Litton La
71
Bachelor's Walk
Aston Quay
O'Connell
Bridge
Burgh Quay
Westmoreland St
D'Olier St
Tara St
Townsend St
Tara St
Station
Moss St

Wellington Quay
Temple Bar
See map
p240
Fleet St
College St
Trinity
College
See map
p256

NORTH OF THE LIFFEY *Map on p252*

DOCKLANDS

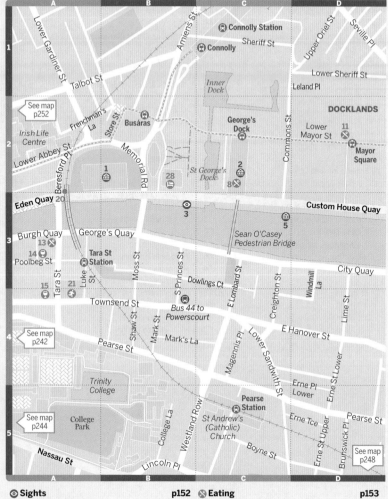

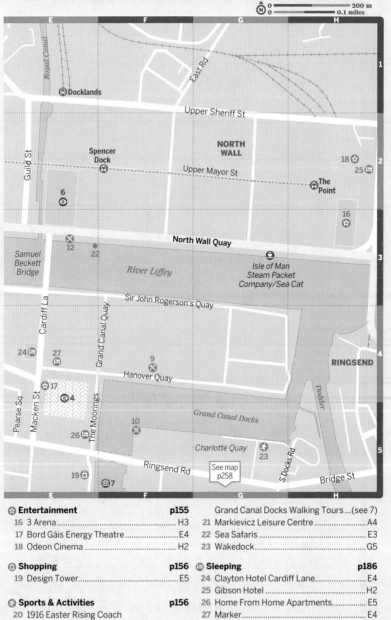

GRAND CANAL & BEYOND

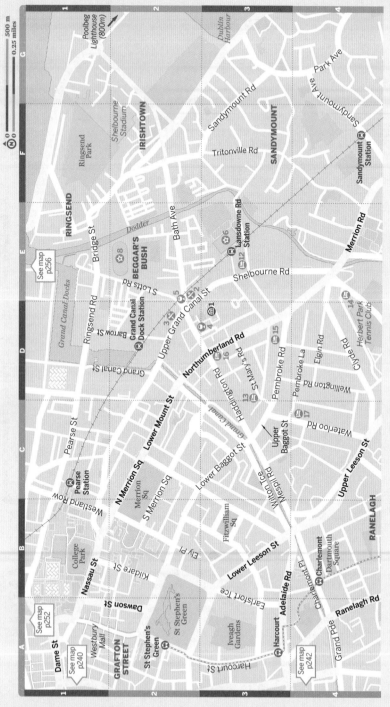

500 m
0.25 miles

See map p256

See map p252

See map p240

See map p242

Poolbeg Lighthouse (800m)

Dublin Harbour

RINGSEND

IRISHTOWN

SANDYMOUNT

Ringsend Park

Shelbourne Stadium

Park Ave

Sandymount Ave

Sandymount Station

Sandymount Rd

Tritonville Rd

Merrion Rd

BEGGAR'S BUSH

Dodder

Bath Ave

Lansdowne Rd Station

Bridge St

S Lotts Rd

Grand Canal Docks

Ringsend Rd

Barrow St

Grand Canal Dock Station

Upper Grand Canal St

Grand Canal St

Shelbourne Rd

Northumberland Rd

St Mary's Rd

Pembroke Rd

Elgin Rd

Clyde Rd

Herbert Park Tennis Club

Lower Mount St

Haddington Rd

Grand Canal

Pembroke La

Wellington Rd

Upper Baggot St

Lower Baggot St

Waterloo Rd

Pearse Station

Pearse St

Westland Row

N Merrion Sq

Merrion Sq

S Merrion Sq

Fitzwilliam Sq

Wilton Tce

Nespil Rd

Upper Leeson St

RANELAGH

College Park

Nassau St

Kildare St

Ely Pl

Lower Leeson St

Earlsfort Tce

Adelaide Rd

Charlemont Pl

Charlemont

Dartmouth Square

Ranelagh Rd

Dame St

Westbury Mall

GRAFTON STREET

Dawson St

St Stephen's Green

St Stephen's Green

Iveagh Gardens

Harcourt St

Harcourt

Grand Pde

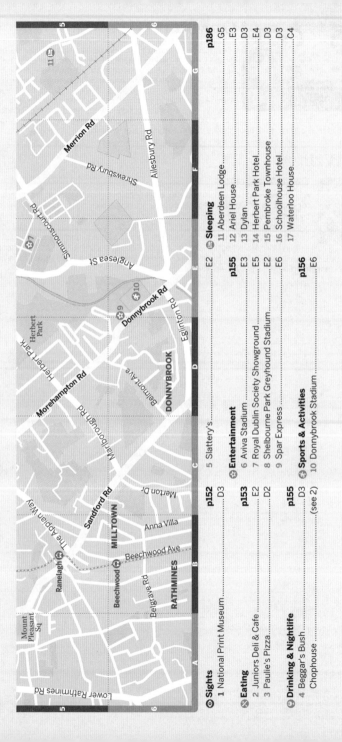

GRAND CANAL & BEYOND

Our Story

A beat-up old car, a few dollars in the pocket and a sense of adventure. In 1972 that's all Tony and Maureen Wheeler needed for the trip of a lifetime – across Europe and Asia overland to Australia. It took several months, and at the end – broke but inspired – they sat at their kitchen table writing and stapling together their first travel guide, *Across Asia on the Cheap*. Within a week they'd sold 1500 copies. Lonely Planet was born.

Today, Lonely Planet has offices in Franklin, London, Melbourne, Oakland, Dublin, Beijing and Delhi, with more than 600 staff and writers. We share Tony's belief that 'a great guidebook should do three things: inform, educate and amuse'.

Our Writers

Fionn Davenport

A Dubliner by birth and conviction, Fionn has been writing about his native city for more than two decades. He's come and gone over the years, pulled abroad by stasis and by the promise of adventure, but it has cemented his belief that 'dear dirty Dublin' (in the words of Lady Morgan and, later, Joyce) is still his favourite city in the world. These days, he has a weekly commute home to Dublin from Manchester, where he lives with his partner Laura and their car Trevor. In Dublin he presents Inside Culture on RTE Radio 1 and writes travel features for a host of publications, including the *Irish Times*.

Published by Lonely Planet Global Limited
CRN 554153
10th edition – November 2016
ISBN 978 1 78657 129 8
© Lonely Planet 2016   Photographs © as indicated 2016
10 9 8 7 6 5 4 3 2 1
Printed in China

Although the authors and Lonely Planet have taken all reasonable care in preparing this book, we make no warranty about the accuracy or completeness of its content and, to the maximum extent permitted, disclaim all liability arising from its use.

All rights reserved. No part of this publication may be copied, stored in a retrieval system, or transmitted in any form by any means, electronic, mechanical, recording or otherwise, except brief extracts for the purpose of review, and no part of this publication may be sold or hired, without the written permission of the publisher. Lonely Planet and the Lonely Planet logo are trademarks of Lonely Planet and are registered in the US Patent and Trademark Office and in other countries. Lonely Planet does not allow its name or logo to be appropriated by commercial establishments, such as retailers, restaurants or hotels. Please let us know of any misuses: lonelyplanet.com/ip.